INTRODUCTION TO PHYSICAL EDUCATION, EXERCISE SCIENCE, AND SPORT STUDIES

Introduction to Physical Education, Exercise Science, and Sport Studies

FIFTH EDITION

Angela Lumpkin, B.S.E., M.A., M.B.A., Ph.D.
Dean, School of Education
University of Kansas

Boston   Burr Ridge, IL   Dubuque, IA   Madison, WI   New York
San Francisco   St. Louis   Bangkok   Bogotá   Caracas   Kuala Lumpur
Lisbon   London   Madrid   Mexico City   Milan   Montreal   New Delhi
Santiago   Seoul   Singapore   Sydney   Taipei   Toronto

McGraw-Hill Higher Education ✎

A Division of The **McGraw-Hill** Companies

INTRODUCTION TO PHYSICAL EDUCATION, EXERCISE SCIENCE, AND SPORT STUDIES, FIFTH EDITION

Published by McGraw-Hill, a business unit of The McGraw-Hill Companies, Inc., 1221 Avenue of the Americas, New York, NY 10020. Copyright © 2002, 1998, 1994, 1990, 1986 by The McGraw-Hill Companies, Inc. All rights reserved. No part of this publication may be reproduced or distributed in any form or by any means, or stored in a database or retrieval system, without the prior written consent of The McGraw-Hill Companies, Inc., including, but not limited to, in any network or other electronic storage or transmission, or broadcast for distance learning.

Some ancillaries, including electronic and print components, may not be available to customers outside the United States.

This book is printed on acid-free paper.

2 3 4 5 6 7 8 9 0 QPF/QPF 0 9 8 7 6 5 4 3 2 1

ISBN 0–07–232901–7

Vice president and editor-in-chief: *Thalia Dorwick*
Executive editor: *Vicki Malinee*
Developmental editor: *Carlotta Seely*
Senior marketing manager: *Pamela S. Cooper*
Project manager: *Christine Walker*
Production supervisor: *Enboge Chong*
Coordinator of freelance design: *Michelle M. Meerdink*
Freelance cover/interior designer: *Rokusek Design*
Cover image: *Allsport Photography*
Supplement producer: *Jodi K. Banowetz*
Media technology producer: *Judi David*
Compositor: *Interactive Composition Corporation*
Typeface: *10/12 Garamond*
Printer: *Quebecor World Fairfield, PA*

The credits section for this book begins on page 413 and is considered an extension of the copyright page.

Library of Congress Cataloging-in-Publication Data

Lumpkin, Angela.
    Introduction to physical education, exercise science, and sport studies / Angela
Lumpkin—5th ed.
        p.   cm.
    Rev. ed. of: Physical education and sport. © 1998.
    Includes bibliographical references and index.
    ISBN 0–07–232901–7 (alk. paper)
    1. Physical education and training.   2. Sports.   3. Physical education and
training—Vocational guidance—United States.   I. Lumpkin, Angela. Physical education
and sport.   II. Title.

GV341 .L85   2002
613.7′1′023—dc21   2001030710
                                                                      CIP

The Internet addresses listed in the text were accurate at the time of publication. The inclusion of a website does not indicate an endorsement by the authors or McGraw-Hill, and McGraw-Hill does not guarantee the accuracy of the information presented at these sites.

www.mhhe.com

Contents

UNIT TWO
HISTORY AND DEVELOPMENT OF PHYSICAL EDUCATION, EXERCISE SCIENCE, AND SPORT

UNIT THREE

THE CHANGING NATURE OF PHYSICAL EDUCATION, EXERCISE SCIENCE, AND SPORT

Preface

Introduction to Physical Education, Exercise Science, and Sport Studies provides students with an exciting opportunity to discover the diversity of physical education, exercise science, and sport and the wealth of careers available in these fields. Students will be introduced to the heritage, current programs, and future potential of the field that they are considering entering. The purpose of this book is to introduce students to these multifaceted fields and to involve students in assessing potential careers in physical education, exercise science, and sport.

The intent of this book is to broaden students' understanding of how the philosophies and programs of physical education, exercise science, and sport evolved as well as to present the current status of these fields. Inherent within the changing nature of physical education, exercise science, and sport is a need to examine how Title IX of the 1972 Education Amendments, the inclusion into classrooms of physically and mentally challenged individuals, the increased emphasis on physical activity and fitness for all ages, past programs in this country and in Europe, and traditional philosophies have affected and will influence what you do as a professional in this field in the twenty-first century.

No longer are physical education, exercise science, and sport just for schools or colleges, although teaching in these settings is certainly an important endeavor. By learning about careers in leisure services, athletic training, corporate fitness, sport management, fitness club instruction and management, recreation for all ages and abilities, coaching, and a variety of other activity-related pursuits, students will gain a clearer perspective of the future role physical education, exercise science, and sport should play in American society. Individuals who accept the challenges of these careers will help women, minorities, senior citizens, individuals in lower socioeconomic classes, students, and many others benefit from active, fit lifestyles. Practical suggestions are provided to students as you choose and prepare for careers. To enhance this process, throughout the book the importance of physical education, exercise science, and sport as expanding and diverse fields of service, enjoyment, and employment is emphasized.

NEW TO THIS EDITION

The new title for this edition, *Introduction to Physical Education, Exercise Science, and Sport Studies,* reflects a new emphasis on exercise science and sport studies, fields that are becoming increasingly connected to all aspects of physical education. New information on exercise science, physical activity, and fitness has been woven throughout this book. In addition, every chapter has been updated, with extensive revisions made to several key topics. Chapter 10 has been completely revised and rewritten to make it more relevant to students studying physical education and exercise science. New photographs have been added throughout the book to help reinforce student learning about key concepts. The Review Questions, Student Activities, and Suggested Readings have also been revised and updated.

Research View

Except for the historical chapters, each chapter features at least one Research View box, which offers questions designed to stimulate students toward critical thinking and continued study. These boxes encourage students to think beyond the text page and relate what they are learning to what could be in the future.

Web Connections

Each chapter also includes a Web Connections box, which lists websites that students can explore to find chapter-related information on the Internet. This feature allows students to expand their knowledge according to their individual abilities and goals and offers a springboard for independent learning.

New or Expanded Topics

This new edition has been significantly revised and updated. The following list is a sampling of the topics that are either new to this edition or have been explored in greater depth than in the previous edition:

Chapter 1: Physical Education, Exercise Science, and Sport Studies—Dynamic Fields

- Greater emphasis on exercise science
- Expanded discussion of the importance of physical activity for all
- Public attitudes toward physical education
- New section on non-teaching fields
- Physical activity patterns of American youth
- New information about Healthy People 2010

Chapter 2: Exercise and Sport Sciences

- Significantly revised chapter with increased focus on the scientific foundation of the exercise and sport sciences
- Expanded discussion of exercise physiology
- New section on motor control and learning
- New section on motor development
- New information on sport biomechanics, sports medicine, sport and exercise psychology, sport history, sport philosophy, sport management, and sport sociology
- New model for illustrating interface of the exercise and sport sciences

- List of films and videos related to sport history and sport philosophy
- New section on technology

Chapter 3: The Profession of Physical Education, Exercise Science, and Sport Studies

- Pedagogy and adapted physical education
- New section on student involvement in professional organizations
- Updated information on certification in athletic training
- Issues facing professionals working with physical activity fields

Chapter 4: Philosophy of Physical Education, Exercise Science, and Sport

- Developing a personal code of conduct
- Code of Ethics of the National Athletic Trainers' Association
- Expanded information about related philosophies
- Sample philosophy of teaching

Chapter 5: Selecting a Career

- Greater emphasis on careers in fitness, exercise, and sport
- National Standards for Athletic Coaches

Chapter 6: Preparation for a Career

- Greater emphasis on internships
- New sample resumes and letters of application
- Contents for a teaching portfolio
- Questions to answer in preparing for potential careers

Chapter 7: Sport in the Ancient World and Our European Heritage

- Updated information on sport and physical activity in early cultures
- Revised discussion of influence of sports played in Great Britain

Chapter 8: Early American Physical Education and Sport

- Updated information on major developments in American physical education and sport
- Expanded section on contributions of Dioclesian Lewis
- Contributions of Carl Fitz and the Lawrence Scientific School

Chapter 9: Twentieth Century Physical Education and Sport

- Recent developments in school and non-school physical education and sport programs
- New section about commercialization in collegiate sports
- Title IX timeline for women's sports

Chapter 10: Opportunities and Challenges in Physical Education and Exercise Science

- Completely revised chapter that focuses on the value of physical activity
- New section on recreation and leisure services
- Emphasis on exercise science
- Elementary, middle, and secondary school programs
- Emphasis on accountability, standards, and assessments in all physical activity programs
- Assessment model for physical education professionals
- Legal duties owed to physical activity participants
- New section on commercialization of physical fitness

Chapter 11: Issues in Sports

- Threats to the integrity of sport
- Drug testing
- Equality of physical activity opportunities for senior citizens and individuals with disabilities
- Citizenship Through Sports Alliance
- Recent sports timeline
- Updated discussion of impact of Title IX on sports for females

Chapter 12: Living Actively in the Twenty-First Century

- New section on leadership
- Revised and updated forecast about living in the twenty-first century
- Changing identify from physical education to exercise science and sport studies
- Emphasis on physical activity throughout life
- Impact of technology and aging population

Appendix A features a revised and updated listing of professional journals with contact addresses and websites. Appendix B includes a revised and updated listing of certifying organizations. The Glossary has been expanded to include 30 new definitions.

CONTENT DESIGN

Written in a conversational and personal style, *Introduction to Physical Education, Exercise Science, and Sport Studies* is designed for students enrolled in their first course related to exercise science, sport management, physical education, athletic training, or other related majors.

An overview of the field is stressed rather than an in-depth examination of the disciplinary areas. Some of these relevant topics discussed include practical suggestions for selecting and obtaining a job in the chosen career; current issues affecting job selection; girls and women in sport; minorities in physical education and sport; the standards and assessment movement; teacher, coach, athletic trainer, and exercise specialist certifications; educational values of sports; and the importance of physical activity for all.

The book's three units are self-contained and may be read in any order, although each is important to a full understanding of the field. Unit One provides foundational information in the first four chapters before focusing on careers. As defined in Chapter 1, *physical education is a process through which an individual obtains optimal physical, mental, and social skills and fitness through physical activity. Exercise science is broadly defined as the scientific analysis of the human body in motion and encompasses exercise physiology, biomechanics, kinesiology, anatomy, physiology, motor behavior, and some aspects of sports medicine.* Sport is operationally defined as *physical activities governed by formal or informal rules that involve competition against an opponent or oneself and are engaged in for fun, recreation, or reward.* The cognitive, affective, and physical fitness and motor skill development objectives of physical education and sport indicate how physical education and sport can contribute to improvements in quality of life for all. Chapter 2 provides an in-depth look at the exercise and sport sciences, such as exercise physiology, sports medicine, and sport management. An explanation of organizations in the field precedes a discussion about preparation programs for school and nonschool careers in Chapter 3. The five traditional philosophies and discussion of ethics presented in Chapter 4 provide reference points for the development of a personal philosophy.

A career emphasis is integrated throughout, and given special attention in Chapters 5 and 6. Chapter 5 describes more than 50 careers in education, recreation, fitness, sports, business, and athletics. Students can learn about job responsibilities, prerequisite education and preparation, and the potential availability of positions. Chapter 6 provides practical ideas for preparing for careers, with an emphasis on the importance of internships, volunteer experiences, and obtaining certifications. Recommendations for writing a resume, developing a portfolio, and seeking a job are provided.

Unit Two covers the history and development of physical education and sport from early cultures through today. Athletics in Athens and Sparta, European gymnastics programs, and sports and games in Great Britain are emphasized in Chapter 7 in terms of their influence on programs in the United States. In Chapter 8, early American physical education and sport is traced from early sporting diversions through the formalized gymnastics programs of the late 1800s. Chapter 9 completes the chronology of evolving programs that are diverse in philosophy, clientele, and activity.

Unit Three describes issues and trends in physical education, exercise science, and sport. Chapter 10, examines the value of physical activity for everyone, exercise science program developments, unique features of elementary, middle, and secondary school physical education, standards and accountability, legal liability, career burnout, and instructional challenges facing physical educators. The beneficial outcomes and associated issues of sports for girls and women, minorities, youth, school and college students, and Olympic athletes are addressed in Chapter 11. The final chapter looks at the image and role of physical education, exercise science, and sport in all settings in the twenty-first century.

SUCCESSFUL FEATURES

Key Concepts

Each chapter begins with statements that highlight the major topics to be discussed. These provide students with both a focus and direction as you read.

Introductions

The first paragraphs in the chapters briefly set the stage for and preview the text. They help students gain further perspective on the relevance of the content.

Illustrations

More than 140 photographs help students see the diversity of physical education, exercise science, and sport and potential careers therein. These photographs also reemphasize the popularity of sports and activities for all and help teach important concepts.

Boxed Material

Throughout the text, specially highlighted information is designed to enhance students' understanding and provide additional insights into these professions.

Summaries

A summary paragraph at the conclusion of each chapter emphasizes the primary areas of importance, thus complementing the initial key concepts. These summaries help students focus on the major items discussed.

Career Perspective

A unique feature of this book is the integration of biographical sketches of sport, exercise science, and physical education professionals in several diverse careers. The featured individuals list their job responsibilities, hours, course work, and degrees, discuss experience needed for their careers, satisfying aspects of their careers, and job potential, and offer suggestions for students.

Review Questions

To enhance retention of each chapter's content, students are encouraged to answer the review questions. Rather than seeking rote memorization of facts, these questions stress understanding the concepts.

Student Activities

Like the review questions, student activities encourage students to think about and use the chapter content in greater depth and to extract practical ideas for career application. These activities also encourage an active participation in the learning process.

Suggested Readings

Suggested readings furnish students with additional information and potential resources for further study. The annotations are especially beneficial to expanding students' knowledge.

Glossary

A comprehensive glossary of important terms reinforces students' understanding of the terminology used in the book and in physical education, exercise science, and sport.

Appendixes

An appendix of professional journals, mailing addresses, websites, and foci provides easy references for purchasing these periodicals or learning more about their availability. A second appendix gives addresses for several organizations that certify coaches, athletic trainers, and fitness leaders.

ANCILLARIES

Instructor's Manual and Test Bank

An *Instructor's Manual and Test Bank* accompanies the text and is available to those who adopt it. The manual includes practical teaching suggestions, chapter overviews, instructional objectives, additional annotated readings, more than 450 multiple choice, true/false, matching, and essay test items with answer keys, and suggested audiovisual materials.

Online Learning Center

This website offers resources for both instructors and students. It features downloadable ancillaries, web links, student quizzing, additional information on topics of interest, and more.

Resources for the instructor include:

- Downloadable PowerPoint presentations for each chapter
- Lecture outlines
- Links to professional resources
- Additional web links

Resources for the student include:

- Flashcards
- Learning objectives
- Internet activities
- Career opportunities

The Online Learning Center can be found at this website: www.mhhe.com/lumpkin.

PowerWeb

This edition of *Introduction to Physical Education, Exercise Science, and Sport Studies* has been packaged with PowerWeb, a tremendous learning tool. Power Web is an easy-to-use online resource from McGraw-Hill that provides current articles, curriculum-based materials, weekly updates with assessment, informative and timely world news, related web links, research tools, student study tools, interactive tools, and more.

Access to PowerWeb also offers:

- Study tips with self-quizzes
- Links to related sites
- Weekly updates
- Current news
- Daily newsfeed of related topics
- Web research guide

PowerWeb is a password-protected website. Your McGraw-Hill Sales Representative can guide you in creating a student package with PowerWeb. Preview this website at: www.dushkin.com/powerweb.

ACKNOWLEDGMENTS

Without the help of numerous individuals, this book would not exist. First and foremost, my parents, Janice and Carol Lumpkin, instilled in me a love for learning, provided me with many educational opportunities through personal sacrifice, and continually encourage all of my endeavors. I dedicate this book to them with my love. My sister, Vernell Berry, and my brother, Phillip Lumpkin, who are dear friends, and their families provide me with love and encouragement, too.

I am also appreciative of the invaluable help given to me by the reviewers who have provided valuable suggestions for this revision:

B. Sue Graves
Florida Atlantic University

David Cutton
Aquinas College

Harry Krampf
Minnesota State University-Mankato

Jeff Martin
Wayne State University

Alison M. Wrynn
State University of New York-Cortland

Last, but significantly, I want to thank the outstanding professionals at McGraw-Hill Higher Education, and especially Carlotta Seely. It has been a pleasure to be associated with each of them. Their commitment to the publishing of quality books is unmatched. It is my hope that this book will awaken and kindle the interest of those who read it to select careers in physical education, exercise science, and sports.

Angela Lumpkin

1

PRINCIPLES AND SCOPE OF PHYSICAL EDUCATION, EXERCISE SCIENCE, AND SPORT STUDIES

© Corbis/Vol. 103

CHAPTER

1

PHYSICAL EDUCATION, EXERCISE SCIENCE, AND SPORT STUDIES— DYNAMIC FIELDS

KEY CONCEPTS

- Today's physical education, exercise science, and sport studies programs have the potential to improve the quality of life for everyone.
- The purpose of physical education, exercise science, and sport studies is to enhance lives through participation in physical activity. The growing interest in health and fitness contributes to the achievement of this purpose.
- Cognitive development, affective development, physical fitness and motor skill development objectives are achieved through today's programs in these dynamic fields.
- The allied fields of health, recreation, and dance share some curricula and purposes.
- The continual challenge facing physical educators, exercise scientists, and leaders in sports programs remains to instill in Americans of all ages the importance of participating in regular physical activity.

Children love to move because it is fun. Adults choose to engage in physical activity because they find it enjoyable. With increased leisure time, people of all ages are seeking out instructional, recreational, and competitive physical activity and sport programs. This interest promises a dynamic future for professionals who want to contribute to the well-being and quality of life of others. The millions who enroll in aerobic dance classes, join fitness clubs, bowl in leagues, hike, camp, swim, jog, climb, sail, walk, skate, and engage in many other physical pursuits already have determined that these activities are fun. Many also value the mental, social, and physical development resulting from their regular participation.

Although maintaining a physically active and fit lifestyle is highly esteemed by many, others have yet not been convinced. Motivating this latter group is

2

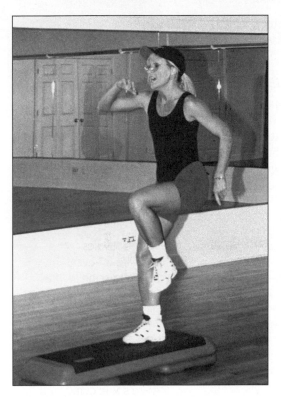

Aerobic activities are important. (Photo courtesy Bob Hilliard.)

the challenge awaiting you when you begin your career. Historically, the term physical educator has been used to encompass professionals in various careers who teach fitness and sport skills. This descriptor identifies individuals who are committed to using physical activities to develop the whole person.

To help you meet the challenge to contribute to the wellness of others, this text will introduce you to both the current concepts and objectives in the dynamic fields of physical education, exercise science, and sport studies and to their rich heritage. Past physical education programs provide the foundation for today's broader programs in the United States, shaping the way we structure and describe these fields. Understanding the definition and objectives of physical education today and in the past will help you conceptualize the breadth and depth of these fields. Understanding current affective, cognitive, and psychomotor domains of learning will ensure that you know what physical education, exercise science, and sport studies programs seek to accomplish.

WHAT IS PHYSICAL EDUCATION? WHAT IS EXERCISE SCIENCE? WHAT IS SPORT?

Physical education, exercise science, and sport are allied fields that share a common heritage and have grown more distinctive with the knowledge explosion and disciplinary specificity. They relate to, but are not synonymous with, exercise, play, games, leisure, recreation, and athletics. Defining each of these terms can help clarify the distinctions and similarities. **Exercise** means to practice, to strengthen, or to condition through physical activity. **Play** refers to amusements engaged in freely, for fun, devoid of constraints. **Games,** usually implying winners and losers, can range from simple diversions to cooperative activities to competitions with significant outcomes governed by rules. Freedom from work or responsibilities describes **leisure,** which may or may not include physical activity. Similarly, **recreation** refreshes or renews one's strength and spirit after toil, again with or without activity. **Athletics** are organized, highly structured, competitive activities in which skilled individuals participate. The physical activity matrix shown in Figure 1.1 helps differentiate among these similar terms.

Definitions

Sports may be played both for exercise and as a game. Sports participants may use their leisure time to play games recreationally. Some describe bridge and chess games as sports, while others claim that rock climbing, fly fishing, and skydiving are sports. When the rules governing the skill levels required of participants, and the significance placed on the outcome are rigidly structured, sport becomes athletics. Usually, sport refers to contests in which the outcome is viewed as important by the players, who will emerge as either winners or losers. Broadly

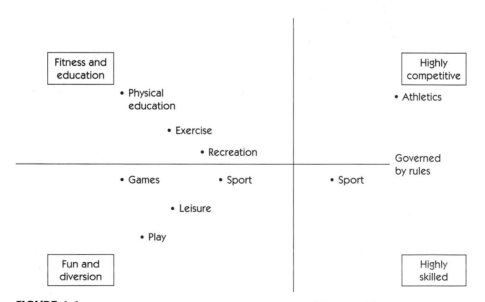

FIGURE 1.1

This matrix shows how various types of physical activity relate to each other and the specified areas of emphasis.

RESEARCH VIEW

Public Attitudes toward Physical Education

The National Association for Sport and Physical Education in 2000 conducted a survey of adults and teens to gain a better understanding of their attitudes about physical education and physical activity. The major findings of this study included the following:

- Daily physical education should be mandatory in schools
    - 81% of adults agree
    - 71% of teens agree
- Physical education helps children prepare to become active, healthy adults
    - 64% of adults agree
    - 54% of teens agree
- Physical education helps children build social skills as well as physical strength and coordination
    - 64% of adults agree
    - 53% of teens agree
- Physical education classes do not interfere with children's academic needs
    - 91% of adults agree
- Participation in team sports helps children learn lessons about discipline and teamwork that are important and will help them in the future
    - 67% of adults agree
    - 69% of teens agree
- What students like about physical education classes
    - 20% like the opportunity to exercise
    - 18% like getting fit
    - 16% say it is fun
    - 16% like the activities offered
- What students dislike about physical education classes
    - 13% indicated running
    - 9% indicated boring activities
    - 7% indicated dressing and undressing
- It is important for children to be physically fit
    - 99% of adults agree
- American children are physically fit
    - 69% of adults agree
    - 54% of teens agree

(continued)

- What things prevent youth from getting enough physical activity according to adults
  - 24% stated a lack of interest or motivation
  - 13% stated not enough time
  - 13% stated watching television
- What things prevent youth from getting enough physical activity according to teens
  - 24% stated not enough time
  - 19% stated doing homework
  - 13% stated a lack of interest or motivation

---

defined, **sports** are physical activities governed by formal or informal rules that involve competition against an opponent or oneself and are engaged in for fun, recreation, or reward.

Traditionally, the definition of physical education has been restricted to formal instruction in a school or college. Yet, instruction in physical activities also can occur in an aerobics center, a sports club, a corporate fitness program, or a recreational league. In these settings, people learn skills, develop fitness, and commit to enhancing their physical well-being. The National Association for Sport and Physical Education, in its *National Standards for Physical Education* (1995), has identified seven components of a physically educated person that answer the question "What should students know and be able to do?" These include:

- Demonstrates competency in many movement forms and proficiency in a few movement forms.
- Applies movement concepts and principles to the learning and development of motor skills.
- Exhibits a physically active lifestyle.
- Achieves and maintains a health-enhancing level of physical fitness.
- Demonstrates responsible personal and social behavior in physical activity settings.
- Demonstrates understanding and respect for differences among people in physical activity settings.
- Understands that physical activity provides opportunities for enjoyment, challenge, self-expression, and social interaction.

To encompass the various outcomes experienced by all people in diverse programs, **physical education** is defined as a process through which an individual obtains optimal physical, mental, social, and fitness skills through physical activity. In recent years, many colleges have chosen to rename their departments, using terms such as kinesiology, exercise science, human movement, and sport studies.

Exercise science describes the scientific analysis of the human body in motion. This broad term encompasses exercise physiology, biomechanics, kinesiology, anatomy, physiology, motor behavior, and some aspects of sports medicine. Researchers are exploring how to maximize the potential of human movement through physiological, biomechanical, and psychological studies. Practitioners are applying these findings to improve the quality of life for all who incorporate physical activity into their lives. Thus, the term exercise science rather than physical education may more broadly define what people know and do relative to human movement.

QUALITY OF LIFE

What does "quality of life" mean? Is it happiness, wellness, health, fitness, or fun? Maybe it refers to leisure time, relief from stress, safety from harm, or the absence of disease. Quality of life, although defined individually, in today's world increasingly means a long and healthy life. Inherent therein is the concept that a feeling of well-being or some level of fitness enhances life. Maybe it is an outgrowth of Americans' search for the fountain of youth, but it seems that fitness, or at least the appearance of fitness, is valued.

Not a fad, this commitment to fitness has become an integral part of life for many. Executives may choose where to take a job based on the availability of exercise programs, or employers may hire employees only if they are healthy and fit. Families often plan vacations and leisure time around various recreational and sports activities. Thousands of people sign up for marathons, 10-kilometer road races, and fun runs. Walking has become popular for people of all ages. Sporting goods and sports clothing sales continue to gross millions of dollars. Sports facilities, such as health clubs, aerobics centers, tennis courts, swimming pools, and golf courses, increasingly attract people who take both their health and sports seriously.

A number of factors in contemporary life have reemphasized the importance of physical activity. The threat of cardiovascular disease has contributed to a realization of the need to exercise the heart muscle. Poor nutritional habits have adversely affected the health of thousands. Longer life expectancies have raised the consciousness levels of many who not only want to live longer, but who also want to enjoy their later years. Technological advances have reduced the amount of exercise inherent in our daily lives while simultaneously providing greater amounts of leisure time and discretionary income. Stress proliferates as a frequent by-product of technology and a highly competitive business world. In each case, exercise, along with a knowledge of how the body functions in response to activity, can enhance fitness and the overall quality of life. R. Tait McKenzie's "The Joy of Effort" depicted on page 8 certainly captures the ecstasy of participating in sport for the pleasure it offers.

Millions of people in the United States, however, do not participate in any physical activity because of lack of motivation, time, money, skills, or knowledge. To encourage participation is the role of physical educators, exercise scientists,

R. Tait McKenzie's *The Joy of Effort* won the King's Medal at the 1912 Stockholm Olympic Games. (Courtesy the University of Tennessee Press.)

and leaders of sports programs. Are you willing to accept responsibility for changing attitudes and developing programs to get the inactive involved? Teachers, can you sell your students on the value of physical activity? Sports leaders, can you get participants to adhere to, rather than drop out of, their sports programs? Exercise scientists, can you activate the lethargic? The opportunity to make a difference is boundless since less than 50 percent of our population exercises regularly.

The contribution of physical education, exercise science, and sport to the quality of life can be enhanced by encouraging participation in team sports and individual sports. Schools, recreation departments, and large corporations offer league competitions in baseball, volleyball, basketball, football, soccer, and softball. Within these settings, team members learn and demonstrate teamwork, cooperation, communication skills, and the ability both to lead and to follow. Team camaraderie may lead to lifelong friendships and the willingness to place the team's benefit above individual goals. Although some of these sports can become ageless pursuits, many individuals discontinue participation because they lack sufficient players or because of the physical demands of the sport.

Individual sports are often called lifetime sports because of the greater likelihood of continued participation throughout life. Most of these sports can be

Aerobic activities are important for all ages and both genders. (Photo courtesy Lisa Sense.)

engaged in by an individual either alone or with only one other person. Aerobics, bowling, fishing, golf, hiking, jogging, racquetball, swimming, tennis, walking, and weight lifting are the most popular of these sports and activities. They can be engaged in recreationally, or participants can become competitive through leagues, tournaments, and organized events. Individual sports, like team sports, can teach fair play, self-confidence, how to win and lose, as well as specific sports skills.

Typically, school athletic teams and city or business recreational leagues attract skilled participants or those at least moderately comfortable with their skills. Those lacking skills, however, are often relegated to spectator roles or to their easy chairs in front of their televisions, video games, or computers. More instructional programs and beginning level leagues and teams are needed for individuals of all ages. Unfortunately, there is frequently an overlap between the lower skilled and the economically disadvantaged. Because of the cost of tennis, golf, and swimming, for example, these have often been categorized as upper-class sports. Therefore, tax-supported recreation departments need to provide opportunities for these and other activities for all individuals.

Senior citizens, a growing percentage of the population of the United States, also have recreational needs. For example, exercise has been found to reduce osteoporosis (a breakdown of the calcium in the bones), especially for women in their postmenopausal years. Senior citizens need activities matched with their capabilities. On the other end of the spectrum, children have many needs for physical activity that remain unfulfilled. Daily physical education from kindergarten through the twelfth grade would greatly enhance children's movement skills and fitness capacities. Nonschool sport programs can also provide opportunities for physical activity and play. For each of these groups, increased fun-filled opportunities for physical activities will contribute to the development of a healthy lifestyle. You, as a coach, recreation leader, personal trainer, or teacher hold the key to unlocking this door of opportunity for others.

Moderate activity often meets both the social and the recreational needs of senior citizens.

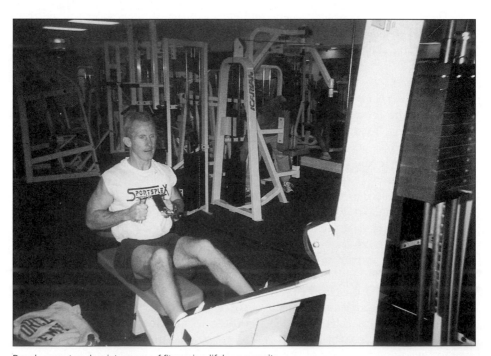

Development and maintenance of fitness is a lifelong pursuit.

IMPORTANCE OF PHYSICAL ACTIVITY

In 1992, more than 60 percent of adults in this country did not achieve the recommended amount of regular physical activity. That same year, nearly half of the 12 to 21 year olds were not vigorously active on a regular basis. Nearly a quarter of American adults in 1992 engaged in no leisure-time, physical activity; many of these live in families whose annual family income is less than $20,000, and some are individuals with disabilities. Approximately 30 percent of adult American women and 25 percent of adult American men are overweight. By age 18, most students will have spent more hours watching television than they will have been in classes.

Healthy People 2000, published by the federal government in 1990, reported disturbing statistics and proposed a national plan to improve the health of all Americans. One of its three principal goals was to increase the span of healthy lives of Americans, and seven of its objectives specifically addressed physical activity and fitness. Limited progress was achieved in meeting these objectives. Therefore, a decade later another set of goals was established.

The *Healthy People 2010* goals listed in the box on pages 12–14 are important guidelines for the work of physical educators, exercise scientists, and sports leaders.

In 1996, the first ever Surgeon General's *Report on Physical Activity and Health* emphasized that Americans could substantially improve their health and the quality of their lives by participating in regular physical activity. Despite the *Healthy People 2000* goals, the patterns and trends in physical activity reported in

Daily physical education leads to skill development so that individuals can play at high skill levels as adults. (Photo courtesy Lisa Sense.)

HEALTHY PEOPLE 2010

Healthy People 2010 is a national health promotion and disease prevention initiative that seeks to unite agencies at all levels in their efforts to improve the health of all Americans, eliminate disparities in health, extend lives, and improve the quality of life. Healthy People 2010 builds on initiatives pursued over the past two decades to achieve national health objectives. Healthy People 2010 seeks to attain 2 overarching goals in 28 focus areas through 467 specific objectives.

Goal 1: Increase Quality and Years of Healthy Life

Healthy People 2010 seeks to help individuals of all ages increase life expectancy and improve their quality of life.

Goal 2: Eliminate Health Disparities

Healthy People 2010 seeks to eliminate health disparities among different segments of the population. These include differences that occur by gender, race or ethnicity, education or income, disability, living in rural localities, or sexual orientation.

Healthy People 2010 Focus Areas

- Access to Quality Health Services
- Arthritis, Osteoporosis, and Chronic Back Conditions
- Cancer
- Chronic Kidney Disease
- Diabetes
- Disability and Secondary Conditions
- Educational and Community-Based Programs
- Environmental Health
- Family Planning
- Food Safety
- Health Communication
- Heart Disease and Stroke
- HIV
- Immunization and Infectious Diseases
- Injury and Violence Prevention
- Maternal, Infant, and Child Health
- Medical Product Safety
- Mental Health and Mental Disorders
- Nutrition and Overweight
- Occupational Safety and Health
- Oral Health
- Physical Activity and Fitness
- Public Health Infrastructure
- Respiratory Diseases
- Sexually Transmitted Diseases

HEALTHY PEOPLE 2010 (CONTINUED)

- Substance Abuse
- Tobacco Use
- Vision and Hearing

Objective 22 Deals with Physical Activity and Fitness—to Improve Health, Fitness, and Quality of Life through Daily Physical Activity

Physical Activity in Adults

22-1. Reduce the proportion of adults who engage in no leisure-time physical activity.
   Target: 20 percent.
   Baseline: 40 percent of adults aged 18 years and older engaged in no leisure-time physical activity in 1997 (age adjusted to the year 2000 standard population).

22-2. Increase the proportion of adults who engage regularly, preferably daily, in moderate physical activity for at least 30 minutes per day.
   Target: 30 percent.
   Baseline: 15 percent of adults aged 18 years and older were active for at least 30 minutes 5 or more days per week in 1997 (age adjusted to the year 2000 standard population).

22-3. Increase the proportion of adults who engage in vigorous physical activity that promotes the development and maintenance of cardiorespiratory fitness 3 or more days per week for 20 or more minutes per occasion.
   Target: 30 percent.
   Baseline: 23 percent of adults aged 18 years and older engaged in vigorous physical activity 3 or more days per week for 20 or more minutes per occasion in 1997 (age adjusted to the year 2000 standard population).

Muscular Strength/Endurance and Flexibility

22-4. Increase the proportion of adults who perform physical activities that enhance and maintain muscular strength and endurance.
   Target: 30 percent.
   Baseline: 19 percent of adults aged 18 years and older performed physical activities that enhance and maintain strength and endurance 2 or more days per week in 1997 (age adjusted to the year 2000 standard population).

22-5. Increase the proportion of adults who perform physical activities that enhance and maintain flexibility.
   Target: 40 percent.
   Baseline: 30 percent of adults aged 18 years and older did stretching exercises in the past 2 weeks in 1995 (age adjusted to the year 2000 standard population).

Physical Activity in Children and Adolescents

22-6. Increase the proportion of adolescents who engage in moderate physical activity for at least 30 minutes on 5 or more of the previous 7 days.
   Target: 30 percent.
   Baseline: 20 percent of students in grades 9 through 12 engaged in moderate physical activity for at least 30 minutes on 5 or more of the previous 7 days in 1997.

(continued)

HEALTHY PEOPLE 2010 (CONTINUED)

22-7. Increase the proportion of adolescents who engage in vigorous physical activity that promotes cardiorespiratory fitness 3 or more days per week for 20 or more minutes per occasion.

Target: 85 percent.

Baseline: 64 percent of students in grades 9 through 12 engaged in vigorous physical activity 3 or more days per week for 20 or more minutes per occasion in 1997.

22-8. Increase the proportion of the nation's public and private schools that require daily physical education for all students.

Target: 25 percent of students in middle and junior high school and 5 percent in senior high school.

Baseline: 17 percent of students in middle and junior high school and 2 percent of students in senior high school were required to take daily physical education in 1994.

22-9. Increase the proportion of adolescents who participate in daily school physical education.

Target: 50 percent.

Baseline: 27 percent of students in grades 9 through 12 participated in daily school physical education in 1997.

22-10. Increase the proportion of adolescents who spend at least 50 percent of school physical education class time being physically active.

Target: 50 percent.

Baseline: 32 percent of students in grades 9 through 12 were physically active in physical education class more than 20 minutes 3 to 5 days per week in 1997.

22-11. Increase the proportion of children and adolescents who view television 2 or fewer hours per day.

Target: 75 percent.

Baseline: 60 percent of persons aged 8 to 16 years viewed television 2 or fewer hours per day in 1988 to 1994.

See the Healthy People 2010 website for more information:
www.health.gov/healthypeople/default.htm

---

the Surgeon General's report indicated little progress and even some decreases in activity. A few of these low participation levels included:

- Approximately 15 percent of adults and about 50 percent of individuals 12 to 21 years old in this country engage in vigorous physical activity at least three times a week for at least 20 minutes.

- Approximately 22 percent of adults in this country engage in sustained physical activity at least five times a week for at least 30 minutes.

- About 25 percent of adults and 25 percent of individuals 12 to 21 years old in this country engage in no physical activity.

- Daily attendance in high school physical education classes between 1991 and 1995 declined from approximately 42 percent to 25 percent.

These data verified the significant challenge facing this nation and confirmed a national concern for the physical welfare of most citizens.

As the Surgeon General's *Report on Physical Activity and Health* concluded, people of all ages and both genders can benefit from regular physical activity. Significant health benefits can be obtained by including a moderate amount of physical activity in our weekly routines (e.g., 30 minutes of brisk walking, 15 minutes of running, or 45 minutes of playing volleyball on most, if not all, days of the week). Regular physical activity improves health by reducing the risk of premature death, dying from heart disease, developing diabetes, developing high blood pressure, or developing colon cancer. Daily, moderate physical activity helps reduce blood pressure in people who already have high blood pressure, reduces feelings of depression and anxiety, helps control weight, helps older adults become stronger and better able to move about without falling, and promotes psychological well-being.

Physical activity has numerous beneficial physiological effects on the cardiovascular and musculoskeletal systems, but it also benefits the metabolic, endocrine, and immune systems. Maintaining normal muscle strength, joint structure, and joint function only occurs when activity is sustained. Many of the beneficial effects of endurance and resistance activities diminish within two weeks if physical activity is substantially reduced, and effects disappear within two to eight months if physical activity is not resumed. Thus, the health benefits can only be enjoyed if physical activity becomes a regular part of a person's life.

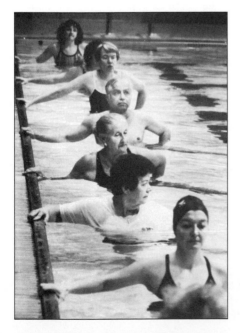

Individuals of all ages are seeking to achieve the healthy benefits of physical activity. (Photo courtesy Lisa Sense.)

PURPOSE

What exactly do physical education, exercise science, and sport programs seek to accomplish? A **purpose** is a stated intention, aim, or goal. Used interchangeably, these terms describe desired long-range achievements that will only occur after many hours of effort and incremental progress. Working to make the dean's list this semester, earning a grant-in-aid based on performance as a walk-on athlete, getting invited into an academic honor society, and saving money from a part-time job to purchase a car are all examples of goals. Whether you call it an aim, a goal, or a purpose, each is achieved by meeting several objectives, such as spending long hours studying or perfecting athletic skills.

Historically, physical educators have been challenged to significantly improve the quality of life of each person taught. Physical education, exercise science, and sport-related positions, inside and outside of educational institutions, provide opportunities to teach motor and sports skills and to dynamically affect

 # WEB CONNECTIONS

1. www.health.gov/healthypeople/default.htm
   This site includes the entire document and related information for the Healthy People 2010 initiative.

2. www.cdc.gov
   Welcome to a plethora of information and data about health topics from the Centers for Disease Control.

3. www.nih.gov
   The National Institutes for Health provide fact sheets, results from clinical trials, health information via hotlines, MEDLINEplus, and other resources.

4. www.surgeongeneral.gov/ophs/pcpfs.htm
   Visit this site of the President's Council on Physical Fitness and Sports to learn more about its activities to coordinate and promote opportunities in physical activity, fitness, and sports for all Americans.

5. www.cdc.gov/nccdphp/sgr/sgr.htm
   Read the text of the Surgeon General's *Report on Physical Activity and Health* as well as gain access to other publications from this office.

6. www.healthfinder.gov
   This service of the U.S. Office of Health and Human Services provides a wealth of information about health and nutrition topics.

the physical, psychological, and emotional well-being of others. Physical activity experiences aim to benefit every individual physically, mentally, and socially and to develop healthy lifestyle skills and attitudes. To help each person make these attitudinal and behavioral changes, the purpose of physical education, exercise science, and sport programs is to optimize the quality of life through a long-term commitment to enjoyable physical activity and sport experiences that will meet varied needs in a changing world.

A purpose provides the answer to the question why. Physical education, exercise science, and sport programs must add value to the lives of participants, or they cannot be justified. A "roll out the ball" physical education class that results in no development of physical fitness or motor skills should be changed. A school sports program that fails to teach fair play, cooperation, and self-control cannot be defended. A corporate or community fitness or sport program that is poorly organized, results in injuries and attrition because it is not based on sound physiological principles, and is not fun for the participants is doomed to failure. Conversely, the purpose of physical education, exercise science, and sport programs is to ensure that each person benefits physically, mentally, socially, and emotionally. Most people enjoy being active, which is the reason why these opportunities exist. An improvement in the quality of their lives will be the desired and valued outcome that you can help them achieve.

Physical activity, physical fitness, health, and wellness are components essential to the achievement of the purpose of physical education, exercise science, and sport. **Physical activity** includes all movements that can contribute to improved health. **Physical fitness** is developed through endurance and resistive exercises of sufficient frequency, duration, and intensity to enhance heart and other body functions. **Health-related fitness** refers to attaining the level of well-being associated with heart function (cardiovascular endurance) and muscular

Tennis skills learned at a young age can be used throughout life. (Photo courtesy Lisa Sense.)

function (strength, endurance, and flexibility) as a deterrent to debilitating conditions. **Skill-related fitness** refers to achieving levels of ability to perform physical movements specific to a sport, such as serving a tennis ball effectively, or a physical activity, such as executing safe and proper technique in a step aerobics class. **Health** refers to the well-being of body and mind. It also encompasses the absence of disease and illness, such as coronary heart disease, high blood pressure, and depression. **Wellness** includes the mental, emotional, spiritual, nutritional, and physical factors that lead to healthy behaviors. Each of these is vital to a person's quality of life.

OBJECTIVES OF PHYSICAL EDUCATION, EXERCISE SCIENCE, AND SPORT PROGRAMS

The objectives of physical education, exercise science, and sport programs are often stated more specifically than the purpose because they consist of particular learning outcomes. Professional colleagues and the general public often learn about a program's worth through an examination of its objectives and their fulfillment.

Through the years, physical education, exercise science, and sport objectives have increasingly focused on the whole person. Dudley Sargent, a recognized leader in physical education for college students in the late 1800s and early 1900s, suggested that physical education achieved hygienic, educative, recreative, and remedial objectives. Outcomes that he noted in his programs included improved health, fun, reduction of illness and injury, and enhanced knowledge about how the body moved and learned. Clark Hetherington, one of the "new physical educators," helped to lead the transition from exercising methodically to developing the entire person. In 1910, he recommended that physical education programs seek to achieve organic, psychomotor, character, and intellectual objectives.

In 1934, the American Physical Education Association's (today's American Alliance for Health, Physical Education, Recreation and Dance) Committee on Objectives listed:

- physical fitness,
- mental health and efficiency,
- social and moral character,
- emotional expression and control,
- appreciation

as the desired objectives. In 1950, these were restated:

- to develop and to maintain maximum physical efficiency,
- to develop useful skills,
- to conduct oneself in socially useful ways
- to enjoy wholesome recreation.

In 1965, the American Association for Health, Physical Education and Recreation stated five major objectives (*This is physical education,* 1965):

- To help children move in a skillful and effective manner in all the selected activities in which they engage, in the physical education program, and also in those situations that they will experience during their lifetime.
- To develop an understanding and appreciation of movement in children and youth so that their lives will become more meaningful, purposive, and productive.
- To develop an understanding and appreciation of certain scientific principles concerned with movement that relate to such factors as time, space, force, and mass-energy relationships.
- To develop through the medium of games and sports better interpersonal relationships.
- To develop the various organic systems of the body so they will respond in a healthful way to the increased demands placed on them.

Before examining the objectives that guide physical education, exercise science, and sport programs, it is essential to understand how these objectives relate to those of education.

In 1918, the Educational Policies Commission stated seven objectives of education:

- health,
- command of fundamental processes,
- worthy home membership,
- vocation,
- citizenship,
- worthy use of leisure time,
- ethical character.

In 1938, these were consolidated into:

- self-realization,
- human relationship,
- economic efficiency,
- civic responsibility.

Through all of these objectives, educational leaders sought to develop the whole child. Justification for any educational program was based on what contributions it could make. Since the 1930s, physical education has verified its value as a school subject by demonstrating its alignment with Benjamin Bloom's domains of learning—cognitive, affective, and psychomotor objectives. Educators, physicians, legislators, and parents have affirmed that school programs have helped achieve the educational objectives listed in the box on page 20. The domains of learning encompass mental, physical, social, and emotional components. School

EDUCATIONAL OBJECTIVES WHOSE ACHIEVEMENT IS ENHANCED THROUGH PHYSICAL EDUCATION, EXERCISE SCIENCE, AND SPORT PROGRAMS

Physical

- Reduces risk of coronary heart disease, diabetes, obesity, high blood pressure, and colon cancer
- Improves muscular strength and endurance, flexibility, and cardiovascular endurance
- Regulates weight, tones bodies, and improves body composition
- Promotes overall health and fitness
- Strengthens bones
- Develops movement skills

Mental

- Improves academic performance
- Increases interest in learning
- Improves judgment
- Promotes self-discipline
- Encourages goal setting and achieving these goals

Psychological and Social

- Improves self-confidence, self-esteem, and self-control
- Provides an outlet for stress
- Strengthens peer relationships
- Reduces the risk of depression
- Promotes healthier lifestyles

physical education and sport programs are unique because they contribute to the all-around person. The psychomotor objective focuses on the development of motor skills and physical fitness. Activities in these programs include an integration of cognitive abilities for optimal learning. Through participation in physical activities, individuals learn to value and appreciate themselves and others, as well as the experiences.

Cognitive Development

Cognitive objectives focus on the acquisition, comprehension, analysis, synthesis, application, and evaluation of knowledge. Preparation in physical education, exercise science, and sport studies includes studying the body's structure and function, history and philosophy, growth and development, sport marketing, sport finance, sport ethics, sport law, motor learning, biomechanics, sport psychology, sport sociology, and exercise physiology. Regardless of the setting, content learned in such courses is essential for teachers and leaders to understand and disseminate information and for program participants to comprehend and apply what they have learned.

Increased cognitive involvement usually leads to better execution of a skill and to a better understanding of the activity. In meeting cognitive objectives, teachers in all settings need to explain not only *how* but especially *why* the body's movements result in certain outcomes. For example, they can explain why hand position, release technique, and follow-through are critical to the success of throwing a ball. Teachers in all settings need to emphasize learning rules, strategies, skills, safety principles, and proper etiquette. An example of a measurable cognitive learning outcome would be—"a participant will demonstrate knowledge of the rules of tennis by answering at least 15 out of 20 questions correctly."

Thus, physical activity often enhances cognitive development. Not only may performance in reading, math, language, and other subjects be enhanced through participation in certain physical activities, but the content of these areas can also be incorporated into physical activities. In addition, mental fatigue from studying or working can be reduced through exercise, so that a subsequent classroom session or job task is more productive. Stress can impede cognitive processes, but activity can reduce stress and enhance productivity.

Affective Development

Affective objectives emphasize the development of attitudes, appreciations, and values; this domain contains both social and emotional dimensions. In the social realm, both individual and group needs are met while positive characteristics are developed. Learning self-confidence, courtesy, fair play, sportsmanship, and how to make value judgments through cooperative activities benefits all students. In team sports, decision-making abilities, communication skills, and affiliation needs are enhanced, as long as the outcome of the event is not overemphasized. Individuals' values and attitudes toward involvement in physical activity are solidified, as are appreciations for participation and performance when the achievement of realistic personal goals is paramount. On the emotional side, self-discipline, fun, learning how to win and lose, tension release, self-control, and self-expression are enhanced through the give-and-take of challenging oneself and competing with and against others. An example of an affective learning outcome would be "students take turns tossing balls to classmates in such a way that the classmate can catch at least 8 out of 10."

Physical Fitness and Motor Skill Development

Movement undergirds all physical education, exercise science, and sport programs that seek to achieve the objectives of physical fitness and motor skill development. Although any person can learn fundamental movement skills, children learn more easily because they do not have to break habitual inefficient motor patterns. Also, if the basic locomotor, manipulative, and perceptual-motor skills are learned early, they provide the foundation for lifelong enjoyment of physical activity.

Movement concepts include body awareness; spatial awareness including space, direction, level, and pathways; qualities of movement such as time, force, and flow; and relationships with objects and with people. Walking, running,

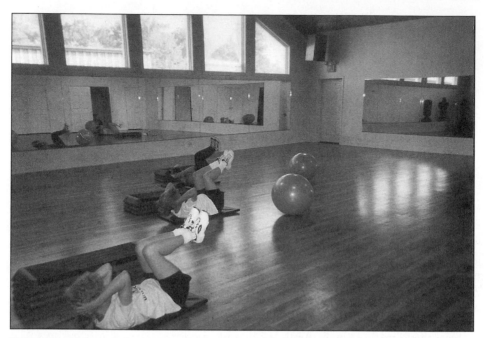

Flexibility, muscular strength and endurance, and cardiovascular endurance are the essential components of physical fitness.

jumping, leaping, and sliding are some of the basic locomotor movements; conversely, stretching, twisting, pushing, lifting, and swinging are nonlocomotor movements. Manipulative skills, involving propelling or absorbing force from an object, include throwing, catching, striking, and kicking.

Developing and improving fundamental movement skills and game or sport skills are important objectives, since sport, aquatic, and dance skills begin with learning basic and efficient movement patterns. Children need to explore their bodies' capabilities as they learn to walk, run, or jump independently, in conjunction with others, or by using a piece of equipment. Similar principles can apply as individuals experiment with solving other movement challenges. Manipulative skills are developed by exploring the potential of hoops, ropes, balls, rackets, bats, and other implements. Perceptual-motor skills, such as the eye/hand coordination needed to strike a ball with a racket or the reaction time needed to judge how quickly a partner's thrown ball will arrive, are also important skills. Once these abilities are mastered developmentally and independently, then skills, such as catching, throwing, and batting, can be incorporated into lead-up games and sport situations. An example of a motor skill development learning outcome would be—"the participant will use the proper technique in successfully executing at least 7 out of 10 dominant-hand basketball layups."

Physical fitness includes cardiovascular endurance, muscular strength and endurance, flexibility, and body composition. The ability to sustain physical activity that requires oxygen for exertion indicates cardiovascular endurance, the

Physical education helps children develop fitness and psychomotor skills as they learn to enjoy activity. (Photo courtesy Bob Hilliard.)

most essential component of physical fitness. Similarly, the ability to exert and sustain maximal force against a resistance constitutes muscular strength and endurance. Flexibility gained by statically stretching the muscles improves the range of motion in the joints. Body composition refers to the percentage of fat in the body. Caloric expenditure through exercise helps regulate body composition. Agility, balance, neuromuscular coordination, speed, and power also contribute to physical fitness. Agility permits quick changes in direction during activity. A person's balance, or state of equilibrium, stabilizes the body in preparation for future movements or actions. Neuromuscular coordination, including reaction time, integrates the senses with motor function. Speed permits rapid execution of a movement, while power combines speed with muscular strength.

Figure 1.2 summarizes the objectives of physical education, exercise science, and sport. It is essential to recognize that these objectives interrelate rather than exist in isolation. For example, while learning to hit a tennis ball, people not only enhance their eye/hand coordination but also learn proper body position for a level swing and cooperation with those with whom they take turns tossing the ball. The box on page 25 provides several examples of how the objectives of physical education and sport are achieved and interrelated. It should also be emphasized that the breadth of the outcomes sought in physical education, exercise science, and sport programs make it challenging to maintain a focused field of study.

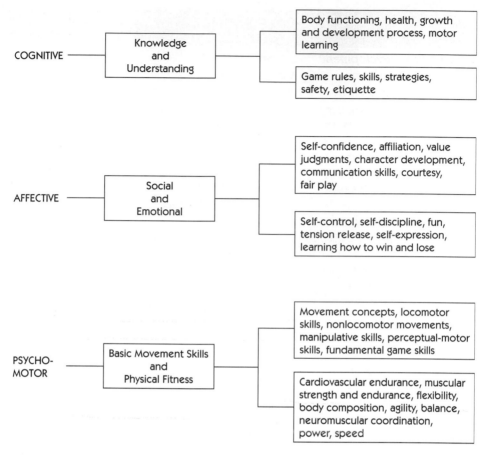

FIGURE 1.2

Objectives of physical education, exercise science, and sport studies.

ALLIED FIELDS

Health, recreation, and dance have traditionally been allied in purpose with physical education, exercise science, and sport, although their programs differ somewhat in emphasis. Coaching, another allied field, is often a combined career with teaching physical education in the schools. Today, personal trainers, athletic trainers, sport managers, sport psychologists, exercise physiologists, and others help achieve the purpose and objectives of physical education, exercise science, and sport programs.

Health

Many of the early school and college physical education programs in the 1800s emphasized health benefits as their primary justifications. For example, at Amherst College, beginning in the 1860s, the president supported a physical education

EXAMPLES OF PHYSICAL EDUCATION, EXERCISE SCIENCE, AND SPORT OBJECTIVES

Cognitive Development

- The participant will explain the principles for playing zone defense in basketball.
- The participant will analyze the technique for executing a flat tennis serve.
- The participant, using the entire stroke (whole teaching method), will synthesize the principles of learning the crawl stroke in swimming.
- The participant will apply knowledge of cardiovascular functioning in establishing a personal fitness program.
- The participant will evaluate another person's weight-lifting technique and provide corrective feedback.

Affective Development

- The participant will express appreciation for the excellence of an opponent's high-level performance.
- The participant will enjoy playing hard and doing his or her best, regardless of the outcome of the contest.
- The participant will cooperate and take turns with others.
- The participant will demonstrate fair play in unsupervised activities.
- The participant will value the rights of others and the regulations governing the situation.

Physical Fitness and Motor Skill Development

- The participant will improve eye/hand coordination by weekly practicing racquetball forehand and backhand shots.
- The participant will explore ways to manipulate a ball without using the hands.
- The participant will design and perform a one-minute dance that includes the use of two locomotor movements and two objects.
- The participant will demonstrate the proper technique for executing a volleyball spike.
- The participant will execute four exercises designed to improve flexibility of the shoulders.

program to help students become and stay healthy. As was the case with many other institutions, the person charged with directing this program was a physician. In the twentieth century, the dual role of the health/physical educator separated as colleges prepared physical education teachers for jobs that focused on teaching physical activities, especially in alignment with educational objectives rather than health objectives. Because health and physical education programs share the goal of good health, and because school health classes are often assigned to physical educators (who at best have minimal academic preparation in this field), acceptance of health as a separate discipline in schools has been gradual.

Although the disciplines of health and physical education share some content and objectives, each also seeks to achieve unique outcomes. Physical activity and sports participation contribute to fitness and overall well-being. Health, in addition to being the traditional absence of disease, also encompasses soundness

Soccer helps develop many of the components of physical fitness. (Photo courtesy Lisa Sense.)

of body, mind, and spirit. School health curricula include the study of nutrition, mental and emotional health, avoidance of the abuses of tobacco, alcohol, and other drugs, and human sexuality. Community and corporate health programs focus on disease prevention, smoking cessation, safety and first aid, child care, weight loss and control, and stress management.

Hypokinetic disease refers to those diseases and health problems associated with physical inactivity and a sedentary lifestyle. Coronary heart disease, high blood pressure, stress, ulcers, obesity, and low back pain often affect individuals who fail to engage in regular exercise. When school, work, and family place few physical demands on our bodies, these degenerative diseases may develop. Health education and physical activity can help alter or deter the disease process.

In 1992, the American Heart Association identified physical inactivity (along with high blood pressure and high cholesterol) as a primary risk factor for coronary heart disease. Now maybe thousands more will realize that participating in regular physical activity and exercise is essential to good health (see Research View box "National Physical Activity Status and Goals").

Recreation

Recreation, a diversion that occurs during leisure hours, renews and refreshes one's strength and spirits after work. Today, most recreation programs are separate from physical education, exercise science, and sport studies programs, although they share many objectives. This change reflects the important role of recreational activities for people of all ages. Schools, businesses, communities, and families have increasingly offered activities for fitness and pleasure as each of these groups accepts some responsibility to educate for leisure. Businesses provide work-site fitness centers, sponsor sports teams, and offer a variety of fitness activities for employees and their families.

⌕ RESEARCH VIEW

National Physical Activity Status and Goals

Date	Agency/ Initiative	Status/Goals
1987	U.S. Congress	Resolution 97 encouraged educational agencies and governments to provide quality, daily physical education programs for all K-12 children.
1990	*Healthy People 2000* Goals	Increase to at least 50% the proportion of children and adolescents in first through twelfth grade who participate in daily physical education at school. Increase to at least 50% the proportion of physical education class time that students spend being physically active, preferably in lifetime physical activities.
1996	Surgeon General's *Report on Physical Activity and Health*	Nearly half of American youths 12–21 years of age are not vigorously active on a regular basis. Moreover, physical activity declines dramatically during adolescence. Daily enrollment in physical education classes has declined among high school students from 42% in 1991 to 25% in 1995. Only 19% of all high school students report being physically active for 20 minutes or more in daily physical education classes.
1997	*Shape of the Nation* from the National Association for Sport and Physical Education	Only one state (Illinois) requires daily physical education for all K-12 students. Alabama and Washington require daily physical education for all K-8 students. Most high school students between grades 9–12 take physical education for only one year. Three states (Colorado, Mississippi, and South Dakota) have no state mandates for physical education.
2000	*Healthy People 2010* Goals	Increase the proportion of adolescents who engage in moderate physical activity for at least 30 minutes on 5 or more of the previous 7 days. Increase the proportion of the nation's public and private schools that require daily physical education for all students. Increase the proportion of adolescents who spend at least 50% of physical education class time being physically active.

The recreation services industry is growing rapidly in the United States because of increased leisure time and larger discretionary incomes for many. Also, as the American population ages, more and more retired persons are seeking appropriate recreational outlets. No longer can municipal recreation departments fulfill their missions simply by sponsoring youth leagues in the traditional

Rafting has become a popular recreational activity. (Photo courtesy Terry Dash.)

team sports. Americans also want adult competitive leagues, instructional clinics, open facilities for family outings, organized trips and moderate exercise programs for seniors, and child care so that a parent can recreate. Environmental concerns have led many people to expect resource management by state and national authorities so that the beauty of nature and access to it will not be impaired for outdoor recreators. Schools and colleges have expanded their curricula to include the lifetime activities of backpacking, canoeing, rock climbing, and downhill skiing. Thus, some shared outcomes with recreation programs are evident.

Dance

Bodily movements of a rhythmical and patterned succession usually executed to the accompaniment of music constitute **dance.** Both as physical activity and as performing art, dance varieties include aerobic, ballet, ballroom, folk, clogging, jazz, modern, square, and tap. Dance can provide participants opportunities for aesthetic expression whether in a beginner's class or on stage. People of all ages can dance for fitness and for fun. Some schools and most colleges have dance specialists, yet many dance classes, especially for females, are taught by physical educators who sometimes have had minimal preparation in this field.

Introduction to Nonteaching Fields

Many individuals are interested in careers in exercise science, sport, and physical activity programs that do not involve teaching. Opportunities certainly abound in these areas as will become evident in reading this book and in exploring the plethora of learning experiences you will experience during college years. While historically a common heritage is shared, in recent decades the information explosion has created new venues for working in fields that contribute to human welfare broadly defined. For example, with the increase in life expectancy, providing leisure time programs for senior citizens who are healthy and can energetically engage in human movement activities is an expanding field of employment. With the emphasis on constantly improving motor skills, exercise scientists in exercise physiology, biomechanics, sport psychology, and motor learning conduct research studies to identify approaches that will improve how athletes can perform. To offset our more sedentary lifestyles, more and more individuals are seeking fitness programs that can help them attain and maintain healthy lifestyles. With increased leisure time, people of all ages are participating in a diversity of sporting pastimes as well as being entertained by athletes of all ages. Sport managers and recreation specialists organize these programs.

Each of the nonteaching fields makes its unique contribution to the attainment of shared objectives of physical education, exercise science, and sport. As the table on the next page indicates, the contributions made to others as well as personally enjoyed are extensive for each of the objectives.

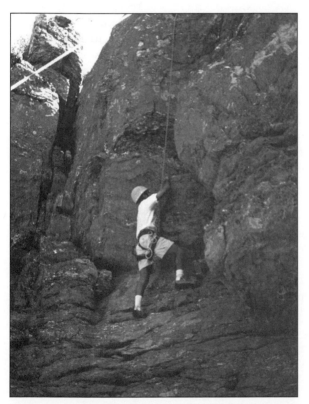

Lifetime recreational activities, such as rock climbing, are now part of some school/college curricula. (Photo courtesy Aram Attarian.)

TABLE 1-1

NONTEACHING PHYSICAL ACTIVITY CAREER CONTRIBUTIONS

Field	Cognitive	Affective	Psychomotor and Fitness
Health director and participants in a corporate fitness program	X	X	X
Coach and athletes on a team	X	X	X
Athletes working with a sport psychologist	X	X	X
Exercise physiologist conducting research on motor performance	X		X
Athletic trainer and services provided to athletes	X	X	X
Sport marketer for a professional team and the athletes and fans served		X	X
Recreational director for senior citizens program	X	X	X
Sporting goods salesperson and customers who purchase products		X	X
Personal trainer at a health and fitness club	X	X	X

SUMMARY

Physical education, exercise science, and sport programs exist to improve the quality of life and the physical well-being of participants. People of all ages enjoy playing games, engaging in recreational activities, and exercising to maintain good health. Competitive, rule-bound sports provide opportunities to test one's skills against opponents. Through all of these, the all-around development of the individual is enhanced during activity. The purpose of these programs is to optimize quality of life through enjoyable physical activity and sport experiences. Educational objectives through cognitive, affective, and physical fitness and motor skill development are sought and achieved. Several of these objectives are shared with the allied fields of health, recreation, and dance. A significant challenge facing physical education, exercise science, and sport professionals is to help all Americans participate in regular physical activity so they can enjoy the associated health benefits.

CAREER PERSPECTIVE

L. FRANKLIN RAGAN
Deputy City Manager for Operations
City of Aurora, Colorado

EDUCATION
B.S., Recreation and Parks Administration, North Carolina State University
M.S., Recreation Resources Administration, North Carolina State University

JOB RESPONSIBILITIES AND HOURS

Frank oversees four departments within the city of Aurora: Planning, Utilities, Public Works, and Parks and Open Space. The responsibilities reflect the organization of a city with tremendous growth opportunities. An objective of this right-sizing structure was to group the major planning and infrastructure components of the municipal government under one leader with the overt intent to gain greater effectiveness and efficiencies with citizen-supported services and facilities. With a previous nineteen-year career focused on the field of parks and recreation and the experience gained in overall leadership and management skills, the opportunity and challenge to assume more responsibilities, albeit more difficult, came more fluidly than Frank had imagined. Although his present responsibilities involve broader areas of citywide planning, development, and management oversight, the various departments operate through the same fundamentals of management common to all park/recreation and related public service organizations. Accountability to the citizens who finance local government operations, as well as one's paycheck, has become more challenging in recent years. Participatory management and community government are the trends of today and the orientation of local government in the future.

The hours of commitment to public service can vary widely, dependent upon one's initiative and the characteristics of the organization for which one works. Frank's weekly schedule of hours devoted to the job can vary from 50 to 70, with an average around 55. Certainly, 40-hour weeks are nonexistent. While there is some semblance of cycles throughout the year, such as budget preparation, long-range capital improvements planning, infrastructure development activities, etc., the pace of an institution and one's desire to either keep up, fall behind, or get out in front of the pack is a strong determinant of hours on the job. With that said, there is a critical need within this profession, and any other for that matter, to balance career goals with other, sometimes more important, goals. Public sector officials work hard to ensure that everyone has the opportunity to enjoy a good quality life; however, these same people sometimes fail to enjoy it themselves. It can be a difficult lesson learning how to balance a career with personal life.

SPECIALIZED COURSE WORK, DEGREES, AND WORK EXPERIENCES NEEDED FOR THIS CAREER

Frank states that his most valuable courses were those with a strong business orientation. He also encourages students to take diversified courses with a strong liberal arts background. While both his undergraduate and graduate degrees were within Parks and

Recreation, which was quite appropriate for careers within the field, it is somewhat difficult to move into a city or county manager's office without an M.B.A., Masters in Public Administration, or closely related degree. Good, recognized experience can overcome some educational preferences by fields outside the mainstream of one's educational orientation. Educational preparation should include courses aimed at information technology, sociology, psychology, research methodology, personnel management, finance/accounting, horticulture, design, planning, zoology, chemistry, and a variety of other courses filling out a broad spectrum of learning activities.

A couple of courses Frank begrudgingly took when he was in college focused on park and recreation facilities maintenance. They ended up being two of the most practical courses to prepare him for real-world responsibilities. Keeping communities clean and beautiful does take some "grunt work." Understanding the various functions and possessing some working knowledge of what makes things work throughout one's organization, even with the least spectacular jobs, leads to a better understanding of the people whom you need to fill those positions and meet your mission. Understanding and listening to people is critical in this business and life in general. Unlike what he felt while attending North Carolina State University, Frank found that virtually every course on his transcript helped in some way or another over the many years of his movement and progression within local government management.

It may be superfluous to mention the role in which information technology is now playing within this field, as it is within most fields. There are space-age technologies being utilized within the public works and community services portion of Frank's city, Aurora, Colorado. From maintenance programming incorporating pinpoint accurate recording of street pothole locations via satellites and computer voice recognition to the entire mapping of infrastructure, demographics, and other data deemed important, to efficient, effective delivery of services. The application of technology into everyday work planning and operations is becoming more routine and essential. Certainly, one cannot learn too much in this field of activity regardless of one's career destination.

SATISFYING ASPECTS

Of most importance to Frank is seeing the direct results of his organization's work and the noticeable, tangible impact made upon individuals' quality of life. He adds that there are few fields of endeavor where the efforts of one's lifework are so evident in day-to-day living. He takes particular pride in working with economic development and redevelopment projects that are major contributing factors to a community's financial prosperity, hence providing stability to the overall health of a community and its interdependent, diversified neighborhoods.

JOB POTENTIAL

Opportunities within local government are great, if one is willing to make some sacrifices. The flexibility to relocate to different parts of the country are imperative for those who want to advance quickly to departmental director positions or higher management/administrative positions. Such drastic moves are unnecessary at lower level positions due to greater availability of positions within a given geographic area, particularly within more urbanized areas of the country. Generally, salaries will tend to be proportionate with the size and priorities of the community and the budget of that jurisdiction. Salaries can also differ significantly in different parts of the country. The cost of living can vary just as greatly, and as a result, one should do research to truly establish whether positions are promotions or merely lateral moves.

SUGGESTIONS FOR STUDENTS

Frank recommends that those considering a career in local government interview people in positions of interest to them. Of particular value is "shadowing" a person during a typical workday and/or evening as the case may be, to directly see what that job or career involves. Once you have chosen a field, he stresses the importance of getting volunteer, part-time and/or seasonal work experiences prior to graduation. Internships are valuable, particularly when you have the opportunity to work with people in a progressive, creative agency who take time to work with interns rather than just take advantage of their budgeted hours. Frank also believes in a strong variation of work experiences and recognizes that the diversity of one's experiences and the professional references drawn from them are often significant deciding factors when going for that first full-time position and everything else that follows. One's opportunities are enhanced exponentially once within a good organization that values and rewards its achieving performers. The responsibility of recognizing good opportunities resides with each person, as well as the requisite education and experiences deemed essential to take full advantage of them.

REVIEW QUESTIONS

1. How can physical education, exercise science, and sport contribute to the improvement of the quality of life of others?
2. How do physical education, exercise science, and sport relate to athletics, leisure, and play?
3. What is the relationship and difference between physical education, exercise science, and sport?
4. How do physical education, exercise science, and sport objectives relate to general educational objectives?
5. What types of knowledge are important within the cognitive domain of physical education, exercise science, and sport? Give examples of each.
6. How are the social and emotional outcomes of the affective objective achieved in physical education, exercise science, and sport programs?
7. What are the three major components of physical fitness?
8. What are the two overarching goals of *Healthy People 2010?*
9. How do health, recreation, and dance relate to physical education, exercise science, and sport?
10. What is the primary recommendation of the Surgeon General's *Report on Physical Activity and Health?*

STUDENT ACTIVITIES

1. Interview three individuals of differing ages (for example, below 18, in their 30s, and over 60) to determine what role physical activity plays in their lives.
2. Ask at least two friends who are not majors in your field what they think physical education, exercise science, and sport are.

3. Write a one- or two-page description of how you would incorporate three movement concepts or skills into a youth soccer program.
4. Write a one-page summary of how the three domains of physical education, exercise science, and sport objectives have influenced your life and career choice.
5. In groups of three to five students, develop several strategies that would effectively change the physical activity patterns of children, teenagers, and adults. Present two-minute reports to the class.

REFERENCES

This is physical education, Washington, D.C., 1965, American Association for Health, Physical Education and Recreation.

Healthy people 2010, Washington, D.C., 2000, U.S. Government.

Moving into the Future-National Standards for Physical Education, Reston, VA, 1995, National Association for Sport and Physical Education.

Physical activity and health, a report of the Surgeon General, Washington, D.C., 1996, Department of Health and Human Services.

SUGGESTED READINGS

Corbin CB, Pangrazi RP: How much physical activity is enough? *JOPERD* 67(4):33, 1996. It is recommended that inactive people need some physical activity; beginners need to start slowly and then progress; adults need at least 30 minutes of moderate intensity physical activity most days; some vigorous activity is recommended. Implementing the FIT formula (frequency, intensity, and time) helps to achieve and maintain high levels of physical fitness and weight control; and some weekly activity designed to build muscular strength and endurance and flexibility is encouraged.

Dorman SM: *Healthy People 2010* online, *J of Sch Health* 70(3): 113, 2000. Health promotion and education resources that are available online from the federal *Healthy People 2010* initiative are presented.

Fernandez-Balboa JM, Barrett K, Solomon M, Silverman S: Perspectives on content knowledge in physical education, *JOPERD* 67(9):54, 1996. The authors describe the pragmatic, cognitive, constructivist, and critical perspective on content knowledge in physical education.

Foret CM, Clemens JM: The elderly's need for physical activity, *JOPERD* 67(4):57, 1996. Based on their entry-level health status, seniors need to participate in properly administered exercise programs that help them improve their functional capacity.

Gill DL (ed.): Quality of life: through movement, health, and fitness, *Quest* 48:245, 1996. This issue contains 14 papers presented at the 1995 meeting of the American Academy of Kinesiology and Physical Education. All of these papers focus on quality of life through movement, health, and fitness.

Haskell WL: Physical activity, sport, and health: toward the next century, *Res Q* 67 Supplement to No. 3: S-37, 1996. The need to promote a physically-active lifestyle has become more critical because of the impact of new technology on work and leisure time and the general aging of the population. The author recommends seven strategies for enhancing health.

Kimiecik JC (ed): A practitioner's guide to exercise motivation, *JOPERD* 62(7):33, 1991. Three articles on children, adults, and older adults stress how to encourage all ages to increase and persist in their physical activity.

Morrow JR, Blair SN: Promoting the Surgeon General's *Report on Physical Activity and Health:* activities of the NCPPA, *Quest* 51(2):178, 1999. The authors advocate for collaborative activities and coalitions to help deliver the message of the Surgeon General's report about the essential relationship between physical activity and health and to work to achieve the goals of *Healthy People 2010.*

Pangrazi RP, Corbin CB, Welk GJ: Physical activity for children and youth, *JOPERD* 67(4):38, 1996. Children should be encouraged to participate in sporadic, high volume, moderate-intensity physical activities. These should be individualized and enjoyable so that youth learn behavioral skills that lead to lifetime activity.

Physical Activity, Health, and Well-Being—An International Scientific Consensus Conference, *Res Q* 66:268, 1995. This special issue published the papers of the eight scientists who were invited to review the current specialist knowledge in their fields at this 1995 conference.

2 EXERCISE AND SPORT SCIENCES

KEY CONCEPTS

- An academic discipline includes a body of knowledge that is scholarly and theoretical and seeks to gain greater insights.
- Ten exercise and sport sciences continue to make significant contributions to the knowledge base of their disciplines.
- As a multidisciplinary field, the exercise and sport sciences share content knowledge with technology and the humanities.

A critical issue in the fields of physical education, exercise science, and sport studies is whether they can be considered academic disciplines. The major question debated in the 1960s (Henry, 1964) was whether physical education possessed a body of knowledge that was formally organized and merited scholarly study. An emphasis on the theoretical and scholarly content of physical education rather than on its practical aspects resulted in attempts starting in the 1980s to rename this field using a more scholarly descriptor. This chapter gives an overview of the contributions of 10 exercise and sport sciences to determine whether physical education, exercise science, and sport studies deserve such a categorization.

WHAT IS AN ACADEMIC DISCIPLINE?

An **academic discipline** is a formal body of knowledge discovered, developed, and disseminated through scholarly research and inquiry. The components of an academic discipline include:

- A body of knowledge
- A conceptual framework
- Scholarly procedures and methods of inquiry
- Both the process of discovery and the end result

If physical education, exercise science, and sport merit the distinction of being called academic disciplines, these criteria must be met.

A body of knowledge refers to an area of study that seeks to find answers to important questions. Participants in a field seek to gain information and to contribute to the knowledge available to others. Physical educators have discovered and reported information that is of value to researchers and practitioners in other fields. Examples of their contributions include studies about the effects of drugs on physical performance, the importance of feedback to learning, and the role of sports in developing cultures. In these and many other studies, the physical educators and exercise scientists examine the physiological, psychological, historical, or sociological impact of physical activity on people.

Similarly, research studies in an academic discipline must be guided by a conceptual framework. Proper hypotheses and experimental designs, strict controls, absence of bias, accurate reporting of findings, and interpretive analyses should characterize each attempt to gain new knowledge. This process requires stringent adherence to protocol to give credibility to the results.

Scholarly procedures and methods of inquiry are built upon this conceptual framework. For example, the sport historian must not rely on secondary, and often inaccurate, sources in examining significant events. Motor development specialists must evaluate the role of genetics and the environment in assessing readiness to learn. The exercise physiologist must control extraneous variables when analyzing the effect of a treatment, such as consuming a different diet or taking a specific drug, on a training regimen.

In seeking knowledge, the process of discovery and the end result are equally important. How the researcher collects data influences the findings; therefore, accuracy in reporting and interpretation is vital. Also, replication studies should verify the results consistently.

Other characteristics of an academic discipline include a substantial history and tradition, a broad scope that is unique in comparison with other fields, and a specific language. Thus, for physical education, exercise science, and sport studies to qualify as academic disciplines, they must contribute to the body of knowledge by using a conceptual framework, scholarly procedures and methods of inquiry, theoretical processes of discovery, and analysis of the end results.

THE SCIENTIFIC FOUNDATION OF PHYSICAL EDUCATION AND SPORT

Before describing the exercise and sport sciences, it is important to realize that our scientific foundation is multidisciplinary. Numerous academic fields of study provide many of the principles and methods of scientific inquiry used by researchers. One cornerstone is biology, the study of life and life processes. Upon these biological facts and information are built anatomy, physiology, chemistry, and physics.

Anatomy and physiology are the studies of the structure and function, respectively, of the human body. Chemistry is the study of the composition, properties, and reactions of matter. The specialization of biochemistry focuses on biological substances and processes, such as how the body's cells use food to obtain energy through respiration. The study of physics examines interactions between matter and energy including various types of motion and forces. These and other sciences rely on applied mathematical concepts and computations.

History, philosophy, psychology, and sociology are often called social sciences because they seek knowledge in more experiential ways than do the "hard" sciences described above. The historian seeks to record and analyze past events. In the pursuit of wisdom through intellectual and logical means, the philosopher investigates the causes and laws underlying reality. The psychologist examines mental processes and behaviors. The sociologist studies human behavior in society. After the 10 exercise and sport sciences are discussed, refer to Table 2-1 to examine the relationships among these and the influencing discipline and to Figure 2.1 to see the interrelations among the 10 exercise and sport sciences.

TABLE 2-1
RELATIONSHIPS AMONG DISCIPLINES

Influencing Discipline	Exercise and Sport Science	Shared Research Interests with
Anatomy Biology Chemistry Physiology	Exercise physiology	Motor control and learning Sport biomechanics Sports medicine Sport and exercise psychology
Physiology Psychology	Motor development	Motor learning
Anatomy Physiology Psychology	Motor control and learning	Exercise physiology Motor development Sport biomechanics
Mathematics	Sport biomechanics	Exercise physiology Motor control and learning Sport medicine
History Philosophy Sociology	Sport history	Sport philosophy Sport sociology
Accounting Finance Law Management Marketing	Sport management	Sport sociology
Anatomy Physical therapy Physiology Psychology	Sports medicine	Exercise physiology Sport biomechanics Sport and exercise psychology
History Philosophy	Sport philosophy	Sport history sport sociology
Physiology Psychology Sociology	Sport and exercise psychology	Exercise physiology Sports medicine Sport sociology

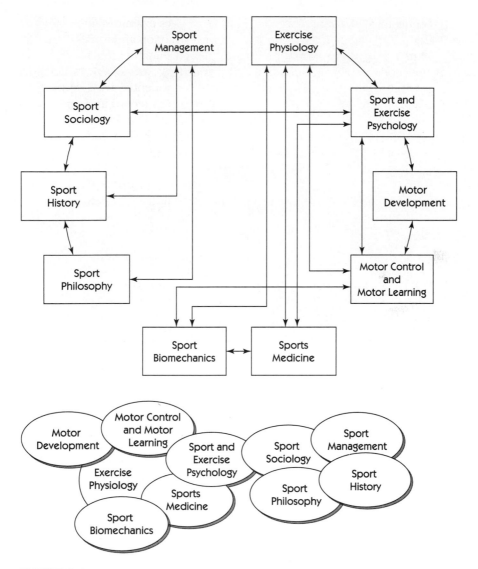

FIGURE 2.1

Exercise and sport sciences—two depictions of their interrelationships.

Exercise Physiology

The study of bodily functions under the stress of muscular activity is called **exercise physiology.** The publications *Healthy People 2000,* the Surgeon General's *Report on Physical Activity and Health,* and *Healthy People 2010,* as discussed in Chapter 1, have thrust exercise physiology research into the national limelight. The Surgeon General's report, for example, completed an exhaustive review of all extant research dealing with the role of physical activity on the health of

Technology has enhanced exercise physiology research.

Americans and concluded that the relationship was integral and that good health through moderate activity was easily within the reach of most citizens. With physical inactivity and other health-risk behaviors at all time highs, it has become paramount that the general public commit to lifestyle changes that can reduce morbidity and improve the quality of life. Exercise physiologists can help through their research in preventative and rehabilitative studies and the publications of their findings that can inform individuals who work with physical activity programs for those of all ages.

One of the first individuals to conduct research on these relationships was George Fitz. As described in Chapter 8, Fitz helped establish the first exercise physiology laboratory at Harvard University over a century ago, through which he advocated using research to substantiate or refute physical activity claims. Exercise physiology, which became the cornerstone of early collegiate physical education programs, grew in stature after the establishment in 1954 of the American College of Sports Medicine. This organization brought together (or rejoined—see Chapter 8) the medical and scientific communities in the shared quest to investigate all aspects of the impact of physical activity on the body.

The study of exercise physiology is built upon an understanding of the anatomical and physiological bases for human movement, including the 206 bones in the human skeleton; the joint structure, which includes cartilage, ligaments, and muscular attachments; the muscular system; the nervous system; and the circulatory and respiratory systems. More than 400 muscles, through a system of levers in conjunction with the skeletal system, provide the physiological key and guide to human movement. This potential for motion is released through the initiation of the nervous system and the biochemical reactions that supply muscles with energy.

Exercise physiologists measure the metabolic responses of the body to exercise and training through various endurance, flexibility, and strength programs. In these projects, they may examine changes in the cardiovascular system, stroke volume, pulse rate, blood composition, and other physiological parameters. Other researchers study how the body utilizes carbohydrates, fats, and proteins during exercise; the effects of diet, smoking, and temperature on performance; and differences between trained and untrained individuals based on a variable such as sleep, diet, and gender.

Exercise physiologists, because of their expertise in understanding bodily functions under the stress of muscular activity, are often consulted about or given the responsibility for prescribing and monitoring exercise programs for cardiac patients. Specialists in cardiac rehabilitation monitor exercise paradigms for individuals who have experienced cardiovascular trauma or prescribe preventive programs for people demonstrating coronary disease risk factors. Biomechanists and exercise physiologists often work together to design the most appropriate training programs for elite athletes, such as those at the United States Olympic Training Center in Colorado Springs.

Researchers in exercise physiology often prescribe workouts on treadmills to monitor oxygen uptake and expired carbon dioxide, to take heart rate and function measurements, and to analyze the chemical activities of the body. Using computers to interface some of these measurements with one another has furnished accurate and immediate results. Exercise physiologists also conduct joint research projects with athletic trainers concerning the prevention and rehabilitation of injuries and with physicians in the areas of muscle biopsies and blood lactate analyses.

Exercise physiologists are interested in studying how the body utilizes food relative to energy output. They have found that numerous factors, such as sleep, drugs, work, and stress influence how the body reacts to a specific diet or an exercise paradigm. Biochemical and physiological tests isolate those nutritional factors that most dramatically affect performance. Studies include the effects of marathon training on nutritional needs, the risks or benefits of vitamin supplementation and the effects of caffeine on various heart parameters. Nutritional information also is vital for the athlete in training who needs to maintain a specific weight, for individuals with disabling conditions who are minimally active, and for the senior citizen whose metabolic rate has slowed.

Exercise physiologists conduct research on how environmental and age factors affect exercise. They also study the interrelationships among disease, bodily functions, and health within the context of exercise. Exercise epidemiology in recent years has emerged to examine how physical activity impacts mortality. Research on the effects on asthma on respiration have helped exercise physiologists develop training programs for athletes who have exercise-induced asthma. Exercise physiologists collaborate with athletic trainers to design rehabilitative programs as well as developmental programs to enhance sport performance (see Research View box "Exercise Physiology").

✐RESEARCH VIEW

Exercise Physiology

In studying how the body functions during muscular activity exercise physiologists conduct research to answer these questions:

- What are the metabolic response of non-fit, adult bodies during endurance training?
- What is the most effective method for developing and maintaining muscular strength for female volleyball players?
- How do various diets or nutritional supplements affect the performance of elite athletes?
- Why and how do individuals respond differently to varying amounts of sleep, caffeine, or temperatures?
- What types of fitness programs are appropriate for senior citizens?
- How do individuals with high levels of cardiovascular fitness differ in their stroke volume, blood lactates, perceived exertion, and pain tolerance to those who engage in no cardiovascular fitness training?
- What kind of routines might an exercise physiologist prescribe for participants in a cardiac rehabilitation program?
- What are the optimal frequency, intensity, and duration for an effective off-season baseball team's conditioning program?
- What affect does ethnicity have on athletic performances such as sprints in track or rebounding in basketball?
- What is the current physical fitness status of school-aged children?

Motor Control and Learning

Motor behavior is a broad term that encompasses motor control, motor learning, and motor development. **Motor control** is an area of study that deals with the neurophysiological factors that impact human movement; **motor learning** is the study of the cognitive processes underlying motor acts associated with skill acquisition through practice and experience. Motor development will be discussed in the next section. Research in solving industrial problems (such as safe and efficient movements in the work place) and military needs (such as pilot selection and training) laid the foundation for the emergence of the fields of motor control and motor learning. Led by Franklin Henry, Alfred Hubbard, Arthur Slater-Hammel, and Dick Schmidt, motor control and motor learning specialists expanded their research and published scholarly manuscripts in journals such as the *Journal of Motor Behavior*. They completed studies dealing with

- Closed-loop theory—how feedback following slow and discrete movements could be used to improve subsequent motor performances;

Motor learning knowledge, such as use of various types of feedback, can enhance an archer's performance. (Photo courtesy Lisa Sense.)

- Open-loop theory—how motor patterns, such as striking skills, could be generalized to a variety of sports or settings, with or without limited feedback;
- Dynamic systems theory—how degrees of freedom in joints and muscles along with neural control can lead to enhanced motor performance;
- Types of practice—investigated the appropriateness and effectiveness of massed or distributed, blocked or random, mental or physical, full or reduced speed, modeling and contextual practice session;
- Cognitive processes in learning motor skills—investigated how knowledge of results and knowledge of performance affect subsequent motor patterns;
- Transfer of learning—investigated how motor skills learned in one setting can be generalized to another sport;
- Types of feedback—investigated how intrinsic, extrinsic, terminal, concurrent, visual, verbal, constant, and interval feedback impact motor performance;
- Special needs—investigated how individuals with special needs, including the aging, can regain and maintain their balance, coordination, reaction time, fundamental movement skills, and fitness levels.

The fields of motor control and motor learning grew out of the area of psychology dealing with human performance and behavior. Whereas motor control focuses on the neurophysiological factors of how and why people move as they do, motor learning integrates the cognitive processing of information with motor skill acquisition. Specialists in motor control and motor learning examine the variables that lead to improved performance of motor skills by responding to questions such as these:

- How and why do the muscles of people respond differently to similar stimuli?

- Describe how massed and distributed types of practice impact motor performance?
- How do neurological responses to cues impact motor performance?
- What type (and with what frequency) of feedback should be provided to enhance motor skill acquisition?
- What type of practice, mental or physical, is optimal for the learning of a skill such as putting a golf ball or shooting a basketball free throw, and why?
- What is the relationship between a student's learning style, this person's information processing system and the ability to learn a motor skill?
- How do varying cognitive abilities impact the learning of motor skills?
- Describe the interrelationship between information processing and skill acquisition.
- How does a person's reaction time influence the learning of motor skills?
- Describe how the aging process affects motor control and motor learning.

The objective of these researchers independently, as well as collectively, is to understand and enhance human movement. In motor control, it is essential to investigate the neuromuscular pathways in order to improve the learning of motor skills. In motor learning, it is essential to build on this information and add knowledge of feedback and optimal practice methods. Motor control researchers may use imaging or manipulation to help the child with special needs learn new motor patterns, whereas motor learning researchers use verbal and kinesthetic cues to help young athletes learn complex motor skills such as heading a soccer ball.

Motor Development

Motor development is the study of the maturation and changes in motor behavior throughout life. Researchers in this field examine factors that influence the performance of motor skills including developmental differences that occur over time. Movement competencies are influenced by contributions from genetics as well as the environment. Throughout life, individuals continually progress from unskilled movements to the demonstration of complex motor skills with accommodations made for age and any physical limitations. Motor development encompasses the process and results of motor behavior as well as the factors that affect it.

Motor development historically has been closely aligned with developmental psychology, such as through studies that examined behavioral sequences and the maturational process. Anna Espenschade's article on "Motor Performance in Adolescence, including the Study of Relationships with Measures of Physical Growth and Maturity" published in 1940 described one of the early models for motor development research. This study and related research by Lawrence Rarick, Vern Seefeldt, and others supported the positive influence of physical growth and development on motor performance. Educational psychology studies into perceptual-motor development concluded that improved motor skills led to an enhancement of academic performance and that cognitive development positively impacted skill acquisition over time. This was especially important because data from studies in this area were used to justify school physical education programs for children. In recent years, researchers have found that dynamic systems, more than cognitive processes, account for enhanced motor performance.

Specialists in motor development investigate questions such as these:

- When are children developmentally ready for weight training and cardiovascular training programs?
- What are the hereditary and environmental factors that most significantly influence obesity in children?
- How and why do weight training and cardiovascular training programs delay the aging process?
- What are the characteristics of children who are developmentally ready for competitive sports?
- What are the developmental stages for learning the fundamental movement skills?
- How does socioeconomic status, which affects nutritional health, impact the development of motor skills?
- How does the developmental level of a person limit his or her ability to learn or to enhance a motor skill?
- What are the factors that determine the relationship between cognitive development and motor development in learning a complex motor skill?
- How does gender affect developmental readiness in motor development?
- What are the developmental stages for learning fundamental sports skills?

Much of the research in motor development is associated with children as they learn fundamental motor skills. Yet, adults also can learn new perceptual-motor skills. Longitudinal studies are especially beneficial in determining the varied factors that impact what, how, and why motor performance emerges. Interdisciplinary research, such as with exercise physiologists or motor learning specialists, not only strengthens present understanding, but also paves the way for improved motor behavior.

Sport Biomechanics

Sport biomechanics is the study of the effects of natural laws and forces on the body through the science and mechanics of movement. Biomechanists study the musculoskeletal system, the principles of mechanics, and activity analyses. They examine the force of muscular contractions; flexion, extension, pronation, and supination of the muscles during activity; the composition of muscle fibers; equilibrium, center of gravity, and base of support; transfer of momentum; and projection of the body or an object. Their findings have contributed to improved

Biomechanical analyses are used to enhance sports performances. (Photo courtesy John R. Stevenson.)

athletic performance and have been used to prevent injuries, which is of special interest to physical therapists and athletic trainers. For example, through biomechanical analysis, minor flaws in throwing technique for the discus or stride length for sprinting can be identified and corrected to enhance distance or to reduce time. Scientific answers can be provided to questions such as: What kind of shoe support is needed for individuals participating regularly in aerobics? What weight of bat is optimal for hitting home runs? What type of weight training is appropriate for judo or volleyball players? What type of exercise program is best for increasing joint flexibility for senior citizens?

Biomechanists explain movement in relation to acceleration, energy, mass, power, torque, and velocity. They rely on mechanical principles such as force application and absorption, leverage, and stability. Use of cinematography (motion-picture photography) has become common among coaches and teachers for the analysis of performance. Electromyography is the measurement of electrical discharges from a muscle to study the action potential and the sequence of muscular activity. An analysis of the position and movements of joints is possible with electrogoniometry. Biomechanists also measure muscular forces using a force platform, determine speeds or frequencies using a stroboscope, and record movements and electrical responses (such as the heart rate) using a telemeter. Computer-assisted analyses have helped isolate components of physical skills that then can be corrected or changed to improve efficiency.

Interest in the science of applying mechanics to human movement can be traced to the early 1900s when the focus was on understanding anatomy and physiology. Notable curricular and research emphases during the following decades included body dynamics, efficiency of work, cinematic studies of sports skills, mechanical analysis of human performance, electromyography, and neurophysiology. Several scholars, such as Ruth Glassow, Thomas Cureton, Gladys Scott, and John Cooper, conducted kinesiological studies grounded in the scientific foundation of physical education and sport that provided the basis for the development of this field. The founding of the International Society of Biomechanics and its publication of the *Journal of Biomechanics* were leading forces in the emergence of biomechanics as a specialty (see Research View box "Sport Biomechanics").

RESEARCH VIEW

Sport Biomechanics

The sport biomechanist inquires into questions such as these:

- What is the optimal design and composition of the pole used in pole vaulting?
- How can a sport biomechanist use computer-enhanced images to analyze and improve the performance of sport skills?
- What are the biomechanical factors that contribute to muscular and joint injuries in baseball pitchers?
- How can fundamental movement skills such as running, jumping, and throwing be taught most effectively and efficiently?
- What mechanical principles are most important for reducing injuries and increasing the attainment of strength goals in weight training programs?
- How does weight transfer affect force and aerodynamics in striking motions?
- Biomechanically, why did the crawl stroke and the Fosbury flop revolutionize swimming and the high jump, respectively?
- What are the most effective approaches for increasing an athlete's vertical jump?
- How and why does the stride length differ for a sprinter versus a distance runner?
- What are the biomechanical factors that contribute to an effective tennis serve?

Sport History

Sport history is the descriptive and analytical examination of the significant people, events, organizations, and trends that shaped the past. Sport historians investigate the past seeking to explain how, what, when, where, and why things occurred. Descriptive history explores events, individuals' contributions, and pivotal happenings using primary sources such as archeological artifacts, original writings, and eyewitness accounts. Such firsthand information is judged to be reliable and accurate, especially when confirmed by other primary sources. When no original information is available, secondary sources must sometimes be used to document history. History reported in secondary sources, however, must be verified meticulously to ensure accuracy. The narrative approach is often used in descriptive history to chronicle events, individual lives, and developments.

Vital to an understanding of why events happened as they did, is the more difficult interpretive or analytical work of historians. Such analysis attempts to explain the significance of each historical event within its historical and social context. Sport historians record biographies, examine organizations and their activities, describe trends and movements, and analyze how and why societal events occurred when they did.

A clear understanding of modern sports depends on an examination of the significant events and practices of the past. Changes in this country that have influenced the emergence and predominance of sport include colonialism, the expanding frontier, rural life, the industrialized age, military involvement, the information age, and the explosion in technology. Seminal works that laid the foundation for the emergence of the field of sport history included Foster Dulles' *Americans Learn to Play* (1940), John Betts' *America's Sporting Heritage, 1850–1950* (1974), and Robert Boyle's *Sport—Mirror of American Life* (1963). Led by physical educators, the North American Society for Sport History was established to legitimize the rising academic interest in this field. Through its *Journal of Sport History,* this organization, which includes individuals from a diverse group of disciplines, serves as the central forum for the promotion of sport history (see Research View box "Sport History").

RESEARCH VIEW

Sport History

The sport historian may examine questions such as these:

- What was the significance of Greek athletes competing in the nude?
- Why were African Americans excluded from Major League Baseball?
- Why were women initially excluded, and only begrudgingly included, in the modern Olympic Games?
- What role did the Industrial Revolution play in the growth and development of organized sport?
- What factors contributed to the establishment of the National Football League? How and why did its relationship with college football evolve as it did?
- How have sports played a role in the americanization of various immigrant groups in this country?
- How and why was basketball spread internationally?
- How did upper-class sport impact the popularity of organized sport in this country?
- What role has gambling played in sports?
- Why is the National Collegiate Athletic Association considered by many to be the most powerful amateur sports organization in this country?

Sport Management

Sport management is the study of the management of personnel, programs, budgets, and facilities in various sports settings. It includes the management functions of planning, organizing, directing, and evaluating, as well as the business components of marketing, accounting, economics, finance, and law. This field encompasses the spectator sport and fitness industries, sporting goods sales, and recreational and educational sport programs.

Academics and practitioners in sport management are interested in learning the answers to questions such as these:

- What amenities are important to increase attendance at sporting events at the high school, college, and professional levels?
- How can private health and fitness clubs attract and retain members?
- What recreational and leisure-time activities are of most interest to individuals of all ages?
- How can professional sports teams in smaller metropolitan areas financially compete with Major League Baseball given the disproportionate revenues in comparison to teams in larger metropolitan areas?
- What are the economic factors involved in joining a major college athletic conference? How does such a change affect the college's revenue- and nonrevenue-producing sports?
- What are the legal liabilities for a professional franchise when fans are injured or cause injury to other fans?
- What leadership and management characteristics or traits are most important for the success of a sport manager?
- What are the costs and benefits for awarding naming rights to a stadium or arena?
- How is market research important in sports?
- What responsibility do sport managers have for the ethical conduct of their athletes?

Professionals working in the management of sport and leisure programs in the 1980s recognized the need to study and develop an essential body of knowledge. The North American Society for Sport Management (NASSM) was established to promote, stimulate, and encourage research, scholarly writing, and professional development in the area of sport management. This cross-disciplinary field encompasses management, leadership, and organizational behavior in sport, sport ethics, sport marketing, sport finance, sport economics, sport business in the social context, legal aspects of sport, and sport governance. NASSM's *Journal of Sport Management* provides a venue for the publication of theoretical and applied aspects of management related to sport, exercise, dance, and play in a variety of settings, such as professional sports, intercollegiate athletics, interscholastic sports, health and sport clubs, and recreational sports.

The sport industry, broadly defined, involves sport products and services, all of which need sport managers. Career options exist in professional sports, intercollegiate athletics, high school sports, recreation programs, the leisure and travel industry, private and public health and sports clubs, and sporting goods businesses.

Sport managers need to be competent in a number of areas to qualify for such careers. These include communication skills, facility and event management abilities, sport marketing skills, financial management skills, and personnel management abilities.

Sports Medicine

Athletic training, or **sports medicine** as it is often called, includes the prevention, treatment, and rehabilitation of sports injuries. Sports medicine involves physicians, who may be general practitioners, orthopedic surgeons, or other specialists. Physicians are responsible for clearing athletes for practice and competition as well as attending to the needs of athletes in events in which the risks of injury are high. Athletic trainers are involved with athletes almost daily. They help design appropriate sport conditioning during the preseason, the postseason, and the off-season; they tape, preventively as well as protectively, athletes before activity; they are responsible for assessing injuries at the time they occur, for providing immediate and appropriate first aid, and for supervising the rehabilitation process upon the recommendation of a physician.

Extensive knowledge of the anatomy and physiology of the body and skill in applying this knowledge to injury situations are essential for athletic trainers. Sometimes they need to be able to console injured athletes and to keep them from trying to return to competition or practices too quickly. At other times, athletic trainers may need to encourage athletes to work more diligently during their rehabilitation (see Research View box "Sports Medicine").

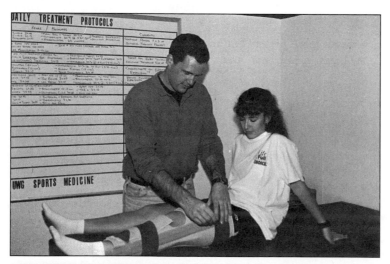

Athletic trainers apply splints to immobilize injured areas such as legs.
(Photo courtesy Bob Hilliard.)

⌕ RESEARCH VIEW

Sports Medicine

The athletic trainer studies the prevention, evaluation, management, and rehabilitation of injuries through seeking answers to questions like these:

- What type of flexibility training will help prevent injuries in football?
- What should be the authority of the athletic trainer in determining the readiness of injured athletes to return to competition?
- Why do more female athletes suffer from anterior cruciate ligament damages than do male athletes?
- What should athletes who seldom play during competitions do to maintain their cardiovascular conditioning?
- What is the optimal type of weight training for youth below the age of 12?
- What is the optimal rehabilitation program for a soccer athlete recovering from a hamstring muscle strain?
- What is the athletic trainer's role in evaluating an injury in the presence of a physician?
- How does an athletic trainer deal with a gymnast who is suffering from anorexia?
- What is the best treatment for ankle sprains?
- What is the athletic trainer's role in the nutrition of athletes?

Athletic trainers, who may also be educated as physical therapists, are expected to use various treatments, such as ultrasound, whirlpool, ice massage or heat. These professionals constantly help athletes play despite minor injuries by using the above treatments or various taping techniques.

The National Athletic Trainers' Association (NATA) seeks to enhance the quality of health care for athletes and those engaged in physical activity as well as advance the profession of athletic training through education and research in the prevention, evaluation, management, and rehabilitation of injuries. NATA was founded in 1950, and has grown to more than 22,000 members; over 100 universities and colleges offer NATA-approved curricula. NATA publishes the *Journal of Athletic Training,* a quarterly scientific journal.

Sport Philosophy

Sport philosophy is the search for, and the analysis of the truths, values, and actions of sport. Every person has a philosophy, although it may be unstated. One's philosophy is revealed in the particular thought patterns, behaviors, and aspirations each has. Sport philosophers analyze concepts, make normative

FILMS AND VIDEOS RELATED TO SPORT HISTORY AND SPORT PHILOSOPHY

- *Bang the Drum Slowly: Friendship and Compassion*—An examination of motivations and actions of major league baseball players
- *The Black Athlete*—Through interviews, the status of African Americans in sport is portrayed
- *Brian's Song*—True story of the deep and courageous friendship between Gale Sayers and Brian Piccolo of the Chicago Bears
- *Chariots of Fire*—Harold Abrahams and Eric Liddell lead the British track and field team to victories in the 1924 Olympic Games
- *Do You Believe in Miracles*—The winning of the gold medal in Olympic ice hockey
- *Eight Men Out*—The scandal of the Chicago White Sox throwing of the 1919 World Series
- *Going for the Gold. . . The Story of Black Women in Sports*—A profile of 17 African American women athletes
- *A Hard Road to Glory*—Compelling story of the early rise of African American athletes
- *Hoosiers*—Small town (Hickory) team wins the Indiana high school basketball championship in 1952
- *A League of their Own*—The story of the beginning of the All-American Girls' Professional Baseball League
- *The Natural*—Roy Hobbs seeks superstardom, but only leads his team to a play-off victory one year
- *Rocky Bleier*—True story of a Vietnam veteran who rehabilitates from a war injury to start for the world champion Steelers
- *"There Was Always Sun Shining Someplace": Life in the Negro Baseball Leagues*—Tells the story of the Negro Baseball Leagues with interviews of some of the stars
- *A Winner Never Quits*—Describes a high school team and the roles of the players, cheerleaders, and coaches
- *Women in Sports: An Informal History*—Reviews the history and development of sport opportunities for women

statements that guide practical activity, and speculate or extrapolate beyond the limits of scientific knowledge. Within the schools, sport philosophers examine how physical education contributes to both educational objectives and social values by explaining the nature, import, and reason for programs. Meeting peoples' needs, relating physical activity to human performance of all kinds, and enhancing the quality of life for others are the roles of sport philosophy outside the schools.

The sport philosopher seeks truth and understanding by investigating questions such as these:

- What is the meaning of competition to the athlete?
- Why do sports fans become so avid in their support of an athletic team?
- How and why does sport lose its element of fun for many competitors?
- Why is sportsmanship considered integral to sport?

- Does participation in sport lead to the development of moral values? And, if so, how does this occur?
- Why is "taking out an opponent" considered ethical by some athletes?
- What is the significance of a feminist sport perspective?
- Why is winning seemingly the only thing that matters in sport?
- Why would over half of the Olympic athletes who responded to a survey say that they would be willing to take a drug that would definitely kill them within five years if it could be guaranteed that they would immediately win a gold medal?
- Why is sport of such paramount interest to millions in this country?

The early roots of today's sport philosophy grew out of an eclectic philosophy of education and, subsequently, physical education. The various factors that have influenced sport philosophy include: the progressive education movement (including developmentalism), traditional philosophical systems (such as idealism, realism, pragmatism, naturalism, and existentialism), and specialized research investigating the nature, relationships, and values of sport. The establishment of the Philosophical Society for the Study of Sport and the publication of the *Journal of the Philosophy of Sport* helped establish the identity of this new field.

Most individuals in physical education and sport use philosophy to analyze issues of today. For example, what are the moral values depicted in films like *Chariots of Fire* or *Hoosiers?* (See other suggested films and videos in the box on page 52.) Why do the problems such as gambling, sports agents, and a lack of sportsmanship plague intercollegiate athletic programs today? Why do so many athletes, even at the high school level, use anabolic steroids? What lesson is learned by youth soccer players when the congratulatory hand-slap at the end of the game is eliminated because members of one team spit on their hands and then slapped their opponents' hands? Sport philosophy seeks to understand why such things exist, and what values they reflect.

Sport and Exercise Psychology

Sport and exercise psychology is the study of human behavior in sports, including an understanding of the mental processes that impact motor skill performance. Theories and laws of learning, the importance of reinforcement, and the linking of perceptual abilities with motor performance contribute to this body of knowledge. Sport and exercise psychologists utilize this information when studying topics such as achievement motivation, arousal, attribution, and personality development. Achievement motivation research examines how to promote self-esteem and self-actualization. Excitement and relaxation (as well as tension reduction), are among the parameters of arousal studies. The study of causal attribution weighs the importance placed on ability, effort, luck, and task difficulty relative to contest outcome. Aggression, competitiveness, anxiety, independence, extroversion, and self-confidence are among the personality traits researched. Sport and exercise psychologists also examine the influence of group dynamics, exercise addiction, and enhanced body image on people who are physically active.

Sports psychologists often use biofeedback techniques to help athletes achieve their potential. (Photo courtesy John Silva.)

The mental aspect of sports has intrigued researchers for years. Some have stated that at the elite level of sport, where all of the athletes are highly skilled, the outcome of the contest is overwhelmingly dependent on mental preparation and cognitive execution. Coleman Griffith is credited with conducting the initial sport psychology research, even though earlier researchers had stated that there were psychological benefits from participating in sport and physical activity. The prolific research coming from Griffith's Athletics Research Lab at the University of Illinois, along with early writings like John Lawther's *The Psychology of Coaching* (1951), Bryant Cratty's *Psychology and Physical Activity* (1967), and Robert Singer's *Motor Learning and Human Performance* (1968), laid the foundation for the emergence of this field of study. The founding of the North American Society for the Psychology of Sport and Physical Activity in 1967 and the Association for the Advancement of Applied Sport Psychology in 1985, and their publications, the *Journal of Sport Psychology* (later, the *Journal of Sport and Exercise Psychology*) and the *Journal of Applied Sport Psychology,* strengthened the development of this discipline.

Applied sport psychology focuses on understanding psychological theories and techniques to help athletes improve their performance. This area has grown in popularity as coaches and athletes seek a competitive edge. Specific strategies assist athletes in managing stress, concentrating more effectively, and maintaining confidence. Sport psychologists help athletes achieve their physical potential by improving their mental state (see Research View box "Sport and Exercise Psychology").

RESEARCH VIEW

Sport and Exercise Psychology

The sport and exercise psychologist studies how to enhance motor performance through an examination of and interventions in areas such as these:

- How does an athlete's self-efficacy impact performance?
- Why is stress reduction essential to success in sport?
- What role does mental imaging play in the execution of motor skills?
- How does participation in physical activity impact performance in cognitive tasks?
- What is the relationship between the body's psychological and physiological responses within sports?
- How does attribution influence the way an athlete deals with winning and losing?
- What is the difference in the arousal states of football linemen and elite golfers and how can these be shaped?
- How does the traditional pep talk given by a coach prior to a competition affect athletes?
- What are the most effective techniques for relaxation training?
- Why are sport psychologists increasingly hired by individual athletes and teams?

The clinical interventions used by sport psychologists include relaxation training, biofeedback, breath control, desensitization, and mental imaging. Through these, athletes are aided in coping with the pressures of competition.

Sport Sociology

Sport sociology is the study of social units and processes within the sporting context. This discipline examines the role of sports in human society by seeking to determine why people play and how participation in various physical activities influences them. The sport sociologist examines play, games, sports, recreational activities, and leisure-time pursuits in analyzing the expected outcomes of fun, relaxation, self-expression, wish fulfillment, and social interaction. The dynamics of socialization may reveal examples of racial and gender integration, exclusion, affiliation, competition, cooperation, conflict, rivalry, teamwork, and fair play.

Sport sociologists investigate sport as a game and as an institution. They examine the concepts of social mobility, class and gender stratification, status, racial and ethnic discrimination, team dynamics, social consciousness, and social values. Understanding the sociology of sport requires dealing with the relationship between sports and social institutions.

Sport is woven into the daily and seasonal fabric of American society. The social significance of sporting pastimes emerged from the British emphasis on sports in private boarding schools for boys in the mid-1800s. Schoolmasters and fathers came to believe that manly virtues learned through playing sports would prepare upper-class youth for their anticipated leadership roles in business, politics, and the military. This emphasis on character development through sports was adopted by organized sports in this country and has influenced attitudes toward sports at all levels. As an outgrowth of these perspectives about the role of sport in society, books such as Thorstein Veblen's *The Theory of the Leisure Class* (1899), Frederick Cozens and Florence Stumpf's *Sport in American Life* (1953), and Roger Caillois' *Man, Play and Games* (1961) blazed the trail for the subsequent development of the discipline of sport sociology. In the 1960s, publications and presentations by Gerald Kenyon, John Loy, and others led to the identification of sport sociology as a unique field of study. Publications such as the *International Review of Sport Sociology* and the *Sociology of Sport Journal,* as well as the establishment of the North American Society for the Sociology of Sport, marked its emergence and acceptance as a distinct discipline. Sport sociology moved from a positivist, empirical-analytical paradigm that focused on describing and analyzing the social order of sport to an interpretive research model. Scholars of this genre examined sport cultures from a variety of theoretical and methodological perspectives with an emphasis on interpretation. Today, many sport sociologists take a critical inquiry approach, where social dynamics are not only analyzed and interpreted, but suggestions are made for transforming social structures.

The sport sociologist addresses questions such as these:

- What sociological factors may have contributed to a mother purchasing a death contract on a girl who beat out her daughter for a spot on the high school cheerleading squad?

- Why did a sophomore in high school commit suicide after leading his team to the state football championship?

- What are the sociological factors that have contributed to the inequitable funding of girls' and women's athletic teams?

- Why are so few African Americans hired to coach professional and college sports teams?

- How are males and females socialized differently in and through sport?

- Why do approximately half of all children drop out of organized sports by age 12?

- Why are athletes permitted to act in violent ways during sporting events that would be illegal if these same acts occurred outside of sport?

- Why has television been allowed to dictate rule changes and starting times for sporting events?

- How does socioeconomic status affect individuals' participation in physical activity and sport?

- Does sport mirror society, or does society mirror sport?

EXERCISE AND SPORT SCIENCES QUIZ

1. Which of the exercise and sport sciences studies oxygen utilization during cardiovascular exercise and metabolic responses to exercise and training?
2. Which of the exercise and sport sciences describes and analyzes the past?
3. Which of the exercise and sport sciences studies how people learn skills, especially through practice and feedback?
4. Which of the exercise and sport sciences studies how sport impacts social units, processes, and institutions?
5. Which of the exercise and sport sciences analyzes the impact of motion, force, and energy on sport performance?
6. Which of the exercise and sport sciences analyzes the developmental patterns associated with movement and skill performance?
7. Which of the exercise and sport sciences uses extensive knowlledge of the body to help athletes stay injury free and return to competition safely?
8. Which of the exercise and sport sciences seeks to understand why people act as they do based on their values?
9. Which of the exercise and sport sciences involves providing sports products and managing sporting events?
10. Which of the exercise and sport sciences uses various mental coping strategies to aid sports performance?

As shown in Figure 2.1, each of these exercise and sport sciences are important disciplinary components. Take the Exercise and Sport Sciences Quiz above to review the key areas of emphasis for each of these. All of the exercise and sport sciences contribute to the greater whole. Rather than being mutually exclusive, they interact with each other.

Humanities

Although the humanities are not a part of the exercise and sport sciences, they have made a significant contribution to sports. The humanities, which encompass the areas of art, literature, and music, are noteworthy from both historical and practical perspectives. Archaeological discoveries from early civilizations verify the significance attached to physical activity for survival, group affiliation, religious worship, and enjoyment. From Myron's "Disco-bolus" during the Greek zenith to R. Tait McKenzie's "The Joy of Effort" (which received the King's Medal in the Fine Arts Competition at the 1912 Stockholm Olympic Games; see page 8) to a wall fresco of the first women's Olympic marathon champion Joan Benoit, art has vividly shown the beauty of human movement.

Homer's *Iliad* and *Odyssey* verify the importance of athletics in Greek times. According to several presenters at conferences of the North American Society for Sport History, some literature in the United States today, as well as that of earlier times, affirm the socialization role of sports.

WEB CONNECTIONS

1. www.nata.org
   This site for the National Athletic Trainers' Association lists all the requirements for obtaining certification and provides other helpful information for individuals interested in sports medicine.

2. www.nassm.org
   Visit this site to learn more about the North American Society for Sport Management.

3. www.naspspa.org
   Learn more about the multidisciplinary North American Society for the Psychology of Sport and Physical Activity and its work to improve the quality of teaching and research in sport psychology, motor development, and motor learning and control.

4. www.pesoftware.com/news.html
   Bonnie Mohnsen publishes this online newsletter for K through 12 physical educators to help them keep abreast of current trends in using technology in physical education.

5. www.nassh.org
   Learn more about the activities of the North American Society for Sport History at this site.

6. http://isb.ri.ccf.org/index.html
   Check out this site for more information about the International Society of Biomechanics, which promotes the study of all areas of biomechanics at the international level, with special emphasis on the biomechanics of human movement.

7. http://playlab.uconn.edu/nasss.html
   Examine this site of the North American Society for the Sociology of Sport, which promotes the sociological study of play, games, and sport.

Music provides the rhythm for movement experiences for all ages. The Greeks exercised to the music of the lyre, and music became a vital component of German school gymnastics in the 1800s. Children in elementary physical education today frequently experiment with and explore movement to the accompaniment of their favorite songs. In the 1980s, the addition of music to exercise routines helped popularize aerobics. Athletic team practice sessions, weight training workouts, and daily jogs often include music. Art, literature, and music can help focus on the development of a fit body, the socializing nature of sport, and the free experimentation of movement, thereby facilitating the application of the body of knowledge comprising the exercise and sport sciences.

Technology

Inseparably linked with the exercise and sport sciences is the use of technology. As mentioned in several of the previous sections, much of today's research relies on technology-based equipment that makes it possible to collect and analyze data. For example, biomechanists use technology to analyze the position and movement of joints to improve the techniques and performances of elite athletes. Exercise physiologists analyze the measurement of oxygen uptake and expired carbon dioxide, heart rate functioning, and chemical reactions to obtain immediate and valid data for exercise prescription. Sport psychologists use biofeedback techniques interfaced with computers to monitor arousal levels. Athletic trainers monitor conditioning programs and injury rehabilitation for thousands of athletes using computers. Sport managers utilize a plethora of software packages to monitor financial and statistical records.

Regardless of the computer platform, the operating system chosen, or the types of software being used, the exercise and sport scientist is limited in

"American Dream Machine"
Steel, 16 Feet Tall
Pat Monk

Pat Monk's *American Dream Machine* in an unusual, yet lifelike, manner depicts one type of sport. (Photo courtesy Pat Monk.)

contributing to the body of knowledge in the field without being technologically literate. In searching for information, exercise and sport scientists and their students can access a wealth of information through Compact Disc Read Only Memory (CD-ROMs), which store about 300,000 typewritten pages of text that can be easily retrieved using word searches. *Medline* (*Index Medicus*), ERIC (Educational Resources Information Center), and *SPORT Discus* offer a wealth of information in the exercise and sport sciences.

Internet (the network of computers that links individuals worldwide) access to the World Wide Web is an essential research tool. Using the browser of a program such as Netscape or Microsoft Explorer, anyone can gain access to an amazing range of resources. This includes the entire Encyclopedia Britannica (www.britannica.com), search engines such as Lycos (http://lycos.cs.cmu.edu), and the Library of Congress (http://lcweb.loc.gov). Also, every student should obtain (free to most students) an electronic mail (e-mail) address to aid their communication with professors and classmates.

SUMMARY

An academic discipline includes a body of knowledge, a conceptual framework, and scholarly procedures and methods of inquiry. Based on the heritage of physical education as a teaching profession, the exercise and sport sciences have drawn from and contributed to the knowledge base in multiple academic disciplines. Integral to the emergence and acceptance of the exercise and sport sciences as recognized academic disciplines have been the extensive scholarly and scientific research studies that have informed the academic community as well as the general public about the importance of physical activity. The exercise and sport sciences have improved the human movement experiences of individuals of all ages and skill levels. Research findings have helped prevent health-related disabilities as well as assisted in the rehabilitation of individuals who have suffered from medical maladies. Despite critics who claim that our fields have no unique body of knowledge, scholars in the exercise and sport sciences have made significant contributions to a broader understanding of the historical, sociological, psychological, and physiological roles of exercise and sport in the lives of everyone.

CAREER PERSPECTIVE

DORIS R. CORBETT
Sport Sociologist
ICHPER.SD President 1991–1999
AAHPERD President 1990–1991
NAGWS President 1980–1981
EDA-AAHPERD President 1987–1988
DCAHPERD President 1976–1978

EDUCATION
B.S., Health and Physical Education, North Carolina College
M.S., Physical Education, North Carolina Central University
Ph.D., Sociology of Sport, Sociology, University of Maryland

JOB RESPONSIBILITIES AND HOURS
As a Howard University professor, Doris' primary duties include teaching and research. She teaches courses in Sociology of Sport, Ethics and Issues in Sport, and History and Philosophy of Physical Education and Sport. She serves on the International Olympic Committee (IOC) Sports for All Commission. Doris dedicates many hours to research and writing in the areas of ethics and sport and women and sport issues. Doris' hours are 7.00 A.M. to 7.00 P.M. on most days of a typical work week, but her hours may be longer depending on departmental research, and international initiatives.

SPECIALIZED COURSE WORK, DEGREES, AND WORK EXPERIENCES NEEDED FOR THIS CAREER
A doctoral degree in one of the social sciences, such as sport sociology, is required for a university professorial rank. The ability to listen to people and to *hear* what the needs are of the various constituencies she serves is vitally important. To prepare for an academic professorship, take courses in the sociology of sport, women in sport, psychology of sport, sport management, history and philosophy of sport, comparative and international physical education and sport, cultural diversity, the Olympics, human relations, research, statistics, and at least one world language.

SATISFYING ASPECTS
Doris values the national and international connection to colleagues throughout the continental USA and abroad, and the opportunity to share information and to gain new knowledge and skills from a global community of professionals.

JOB POTENTIAL
If a professional attains a doctor's degree and engages in scholarly activity, then earning a tenured faculty position is realistic. An experienced, tenured professor in the social sciences of sport can achieve a salary of $50,000 or more. Becoming a dean, department chairperson, or program director is a possibility for interested and competent professionals.

SUGGESTIONS FOR STUDENTS

One must be academically prepared. One must be willing to spend long hours in meetings and travel, be open to learning new information, be flexible, be disciplined, purposeful and responsible, be honest with self and others, be a good listener, and not be afraid to let others know when you need help.

REVIEW QUESTIONS

1. What are the characteristics of an academic discipline?
2. What is exercise physiology, and how has it become the leading disciplinary foundation of sports?
3. What is biomechanics?
4. What is the difference between motor development and motor learning?
5. Within which of the exercise and sport sciences would research studies on mental practice to improve performance be conducted?
6. Why is sport history relevant?
7. Describe the various content areas that comprise sport management.
8. Describe the scope of responsibilities for an athletic trainer.
9. What role would a sport psychologist play with a professional athlete?
10. How would a sport historian and sport sociologist collaborate in research of mutual interest to them?

STUDENT ACTIVITIES

1. Select 1 of the 10 exercise and sport sciences and describe its contributions to sport.
2. Volunteer to help a faculty member or a graduate student conduct a research project specific to 1 of the 10 exercise and sport sciences.
3. Read two research articles that contribute to the body of knowledge in the exercise and sport sciences. Summarize the major points of each article, the scholarly procedures and methods of inquiry used, and the end result of each study.
4. Invite a specialist in each of the exercise and sport sciences to your class or majors club to present an overview of each field of study and how it interrelates with the others.
5. Divide the exercise and sport sciences into the following groups:

   - motor learning, motor development, and sport psychology
   - exercise physiology, biomechanics, and sports medicine
   - sport history, sport philosophy, sport sociology, and sport management

   Conduct a class debate about the relative significance of the contributions of each of these three groups.

6. Interview one of your professors who works in one of the exercise and sport sciences. Describe the type of research conducted by this person.

REFERENCE

Henry FM: Physical education: an academic discipline, *JOHPER* 35(7):32, 1964.

SUGGESTED READINGS

Blinde EM: Teaching sociology of sport: an active learning approach, *Teach Soc* 23(3):264, 1995. Four learning activities designed to help students understand the pervasiveness and significance of sport as a social institution are discussed.

Christina RW, Eckert HM (eds.): Enhancing human performance, *The Academy Papers* 25, 1992. This volume of *The Academy Papers* describes new concepts and developments for enhancing sport performance. It includes discussions about biomechanics, sport psychology, exercise physiology, and other exercise sciences.

Hyllegard R, Mood DP, Morrow JR, Jr.: *Interpreting research in sport and exercise science*, St. Louis, 1996, Mosby. This book provides a wealth of information about how to design, conduct, and analyze research projects in exercise and sport science.

Lehnus DL, Miller GA: The status of athletic marketing in division 1A universities, *Sp Mkt Q* 5(3):31, 1996. Data from questionnaires returned by university presidents, athletics directors, and marketing personnel revealed that the two most important problems facing college athletics in the next decade will be gender equity and inadequate finances. Marketing professionals can help with generating new revenues, but indicate a need for greater understanding by others about the function or concepts of sport marketing.

Masengale J, Swanson RA: *The history of exercise and sport science*, Champaign, IL, 1996, Human Kinetics Publishers. The authors describe the rich history and current status of the exercise and sport science fields.

Park RJ, Eckert HM (eds.): New possibilities, new paradigms?, *The Academy Papers* 24, 1991. The papers in volume 24 of *The Academy Papers* examine a reconceptualization of physical education with a look toward a multi-disciplinary study of human movement.

Pinheiro VED, Simon HA: An operational model of motor skill diagnosis, *J of Teach in PE* 11(3):288, 1992. Processes critical in motor skill diagnosis are discussed along with an operational model of motor skill development.

Sage GH: Physical education, sociology, and sociology of sport: points of intersection, *Soc Sp J* 14:317, 1997. The author describes the linkages between physical education, sociology, and sociology of sport in North

America as well as the connections between social theory and physical education before the sociology of sport developed its unique disciplinary foundation.

Silverman S: Communication and motor skill learning: what we learn from research in the gymnasium, *Quest* 46(3):345, 1994. After discussing the design for research in physical education settings, it is concluded that teachers are important in structuring and communicating expectations to students as they learn motor skills.

Thomas JR: Children's control, learning, and performance of motor skills, *Res Q Exer & Sport* 71(1): 1, 2000. In this text of the 1999 McCloy Lecture, the author discusses the characteristics of children that influence their motor skills, whether children's failure to use cognitive strategies account for deficits in motor performance, and how children develop motor expertise and control their movements.

3

THE PROFESSION OF PHYSICAL EDUCATION, EXERCISE SCIENCE, AND SPORT STUDIES

KEY CONCEPTS

- Careers in physical education, exercise science, and sport are characterized by the components of a profession.
- The American Alliance fulfills its objectives through the programs of its associations and through conventions, publications, and other activities that benefit its membership and the people they serve.
- Many professional organizations promote the study of and involvement in human movement, sports, leisure activities, fitness programs, and other related pursuits.
- Physical education, exercise science, and sport specializations in athletic training, coaching, fitness, sport management, exercise physiology, and therapeutic fields prepare students for diverse careers following the completion of specialized course work.
- Issues facing physical education, exercise science, and sport studies include program viability, teacher/coach conflict, and fragmentation.

Physical education has long been recognized as a part of the teaching profession, evidenced by its affiliation with the National Education Association since 1937. Even earlier, in 1885, a group of teachers and other interested individuals formed the Association for the Advancement of Physical Education to encourage the exchange of program and instructional ideas. Today, the American Alliance for Health, Physical Education, Recreation and Dance along with a multiplicity of allied organizations, promote a broad discipline that encompasses physical education, exercise science, health, sports, dance, and leisure. This chapter describes many of these associations along with their purposes, publications, and services. To understand physical education, exercise science, and sport, it is important to know the requisite educational background needed to enter many physical education, exercise science, and sport careers; therefore, the teaching option and some nontraditional specializations are described.

THE DISCIPLINE/PROFESSION DEBATE

Since the 1960s, a debate has raged within traditional physical education programs at the college level concerning whether it should be classified as a discipline or a profession. Academicians in recent decades claim that the only way that their research can be accepted as meritorious, and thereby their status within academe enhanced, is to disassociate from their historical roots. Conversely, advocates of physical education as a profession stress that our only justifiable uniqueness is "educating the physical." Let us examine this debate more fully.

Physical educators have long viewed themselves primarily as practitioners who taught knowledge, skills, and values. Although many early physical educators in the colleges held medical degrees, most physical educators in the schools and colleges received degrees from teacher training institutions. They studied the scientific foundations, but emphasized the application of this knowledge for the development of movement and sports skills. Physical education starting in the 1930s aligned itself closely with educational goals while specifying that it made a unique contribution to the education of the whole child. Teachers in the schools, who were often the coaches, enthusiastically supported the belief that theirs was a practical field.

In contrast, the acquisition of knowledge for its own sake, rather than for any applied purpose, was the rallying cry of the academicians, and especially those in the sciences. They focused on researching, conceptualizing, and theorizing. Those who emphasized that the broadening field of physical education must defend itself through scholarly writings and publications seemed worlds apart from the practitioners in the gymnasium. As this chasm widened in the 1970s, the academicians established numerous specialized organizations that provided outlets for their research in scholarly journals and through presentations at annual conferences.

The debate continued as those involved in disciplinary research sought knowledge for its own sake, while the teacher desired ways to help improve instruction. As society increasingly became more specialized in all areas, and the quality of the scholarship produced by the academicians improved, this disciplinary approach began to influence students' selection of majors. Simultaneously, many school physical education programs experienced cuts that resulted in a reduced demand for teachers. Students selecting nontraditional career options in physical education, exercise science, and sport, such as in athletic training, corporate and community fitness, and sport management, quickly exceeded the number choosing teacher education. The physical education generalist who could teach, coach, and work in a recreation program or a camp gave way to the disciplinary specialist.

PHYSICAL EDUCATION AS A PROFESSION

Before looking specifically at physical education as a profession, we need to define what a profession is. A **profession** is a learned occupation that requires training in a specialized field of study. The characteristics of a profession include:

- a complex, systematic body of theoretical knowledge
- individuals who have attained extensive knowledge and experience through a formal educational process
- standards and competencies for entry into the profession, often through a certification process
- mechanisms and opportunities for growth and development within the field to ensure adherence to established standards, competencies, and practices
- providing a socially valuable service that has received societal recognition and status
- governance by a code of ethics to protect those served

Physical educators and exercise and sport scientists must have at least a bachelor's degree and frequently have advanced study and training in an extensive body of knowledge that takes considerable time and effort to learn. Individuals in these fields share research findings and new ideas while serving people throughout society.

While the above describes physical education as a profession, Chapter 2 presented the exercise and sport sciences as academic disciplines. Are these contradictory or complementary perspectives? Physical education, exercise science, and sport studies include the 10 specialized disciplines described in the previous chapter, any of which can be a career emphasis. As individuals continue to specialize, they most often take on the identity of exercise physiologists or sport managers, even though their areas of work are based on physical activity. Historically, physical education has been one of the teaching professions. It has retained the characteristics of a profession even though it has expanded into teaching in various nonschool settings and into nonteaching, activity-related careers. Thus, physical education, exercise science, and sport studies have broadened to encompass aspects of an academic discipline and a profession.

NATIONAL ORGANIZATIONS AND SERVICES

The American Alliance for Health, Physical Education, Recreation and Dance (AAHPERD, or the Alliance) has grown from 49 to more than 30,000 members, and served these members for over a century. One reason for the widespread influence of AAHPERD is that many professional groups have merged into its structure. In 1937, as a department of the National Education Association, the former American Physical Education Association became the American Association for

Health and Physical Education. (It became an alliance in 1974.) Recreation was added to its title in 1938; dance was added in 1979.

The Alliance is an educational organization designed to facilitate and promote the purposes and activities of its members, associations, and affiliated groups. The Alliance's mission is to promote and support creative and healthy lifestyles through high quality programs in health, physical education, recreation, dance, and sport, and to provide members with professional development opportunities that increase knowledge, improve skills, and encourage sound professional practices. AAHPERD's mission is achieved through the following purposes:

- to develop and disseminate professional guidelines, standards, and ethics;
- to enhance professional practice by providing opportunities for professional growth and development;
- to advance the body of knowledge in the fields of study and in the professional practice of the fields by initiating, facilitating, and disseminating research;
- to facilitate and nurture communication and activities with other associations and other related professional groups;
- to serve as their own spokespersons;
- to promote public understanding and improve government relations in their fields of study;
- to engage in future planning; and
- to establish and fulfill other purposes which are consistent with the purposes of the Alliance.

The Alliance is headquartered at 1900 Association Drive, Reston, VA 20191-1599. For more information about the Alliance, call 1-800-213-7193 or visit the Alliance web site at www.aahperd.org. The services provided by the Alliance include holding an annual national convention; publishing brochures, research abstracts, conference proceedings, and other information pertinent to its fields of interest; positively influencing public opinion and legislation; and providing consultant services.

Periodicals published by the Alliance include the *Journal of Physical Education, Recreation and Dance,* which includes articles of a broad and practical nature, and the *Research Quarterly for Exercise and Sport,* which reports research findings. *Update,* published in newspaper format, keeps the membership apprised of current events and legislation. Issues of *Update* include notices of job vacancies and information about graduate assistantships.

The Alliance is divided into six national associations through which it accomplishes its goals. The **American Association for Active Lifestyles and Fitness (AAALF)** represents numerous special interest groups that fill particular niches to achieve its purposes as well as those of the Alliance. These councils and societies conduct conferences, publish position papers, and collaborate in promotional initiatives in areas such as aging, aquatics, adapted physical activity, administration, facilities, international relations, measurement, physical fitness, and safety.

The **American Association for Health Education (AAHE)** promotes health education in schools, public and community health agencies, business and industry, and colleges. Among the health issues vigorously addressed by AAHE are drug use prevention, HIV prevention and AIDS education, and cultural awareness and sensitivity. AAHE offers continuing education credits for health education professionals through a credentialing process using its *American Journal of Health Education.*

The **American Association for Leisure and Recreation (AALR)** seeks to enhance the quality of American life through the awareness and promotion of leisure and recreational experiences. In addition to helping integrate the concepts of positive leisure attitudes and values into education, AALR professionals formulate and disseminate leisure knowledge, trends, and delivery methods. This organization's commitment to uplifting the human spirit results in efforts to conserve cultural and natural resources so individuals can enjoy life-enriching experiences. The "Leisure Today" feature in the *Journal of Physical Education, Recreation and Dance* focuses on the provision of leisure and recreational programs for all populations including older individuals and those with special needs. In collaboration with the National Recreation and Park Association, the AALR accredits programs and has developed standards for evaluating services delivered by community, park, and recreation agencies.

The **National Association for Girls and Women in Sport (NAGWS)** seeks to improve and expand sport opportunities for girls and women at all levels of competition. It advocates for the initiation and enhancement of opportunities for sports participation and leadership for females. NAGWS helps coordinate the annual celebration of National Girls and Women in Sports Day. Through collaborative work with other associations, NAGWS is an advocate for equity in sport.

The National Association for Sport and Physical Education of the American Alliance for Health, Physical Education, Recreation and Dance serves over 20,000 members through various projects and programs. (Photo courtesy Mary Ellen Saville.)

NATIONAL ASSOCIATION FOR SPORT AND PHYSICAL EDUCATION

Physical Education Councils
- Council on Physical Education for Children
- Middle and Secondary Physical Education Council
- Council for School Leadership in Physical Education
- Council on Professional Preparation in Physical Education
- College and University Physical Education Council

Academics
- Biomechanics
- Curriculum and Instruction
- Exercise Physiology
- Motor Development
- Sport History
- Sport Philosophy
- Sport Psychology
- Sport Sociology

Sport Councils
- Coaches Council
- National Council of Athletic Training
- National Council of Secondary School Athletic Directors
- National Intramural Sports Council
- Sport Management Council
- Youth Sports Coalition

The **National Association for Sport and Physical Education (NASPE)** supports quality physical activity programs for children and adults. NASPE crusades for quality, daily physical education for each school student through conferences, print ads, public service announcements, and observance of the National Physical Education and Sport Week (May 1–7). Specialized councils serve NASPE members through conferences and workshops, convention programs, and the establishment of guidelines and position statements, such as "Developmentally Appropriate Physical Education Practices for Children." NASPE publishes *Strategies,* which includes practical articles for physical educators and coaches (see "National Association for Sport and Physical Education" box).

The **National Dance Association (NDA)** advocates for standards, assessments, and sound professional practices in dance education. It promotes dance pedagogy and the creative process, movement training, and performance practices. The NDA through its publications, conferences, and collaborations helps disseminate resources in dance curriculum, program development, and professional development.

Each of the national associations comprising the Alliance provides opportunities for student involvement. This begins by joining the Alliance, which can be done online at (www.aahperd.org/ssl/membership-form.cfm). Students are invited to attend the Alliance's annual convention, to participate on committees and councils through the national associations, and to read its journals and other publications. Since the future of physical education, exercise science, and sport studies depends on students who join the profession and take an active role, it is essential that these opportunities remain beneficial and interesting. Involvement often begins at the college level, where clubs for majors in physical education, exercise science, athletic training, sport management, and other fields exist. Through these collegiate experiences, students develop their leadership abilities, learn more about their fields of study from professors and guest lecturers, and have fun with their friends. Oftentimes, these major clubs participate in service activities by providing after-school fitness programs for at-risk kids, conducting events for Special Olympics, or by assisting with fund raising events for the American Heart Association or American Cancer Society. These service activities not only give back to the community but also strengthen and expand one's knowledge and skills.

The Alliance is divided into these six district associations that share the goals and activities of the Alliance while providing leadership opportunities and services within each region. (See Figure 3.1.) Membership in the Alliance and in a district is combined, thus enabling professionals to attend their district conventions and the Alliance's annual conventions. During these conventions, the Alliance provides a job placement service where graduates can learn about vacancies and interview for jobs. Nonconvention workshops, clinics, and seminars provide Alliance members with the latest research findings, innovative activities, and teaching approaches as well as opportunities for personal enrichment and growth. One example of this leadership is the Southern District's position paper on physical education (see box on page 73).

Similarly, state associations provide professionals the opportunity to learn different coaching techniques, acquire new skills, and interact and exchange information with other members at their annual conventions. Students, especially you, should take advantage of state conventions. Not only will you learn from these experiences, but you may also make contacts with individuals who later hire you or help you to get a job.

Thus, physical education, exercise science, and sport studies provide enrichment opportunities to members as they prepare themselves to serve others. They are joined in their efforts by related groups who seek to share knowledge for the benefit of all.

Pedagogy

The pedagogist (or teacher) must provide an effective learning environment that focuses on successful practice opportunities. Each student or participant should spend most practice time "on task," rather than being subjected to management or organizational distractions such as waiting to use the equipment. Each individual needs to be sequentially challenged by the movement experience or sports

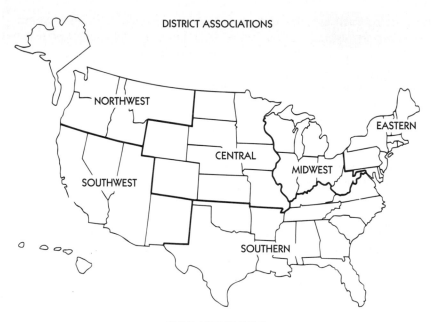

DISTRICT ASSOCIATIONS

STATE ASSOCIATIONS

NORTHWEST DISTRICT
Alaska
Idaho
Montana
Oregon
Washington

CENTRAL DISTRICT
Colorado
Iowa
Kansas
Minnesota
Missouri
Nebraska
North Dakota
South Dakota
Wyoming

SOUTHWEST DISTRICT
Arizona
California
Guam
Hawaii
Nevada
New Mexico
Utah

SOUTHERN DISTRICT
Alabama
Arkansas
Florida
Georgia
Kentucky
Louisiana
Mississippi
North Carolina
South Carolina
Oklahoma
Tennessee
Texas
Virginia

MIDWEST DISTRICT
Illinois
Indiana
Michigan
Ohio
West Virginia
Wisconsin

EASTERN DISTRICT
Connecticut
Delaware
Washington, D.C.
Maine
Maryland
Massachusetts
New Hampshire
New Jersey
New York
Pennsylvania
Puerto Rico
Rhode Island
U.S. Virgin Islands
Vermont

FIGURE 3.1

District and state associations.

SOUTHERN DISTRICT AAHPERD POSITION PAPER ON PHYSICAL EDUCATION

Physical education contributes to the growth, development, motor skill acquisition, and fitness of students through physical activity/movement and health-related activities. Participation in physical education can contribute to awareness and positive attitudes that regular vigorous activity is essential throughout life to maintain health and to enrich the quality of life. Because of its unique and essential contribution to the total education program, daily quality physical education should be required in grades K–12.

In grades K–5, classes should be a minimum of 30 minutes each for a minimum total of 150 minutes per week. In grades 6–12, classes should be the length of a regular class period for a minimum total of 250–300 minutes per week. Class size should be consistent with other subjects in the school curriculum.

Classes should be scheduled by grade level and, whenever possible, by ability and physical maturation level. Classes should be designed to accommodate differences in ability among all students including those with identified special needs. Students with identified special needs should be placed in special classes only when it is demonstrated that there is not a reasonable opportunity for success in regular classes through the use of appropriate modifications and accommodations.

No substitutions should be permitted for participants in marching band, interscholastic sports, ROTC, and other extracurricular activities.

Both indoor and outdoor physical education facilities should be provided and should be maintained to meet safety standards. Quality equipment and supplies should be provided in sufficient quantity to meet the needs of all students. Appropriate clothing designed for free and safe movement should be worn in all physical education classes.

Physical fitness, including concepts, should be emphasized as a vital component of the curriculum at all levels. The elementary school curriculum should emphasize the development of basic movement awareness, fundamental motor skills, and fitness, as applied to educational games, educational dance, and educational gymnastic contexts. The middle school/junior high school curriculum should emphasize gymnastics, stunts, and tumbling, aquatics, dance, individual, dual, and team activities/games, recreation, and outdoor education. The secondary/senior high school curriculum should emphasize progressive lifetime-leisure activities and individualized fitness-related theory and exercise programs.

Elementary classes should be taught by instructors certified in physical education with an elementary physical education emphasis. Secondary physical education should be taught by instructors certified in physical education with a secondary physical education emphasis.

(Courtesy the Southern District of the American Alliance for Health, Physical Education, Recreation and Dance.)

---

skill to achieve success while being motivated to pursue additional learning. These components of effective teaching are so critical that each will be explained in greater depth (see Research View box "Pedagogy").

The first objective is to use class or practice time efficiently and effectively. Each teacher must plan extensively to ensure that equipment is readily accessible, handouts explaining the day's lesson are prepared for distribution, and instructional learning cues appropriate for students with heterogeneous abilities are ready for use. The good teacher is also prepared to handle management tasks (such as calling roll and passing out equipment) and discipline problems with

RESEARCH VIEW

Pedagogy

Teachers, in their continuous process to enhance their pedagogical practices, seek answers to questions like these:

- What instructional strategies should be used to meet the various learning styles and multiple intelligences of a diverse class of students?

- How much of class time is devoted to providing instruction, allowing for practice, giving feedback, dealing with discipline problems, managing equipment distribution, and checking attendance? What adjustments, if any, should be made to provide the optimal learning environment?

- How do the genders of teachers and students affect the number and quality of interactions?

- How can students become engaged in developing personalized fitness programs?

- What role should students have in the selection and implementation of their physical education curriculum?

- What type of grouping, homogeneous or heterogeneous (or both), should be used to increase student learning?

- How can a middle school coach design and implement an athletic program focused on skill development and fun?

- Why and how should a personal trainer adapt strength training programs for adolescents, unfit adults, or senior citizens in cardiac rehabilitation programs?

- What is the most effective method of giving feedback to students learning new motor skills?

- Describe how to develop and implement an accurate and effective assessment process.

---

minimal loss of instructional and practice time. Each day's lesson is sequentially structured to provide maximal opportunities to practice each new skill.

The second essential criterion of exemplary teaching focuses on helping students or participants achieve success and challenge themselves to higher levels of skill development. Specific, corrective feedback and positive reinforcing comments about proper execution of a skill or movement must be provided by the teacher. Only when each participant, with his or her individual limitations, enjoys learning will they want to continue. A feeling of success is the key to this enjoyment.

The primary reason that people choose a career in teaching is the pleasure and reinforcement they receive when their students learn, enjoy the learning

An essential component of practice time is receiving specific, positive feedback from teachers. (Photo courtesy Bob Hilliard.)

process, and continue to participate and to develop their skills. Teaching is personally, more than financially, rewarding. This feeling of success occurs when teachers plan and implement innovative curricula, commit to the improvement of student-to-student and teacher-to-student interactions, assess students' performance in order to ensure that learning is occurring, and continually evaluate their work and make enhancements.

Pedagogy researchers seek to improve the instructional process through observation, analysis, and evaluation. By examining the amount of academic learning, direct instruction, and management time, one can determine how teachers' and students' behaviors influence learning. Research studies also look at teachers' expectations for students, the classroom learning climate, and the type and amount of feedback—all critical to student learning.

Adapted Physical Education

Adapted physical education prepares teachers to provide specialized programs for individuals with diverse abilities and limitations. Based on federal protection of individuals' rights and changing societal attitudes, increasingly school children with disabilities are being placed in regular classes, including physical education. **Inclusion** is the placement of students with physical, mental, behavioral, or emotional disabilities or limitations into regular classes with their peers. The inclusion of students who may have hearing limitations, are wheelchair-bound, have attention deficit disorders, suffer from cerebral palsy, or who are autistic presents significant challenges to the physical educator who must help these and all other students achieve cognitive, affective, motor skills, and physical fitness goals (see Research View box "Adapted Physical Education").

RESEARCH VIEW

Adapted Physical Education

Adapted physical educators seek to provide specialized programs for individuals with special needs based on research questions such as these:

- What are the most effective adaptations that can be made for the wheelchair-bound student during a softball unit of study?

- How can instructional strategies be used to accommodate students with attention deficit disorder?

- What curricular planning and implementation methods should the classroom teacher and the adapted physical educator utilize to meet the needs of children with emotional and behavioral disorders?

- Why are equipment adaptations essential for children with intellectual limitations? Which of these are most effective for the learning of fundamental movement skills?

- What types of evaluations and assessments should be used with children with learning disabilities who are placed in inclusion physical education classes?

- How can learning outcomes other than those associated with physical development be designed so that children with special needs can succeed?

- What are the most effective instructional strategies for the physical education curriculum portion of an Individualized Education Program for a child with cerebral palsy?

- Describe the conditions under which a child with special needs would be placed into a "pull out," adapted physical education class.

- What curricular adaptations should be made to help a gifted child who is obese become physically fit?

- What are the pros and cons of pairing a student with special needs with a student without any special needs during physical education classes?

Individualized programs or modified activities are needed to help all students have successful learning experiences. To make this approach effective, differently-sized and weighted pieces of equipment, choices in task dimensions and goals, and variety in evaluation measures should be used. Peer tutors, collaborative teaching, and cooperative learning activities have proven effective in inclusion classes.

Adapted physical educators can work with "regular" physical educators to reap the benefits of inclusion classrooms. Students gain respect for those who may be different. They demonstrate greater social acceptance, display changed

WEB CONNECTIONS

1. www.ashaweb.org
   Learn more about the American School Health Association and its
   programs and services for promoting the health of our nation's youth
   at this web site.

2. www.aahperd.org
   The American Alliance for Health, Physical Education, Recreation and
   Dance offers a huge array of information and services via this
   comprehensive web site.

3. http://pe.central.vt.edu/pecinfo/generalinfo.html
   This PE Central site contains a plethora of information to assist teachers
   in helping children become physically active and healthy for a lifetime.

4. www.pelinks4u.org
   This site provides a wealth of information for developing skillful and
   healthy movers.

5. www.activeparks.org
   Learn about all the programs and services offered by the National
   Recreation and Park Association.

6. www.pecentral.org/adapted/adaptedmenu.html
   A plethora of information about adapted physical education awaits
   the visitor to this site.

attitudes, and recognize their fellow students as having equal status. The collaboration among students as well as among the teachers who design curricula positively impacts learning. Inclusion implies that special resources, personnel, and curricular adaptations make it possible to educate all children with special needs, mild to severe, in regular classrooms.

Physical educators are increasingly sharing their expertise with and borrowing from the various therapeutic fields. The value of exercise in retarding osteoporosis and other degenerative diseases carries broad implications for recreational activities for senior citizens. Physical therapists and athletic trainers are seeking the best programs for injury rehabilitation. Exercise physiologists are working with physicians in the prescription of exercises for individuals who have suffered heart attacks. Recreational therapists and adapted physical educators together may provide appropriate activities for disabled employees and school children. In each of these cases, the medium of exercise is involved and, through consultation, the best activities are prescribed.

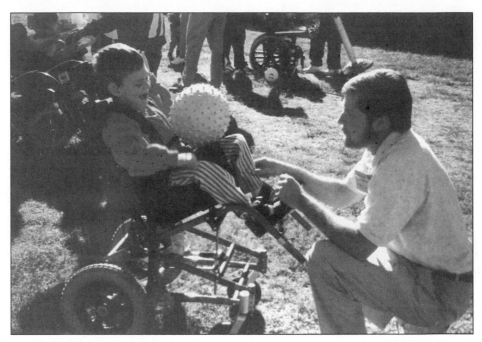

Through adapted physical education, persons with disabling conditions can develop physically by achieving their individual goals. (Photo courtesy Bob Hilliard.)

ALLIED ORGANIZATIONS

Although AAHPERD is the largest organization of professionals supporting those involved with physical education, health promotion, fitness, leisure, dance, and related specialties, it shares its interests with numerous other groups. The discussion that follows briefly describes some of these organizations.

Higher Education

In 1978, the National Association for Physical Education in Higher Education (NAPEHE) was formed by a merger of the National Association for Physical Education of College Women and the National College Physical Education Association for Men. Since the merger, NAPEHE has continued the publication of *Quest* and its conference proceedings.

Since 1930, the American Academy of Kinesiology and Physical Education has been the highest honorary group in health, physical education, and recreation. Its more than 125 active members have contributed scholarship and professional service, especially in colleges and universities. Some research studies are published annually in *The Academy Papers*.

Health

Since 1926, the American School Health Association has sought to improve health instruction, healthful living, and health services in the schools. Although originally only for physicians, membership is now open to anyone engaged in school health work. This association publishes the *Journal of School Health*.

Recreation

The National Recreation and Park Association (NRPA) is dedicated to improving the human condition through improved park, recreation, and leisure opportunities as well as developing and expanding their programs and services and addressing environmental concerns. NRPA facilitates the training of personnel who conduct community recreation programs. *SCHOLE: A Journal of Leisure Studies and Recreation Education, Journal of Leisure Research, Therapeutic Recreation,* and *Parks and Recreation* are NRPA publications.

The National Intramural-Recreational Sports Association (NIRSA) was begun in 1950 to provide an opportunity for college intramural directors to meet annually to exchange ideas and information. With the expansion of college programs into recreational services of all kinds, the Association assumed its present name in 1975. Sharing innovative program ideas, reporting research, and discussing policy and procedures highlight its annual convention and the *NIRSA Journal.*

Sports Medicine

The need to establish professional standards and to disseminate information led to the establishment, in 1950, of the National Athletic Trainers' Association (NATA), which publishes the *Journal of Athletic Training* for its members, who serve as athletic trainers at all levels of sport. The NATA Board of Certification accredits all approved undergraduate and graduate athletic training programs.

Rehabilitation is an important responsibility of athletic trainers. (Photo courtesy Bob Hilliard.)

The American College of Sports Medicine (ACSM) was founded in 1954 by individuals drawn from medicine, physiology, and physical education. Among its objectives are advancing scientific research dealing with the effects of physical activities on health and well-being; encouraging cooperation and professional exchange among physicians, scientists, and educators; initiating, promoting, and applying research in sports medicine and exercise science; and maintaining a sports medicine library. The ACSM encourages research publications on injury prevention and rehabilitation and on the environmental effects of exercise, nutrition, and other factors through its *Medicine and Science in Sports and Exercise.*

Other Exercise and Sport Sciences

Psychologists and physical educators founded the North American Society for the Psychology of Sport and Physical Activity in 1967 to promote this increasingly popular field of study. The Association for the Advancement of Applied Sport Psychology, founded in 1986, promotes research and intervention strategies in sport psychology. It publishes the *Journal of Applied Sport Psychology.* Since 1973, the North American Society for Sport History has encouraged scholarly research in all aspects of this discipline of sport, conducted an annual conference, and published the *Journal of Sport History.* The North American Society for Sport Management, established in 1985, focuses on the professional development of practitioners and researchers in this specialization. Articles in the *Journal of Sport Management* encompass both the theory and application of management to sport

Maintaining muscular strength and endurance are important throughout life.

settings. The National Strength and Conditioning Association (NSCA), founded in 1978, is comprised of teachers, personal trainers, physical therapists, sports medicine physicians, and sport science researchers. It promotes the total conditioning of athletes for optimal performance. It publishes the *Journal of Strength and Conditioning Research* and *Strength and Conditioning Journal.* Appendix B lists several organizations, like the NSCA and ACSM, should you seek to obtain certification to work in the fitness industry.

Athletics

In the realm of college athletics, the regulatory bodies include the National Collegiate Athletic Association (NCAA; founded in 1906), the National Association of Intercollegiate Athletics (NAIA; founded in 1940), and the National Junior College Athletic Association (NJCAA; founded in 1938). The NCAA, with approximately 1200 members, promotes competition through championships for women and men. The *NCAA News,* published in newspaper format, provides updates on issues and events for its members along with numerous job announcements. Athletes in small colleges that hold membership in the NAIA compete in 23 women's and men's championships. The NJCAA, representing approximately 500 institutions, conducts championships in the major sports for women and men. Other athletic organizations that encourage the exchange of ideas include the College Sports Information Directors of America, the College Athletic Business Management Association, and the National Association of Collegiate Directors of Athletics.

The Amateur Athletic Union was founded in 1888 to promote amateur sports and to check the spread of problems associated with professional sports. Its over 3,000,000 members participate in and conduct local, regional, and national sports events for athletes ages 3 to 19.

The National Federation of State High School Associations (founded in 1920) and the 50 state and associated high school athletic and activities associations work to protect the activity and athletic interests of high schools, to promote the growth of educational interscholastic athletics, and to protect high school students from exploitation. It publishes *Interscholastic Athletic Administration.*

Many states also have coaches' associations that either are specific to one sport or have coaches from all sports in their memberships. These groups usually sponsor statewide or regional workshops or clinics about specific coaching techniques or strategies, rule changes, values and ethics in school athletics, and sport psychology. The National High School Athletic Coaches Association (founded in 1965) and the National Federation Interscholastic Coaches Association (founded in 1981) combined have nearly 100,000 members. Many volunteer coaches join the National Youth Sports Coaches Association.

•   •   •   •

The value and importance of joining and participating in a professional organization are multifaceted. First, membership entitles each person to receive journals, newsletters, directories, and other materials. If read, these keep the practitioner up to date with the latest techniques, research, methodology, and applications. Second, many of these organizations sponsor conferences and workshops, which provide additional opportunities to stay current through timely updates and to interact with and learn from colleagues in similar careers. Third, organizational affiliation may lead to service on committees and leadership opportunities where you can contribute to the promotion of standards and share your expertise with others. Fourth, job announcements in newsletters and placement centers at conferences may lead to career advancement. Thus, professional involvement enlivens your career.

The basic objectives of all professional groups are to exchange information, to learn, and to serve. To enhance both your knowledge about and commitment to your chosen career, you should seek opportunities through these organizations to grow professionally. By exchanging program ideas and instructional and motivational techniques, members can improve their abilities to serve others and to learn how to communicate their goals and activities to colleagues and to the general public. Through the sharing of experiences and research, many ideas for further study are generated. Therefore, as a young professional, you are encouraged to join your college, state, and national associations and one or more of the organizations in your interest area. You also should begin to read physical education and sport periodicals, as listed in the box on page 83, to help you more fully understand your profession.

UNDERGRADUATE SPECIALIZATIONS

Assuming that you are considering a career in physical education, exercise science, or sport, the following section of this chapter introduces you to the various options or specializations that exist in many colleges and universities. This discussion will prepare you for Chapter 5, which describes many careers related to physical education and sport, and Chapter 6, which explains many specific programs and certifications.

Professional preparation programs in physical education traditionally have been oriented toward teacher education, although today most colleges offer a variety of specializations, such as exercise science, sport management, and athletic training. As the demand for teachers decreased dramatically in the late 1970s, colleges and universities revised their curricula to include the increasingly popular sport and fitness-related specializations. This expansion in the fields of fitness, leisure, recreation, athletics, and sport resulted in diverse career opportunities for students specializing in these areas.

Athletic Training

Many students opt to specialize in athletic training, which deals with the prevention, treatment, and rehabilitation of sports injuries. Athletic trainers work with coaches to develop conditioning programs to optimally prepare athletes for competition. Trainers also provide supportive taping to help ensure safe participation. When injuries occur, athletic trainers are the primary caregivers, conducting onsite assessments about the severity of injuries. If these injuries are minor, first aid

PHYSICAL EDUCATION, EXERCISE SCIENCE, AND SPORT JOURNALS

ACE Fitness Matters
Adapted Physical Activity Quarterly
American Fitness Magazine
American Journal of Clinical Nutrition
American Journal of Health Education
American Journal of Physiology
American Journal of Sports Medicine
Clinical Exercise Physiology
Clinics in Sports Medicine
Exercise and Sport Sciences Reviews
Fitness Management Magazine
Health and Fitness Journal
Journal of Aging and Physical Activity
Journal of Biomechanics
Journal of Applied Biomechanics
Journal of Applied Physiology
Journal of Applied Sport Psychology
Journal of Athletic Training
Journal of Cardiopulmonary Rehabilitation
Journal of Leisure Research
Journal of Orthopedic and Sports Physical Therapy
Journal of Motor Behavior
Journal of the Philosophy of Sport
Journal of Physical Education, Recreation and Dance
Journal of Sport Behavior
Journal of Sport and Exercise Psychology
Journal of Sport History
Journal of Sport Management
Journal of Sport Rehabilitation
Journal of Sport and Social Issues
Journal of Strength and Conditioning Research
Journal of Teaching in Physical Education
Measurement in Physical Education and Exercise Science
Medicine and Science in Sports and Exercise
Palaestra
Parks and Recreation
Pediatric Exercise Science
Quest
Research Quarterly for Exercise and Sport
SCHOLE: A Journal of Leisure Studies and Recreation Education
Sociology of Sport Journal
Sport Psychologist
Strategies: A Journal for Sport and Physical Education
Strength and Conditioning Journal
The Physical Educator
The Physician and Sportsmedicine
Therapeutic Recreation

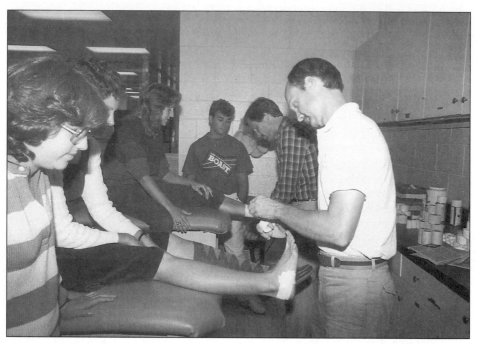

Careers in athletic training are available in schools, colleges, professional leagues, and clinical settings.

measures and the administration of ice, whirlpool, ultrasound, or other treatments fall within their purview. Under a physician's supervision, athletic trainers rehabilitate athletes suffering from more serious conditions, such as loss of mobility due to a broken bone or surgery. In addition, athletic trainers often counsel athletes to help them deal with injuries and rehabilitation.

Most states do not require certification as a prerequisite for athletic trainers to work in schools. This situation, however, places the trainers, athletes, and schools at risk when proper care is not given. Almost all colleges, professional teams, and sports medicine clinics stipulate that applicants must hold certifications from the National Athletic Trainers' Association (NATA) for employment (see box on page 85).

In schools, athletic trainers can expect to teach at least a partial load of classes (if they hold a teaching certification) because these positions are seldom full-time. Salaries are determined by the local school district's salary schedule and are based on years of experience and educational degrees. Additional stipends for extracurricular work are possible. Annual salaries range from $30,000 to $80,000.

College athletic trainers, depending on the size of the institution and the number of trainers, may be full- or part-time. They may teach in a NATA-approved program or in some other field. They may serve one team (such as football) or be responsible for all of the intercollegiate sports teams. Depending on the job description, salaries can vary widely, from $30,000 to $100,000 a year.

CERTIFICATION IN ATHLETIC TRAINING

The National Athletic Trainers' Association, through certification programs conducted by its Board of Certification (NATABOC), upholds the standards for entry into the field of athletic training. Candidates must satisfy the following:

Basic Requirements

- Obtain a baccalaureate degree from an accredited college or university
- Hold a current certification in cardiopulmonary resuscitation
- Verify that at least twenty-five percent (200 hours for accredited curriculum or 375 hours for internship applicants) of the required athletic training experience hours credited in fulfilling the certification requirements were obtained in actual (on location) practice and/or game coverage with one or more of the following sports: football, soccer, hockey, wrestling, basketball, gymnastics, lacrosse, volleyball, rugby, or rodeo
- Receive endorsement by an NATABOC certified athletic trainer

Section Requirements

- Graduate in no less than two academic years from an entry-level Commission on Accreditation of Allied Health Education Program's (CAAHEP) accredited curriculum. This program must include 800 hours of athletic training experience under the supervision of a NATABOC certified athletic trainer. The athletic training experience must be obtained from athletic training settings associated with the accredited curriculum.

OR

- Complete, as an internship applicant, at least 1500 hours of athletic training experience under the supervision of an NATABOC certified athletic trainer. The applicant must show proof that the athletic training experience was gained over a period of at least two academic years. Of these 1500 hours, at least 1000 hours must be attained in a traditional athletic training setting at the interscholastic, intercollegiate, or professional sports level. The additional 500 hours may be attained from an allied clinical setting and/or sport camp setting under the supervision of an NATABOC certified athletic trainer. Also, the applicant must submit an official transcript that verifies successful completion of at least one formal course in each of the following areas:
  - Health (Nutrition, Drugs/Substance Abuse, Health Education, Personal Health and Wellness); a course in Pathology is considered an acceptable substitution.
  - Human Anatomy
  - Kinesiology/Biomechanics
  - Human Physiology
  - Physiology of Exercise
  - Basic Athletic Training
  - Advanced Athletic Training
- Pass a three-part national certification examination

See www.nataboc.org for additional information

Another popular career choice for athletic trainers is in a clinical setting. These jobs may be affiliated with a hospital (with a rehabilitative focus) or in a private clinic that serves the public. Individuals helped by athletic trainers may have suffered sports-related injuries or need assistance in returning to activity after inactivity or some nonsports-related injury.

Coaching

Coaching specializations or minors are popular choices for undergraduates who want to continue their involvement with sports. Interscholastic and youth programs need individuals who want to coach young athletes. The demand for coaches of school teams exceeds the supply because of increased numbers of girls' teams, the hiring of fewer new teachers, and the resignation of tenured physical educators from coaching, but not from teaching. The millions of children competing on youth sport teams deserve coaches who know how to teach fundamental skills while making sports fun.

Almost all youth league coaches, however, are volunteers. Regardless of the type of employment of these volunteers, they need a basic knowledge in first aid, coaching concepts, human growth and development, and exercise and sport sciences. Although a few independent programs offer educational opportunities and certifications for these coaches, most volunteers demonstrate minimal competence.

Few individuals only coach in the schools; the dual role of teacher/coach characterizes most. Whereas states require subject matter certifications for teachers, only a few specify that coaches show competencies or complete certain courses.

Coaching and teaching are often combined into one career in schools and colleges.

Coaching curricula typically include courses in first aid, care and prevention of athletic injuries, anatomy, physiology, exercise physiology, coaching theory, coaching techniques in specific sports, human growth and development, sport management, and sport psychology. Typically the teacher/coach is paid according to a state or district salary scale along with a stipend for coaching. These amounts and salaries vary widely.

Fitness

A specialization in fitness prepares students to enter myriad careers in this growing field. One appealing feature is the opportunity to help others attain and maintain healthy lifestyles. Another is the pleasure of associating with people who value fitness. Although fitness specialists avoid most of the discipline problems and management minutiae in the schools, they typically work during the leisure hours of others.

Regardless of the setting, the fitness specialist must have a strong scientific background, such as in biomechanics and exercise physiology, especially if any activity programs are being designed and prescribed. A knowledge of business and management not only helps in entry-level positions but is essential for career advancement. Fitness specialists typically find jobs in corporate and industrial fitness settings; commercial aerobics; health, fitness, and sports clubs; or recreation departments. However, there are also job opportunities on cruise ships, in resorts, or as personal trainers. Salaries in the fitness industry vary from hourly rates at minimum wage to over $100,000 for some personal trainers.

Sport Management

The burgeoning sports industry attracts graduates who seek to apply business and management knowledge to sports settings. The best academic preparation encompasses the triad of management foundations, sports applications, and an internship or work experience within the field. It is imperative that students understand that careers in this area are "bottom-line," or profit-oriented. Therefore, courses in accounting, economics, finance, organizational behavior, and law are important. Built on these should be applications courses such as sport management, sport law, facility management, sport ethics, and personnel management. The culminating experience that links this knowledge and application is the internship.

Exercise Science

The academic preparation of the exercise science student focuses on the sciences. Usually courses are completed in biology or zoology, anatomy, physiology, chemistry, exercise physiology, biomechanics, and possibly biochemistry. Also beneficial is the development of strong statistical and computer technology skills along with a background in nutrition. This strong scientific foundation also helps prepare a student to pursue advanced degrees for a college professorship.

On the practical side, exercise prescription skills are necessary to qualify for many positions, such as those in corporate fitness programs, clinical settings, or cardiac rehabilitation centers. Experiences gained through an internship or part-time work are decided advantages when entering this specialization.

Physical Therapy, Adapted Physical Education, and Therapeutic Recreation

The therapeutic field encompasses physical therapy, adapted physical education, and therapeutic recreation. Whether in the schools or in clinics, specialists in these fields help individuals with disabling conditions. Majors in physical therapy prepare for the licensing exam through course work based on the sciences and extensive clinical experiences. The adapted physical educator may instruct one-on-one, in a special school, or within inclusion classrooms. Activities outside of schools are used by the therapeutic recreation professional to enhance mobility, self-confidence, and independence. Internships or experiences working with people with different disabling conditions facilitate the application of therapeutic knowledge and skills.

Teaching Option

Teacher certification following graduation from an accredited degree-granting institution is the goal of graduates choosing a teaching option. Teacher preparation courses may be taken throughout the undergraduate years or may be concentrated in just two years following the completion of general education courses taken at a junior or community college or at a four-year institution. Certifications for physical education may include those for pre-kindergarten (P) through grade 6, grades 5 through 8, grades 7 through 12, P through grade 12, health education, and dance.

The National Council for Accreditation of Teacher Education (NCATE) allows learned societies, such as the National Association for Sport and Physical Education, to recommend guidelines for the professional studies component of its standards. These guidelines, containing all the attitudes, knowledge, and skills required of a physical education teacher, have been subdivided into three elements: academic, professional, and pedagogical. Aquatics, dance, exercise, games, sports, and other leisure pursuits are components of the unique academic content of physical education. Motor development, sport management, motor control and learning, sport philosophy, sport biomechanics, exercise physiology, sport history, sport and exercise psychology, sport sociology, and sports medicine, as discussed in Chapter 2, provide the intellectual and theoretical bases for studies in physical education. The professional aspect of the undergraduate program develops an awareness of and commitment to the various educational, research, and service activities of physical education, exercise science, and sport studies. These include studies of curriculum models, organizational structures, diagnostic and evaluative procedures, and problem-solving techniques. Knowledge about teaching and learning physical skills constitutes the pedagogical element. Abilities to

Teachers need expertise to instruct in nontraditional activities.

plan, implement, and evaluate learning are observed in a supervised student teaching experience.

• • • •

These specializations, while not the only ones available, illustrate the variety of alternative career choices in physical education, exercise science and sport. Chapter 5, Selecting a Career, will assist in your career choice and career development process.

ISSUES FACING PHYSICAL EDUCATION, EXERCISE SCIENCE, AND SPORT

The issues facing physical education, exercise science, and sport today include program viability, role conflicts between physical educators and coaches, an identity dilemma in name and image, and fragmentation in the field. Each of these situations and some suggestions for actions that can be taken to ameliorate them will be briefly described.

Program Viability

The greatest challenge for most physical education programs rests with inadequate resources. No longer can schools and colleges expect to receive budgetary increases. In many states, educational budgets have been cut, some substantially. During tight economic times, the so-called nonessential subjects, such as physical education, art, and music, are reduced, if not eliminated. Corporate fitness programs, public recreation agencies, and even private clubs may reduce their leagues, operating hours, and staff to withstand financial shortfalls or zero-growth budgets. No longer can leaders in our field expect an ever-increasing revenue stream. Rather, we must expect to meet our goals with the same or fewer resources. We may have to eliminate excesses in big-time college athletics or simply be more frugal with our meager equipment allocation through careful maintenance and repair. We may have to charge increased fees for participation, while always providing alternative payment methods for those who would otherwise be excluded. We may have to market our programs better to increase participation volume and donations.

Role Conflicts Between Physical Educators and Coaches

Many physical educators in the schools and small colleges also coach. In fact, some obtain degrees in physical education to increase the likelihood of obtaining coaching positions. Because of the overlap in instructional knowledge and skill content, this joint career seems most appropriate. When these individuals commit equally to teaching students of heterogenous ability levels and to coaching the highly skilled, all students benefit.

Conflicts occur, however, because of time and energy constraints, unequal rewards, self-imposed and external pressures, and personal preferences. Most physical educators are expected to teach a full class load and then to coach after school. This schedule results in long days. For those coaching multiple sports, these long days continue season after season. Some coaches rapidly experience burnout, causing them to quit. Others compensate by losing enthusiasm and not preparing for one of their roles—usually their classes.

Compensation for the teacher/coach varies widely. Teaching salaries are usually established by the school district based on years of experience and academic degree(s). Coaching stipends usually are salary supplements. In small colleges, there will likely be more equity in salary and workload for the teacher/coach. Fringe benefits, such as bonuses, use of a car, or club memberships may help compensate a person for their coaching duties.

Pressures to win, whether self-imposed or from external sources, accompany sports competitions. Although most people have no interest in the quality of classroom instruction provided by the teacher/coach, hundreds or even thousands may pass judgment on one's ability to develop a successful team. Accompanying these pressures, which in the worst case may cause one to be fired, are the public prestige and status of being a coach.

Another potential source of conflict is preference for one role. Often, the teacher/coach finds coaching the highly skilled and building a strong team more rewarding than the daily routine of teaching, especially when many students, unlike most athletes, do not want to learn. A personal preference often leads to a disproportionate allocation of time and energy to the coaching role.

Resolution of this role conflict is difficult because the conflict usually develops gradually. The teacher/coach needs to continually assess the commitment given each responsibility to ensure that it is equitable. Regardless of the pressures, rewards, constraints, and preferences, the teacher/coach as a professional is ethically expected to serve competently in both roles. Suggested strategies to ameliorate some of the teacher/coach conflict might include:

- encouraging school administrators to define, evaluate, and reward teaching and coaching roles separately;

- allowing the athletic director to specify team responsibilities and lines of authority to preclude potential conflicts between teaching and coaching duties;

- urging school administrators and athletic directors to work together to relieve the excessive pressures placed on coaches by athletes, parents, and team supporters;

- helping coaches balance the time and energy spent in meeting the responsibilities of both teaching and coaching.

Identity Dilemma in Name and Image

The field is no longer singularly unified by its traditional name—*physical education*. Although schools continue to use the term, many people disparagingly refer to the instruction occurring in its classes as "gym," "phys ed," "recess," or "play." Many fail to respect the profession because physical educators have sometimes failed to teach its skills, knowledge, and values.

Most colleges and universities, in attempting to align themselves with a multidisciplinary content that is recognized as academic, have chosen names such as kinesiology, human performance, and exercise science. This disassociation from physical education has also grown out of the dramatic shift in students' major fields of study from preparing to teach physical education in the schools to specializing in exercise science, athletic training, and sport management. Although many outside the schools educate others in performing physical activities, they prefer titles such as tennis pro, aerobics leader, personal trainer, exercise physiologist, athletic trainer, and coach.

Changing the public's perception of physical education rests squarely on the shoulders of those in the field. School physical educators must design and teach quality programs that they proudly demonstrate to parents, school administrators, school board members, and legislators. College physical education instructional programs also must provide quality instructional opportunities for their students in a variety of activities. These may become the only two groups that retain the name of physical education.

College academicians will continue to conduct research and to educate their students in specialized subdisciplines such as exercise physiology, sport and exercise psychology, and athletic training. As long as the focus remains on enhancing the physical well-being of those served, the name is probably irrelevant. What is essential, though, is that each specialist, regardless of the title, demonstrates a commitment to physical activity for all.

Fragmentation

Beginning in the 1960s, the field of physical education has divided into special-izations that focus on the research-based exercise and sport sciences described in the previous chapter. Moving away from an instructional emphasis in school and college programs of physical education, these theoretical fields have sought to gain recognition and status as academic disciplines with unique contributions. While these academic disciplines investigate various aspects of human move-ment, they emphasize gaining deeper understandings rather than limiting their work primarily to the teaching of physical activity.

Primarily associated with universities, this fragmentation has divided the tra-ditional field of physical education into narrowly defined areas of study and en-couraged professors to specialize in one of these exercise and sport sciences. With this new commitment to the creation of new knowledge, a dissonance has occurred between practitioners in the schools and researchers in the universities. Oftentimes, research studies in exercise science and sport studies fail to have practical application to helping children learn and achieve the objectives of phys-ical education. Within the profession, fragmentation has resulted in the establish-ment and growth of specialized organizations and in a loss of membership and involvement in the American Alliance for Health, Physical Education, Recreation and Dance. These discipline-specific organizations are attractive to specialists be-cause colleagues nurture and encourage strong research and conduct confer-ences with singular foci.

SUMMARY

This chapter focuses on being a professional, not on joining a profession. Physi-cal education, exercise science, and sport studies are characterized by extensive training in a disciplinary body of knowledge and service; therefore, communica-tion among colleagues is essential. The services provided by the Alliance will en-hance development of each of the component parts of the profession. The Al-liance's six national associations are composed of professionals in leisure and recreation, health, fitness, sport, physical education, dance, and related fields. Numerous other professional associations provide avenues for collaboration and individual career development. Journals and conferences are the two most note-worthy services provided by these organizations. Become involved while you are a student. Participate in conferences, attend workshops, and read publications of professional organizations to prepare for your chosen career.

Undergraduate specializations include athletic training, coaching, fitness, sev-eral exercise and sport sciences, and teaching. Various career options await grad-uates with specialized knowledge and skills in one of these fields.

As a young professional, you can make a significant contribution to the qual-ity of life of those you serve as a teacher, researcher, or program leader. You have the opportunity to become a role model by planning and implementing effective programs that meet the activity needs of diverse groups. Rather than reacting, you can become proactive by promoting the values of physical education, exercise science, and sport and by implementing exemplary programs.

CAREER PERSPECTIVE

LONNIE EDWARDS
Health and Physical Education Teacher
Chapel Hill Middle School
DeKalb County Schools, Georgia

EDUCATION
B.S.Ed., Health and Physical Education, State University of
West Georgia

JOB RESPONSIBILITIES AND HOURS
Lonnie's primary job responsibilities are to plan for and provide classroom instruction in health and physical education to students in grades seven and eight. He also fulfills other assigned duties associated with monitoring students in and around the school. He normally works from 7:15 am to 4 pm since some of his duties occur before classes begin each day. The salary range for teachers like Lonnie start around $33,000 but can increase to around $63,000.

SPECIALIZED COURSE WORK, DEGREES, AND WORK EXPERIENCE NEEDED FOR THIS CAREER
Teachers are expected to hold a bachelor's degree in health and physical education as well as successfully complete a student teaching internship. In addition, prospective teachers must pass the state required teacher certification test. Courses that were most helpful to Lonnie included the internship, instructional methods, history and philosophy of physical education and sports, biomechanics, middle grades physical education, and other required professional courses.

SATISFYING ASPECTS
To Lonnie, the most satisfying aspect of his career is watching students become more physically fit as they learn life skills that will benefit them now and in the future. While teaching is challenging and sometimes instructional situations are difficult, he is committed to always finding ways to offset these conditions and providing enjoyable learning experiences for his students.

JOB POTENTIAL
Advancement within education is possible if a person chooses to return to college and obtain a higher degree or to coach a sport.

SUGGESTIONS FOR STUDENTS
Lonnie believes that a teacher must care about children and have a genuine interest in the success of each child. The reward cannot be the paycheck or the financial gain, but it must be the joy of watching children improve and succeed. The best reward a teacher can get is the reward of a child's success.

REVIEW QUESTIONS

1. What are the characteristics of a profession?
2. How can you justify physical education, exercise science, and sport studies as professions?
3. How has the American Alliance for Health, Physical Education, Recreation and Dance sought to achieve its mission?
4. What types of services are provided by the National Association for Sport and Physical Education?
5. What opportunities are available for students through majors clubs?
6. What are the purposes of the American College of Sports Medicine?
7. What is the purpose of the National Strength and Conditioning Association?
8. According to the National Council for Accreditation of Teacher Education, in what three elements of physical education must a prospective teacher gain knowledge?
9. What is required for certification as an athletic trainer?
10. What are several career possibilities for individuals specializing in the exercise and sport sciences?

STUDENT ACTIVITIES

1. Join the American Alliance for Health, Physical Education, Recreation and Dance.
2. Write to one physical education, exercise science, or sport organization that interests you (other than the AAHPERD) and request information about possible careers.
3. Read at least one article from any two of the periodicals listed in the box on page 83. Describe its key points.
4. Write a one-page statement defending the importance of being a professional.
5. Attend at least one professional workshop or clinic during this school year.
6. In small groups, prepare a five-minute defense for the importance and advantages of joining a professional organization.
7. Interview one person in each of the undergraduate specializations to learn more information about their careers. Write a one-page report about each or share this information in a two-minute class presentation.
8. Select one of the professional organizations and give a two-minute presentation about its unique programs and services.
9. Read one position paper or publication of one of the six Alliance organizations and write a one-page report about it.
10. Discuss and debate this situation: The Board of Trustees of Midwest College has directed the President to cut programs on campus due to the current financial crisis. The President has decided that physical education, intramurals, and athletics are expendable because they contribute little to achieving the mission of the college. The President has formed three task

forces, one composed of student physical education, exercise science, and sport majors, another of physical education faculty, and another of athletic department personnel. Each is charged with justifying why these programs should NOT be eliminated. (The city has offered to buy the existing physical education and athletic facilities, thereby eliminating the financial burden.) Form three groups representing these task forces and prepare responses. The task forces may proceed in any way they choose to collect pertinent data and information to justify the importance of these programs. Each task force should also prepare and present alternative strategies for the President to consider. Each task force will be chaired by a person responsible for delivering a five-minute defense during class.

REFERENCE

American Alliance for Health, Physical Education, Recreation and Dance: Reston, VA, 2000, the Alliance.

SUGGESTED READINGS

Brunner R, Hill D: Using learning style research in coaching, *JOPERD* 63(4):26, 1992. After discussing the learning style approach in coaching, where coaching methods are matched to athletes' learning preferences, the authors describe how this approach helped one high school wrestling coach develop a winning team.

Bunker LK: Virtual reality: movement's centrality, *Quest* 46(4):456, 1994. Human movement should be the central focus of physical education as a profession. To facilitate this transformation, the author suggests several key principles—uniqueness, communication, accountability, diversity, teamwork, ethics, change, and the production of theoretical and practical knowledge.

Clark DE: A new code of ethics for NRPA, *Parks and Rec* 30(8):38, 1995. The National Recreation and Park Association has addressed concerns about ethical violations of public trust and how to educate its members about the value of ethical behavior.

Corbin CB: The field of physical education—common goals, not common roles, *JOPERD* 64(1):79, 1993. Based on historical developments characterized by professional and disciplinary influences and conflicts, the author advocates that physical education should be a field encompassing both.

Corbin CB, Eckert HM, (eds): The evolving undergraduate major, Champaign, 1990, Human Kinetics Publishers, *The Academy Papers* 23. Physical education as a discipline and as a profession is described and contrasted. The name and image crisis issue is also examined.

Grunbaum JA, et al.: A comprehensive approach to school health program needs assessment, *J of Sch Health* 65(2):54, 1995. This article describes one approach using surveys, interviews, and observation for assessing whether school health programs are effectively addressing topics such as violence, smoking, substance abuse, sexual behavior, nutrition, and physical activity.

Hester D, Dunaway D (eds.): NAGWS: paths to advocacy, recruitment, and enhancement, *JOPERD* 62(3):29, 1991. Nine articles explain how the National Association for Girls and Women in Sport has achieved its three goals: advocacy for women's full participation in physical activity and sports leadership; recruitment, development and promotion of female leadership positions; and advocacy for initiating and enhancing quality sport and physical activity programs for all females.

Lambrecht KW: A study of curricular preparation needs for sport club managers, *J of Sp Mgmt* 5:47, 1991. Based on responses to a national questionnaire, sport club managers, regardless of the number of members served, identified the eight leading curricular preparation needs. These included marketing, business management, sales communications, public relations, budgeting, communication (speaking) skills, internship in club management, and facility and equipment management.

Sherrill C: *Adapted physical activity, recreation and sport: crossdisciplinary and lifespan* (5th ed.), 1997, New York: McGraw-Hill. This comprehensive book describes the curricular, instructional, assessment, and legal aspects of providing activity programs for individuals with special needs.

Stroot SA (ed.): Socialization into physical education, *J of Teach in PE* 12(4):337, 1993. This issue focuses on the socialization of preservice and beginning teachers. Among the topics are teachers' perspectives, beliefs about teaching during educational training, induction of physical educators, faculty consensus concerning teacher education, and perspectives on socialization research.

4

PHILOSOPHY OF PHYSICAL EDUCATION, EXERCISE SCIENCE, AND SPORT

KEY CONCEPTS

- Philosophy is the pursuit of truth, knowledge, and values.
- Idealism, realism, pragmatism, naturalism, and existentialism have influenced the growth of physical education, exercise science, and sport programs.
- Ethics is a branch of philosophy that deals with moral values.
- The practical application of philosophical theories will help you develop a personal philosophy of physical education, exercise science, and sport.
- Philosophy, though often misunderstood and neglected, can provide focus, a communication bond, a clarity of vision and direction, and an opportunity to analyze the present to expand one's horizons for the future.

The pursuit of truth is as pervasive today as it was during the development of diverse philosophies in the past. This chapter examines the importance of philosophy by focusing on five of the traditional philosophies, with emphasis on how they have influenced physical education, exercise science, and sport. Other philosophies, and especially ethics, are discussed because of their impact on today's programs. Based on the knowledge gained from this study, you are encouraged to develop a personal philosophy of physical education, exercise science, or sport.

WHY STUDY PHILOSOPHY?

Philosophy can be defined as a love of wisdom or more broadly as the pursuit of truth. Philosophy is both the developmental process and the resultant factors, theories, and values. Philosophy is an attempt to understand the meaning of life by analyzing and synthesizing why; simply having a purpose and objectives, as discussed in Chapter 1, is not sufficient. You must know why these are of value to yourself and to others, and you need to be able to articulate their importance.

What is the worth of physical education to a school child? What is the value of learning a lifetime sport? What constitutes a healthy lifestyle? What is the role of play? These are just a few of the questions that your philosophy can help answer.

Developing a personal philosophy can improve teaching effectiveness, influence your behavior, provide direction in program development, contribute to society's awareness of the value of physical activity, and encourage a feeling of commonality among co-workers. How, you might ask, could a personal philosophy help accomplish all this? When you determine what goals you want your students or those with whom you work to attain, it will influence what you include in your curriculum or program and how you proceed. For example, if you value the development of physical fitness for your students, you will emphasize content and activities that can contribute to improving their fitness levels. Conversely, if

🔎 RESEARCH VIEW

Developing a Personal Code of Conduct as a Physical Education, Exercise Science, and Sport Professional

What is the responsibility of the physical education, exercise science, or sport professional to each of the following?

- Program content relative to standards
- Delivery of instruction and dissemination of information
- Professional knowledge and expertise
- Treatment of individuals from various socioeconomic backgrounds, ages, genders, ethnicities, or ability levels
- Utilization of equipment and other resources
- Responsibilities relative to moral values
- Personal health and well-being

The National Association for Sport and Physical Education's Code of Conduct (www.aahperd.org/naspe/publications-resource_code.html) suggests eight principles to guide responsible ethical practice and provide a framework for the resolution of ethical dilemmas. Among these are maintaining the highest standards of ethical behavior, promoting activities that contribute to overall human welfare, emphasizing best practices and standards of excellence in programs, and completing responsibilities with competence and integrity.

you prioritize the development of movement and sport skills, then you will focus on instructing and having students practice these skills. Another example of how a personal philosophy influences what is accomplished would be to consider whether you will emphasize fair play as a coach. If you believe in playing by the rules and living ethically, you can serve as a positive role model for your students, athletes, and co-workers. (See the Research View box on page 98 to help you in developing your personal philosophy.)

The discussion of the traditional philosophies that follows will challenge your thinking as you decide what you value and how to formulate your personal philosophy. By articulating what you believe in and what is important, you are laying the foundation for your personal philosophy.

FIVE TRADITIONAL PHILOSOPHIES

Idealism, realism, pragmatism, naturalism, and existentialism provide the foundation for educational philosophy, including that of physical education. These five traditional philosophies are defined in the box below. A brief overview of the basic tenets of each philosophy and their application to physical education is provided. Table 4-1 delineates these five philosophies, and Table 4-2 applies the tenets of these philosophies to physical education, exercise science, and sport. The box below further clarifies specific characteristics of each philosophy. To assess your understanding of the five traditional philosophies, after you have studied them, take the philosophy quiz in the box on page 108.

Idealism

Idealism centers on the mind as critical to understanding, since only through reasoning and mental processes can truth emerge. Never-changing ideals, not things, constitute the ultimate reality. Idealists since the Greek philosopher Plato have stressed that only the reflective and intuitive individual can arrive at truth.

FIVE TRADITIONAL PHILOSOPHIES THAT HAVE INFLUENCED THE DEVELOPMENT OF PHYSICAL EDUCATION, EXERCISE SCIENCE, AND SPORT

Idealism—A philosophical theory advocating that reality depends on the mind for existence and that truth is universal and absolute.

Realism—The philosophical system stressing that the laws and order of the world as revealed by science are independent from human experience.

Pragmatism—An American movement in philosophy emphasizing reality as the sum total of each individual's experiences through practical experimentation.

Naturalism—A belief that the scientific laws of nature govern life and that individual goals are more important than societal goals.

Existentialism—A twentieth-century philosophy that centers on individual existence and advocates that truth and values are arrived at by each person's experiences.

TABLE 4-1

FIVE TRADITIONAL PHILOSOPHIES

	Idealism	Realism	Pragmatism	Naturalism	Existentialism
Source of Truth	Ideas	Scientific reality	Human experiences	Nature	Human existence
Most Important	People	Physical world	Society	Individual	Individual
How to Arrive at Truth	Reasoning and intuition	Scientific method	Experiencing changes	Laws of nature	Individual determination
Importance of the Mind	Emphasized	Reasoning powers and scientific method used	Learning by inquiring, observing, and participating	Physical and mental balance for whole person	The individual's determination of the subject matter and the learning method
Importance of the Body	Simultaneous development with mind	Emphasis on the whole individual	Variety of activities for effective functioning in society	Physical activity essential for optimal learning	Freedom to choose activity and to be creative
Curricular Focus	Teacher centered through examples for students; qualitative	Subject centered; quantitative	Student centered; based on individual differences	Individual readiness to learn	Individual centered; based on self-realization
Importance of the Teacher	Model and example	Orderly presentation of facts; drills and scientific method used	Motivator, especially through problem solving	Guide and helper	Stimulator and counselor
Importance of the Personality	Moral and spiritual values stressed	Learn for life adjustment	Development of social skills and meeting one's needs	Development of social skills important	Learning self-responsibility and knowing oneself
Education	Self-development	To meet realities of life	For social efficiency	Natural process	Teaching acceptance of individual responsibility

TABLE 4-2

APPLICATION OF FIVE PHILOSOPHIES TO PHYSICAL EDUCATION, EXERCISE SCIENCE, AND SPORT

	Idealism	Realism	Pragmatism	Naturalism	Existentialism
Objectives	Development of personality and mind	Training students to meet realities of life	Helping students to become better functioning members of society	Development of whole person	Assisting students to become self-actualizing, independent beings
Subject Matter	Utmost importance	Required; the focus of learning	Experiences in a wide variety of activities	Play; self-directed individual activity	Wide selection of alternatives, especially individual activities
Methodology	Lecture; question-answer; discussions	Use of real world; drills, lectures, and projects	Problem solving	Informal; problem solving	Questions raised, thoughts provoked, and freedom of action encouraged by the teacher
Teacher's Role	More important than process	Selects knowledge to learn	Guide	Guide; nature teaches	Guide
Student's Role	Development of total person	Emphasizes the whole individual	Learning about the moral self	Individualized rate of learning	Self-realization
Evaluation	Subjective; qualitative	Quantitative; use of scientific means	Subjective and self-evaluation	Based on attainment of individual goals	Unimportant in the traditional sense
Weaknesses	Resistance to change; development of the physical secondary to the mind	Too narrow a view; everything must conform to natural laws or it is wrong	Lack of fixed aims to give students' stability and direction	Too simple of an approach for the complex world	Overemphasis on individuality precludes preparation for social life

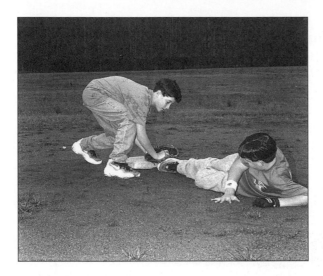

The mental side of sports, such as knowing when and how to slide or how to apply the tag to a sliding runner, is valued by the idealist. (Photo courtesy Bob Hilliard.)

Ideals, virtues, and truths are universal and external and remain the same regardless of how individual interpretations may vary. As people develop and exercise their free will, they make choices through their intellectual powers. These decisions, whether right or wrong, do not alter the values important to the idealist.

The development of the total person is the objective of idealism as applied to physical education, exercise science, and sport. The individual is important and should be nurtured through an emphasis on the mind and its thought processes. Because reality is mental rather than physical, sometimes physical activity is relegated to a secondary status, even though optimally the mind and the body are to be developed simultaneously.

Since the curriculum focuses on ideas, teachers and leaders who are more important than the process, are free to use any methods that would help students or others being served achieve their optimal levels of personality and character development. Outcomes of the affective domain, such as creativity and fair play, are also values upon which idealism places emphasis.

Relative to physical education, exercise science, and sport, the idealist requires students, athletes, and others engaged in physical activity to learn how and why any skill or movement is important and how it is executed. The idealist stresses that while there is one correct way to perform an overhead shot in tennis or to putt a golf ball, it is important that the participant understands why this is the proper technique. The teacher or exercise leader will model how to execute a specific movement and through questions and answers ensure that the person being taught conceptualizes how to execute the skill.

Realism

As a revolt against some of the tenets of idealism, the Greek philosopher Aristotle and today's advocates of realism state that the laws of nature, rather than existing truths, are in control. The scientific method provides the realist with the process for acquiring and applying truth (i.e., the knowledge that originates in the physical

Realism advocates using scientific methods such as electrical stimulation for the rehabilitation of injuries. (Photo courtesy Bob Hilliard.)

world but emerges through experimentation). Scientific investigation examines the material things of the world when seeking truth.

The role of education, according to the realist, is to train the student to discover and to interpret the real things in life (i.e., things that can be shown by the scientific method) to ensure adjustment of the individual in the real world. Since the emphasis is on the whole individual, physical activity, including the traditional objectives of organic fitness, neuromuscular development, intellectual ability, and social and emotional development, has a vital contribution to make.

An orderly progression in learning, extensive use of drills, and objective evaluation are important methodologies used by the realist teacher. Learning is subject centered. The curriculum includes activities and experiences that enable students to understand the laws of the physical world.

Relative to physical education, exercise science, and sport, the realist does not assume that physical fitness is developed just because this is a curricular or program focus. Rather, the realist administers fitness tests to verify that an increase in fitness parameters such as cardiovascular endurance or flexibility has occurred. The realist presents factual information, such as how to execute a forearm pass in volleyball, uses a variety of drills so that all students can progress naturally in learning how to do this skill and administers an objective test to assess skill development.

Pragmatism

Pragmatism states that experiences, not ideals, provide the key to seeking truth. Ultimate reality must be experienced and is not absolute. Circumstances and situations constantly vary from person to person; thus, pragmatism is characterized as dynamic and ever changing.

The pragmatist learns through experiences, such as participating in a personal fitness program.

In seeking knowledge, the pragmatist looks for truth that works in a given situation. If it does, then it is true at that moment. Truth is a function of the social and historical context, and is considered good if it is successful. Values are also relative and result from judgments about one's experiences as long as they are evaluated in terms of the good of the group, not selfishly. Pragmatists emphasize social responsibilities since it is essential that every individual functions within, and hopefully, contributes to, society.

The overall objective of a pragmatic education is the development of social efficiency in students, according to the most famous American pragmatist, John Dewey. That is, students need to have opportunities to experience solving the problems of life and to learn how to become better functioning members of society. Through the use of problem solving, the teacher focuses on the needs and interests of the students. This student-centered curriculum encourages students to apply the scientific method and to experience a wide variety of activities. Team sports stress cooperation and the development of interpersonal skills, and movement activities provide opportunities for exploring numerous solutions to problems.

Relative to physical education, exercise science, and sport, the pragmatist loves to play sports and experience physical activities, especially with others. Pragmatists enjoy developing their social skills through sports and other activities because these interpersonal skills can help them in various situations in life. Self-pacing and self-evaluation activities, such as developing and implementing a personal weight training program, lead to achieving the pragmatic goal of improved health and fitness.

Naturalism

The naturalist believes in things that exist within the physical realm of nature, which is itself the source of value. Since naturalism emphasizes the individual more than society, education should focus on meeting each student's needs.

Stressing "everything according to nature," the eighteenth-century philosopher Jean-Jacques Rousseau echoed the oldest known philosophy of the Western world (dating back to certain pre-Socratic Greek philosophers). Rousseau advocated that education must use the physical world as the classroom and that teachers by example should guide students through inductive reasoning to draw their own conclusions. The laws of nature dictate to the teacher and to the student the logical pattern of growth, development, and learning. Rousseau also encouraged education of the mind and body simultaneously. Physical well-being should then enhance a readiness to learn mental, moral, and social skills.

Naturalism also declares the importance of individualized learning through self-education and self-activity. Exploration of one's capabilities and interests leads directly to greater skills and adjustments to nature. Noncompetitive team, individual, and outdoor activities provide play opportunities that benefit students physically, psychologically, and, especially, socially. Through physical activities, the individual develops in an all-around way.

A natural setting provides an excellent learning environment for developing social, intellectual, and physical skills. (Photo courtesy Aram Attarian.)

Relative to physical education, exercise science, and sport, the naturalist prefers to use nature as the teacher, such as learning about preserving the environment while backpacking and learning about marine biology while scuba diving. The naturalist encourages students to explore how to execute a locomotor movement like jumping or to discover through trial and error the most effective technique for catching a ball. Through problem solving, individuals progress at their own rates to learn how to do a forward roll or to hit a ball tossed to them. The naturalist in physical education uses the principles of movement education and individualized instruction.

Existentialism

According to existentialism, human experiences determine reality. Emerging in the 1900s as a reaction against societal conformity, this philosophy subjugated everything to the individual as long as acceptance of responsibility for oneself was recognized. Leaders of existential thought include Jean Paul Sartre and Karl Jaspers.

Reality for the existentialist is composed of human experiences and is determined by the choices being made. One's experiences and free choices result in truth and are uniquely personal. An individual's value system, while totally controlled by choice, must be tempered by an understanding of social responsibility. No values are imposed by society; instead, each person is free to think and to act as personal desires dictate.

The self-actualizing person is the desired educational outcome, as each student is given freedom to choose. However, students must accept the

The existentialist teaches acceptance of individual responsibility, such as self-motivation in designing and implementing a personal fitness program. (Photo courtesy Bob Hilliard.)

consequences of their actions. In the curriculum, students are presented with a wide variety of activities, especially individual ones, through which to develop creativity, self-awareness, self-responsibility, and realization of individual essence. The teacher raises questions and provokes reflective thinking but leaves students free to choose their own courses of action.

Relative to physical education, exercise science, and sport, the existentialist emphasizes individuality so the curriculum or program will focus on individual activities. The existentialist will allow students choices, such as in-line skating, aerobic dance, and self-challenging or adventure activities, so that they can enjoy their experiences and will persist in their participation. The individual is given tremendous self-responsibility for learning by the existentialist, such as through self-paced instruction and contract grading (see box below for other comparisons.).

COMPARISONS OF THE FIVE TRADITIONAL PHILOSOPHIES RELATIVE TO PHYSICAL EDUCATION, EXERCISE SCIENCE, AND SPORT

Curriculum
- The idealist will select the curriculum without student input.
- The realist will allow students to select activities from various options.
- The pragmatist will pace each curricular offering based on students' individual differences.
- The naturalist will offer those activities that students indicate a readiness to learn.
- The existentialist will focus on each child's progress regardless of the activity.

Teaching Fitness and Sports Skills
- The idealist and the realist focus on content.
- The pragmatist and the existentialist emphasize experiencing a wide variety of activities.
- The naturalist advocates play and self-directed activity for students.

Teaching Methodology
- The idealist controls learning through lectures and some interactions with students.
- The realist maintains control using drills.
- The pragmatist uses a variety of instructional approaches because students have multiple learning styles.
- The naturalist encourages problem solving with the teacher as a guide.
- The existentialist guides by asking questions and offering challenges.

Evaluation
- The idealist's qualitative assessments always subjugate the physical to the mental.
- The realist overemphasizes testing using scientific means for quantitative results.
- The pragmatist advocates subjective self-evaluation that, in the absence of specific goals, often leaves students without any sense of accomplishment.
- The naturalist focuses singularly on the attainment of individual goals.
- The existentialist views evaluation as nonessential because only self-realization is important.

Other Philosophies

Within physical education, exercise science, and sport studies, professionals also need to be knowledgeable of other philosophies that might help them respond to questions and deal with circumstances in their careers. Four of these will be briefly described, while a fifth will be expanded upon more fully. **Metaphysics** refers to the nature of things, how actions or events are related to each other. This philosophical study examines the qualities and characteristics of physical as well as nonphysical things. Metaphysical philosophers might seek to answer questions such as, "What is the nature of sport or play?" or "How does creativity play a role in sport, play, or dance?" **Axiology** deals with the value of things and discovering whether actions are good and virtuous. In seeking truth, the axiologist attempts to answer the question of how people should act in certain situations. Questions that relate to axiology include, "What is the value of competitive sports?" or "Is intentionally harming an opponent right?" The philosophy that examines what people know and how and why they hold certain beliefs is called **epistemology.** This philosophy looks at various aspects of understanding. The epistemologist might ask, "Does being a former successful athlete make this person an effective teacher of sport skills or a successful coach?" **Aesthetics** is the philosophical area that focuses on the artistic or the beautiful, including artistic movement. The person interested in aesthetics is pleased more by the beauty of the human body in motion rather than caring about the outcome of a contest or

---

PHILOSOPHY QUIZ

Fill in the blanks with one of the following: *existentialist, idealist, naturalist, pragmatist,* or *realist.*

1. The _____ advocates that students must indicate their readiness to attempt a cartwheel.
2. The _____ models or provides demonstrations of exactly how to serve a volleyball.
3. The _____ encourages students to use their reasoning powers to decide how to align defensive players to stop an opposing team that fast breaks.
4. Since a curriculum based on this philosophy focuses on the individual, the _____ focuses on teaching the acceptance of responsibility for self-discipline, cooperation, and fair play.
5. The _____ emphasizes learning team sports where social skills are developed.
6. An exercise scientist is sometimes called a/an _____ because he or she utilizes the scientific method of inquiry.
7. The _____ encourages students to select their own movement activities and to be creative, such as designing a new cooperative game or exploring playground apparatus.
8. The wholeness rather than duality (mind versus body) of people is stressed by the _____ and the _____ by their seeking to achieve psychomotor, cognitive, and affective outcomes in all classes.
9. Since to the _____ experience is critical for learning, students are encouraged to experiment with their own techniques in executing body movements.

the skills of the athletes. Appealing questions might include "What is the beauty of the movements of the figure skater," not "how athletic are the jumps displayed?" or "What is the rhythm of the gymnast's movement during a floor exercise routine?" **Ethics** refers to the study of moral values or the doing of good toward others and oneself.

ETHICS

You be the judge:

- A high school defensive tackle sharpens the edges of the fasteners that hold his chin guard to his helmet. After he plays a few downs, several of the opposing players have been cut and are bleeding. Is this action ethical? Is suspending this player from the team and school ethical?

- An elementary school student in a physical education class records that she walked one mile each day to help her team win the special field trip to the zoo, even though she did not do all of this exercise. Is this action ethical? Is suspending this student from school ethical?

- An athletic trainer gives a track athlete amphetamines to help boost his energy level. Is this action ethical? Is this athletic trainer violating the National Athletic Trainers' Association Code of Ethics on page 114?

- A high school athlete cheats on a test in order to maintain eligibility to play on a school team. Is this action ethical? Does it make any difference if other students (nonathletes) in the class cheated on the same test?

- An exercise scientist inaccurately reports data from a research study in a journal article. Is this action ethical? What action, if any, should be taken?

These scenarios deal with ethics, which is related to axiology and is the study of moral values. It deals with good and bad, right and wrong, obligation and choice, and principles of conduct. From the time of the ancient Greeks until today, educators have been held responsible for the nurturance and enhancement of ethical

Ethical dilemmas are often associated with whether behaviors are within the spirit of the rules. (Photo courtesy Lisa Sense.)

behavior. Character development, for example, has traditionally been a vital concern of educators, including physical educators, exercise scientists, and sports leaders. Drawing from the fields of religion, philosophy, and psychology, values serve as the foundation of a way of life; people are expected to conduct themselves in accordance with certain values.

Moral reasoning consists of determining what is the right thing to do. In this moral reasoning process, a person has to assess what he or she knows and values about a particular moral issue before acting on what is decided. Kohlberg (1981) suggested that all people learn and develop morally in a six-stage sequence, organized into three levels:

Preconventional

- Stage One focuses on actions done to avoid punishment.
- Stage Two emphasizes following rules for self-interest.

Conventional

- Stage Three suggests that people react to the expectations of parents, peers, and authority figures.
- Stage Four assumes that people conform to the social system and social order.

Postconventional

- Stage Five expects people to fulfill contract and individual rights.
- Stage Six posits universal ethical principles as the basis for all actions.

Kohlberg stated that the higher stages require more complex moral reasoning, and that moral development could stagnate at any stage.

A moral reasoning strategy begins with what a person believes. These beliefs lead to the development of values about ourselves, society, and others. Values are the answer to the question of what is most important or what has relative worth? Moral values can be described as the relative worth associated with something virtuous and good. Examples of these moral values include justice, honesty, responsibility, and beneficence.

Most ethical theories are based on teleology, deontology, or a combination of the two. **Teleological** theories focus on the end results or consequences of processes or occurrences. For the most prominent of these theories, John Stuart Mill's **utilitarianism,** the goal is the creation of the greatest good for the largest number of people. Since the benefit of the group or society as a whole is the goal, actions are judged to ensure that the good effects outweigh the bad. The utilitarian, however, lacks concern for how the results are produced and may have difficulty determining what society values most highly.

Immanuel Kant helped formulate the theory of moral obligation known as **deontology.** According to this ethical theory, actions must conform to absolute rules of moral behavior, which are characterized by universality, respect for the individual, and acceptability to rational beings. That is, deontology argues that regardless of the particular situation, moral action should make sense to each person and lead to the same behavior. Kant's **categorical imperative** stated that

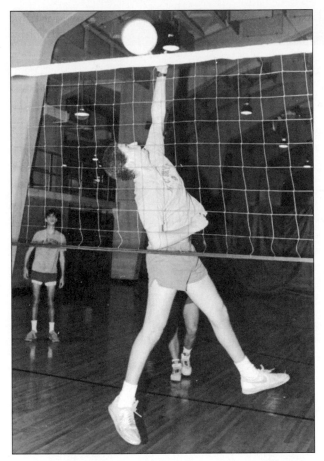

Sport participants often face ethical choices, such as whether to acknowledge touching the net during a volleyball match.

EXAMPLES OF CATEGORICAL IMPERATIVES IN SPORT

- Fair play means playing within the letter and spirit of the rules.
- Seeking to win within the letter and spirit of the rules is acceptable while winning "at-all-costs" is unacceptable.
- An opponent should be treated with respect and exactly as everyone would wish to be treated.
- Games are to be played as mutual quests for excellence where intimidation is inappropriate.
- Retribution for a violent or unfair action done by an opponent or an official is never acceptable.

ETHICAL CHOICES IN SPORTS

1. Should every child play in every contest in youth sports programs?
2. Should extrinsic awards (such as trophies, plaques, or money) be given to sports champions?
3. Should alumni be allowed to give money or tangible gifts to prospective college athletes during their recruitment?
4. Should athletes be allowed to befriend their opponents before or after a competition?
5. Should a coach be allowed to verbally abuse officials?
6. Should strikes (refusal to complete) for more benefits or rights by professional athletes be allowed?
7. Should males and females receive identical treatment in school and college sports?
8. Should all college students be required to pay athletic fees?
9. Should a coach have the right to require that an athlete (at any age) compete in only one sport (e.g., specialize)?
10. Should an athlete be allowed to use drugs (such as amphetamines or anabolic steroids) to enhance performance?
11. Should sports competitions be open to individuals of both sexes playing together?
12. Should an athlete be required to pass all school subjects in order to play on an interscholastic team?
13. Should a coach teach athletes how to circumvent sports rules to their advantage?
14. Should college coaches who violate recruiting regulations be banned from coaching?
15. Should fans be protected from the misbehavior of other fans?
16. Should a coach have the right to verbally or physically abuse an athlete?
17. Should an athlete ever be allowed or required to play when injured?
18. Should children ever be cut when trying out for a youth sports team?
19. Should high school or college alumni or donors be able to influence the hiring and firing of coaches?
20. Should every child get an opportunity to play all positions in youth sports programs?
21. Should sports gambling be legalized?
22. Should fans have to pay to view major sporting events on television?
23. Should colleges be allowed to generate millions of dollars of revenues from their football and basketball programs, while the athletes who help generate these revenues receive only grants-in-aid?
24. Should a television network be allowed to dictate the date and time of a college or professional competition?
25. Should athletes be punished for breaking team rules or federal or state laws during the season?

moral duties are prescriptive and independent of consequences. The box on page 111 provides examples of how categorical imperatives relate to sport.

How to teach ethical standards most effectively has been a dilemma for educators and coaches for a long time. Since fair play is not an inherent characteristic of physical activities, how does it occur? When play, games, sports, and other physical pursuits are engaged in for their inherent pleasure, ethical problems seldom emerge. When the outcome becomes so highly significant that some or all of the participants employ whatever means possible to achieve success, then questionable behavior is readily evident, to the detriment of values. A person's moral values do not preclude seeking to perform to the best of one's ability. But doing so at the risk of impinging on what is good, on one's obligation to others, or on principles of proper conduct violates these values.

Can ethical decision making be taught and modeled by physical educators, exercise scientists, and sport leaders? In spite of our materialistic and pragmatic world, professionals have an obligation to teach and to perpetuate moral and ethical principles that are basic to society. Among these principles are sensitivity to individual needs and differences, responsibility for our personal conduct, concern for others, and devotion to honesty, integrity, and fair play. Educators and leaders in all settings should exemplify ethical behavior and treat everyone fairly so that others are positively influenced. We must constantly be aware that our actions will teach character louder than our statements.

The 25 questions on page 112 challenge you with several ethical choices. These can be discussed in class or with others. Each question may have multiple alternatives, or you may believe there is only one response. Your answer is a direct reflection of the ethical values that are uniquely yours. You also should realize that your attitudes toward and reactions to these and similar situations will influence those with whom you work in a physical education, exercise science, or sport career. The box on page 114 illustrates how the National Athletic Trainers' Association emphasizes the importance of ethical conduct through its code of professional practices.

DEVELOPING A PERSONAL PHILOSOPHY OF PHYSICAL EDUCATION, EXERCISE SCIENCE, AND SPORT

Everyone who plans a career in physical education, exercise science, and sport needs to develop a personal philosophy as a guide to future actions. For example, if fair play is essential to your philosophy, you will stress this in your own behavior, your instruction of others, and the programs you lead. A personal philosophy forces you to think logically and analytically and to explain the worth and the value of what you do and how you serve others. This developmental process will help you relate physical education, exercise science, and sport to general education and will enhance your professional growth. Too frequently, professionals have failed to develop definite personal philosophies, resulting in the loss of career direction and purpose. Therefore, it is essential that you formulate principles, guidelines, and directions for your career. If you do not know where you are going, it is unlikely that you will end up where you want to be (wherever that is!).

Some of the philosophical tenets discussed in this chapter differ significantly. For example, pragmatists advocate helping students become better functioning members of society, while existentialists focus on students becoming self-actualizing, independent beings. In light of this potential disagreement in values and knowledge, you must proceed logically and specifically.

NATIONAL ATHLETIC TRAINERS' ASSOCIATION CODE OF ETHICS

Preamble

The Code of Ethics of the National Athletic Trainers' Association has been written to make the membership aware of the principles of ethical behavior that should be followed in the practice of athletic training. The primary goal of the Code is the assurance of high quality health care. The Code presents aspirational standards of behavior that all members should strive to achieve.

The principles cannot be expected to cover all specific situations that may be encountered by the practicing athletic trainer, but should be considered representative of the spirit with which athletic trainers should make decisions. The principles are written generally and the circumstances of a situation will determine the interpretation and application of a given principle and of the Code as a whole. Whenever there is a conflict between the Code and legality, the laws prevail. The guidelines set forth in this Code are subject to continual review and revision as the athletic training profession develops and changes.

Principle 1

Members shall respect the rights, welfare and dignity of all individuals.

1.1   Members shall not discriminate against any legally protected class.

1.2   Members shall be committed to providing competent care consistent with both the requirements and the limitations of their profession.

1.3   Members shall preserve the confidentiality of privileged information and shall not release such information to a third party not involved in the patient's care unless the person consents to such release or release is permitted or required by law.

Principle 2

Members shall comply with the laws and regulations governing the practice of athletic training.

2.1   Members shall comply with applicable local, state, and federal laws and institutional guidelines.

2.2   Members shall be familiar with and adhere to all National Athletic Trainers' Association guidelines and ethical standards.

2.3   Members are encouraged to report illegal or unethical practice pertaining to athletic training to the appropriate person or authority.

2.4   Members shall avoid substance abuse and, when necessary, seek rehabilitation for chemical dependency.

Principle 3

Members shall accept responsibility for the exercise of sound judgment.

3.1   Members shall not misrepresent in any manner, either directly or indirectly, their skills, training, professional credentials, identity or services.

3.2   Members shall provide only those services for which they are qualified via education and/or experience and by pertinent legal regulatory process.

3.3   Members shall provide services, make referrals, and seek compensation only for those services that are necessary.

(continued)

NATIONAL ATHLETIC TRAINERS' ASSOCIATION CODE OF ETHICS (CONTINUED)

Principle 4

Members shall maintain and promote high standards in the provision services.

4.1   Members shall recognize the need for continuing education and participate in various types of educational activities that enhance their skills and knowledge.

4.2   Members who have the responsibility for employing and evaluating the performance of other staff members shall fulfill such responsibility in a fair, considerate, and equitable manner, on the basis of clearly enunciated criteria.

4.3   Members who have the responsibility for evaluating the performance of employees, supervisees, or students are encouraged to share evaluations with them and allow them the opportunity to respond to those evaluations.

4.4   Members shall educate those whom they supervise in the practice of athletic training with regard to the Code of Ethics and encourage their adherence to it.

4.5   Whenever possible, members are encouraged to participate and support others in the conduct and communication of research and educational activities that may contribute knowledge for improved patient care, patient or student education, and the growth of athletic training as a profession.

4.6   When members are researchers or educators, they are responsible for maintaining and promoting ethical conduct in research and educational activities.

Principle 5

Members shall not engage in any form of conduct that constitutes a conflict of interest or that adversely reflects on the profession.

5.1   The private conduct of the member is a personal matter to the same degree as is any other person's except when such conduct compromises the fulfillment of professional responsibilities.

5.2   Members of the National Athletic Trainers' Association and others serving on the Association's committees or acting as consultants shall not use, directly or by implication, the Association's name or logo or their affiliation with the Association in the endorsement of products or services.

5.3   Members shall not place financial gain above the welfare of the patient being treated and shall not participate in any arrangement that exploits the patient.

5.4   Members may seek remuneration for their services that is commensurate with their services and in compliance with applicable law.

Many educators and philosophers have adopted an eclectic approach rather than accepting all aspects of one particular philosophy. **Eclecticism** is a combination of theories and doctrines from several philosophies into a consistent and compatible set of beliefs. For example, you may believe that the teacher should model correct skill performance, like the idealist would, yet encourage problem solving as the pragmatist and naturalist advocate. You may design your program to focus on individualized learning (naturalism) that allows for individuality

WEB CONNECTIONS

1. www.sportsethicsinstitute.org
   The Sports Ethics Institute encourages the exploration of ethical issues, an examination of the ethical dimensions of sports, and a heightened understanding of ethical behavior in sports.

2. www.dmu.ac.uk/dept/schools/pesl/affiliat/iaps.htm
   Check out the site of the International Association for the Philosophy of Sport, which fosters philosophical interchange among scholars interested in gaining a better understanding of sport.

3. www.britannica.com/bcom/eb/article/6/0,5716,115433+1,00.html
   Gain a deeper knowledge about idealism by reading this article.

4. www.britannica.com/bcom/eb/article/6/0,5716,64476+1+62873,00.
   html?query=realism
   Read this article to learn more about the philosophy of realism.

5. www.britannica.com/bcom/eb/article/6/0,5716,56426+1+
   55048,00.html?query=naturalism
   Expand your understanding about naturalism at this site.

6. www.britannica.com/bcom/eb/article/5/0,5716,115437+1,00.html
   Learn more about the philosophy of pragmatism at this site.

7. www.britannica.com/bcom/eb/article/2/0,5716,115432+1+108678,00.
   html?query=existentialism
   Check out this article for more insight into existentialism.

8. www.ets.uidaho.edu/center_for_ethics
   This site of the Center for ETHICS at the University of Idaho describes some of the leading research being conducted in the area of sport ethics.

(existentialism), yet also emphasizes developing social skills valued by pragmatists. You may choose to evaluate your students using subjective (idealist) and quantitative (realist) measures. Based on your experiences and established values, an eclectic philosophy may emerge as the foundation for your personal philosophy. Again, the key is to realize the importance of examining what you believe, why you believe it, and what your values mean (see "Sample of a Teaching Philosophy" box on page 117.

Before developing your personal philosophy (and to show how your attitudes, beliefs, and values influence your moral reasoning process), read the

SAMPLE OF A TEACHING PHILOSOPHY

Student learning is my primary focus. I seek first to learn who my students are and what they know, because only then can we jointly work to help them learn what they need to know. This student-centered approach makes teaching a creative and complex journey as we challenge and stimulate each other to a deeper understanding of the content in the course.

I model a variety of instructional strategies and behaviors as I communicate information attempting to integrate this with their existing knowledge as they enjoy the process of learning. In every class I demonstrate my personal enthusiasm for the course content, thereby helping students realize the importance of, excitement for, and continual nature of learning. I seek to teach students collectively and individually the foundational concepts and skills in varied, innovative ways that will stimulate them to ask questions and to desire to learn more. Each class is organized to ensure sequential and clear presentations and complete student engagement. I ask questions and encourage dialogue to facilitate critical and creative thinking by involving every student, whom I seek to know by name. Questions are elicited from students to reinforce how valuable their active participation in the learning process is.

To engage students more actively in their learning, I use various grouping for discussing issues, solving learning problems, analyzing case studies, and helping each other learn concepts and applications. I challenge students to think critically, to reflect on what they are learning and how it is relevant to them, and to participate actively in the learning process.

A variety of authentic assessments are used throughout each course to ensure that students are monitoring their learning and demonstrating that they are progressing in the achievement of learning outcomes. Feedback that I seek and gladly receive from students enables me to reflect upon and continually improve my instructional approaches as well as to ensure the relevancy and application of course content to the learning process and their knowledge base.

following situations and give your responses. A composite of your opinions should help you better understand your values and knowledge and how they provide the foundation for your personal philosophy.

- Situation 1—During a basketball game, player 44 (team A) and player 12 (team B) both attempt to control a loose ball, but it goes out of bounds. As the official, you blow your whistle and award the ball to team A. Player 44 acknowledges touching the ball last. Do you change your call? If you were the player, would you have acknowledged causing the ball to go out of bounds? Why or why not?

- Situation 2—During a recreation league softball game, you as the field supervisor learn that one of the teams is playing an individual not on the official team roster. That team is in last place in the league standings. What action, if any, do you take? Would your response differ if this team was in first place?

- Situation 3—As a coach, sporting goods distributors frequently offer you gifts, such as free golf clubs, or special incentives, such as clothing items, if your school purchases from their companies. Should you accept these personal gifts?

- Situation 4—As a collegiate football player you are told by the coach to take anabolic steroids to help build muscle bulk. Do you take the drugs? Is this cheating or gaining a competitive edge?

- Situation 5—Your soccer team of 9- and 10-year-olds is in the last game of the season. If your team wins, it will capture the league championship. Your best player twists an ankle just as the first half ends. The player is in pain, but there is seemingly no fracture and only slight swelling. Do you allow that player to participate in the second half? Should the player be allowed to decide whether to play?

- Situation 6—In applying for a position as an athletic trainer with a rehabilitation clinic, you are told that a preemployment drug test and annual random drug testing are required. Does this violate any of your beliefs or constitutional rights? Would you continue to seek this job?

- Situation 7—The health club at which you just took a position depends on enrolling at least 20 new members monthly to meet its expenses. In your first staff meeting, you are trained how to sell memberships without explaining the required annual fee that is assessed after the first month. You are also told that selling memberships is more important than customer service. Does this contradict any of your values? Is this pragmatic approach offensive to you? Will you assist members less while working more diligently to convince guests to join the club?

- Situation 8—For the recreation department where you serve as special events director, you are planning to conduct a family fun run, walk, and road race. The owner of a local hardware store who has pledged $1000 to fund this event calls one week before the event to notify you that he will not be able to donate the money. You are distraught. Just then you receive a call from the new beer distributor in town offering to provide financial support ($1000) for recreational activities in exchange for advertising. Do you accept this offer even though young people are participating in this event? Should the recreation department have a policy regarding the companies from which support can be received? Is it better to cancel the event or to accept the beer company's offer?

- Situation 9—As you assess the fitness of an employee at a corporate fitness facility, you are told by that person that several employees have been padding their expense accounts to pay for golf outings and sports tickets. Are you bound by any rules of confidentiality in this situation? Should you tell your supervisor? Is this action justified because everyone is doing it, or is it embezzlement?

- Situation 10—As a local sportswriter you are given evidence that a 14-year-old just transferred to a public magnet school because of promised financial benefits. This student happens to be an outstanding athlete. Do you write this story?

Your responses to these real-life situations should help you understand the importance of developing a personal philosophy. Your answers to the following questions can assist you in this developmental process.

- What is the basis for my ethical judgments personally, interpersonally, and programmatically?
  - Is the action honest, fair, responsible, and beneficent?
  - Will the action benefit me?
  - Will the action harm others?
  - Will the action violate a societal tradition, law, or expectation?
  - Will the action violate my personal values?
- Who and what are most important to me in my program?
  - Students
  - Participants
  - Employers
  - Parents
  - Taxpayers
  - Co-workers
  - Athletes
  - Fans
  - Teaching
  - Learning
  - Participation
  - Adherence to the program
  - Fun
  - Skill development
  - Fitness
  - Winning
  - Developing social skills
  - Fair play
  - Classroom management
  - Stress reduction
  - Safety
  - Critical thinking
- How do I determine what the program content should include?
  - Required state curriculum
  - National organization standards
  - Interests of participants
  - Traditional offerings
  - Latest published research findings
  - Popularity of new innovations
  - Something learned at a recent workshop or conference
  - Winning, using whatever means helps achieve this goal
- What instructional and operational approaches will I use?
  - Lecture
  - Problem-solving

- Guided discovery
- Self-pacing
- Mentor
- Guide
- Role model
- Motivator
- Counselor
- Leader
- Facilitator
- Autocrat
- Friend
- Boss

- How will I know if program objectives and personal goals have been achieved?
  - Skills are learned.
  - Participants persist in lifetime activity.
  - Winning occurs.
  - Everyone, including me, has fun.
  - Fitness is developed and maintained.
  - Career advancement occurs.
  - Evaluations are positive.
  - Job security exists.

Hopefully, responding to these questions can start you on the way to developing a personal philosophy that will help guide you into a career that matches what you value. A personal philosophy, though, is an evolving and changing perspective on how a person views those things of most value and the role each will serve in his or her life.

SUMMARY

As you progress in your education and enter your career, your philosophy may change. You may borrow concepts from idealism, realism, pragmatism, naturalism, or existentialism, or you may adopt an eclectic approach. You will face ethical decisions often. Regardless of the values chosen, having a philosophy is essential: it is your personal commitment to what you want to do and become. You can use your philosophy to help you think critically, to examine yourself, to resolve personal and professional issues, and to understand your career better.

CAREER PERSPECTIVE

RICHARD J. CAREY, ATC/L
Health Educator/Athletic Trainer
Lyons Township High School
Western Springs/LaGrange, Illinois

EDUCATION
A.A., Pre-Physical Therapy, Grays Harbor Junior College (WA)
B.A., Health Education, University of Washington
M.S., Health Education, Pennsylvania State University

JOB RESPONSIBILITIES AND HOURS
As the head athletic trainer, Rich is responsible for 26 girls' and boys' teams at two campuses. He covers all home and away football games and home events for all other sports. He prepares athletes for practices and competitions, plans and administers conditioning and rehabilitation programs, and maintains athletes' treatment records, coordinates two training rooms, and supervises 24 student trainers. He also teaches three classes of health education to sophomores and two classes of sports medicine to juniors and seniors. Monday through Friday, Rich works from 7:30 A.M. to 7:00 P.M. and on Saturday, from 7:30 A.M. to 5:00 P.M. These are typical hours for an athletic trainer who also teaches. Additionally, he works longer hours when back-to-back sports competitions occur.

SPECIALIZED COURSE WORK, DEGREES, AND WORK EXPERIENCES NEEDED FOR THIS CAREER
Certification by the National Athletic Trainers' Association and a college degree in education with the appropriate teaching certification are required. Some states also require regulation (Illinois requires licensure) in athletic training. Rich recommends obtaining emergency medical technician training as well as instructor certification in cardiopulmonary resuscitation. He emphasizes the importance of attending sports medicine workshops and symposia whenever possible. Many of these sessions build on one's undergraduate and graduate education and provide the opportunity to obtain required continuing education units.

SATISFYING ASPECTS
Rich enjoys helping others recover from an injury or illness. He likes serving as a counselor for teens during their injury recovery period with its emotional ups and downs. Keeping up-to-date to teach his health education class is a pleasant challenge for him. The two months off in the summer help compensate for the long hours worked during the school year.

JOB POTENTIAL
At Rich's school, one's salary increases with educational hours and years of continuous service in sports. The salary range is $37,000 to $80,000 for teaching, with a $5,000 to $25,000 stipend for athletic training. Professional time is available for speaking and publishing, with the school paying part of the associated expenses.

SUGGESTIONS FOR STUDENTS

Rich recommends accumulating the highest educational degrees possible. You must be willing to relocate from your home in securing a position. Certification in a teaching field other than health and physical education when coupled with athletic training certification may enhance your employment options. Personally, he stresses that one's physical and mental health must be high, with sufficient stamina to work long hours. As an athletic trainer, you must be able to deal with all kinds of people and demonstrate a great sense of humor. You must also show a genuine understanding and supportive attitude during an athlete's convalescence period. In the classroom, you need to use diversified strategies to teach health and decision-making skills. Rich suggests teaching with, not at, your students. He adds that if you work hard and remain dedicated, you can attain any goal you desire as a teacher/athletic trainer.

REVIEW QUESTIONS

1. What does philosophy mean?
2. Using the philosophy of idealism, contrast the role of the teacher with the role of the student.
3. How do realists seek truth?
4. Which philosophy seeks to help students become better functioning members of society, and how is this accomplished?
5. Which philosophy focuses on self-realization for each student?
6. Which philosophies stress using a problem-solving approach?
7. How would naturalism emphasize attaining individual goals?
8. How can a physical educator, exercise scientist, or sport leader teach ethics?
9. Why is a personal philosophy of physical education, exercise science, and sport important?
10. What is an eclectic philosophy?

STUDENT ACTIVITIES

1. Select one of the five traditional philosophies discussed in this chapter and write a two-page paper explaining how it applies to your physical education, exercise science, and sport experiences as a student.
2. Divide the class into five groups with each group adopting one of the five traditional philosophies. Ask each group to prepare and present a five-minute defense, based on their assigned philosophy, of the inclusion of required daily physical education classes in the schools.
3. Respond to each of the 10 situations listed on pages 117–118 and be prepared to discuss them in class. Be ready to justify your opinions.
4. Write your personal philosophy of physical education, exercise science, or sport.
5. Ask a person in a physical education, exercise science, or sport career to explain to you his or her personal philosophy.

REFERENCE

Kohlberg L: *The philosophy of moral development: moral stages and the idea of justice,* New York, 1981, Harper & Row.

SUGGESTED READINGS

Capwell EM, Smith BJ, Shirreffs J, Olsen LK: Development of a unified code of ethics for the health education profession: a report of the national task force on ethics in health education, *Health Ed* 31(4):212, 2000. The members of this task force briefly describe the process of developing the code of ethics for the health education profession. The complete code and an abbreviated version are included.

Conn JH, Gerdes DA: Ethical decision making: issues and applications to American sport, *Phys Educ* 55(3):121, 1998. This article focused on ethical decision making in the context of sport.

Gibbons SI, Ebbeck V, Weiss MR: *Fair play for kids: effects on the moral development for children in physical education, Res Q* 66:247, 1995. This study reported on the effect of participation in educational activities selected from *Fair Play for Kids* on moral judgment, reason, intention, and the social behavior of children. The results validated the *Fair Play for Kids* curriculum for effecting change in the moral development of elementary school students.

Lumpkin A, Stoll SK, Beller JM: *Sport ethics—applications for fair play* (2nd ed.), Boston, 1999, McGraw-Hill. This book describes moral reasoning and fair play behavior as a foundation for chapters on elimination, eligibility, intimidation and violence, ergogenic aids, commercialization, racial equity, gender equity, and morality.

Malloy DC, Zakus DH: Ethical decision making in sport administration: a theoretical inquiry into substance and form, *J of Sp Mgmt* 9:36, 1995. A synthesis of four philosophical approaches to ethics and two psychological approaches to moral reasoning are presented as ways to understand the decision-making behavior of sport managers.

McCallister SG, Blinde EM, Weiss WM: Teaching values and implementing philosophies: dilemmas of the youth sport coach, *Phys Educ* 57(1):35, 2000. This study indicated that youth sport coaches generally have good intentions to provide a positive and wholesome learning environment for children playing baseball and softball, even though external pressures make this difficult.

Miller SC, Bredemeier BJ, Shields DL: Sociomoral education through physical education with at-risk children, *Quest* 49:114, 1997. In 1995, an urban elementary school with at-risk children implemented the moral action model proposed by Shields and Bredemeier to promote empathy, moral reasoning maturity, task motivation, and self-responsibility. Anecdotal evidence of the effectiveness of the intervention was discussed.

Priest RF, Krause JV, Beach J: Four-year changes in college athletes' ethical value choices in sports situations. *Res Q for Exer & Sp* 70(2):170, 1999. Over four years, 631 male and female students attending the United States Military Academy who participated in intercollegiate team and individual sports decreased in making moral choices in sport. In addition, the athletes believed that their coaches were more likely to make unethical choices than they were.

Panagiotopoulos D: The legal aspects of sports ethics and the protection of fair play, *Int J of Phys Educ* 35(3):99, 1998. The author suggests that a legislative approach to sports was necessary to safeguard the spirit of fair play and sports ethics and to punish those who violated sport rules.

Playing hardball: beyond fun and games in interscholastic athletics, *Sch Adm* 55(10):6, 1998. In this special section on high school athletics, there are articles dealing with eligibility issues, the participation of home-schooled students in high school athletics, corporate sponsorship of high school athletics, the use of Title IX of the Education Amendments of 1972 to expand athletics opportunities for girls, and managing the risks of sport to avoid litigation.

SELECTING A CAREER

KEY CONCEPTS

- Self-assessment inventories help identify individual characteristics and desired lifestyles that influence career choices.
- Traditional and nontraditional settings foster the teaching-learning process yet differ in clientele, work hours, and related responsibilities.
- Programs for the development of fitness offer careers for those interested in helping others incorporate healthful habits and practices into their lives.
- Schools, colleges, nonschool agencies, and professional leagues expect coaches, administrators, trainers, officials, and other personnel to direct and to provide quality athletic programs.
- Many schools and public and private organizations need individuals with sport management knowledge to direct their programs.
- Sport marketing has grown to be a multimillion-dollar business as it capitalizes on the nation's enthusiasm for fitness, sports, and leisure activities.

Career choices today are more complex decisions than they were formerly because of the obsolescence of some jobs, the burgeoning of technology, the demographic shifts in population, the acceptance of women and minorities in more jobs in the work force, and economic necessity. People seldom continue with their initial career choices; they change jobs several times during their working years.

The preceding chapters described the broad spectrum of physical education, exercise science, and sport, laying the foundation for the career options presented in this chapter. You should now be prepared to assess objectively your future career. This assessment is not a one-time event, but rather an ongoing process. Your initial career choice is not necessarily a lifetime commitment but one that should be reevaluated periodically. As you read this chapter and assess your interests, abilities, and goals, remember that you are choosing a career pathway, not necessarily a single job.

Before embarking on this process, identify your attitudes and expectations. Your attitude toward a career greatly influences whether you will be successful and happy. A major factor is your self-concept. How do you evaluate your abilities? Are you willing to listen to the advice of teachers, coaches, parents, and others? Can you objectively assess your personal strengths and weaknesses? Are you people oriented? Are you motivated to do your best?

Before considering available careers, analyze the relative importance of some personal and job-related factors. Two self-assessment inventories are provided in the boxes on pages 127–128. Your responses to both of these will help you determine which physical education, exercise science, or sport career best meets your needs and aspirations.

FACTORS INFLUENCING CAREER CHOICES

Family influences regarding a career choice can be positive, negative, or both. Parents may overtly or subtly persuade you to pursue a career on which they place a high value. Many times parents have forbidden their children to major in physical education because they viewed it as frivolous, nonacademic, or not prestigious enough. On the other hand, parents may push their children into a career in sports because of their own rewarding past experiences. Regardless of the situation, remember that your family will not be going to work for you each day or fulfilling the responsibilities of your chosen career. Parents, siblings, and significant others, although they can express their opinions and share their experiences, should not decide for you.

Whether consciously or not, many people select a career because they respect and admire someone who is in a particular position, a role model whom they wish to emulate. This may be a parent, sibling, coach, teacher, or friend who has demonstrated enjoyment of and dedication to a career that you wish to share. One cautionary note: you may not be able to find the same type of position or may not possess the same abilities. Remember, you need to develop your own niche rather than trying to mimic another person.

The skills, knowledge, abilities, and experiences that you bring to your career will influence whether you are successful. This is not to imply that all career preparation precedes employment; certainly there is considerable learning while you are on the job. Your confidence in accepting an initial position is based on two factors, only one of which is prior formal preparation. Always remember the importance of the second factor of gaining experiences, including voluntary or internship experiences, that may enhance your chances of career change or advancement.

An important criterion for continuation in a job is the level of personal fulfillment and satisfaction. If you dread going to work, hate the day-to-day routine, and think the negative aspects far outweigh the positive gains, then it may be time for a change. It is not disastrous to sacrifice job security and material benefits in order to start a career that enhances self-worth and pleasure. One way to make a career change less traumatic is to prepare yourself for a broad physical education, exercise science, and sport career pathway that can offer you numerous alternatives.

FACTORS INFLUENCING CAREER CHOICES

Using the scale below, indicate how you value each of the following in relation to your selection of a career:

5	4	3	2	1
Most highly valued	Strong influencing factor	Average consideration	Weak influencing factor	Not valued at all

_____ Influence of family and significant others

_____ Identification with role model(s)

_____ Knowledgeable about many aspects of this career

_____ Would personally enjoy this career

_____ Enjoy working with people

_____ Desire to serve others

_____ Ease of entrance into this career

_____ Monetary and other benefits from this career

_____ Time compatibility (work hours versus leisure time) meets expectations

_____ Job security available in this career

_____ Job location close to family and friends

From the list above, select the five that you think are most important to you in your career choice and write them (in descending order of importance) in the spaces below.

1. _____
2. _____
3. _____
4. _____
5. _____

Other factors influencing your career choice:

_____

_____

Some people prefer a solitary setting; others need to interact frequently with people. If you are people oriented, you need to identify the ages of those with whom you find the greatest enjoyment and seek a career that includes these opportunities. It is also important for you to identify which aspects of working with people you enjoy the most. Do you prefer to work with large groups, small groups, or one on one? Do you prefer constant or periodic interactions? Can you make decisions with others or concerning others?

Sometimes interaction with others is so highly valued that your personal needs become secondary to those of others. This characteristic is known as altruism. Teachers in traditional and nontraditional settings focus on helping their students develop healthy lifestyles, even though their own material benefits seem small compared with the hours spent in instruction.

LIFESTYLE PREFERENCE ASSESSMENT

1. Where would you prefer to live (state or region)?_____
2. Do you prefer to work for yourself or for others?_____
3. Do you prefer a large or small work environment?_____
4. What ages would you prefer to interact with daily?_____
    _____
5. Do you prefer an outdoor or indoor work environment?_____
6. Do you prefer a sedentary or an active job?_____
7. How much travel (if any) would you want as a regular part of your work?_____
    _____
8. What days of the week would you prefer to work?_____
9. What hours of the day would you prefer to work?_____
10. What salary would you need now?_____ in 10 years?_____
11. How much vacation time would you want each year?_____
12. What fringe benefits would you want as part of your job?_____
    _____
    _____
13. How important to you is career advancement?_____
14. What other job characteristics do you think would be important to your job satisfaction_____
    _____
    _____

One aspect of career satisfaction comes from being able to maintain personal fitness at the health club where you help others do the same.

Career opportunities in physical education, exercise science, and sport are expanding. Your expertise is needed because of increased leisure time, higher standards of living, and the emphasis on fitness. However, your ideal job in the exact location you wish and with the dreamed-for salary may not be available. After realizing that jobs are available for those who actively seek them, you must be willing to accept the probability of starting at the bottom. As a young professional, you can expect to work hard, to volunteer for extra duties, to learn new ideas, to gain experiences, and to accept less desirable responsibilities as a test of commitment to your field. If you do so successfully, you will advance.

You must determine the importance you place on monetary and other material benefits as you choose a career. Your response on the Lifestyle Preference Assessment indicates the value that a certain salary has for you and how it relates to other aspects of your life, such as family, status, location, and travel. The importance that salary has for you is also shown in the hours and days that you prefer to work as well as your desired vacation time. Money, however, is only one type of remuneration. Other benefits, including health insurance, retirement

CAREER OPPORTUNITIES IN PHYSICAL EDUCATION, EXERCISE SCIENCE, AND SPORT

Teaching

Traditional

Elementary school (K–6)
Middle school (5–8)
Secondary school (7–12)
Junior/community college
College/university
Adapted physical education (K–12)

Nontraditional

Sport club
Health club
Sport camp or school
Recreation department
Corporate or industry fitness
Senior citizens' program
Military
Dance studio
Resort
Cruise ship

Fitness

Development

Private sport club
Recreation department
Dance studio
Corporate or industry fitness
Protective services (police and fire.)
Country club
Health spa

Rehabilitative

Therapeutic recreation
Cardiac rehabilitation
Sports medicine clinic
Weight control center
Stress management clinic
Massage clinic
Fitness and nutritional
 counseling

(continued)

CAREER OPPORTUNITIES IN PHYSICAL EDUCATION, EXERCISE SCIENCE, AND SPORT (CONTINUED)

Athletics

School

Coaching
Athletic administration
Athletic training
Sport officiating

College and University

Coaching
Athletic administration
Athletic training
Business management
Facility management
Sports information
Sports marketing
Academic counseling
Sport officiating
Ticket sales
Strength and conditioning coach
Sport psychology

Sport Management

Business and Industry

Sport club
Health club
Sport camp and school
Corporate or industry fitness
Theme park and resort
Sport hall of fame and museum
Public fitness and recreation
Facility management
Equipment design

School

Program/department head
Intramurals/campus recreation
Research

Sport Marketing

Clothing sales
Equipment sales
Club membership sales
Book sales

Sport Communication

Sport broadcasting
Sport journalism
Sport photography

benefits, an expense account, travel, club memberships, and prestige, may offset a lower salary. Only you can decide the importance of money and other benefits, but you must do so honestly, since frequently these are pivotal factors in career selection.

A five-day, 8-to-5 work week is unlikely in most physical education, exercise science, and sport careers. Your career choice could result in working any number of hours a week, nights, holidays, and weekends, and anywhere from 9 to 12 months a year. Only you can weigh your personal preferences versus each job's characteristics. Begrudging time spent working often results in negative feelings toward that task. How important is the amount and scheduling of leisure time for you? How do work hours relate to monetary benefits in importance?

Job security varies dramatically in physical education, exercise science, and sport careers. Competent fulfillment of job responsibilities in some careers results in retention of positions based on merit; careers in education require earning tenure for job security. Some careers carry no guarantee of future employment other than the demand for your services. Associated with the concept of job security is the potential for advancement. Relocation is often necessary for advancement because the position you qualify for or seek may not be available in the same city or with the same employer. Challenge and stimulation are important to many people for continuation in a career, as are recognition for a job well done and increased material benefits.

As you decide on a career, review and weigh all these factors. Take advantage of your institution's career services office, which can assist you in evaluating various career options. Only after evaluating the most influential considerations and your own personal preferences can you objectively select a career pathway. Regardless of your choice, the key is your commitment and motivation.

The box on pages 129–130 provides a broad overview of career opportunities. The rest of this chapter describes these broad categories and some of the options, presenting educational requirements, job availability, and positive and negative aspects. After you have finished this chapter, refer to Figure 5.1 on pages 154–155 for sample questions to ask of professionals in any of the careers you are considering.

TEACHING

Schools and Colleges

Employment for college graduates with majors in physical education has traditionally been in public and private schools. Teaching remains a viable choice for both beginning and lifelong careers. Teachers' salaries are determined by each state's salary schedule and local school district supplements. Additional stipends for extra responsibilities like coaching are possible. Base salaries for beginning teachers with baccalaureate degrees will be at least $20,000, with many school systems paying more and some offering signing bonuses due to teacher shortages. To find jobs, graduates may have to move to smaller communities, urban settings, or different states. In the latter situation, a reciprocal agreement may exist between the certifying state and the new state, or additional course work may be required before full certification is granted.

Many states require *The Praxis Series: Professional Assessments for Beginning Teachers* for certification. This three-part series includes Praxis I (tests reading, writing, and mathematics skills needed by all teachers), Praxis II (measures prospective teachers' knowledge of their major fields of study), and Praxis III (judges actual teaching skill through the use of trained assessors).

Junior high and senior high physical educators in their first years sometimes teach classes outside their major fields. Preparing to teach in a second subject area through taking courses and obtaining certification will enhance the likelihood of securing a teaching position. Willingness to accept these teaching assignments may lead to full-time physical education positions in subsequent years. The physical educator, although perhaps not prepared to teach or interested in teaching health, frequently is assigned classes in this area as well. Some schools hire certified health educators, and others have health consultants, but because of budget constraints many health classes are taught by physical educators in the secondary schools. Physical education teachers work a minimum of seven hours at school, which usually includes one planning period and at least five classes. In addition, the teacher is expected to plan classes; grade papers; monitor the halls, lunchroom, and buses; and complete administrative reports. Some secondary teachers are faced with discipline problems, apathetic students, drug abuse, inadequate facilities and equipment, lack of administrative and community support, and sometimes even violent behaviors. On the other hand, professional involvement and educational enrichment are encouraged by supportive administrators. Low salaries deter some good candidates from choosing teaching careers, while opportunities to positively influence students' lives, retirement and health benefits, summer vacations, and job security are attractive job characteristics.

Adapted physical education specialists are hired most frequently by large systems and state departments of education so that many schools may share the expertise of one individual. This specialist helps classroom teachers and physical educators meet the needs of students with special needs or limitations who have been included in regular classes, or they may individualize instruction for students. Educational background and experience emphasizing adapted physical education is important for this career. Hours and salaries correspond with those of other teachers.

In some states, elementary school physical educators are in demand; in others, jobs are scarce. Their responsibilities vary from teaching daily classes for children at one school to conducting ten 30-minute classes at a different school each day of the week. The intrinsic satisfaction of helping children learn and develop is the reward cited most often by these teachers. The benefits of positively influencing children's attitudes toward movement skills and encouraging healthy lifestyles outweigh problems like inadequate facilities and equipment and limited administrative support.

Teaching physical education in junior or community colleges or in four-year colleges and universities requires education beyond the bachelor's degree. In smaller institutions, faculty with master's degrees are expected to teach pre-major or major courses. Most institutions also require sports and activity instructors to have master's degrees. Since university activity instructors and small college teachers spend most of their time teaching, rather than conducting research, job security or tenure is based primarily on teaching and service rather than on scholarly productivity. (These same teachers are often expected to advise students and to

Teaching fundamental skills to children may lead to their continued participation in physical activity throughout life. (Photo courtesy Bob Hilliard.)

serve on departmental and university committees.) Beginning salaries range widely according to location and status of the institution, with benefits including health insurance, retirement programs, and summer vacations. In their activity and theory classes, these teachers enjoy helping adult students learn healthy lifestyles and relish the generalist approach to teaching physical education three to six hours per day and four to five days a week.

In larger institutions, exercise and sport scientists in specialties such as bio-mechanics, exercise physiology, sport and exercise psychology, and other disci-plines teach undergraduate and graduate courses in addition to conducting research. Research productivity, teaching effectiveness, and professional service are required for tenure, which is granted in five to seven years. For university pro-fessors, conducting research, writing articles for professional journals, and giving scholarly presentations are prerequisites for job security. Lack of time for research and class preparation is cited frequently by university teachers as a problem. Al-though their hours are somewhat flexible, committee meetings, student advising, and other departmental responsibilities besides teaching, research, and service extend the work week well beyond 40 hours.

Noneducational Settings

Opportunities abound for those who want to teach fitness and sports skills out-side a school environment. Dance studios provide instruction in aerobic, jazz, ballet, tap, and modern dance for children and adults. Individuals with dance majors or specialized dance course work teach various dance forms to customers for fees (ranging from $5 per hour for group lessons to $25 per hour for private lessons) at these studios. Classes may be scheduled throughout the day and evening as well as on weekends.

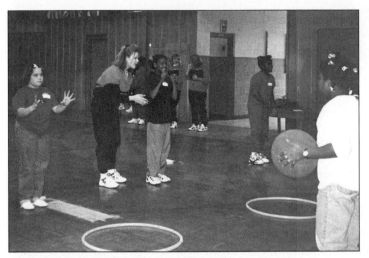

Teachers must be knowledgeable, organized, good communicators, enthusiastic, and respectful of others, as well as possess interpersonal skills and demonstrate professional integrity. (Photo courtesy Bob Hilliard.)

Sport clubs focus on individual sports, such as tennis, aquatics, or racquetball, and need instructors for private and group lessons. Other clubs, which usually have expensive membership fees, may cater to several sports, such as country clubs that offer swimming, golf, and tennis. Vacation resorts are increasingly providing sports instruction for their guests. Health clubs usually offer fitness programs in aerobic conditioning and weight training, sports instruction, such as in racquetball, and possibly classes in stress management and weight control. Because of the tremendous variety in clubs, salaries depend on location, clientele, instructional expertise, and assigned responsibilities. Salaries for instructors may start at $8 to $10 an hour and increase as responsibilities grow.

Sport camps have become booming businesses related to commercial recreation. Both children and adults attend these highly successful ventures in the summer or on weekends and holidays. Sport camps provide excellent opportunities for gaining teaching experience and for making valuable contacts that may lead to permanent positions. For school teachers looking for summer employment, opportunities abound in sport camps. Expertise in teaching one or more activities is important for employment, as is a desire to work with various age and skill levels. Responsibilities, such as those of an instructor or program director, determine salaries, which may vary widely. Day camp instructors may earn $25 to $50 per day, while residence camp instructors can expect salaries at about twice this level.

Concomitant with increasing life spans in the United States is the critical need for professionals trained to provide recreational and leisure activities for senior citizens. Today, approximately 20 percent of the population of the United States is 65 years of age or older. Federal programs, as well as private agencies, increasingly must provide physical activity programs in retirement homes, day care

Golf instruction is popular in schools and colleges as well as in private and public clubs.

centers, and senior citizens' apartment complexes. The job potential for individuals trained to prescribe and to direct activities for this clientele will expand rapidly in the years ahead.

Opportunities to teach and lead sport and fitness programs in the military abound because fitness training is highly valued by the various branches of the armed services. Instructional assignments in physical fitness programs are available to enlistees. Frequently, though, civilians instruct at the service academies, on military installations, and at special training facilities. Programs for the military vary widely—from basic conditioning drills for men and women to broad-based fitness and sport opportunities for career personnel to family-oriented recreational offerings. Highly competitive leagues in a variety of sports are commonplace on most military bases, since skilled, fit servicemen and servicewomen are valued. As an employee of the federal government, your pay would depend on classification, but benefits are excellent.

FITNESS, EXERCISE, AND SPORT SCIENCE

Many large industries and corporations provide fitness centers for their executives. Concerns about work efficiency and loss of time and money from absenteeism have resulted in elaborate facilities for daily aerobic, strength, and flexibility workouts being provided for more and more employees. The directors of

Fitness clubs offer a variety of aerobic exercise machines.

these corporate fitness centers are usually individuals trained in one of the exercise sciences with a bachelor's degree. However, because of the attractiveness of these jobs and the in-depth knowledge needed, holders of master's degrees are often hired. Minimally, each individual should hold a certification as an exercise leader (such as that given by the American College of Sports Medicine), if not a higher certification such as an exercise specialist. Directors of corporate fitness centers are responsible for designing individually prescribed programs that include exercise sessions, nutritional changes, stress management hints, and other recommended lifestyle alterations. Close monitoring is required because for many, these programs dramatically alter their previous habits. Since lack of adherence is the primary reason goals are not achieved, these exercise scientists and leaders, along with their instructional staffs, must constantly motivate participants to adhere to their prescribed programs. In addition, personnel and program management skills are critical in these corporate settings.

Many companies have extended their fitness programs and recreational services to include all of their employees. Although these programs are not as elaborate as those for executives, management has realized the interrelationship of exercise and work efficiency; thus, graduates of physical education, exercise science, and sport studies programs are needed to provide the supervision and instruction for these programs. Working with people in a nonstructured setting appeals to many people in spite of the hours, which are frequently scheduled during workers' leisure time.

Many corporations have chosen to subcontract their fitness programs. In this arrangement, the business provides the site, but all daily administration and staff are provided by an outside supplier. This management firm hires fitness specialists to teach classes and to instruct one on one. Instructors can expect starting salaries of around $20,000, with significant variance depending on the location, number of clients served, and experience.

Related to both industry and job-site fitness is the need for professionals to design and to implement training programs for workers in the protective services (public safety officers). Exercise scientists are being hired to test the fitness levels of these workers and to prescribe exercise programs to meet their individual needs and to prepare them to meet the demands of their jobs. Satisfaction in observing positive lifestyle changes is rewarding; frustration may result when public safety officers fail to achieve their goals.

The fitness mania pervading the United States has led to a proliferation of public facilities and programs promoting lifestyle changes for various groups. Directors and program coordinators organize and implement fitness programs, sport teams, and various social activities. Job security is good, yet few advancement opportunities exist unless management skills learned in this setting are transferred to a related career. The minimal wages earned in many part-time positions in public recreation are offset by the invaluable experiences gained.

Cardiac rehabilitation programs have grown out of the need to help heart attack and heart disease patients regain their health and develop fit lifestyles. Programs at universities, community centers, hospitals, private clinics, and many other settings provide the exercises and activities prescribed by physicians and implemented by individuals with degrees in physical education, exercise science, and sport studies.

LEISURE SERVICES

Programming and Instruction

Recreation and leisure services are allied fields with physical education, exercise science, and sport. Recreation and leisure services professionals provide activities and programs for individuals of all ages and ability levels. The private sector provides millions of jobs in commercial recreation. Many physical education and recreation graduates obtain their first jobs in the following:

- Lodging—management, operation, and programming for individuals associated with housing services, such as resorts, cruise ships, and camps
- Recreation—planning, management, and operation of recreational programs, facilities, and areas for agencies such as commercial/private, governmental, volunteer, industrial, outdoor, and therapeutic institutions
- Entertainment services—management, operation, and programming for such organizations as theme parks, racetracks, and toy and game manufacturers

- Culture services—management, operation, and programming for institutions that deal with the fine arts, such as museums and historical sites
- Sports—management, operation, and programming for athletic areas and facilities, such as racquetball and tennis complexes, health and fitness clubs, and professional athletic organizations

Although numerous opportunities exist in these areas, probably the sports sub-cluster appeals to most individuals, with instruction and program planning being the major types of jobs available. Tennis, golf, and swimming are among the popular types of specific sports clubs; multisport complexes also exist. Health and fitness clubs are examples of these general and specific types of leisure-service organizations.

All of these activity-related clubs or businesses require membership, thereby excluding a segment of the population. Most individuals who work for these organizations are encouraged, if not required, to sell memberships as one of their responsibilities. Hours vary by club but are usually in the afternoons, in the evening, and on weekends, since these are the leisure hours of those who join. Job security varies with each person's expertise, yet potential for advancement into management and even ownership is good. Benefits include working with

The thrill of activities like rock climbing attracts many enthusiasts to careers in recreation. (Photo courtesy Aram Attarian.)

people and seeing their improvement as well as having the opportunity to maintain your own healthy lifestyle in these settings. Social skills, sales ability, and sports expertise are more important than a college degree, although being knowledgeable about the components of physical fitness and having expertise in skill analysis are quite helpful. Attaining a national certification in exercise testing or as a personal trainer can increase career options and lead to a higher salary.

The lodging subcluster includes resorts, condominium complexes, and camps that are increasingly hiring specialists in golf, tennis, swimming, and other sports to organize and to instruct groups and individuals. For these recreation directors, hours vary to meet the needs of the guests, but the pleasant work environment may compensate for a typical schedule.

City and county recreation departments offer a broad spectrum of activities, from instructional classes to league play to trips and nontraditional events. Teachers are especially needed early mornings, afternoons, and evenings, but also throughout the day. Recreational classes are offered in water aerobics, rock climbing, massage, cross-country skiing, karate, arts and crafts, parent and child aerobics, various types of dance, and racquetball. During the summers and evening hours, competitive and recreational leagues abound in basketball, baseball, football, volleyball, softball, soccer, tennis, and other popular sports.

Sponsored trips to museums, art events, state parks, zoos, and other attractions especially appeal to retirees and families. Fun runs, road races, and triathlons attract serious competitors as well as weekend athletes. The availability of facilities for a private swim, weight training session, or workout on a stationary bike or for a pickup basketball game also fall under the responsibility of recreation departments. Therefore, program supervisors and administrators have major responsibilities for providing and scheduling facilities to ensure that events operate smoothly. Increasingly in the future, recreation departments will be charged with the preservation of green space in cities to ensure that park areas are available for use during leisure hours. Recreation professionals who teach can anticipate starting salaries around $20,000. These salaries will grow as management responsibilities increase.

Rehabilitative

An outgrowth of the desire for a healthy lifestyle is the proliferation of specialized clinics and counseling centers, including those for weight control, massage, nutrition, and stress management. Weight-control centers sometimes promote a particular diet or system and usually provide information about nutrition and encourage safe exercise. In massage, a method of tension release and relaxation, one manipulates the body with various stroking, kneading, rubbing, or tapping motions. Wellness programs emphasize the development of nutritional, exercise, and attitudinal lifestyle changes through counseling and participatory sessions. The proliferation of stress management classes, clinics, seminars, workshops, and counseling centers indicates the demand for information and for preventive and corrective strategies. Since these are fee-based businesses, salaries vary dramatically.

In sports medicine clinics on college campuses and in hospitals, physicians, physical therapists, and athletic trainers treat and rehabilitate sports-related injuries. Team physicians for professional, college, school, and community teams must have earned medical degrees before specializing in this field. Physical therapists must be certified.

ATHLETICS

Schools and Colleges

A second career aspiration of many secondary school and some elementary school physical educators is coaching the numerous teams for boys and girls. Many schools have coaching vacancies but no teaching positions in physical education because of the resignations of some physical educators from coaching but not from teaching and because of the increased number of girls' teams. If certified in and willing to teach in a second subject area, the teacher/coach is automatically more marketable. Coaching positions in the more visible sports of basketball and football are not as easy to obtain as those in other sports, and more openings exist for coaches of girls' sports than for boys' teams (see Research View box "National Standards for Athletic Coaches").

In many schools, coaches are expected to work with more than one team and may sometimes have to work with as many as three teams. Some states allow nonteachers or substitute teachers to coach; in others, only employees of the school system can be hired. Monetary supplements (ranging from $500 to $5000) are minimal when compared with the long hours and the innumerable demands on coaches. Job security for football and basketball coaches in some high schools does not exist unless winning teams are consistently produced. Victories are not as critical to job retention for coaches of other sports.

Other athletic opportunities within schools include athletic training, sport officiating, and administration. High school sport officials normally work at other jobs and only umpire or referee as a hobby or as a second job. A former coach or current coach usually serves as the school's athletic director. This individual coordinates team schedules, budgets, and facilities, and supervises the overall athletic program.

Athletic programs vary dramatically depending on the size of a college. In junior or community colleges and small four-year colleges and universities, many coaches teach in physical education or in other departments, with coaching remaining a secondary responsibility. These individuals receive coaching supplements to their salaries and/or reduced teaching loads. Most sports at these institutions are nonrevenue-producing, although for some teams recruiting is expected, since athletic grants-in-aid are awarded. At larger universities, coaches of nonrevenue-producing sports may hold full-time positions in athletics by coaching more than one sport or team or by carrying out assigned administrative responsibilities. Other coaches at larger institutions teach or coach only part-time.

The teacher/coach, administrator/coach, part-time coach, or full-time coach frequently works day and night because of the increasing competitiveness of

RESEARCH VIEW

National Standards for Athletic Coaches

The National Association for Sport and Physical Education in 1995 published its National Standards for Athletic Coaches. The purpose of these standards is to provide coaches, athletic administrators, athletes, parents, and the public with the guidelines for the skills and knowledge that coaches should possess. These standards describe the basic competencies required of coaches with the goal of ensuring enjoyment and skill development of athletes along with their health and safety. The 37 standards are grouped into 8 standards:

Injuries: Prevention, Care, and Management

Standard 1   Prevent injuries by recognizing and insisting on safe playing conditions.

Standard 2   Ensure that the protective equipment is in good condition, fits properly, and is worn as prescribed by the manufacturer; ensure that equipment and facilities meet required standards [American Society for Testing Materials (ASTM) and U.S. Consumer Product Safety Commission (USCPSC)].

Standard 3   Recognize that proper conditioning and good health are vital to the prevention of athletic injuries.

Standard 4   Prevent exposure to the risk of injuries by considering the effects of environmental conditions on the circulatory and respiratory systems when planning and scheduling practices and contests and implementing programs for physical conditioning.

Standard 5   Be able to plan, coordinate, and implement procedures for appropriate emergency care.

Standard 6   Demonstrate skill in the prevention, recognition, and evaluation of injuries and the ability to assist athletes with the recovery/rehabilitation from injuries that are generally associated with participation in athletics in accordance with guidelines provided by qualified medical personnel.

Standard 7   Facilitate a unified medical program of prevention, care, and management of injuries by coordinating the roles and actions of the coach and a National Athletic Trainers' Association (NATA) certified athletic trainer with those of the physician.

Standard 8   Provide coaching assistants, athletes, and parents/guardians with education about injury prevention, injury reporting, and sources of medical care.

(continued)

Risk Management

Standard 9   Understand the scope of legal responsibilities that comes with assuming a coaching position, i.e., proper supervision, planning and instruction, matching participants, safety, first aid, and risk management.

Standard 10   Properly inform coaching assistants, athletes, and parents/guardians of the inherent risks associated with sport so that decisions about participation can be made with informed consent.

Standard 11   Know and convey the need and availability of appropriate medical insurance.

Standard 12   Participate in continuing education regarding rules changes, improvements in equipment, philosophical changes, improved techniques, and other information in order to enhance the safety and success of the athlete.

Growth, Development, and Learning

Standard 13   Recognize the developmental physical changes that occur as athletes move from youth through adulthood and know how these changes influence the sequential learning and performance of motor skills in a specific sport.

Standard 14   Understand the social and emotional development of the athletes being coached, know how to recognize problems related to this development, and know where to refer them for appropriate assistance when necessary.

Standard 15   Analyze human performance in terms of developmental information and individual body structure.

Standard 16   Provide instruction to develop sport-specific motor skills and refer the athletes to appropriate counsel as needed.

Standard 17   Provide learning experiences appropriate to the growth and development of the age group coached.

Training, Conditioning, and Nutrition

Standard 18   Demonstrate a basic knowledge of physiological systems and their responses to training and conditioning.

Standard 19   Design programs of training and conditioning that properly incorporated the mechanics of movement and sound physiological principles taking into account each individual's ability and medical history, avoiding contra-indicated exercises and activities and guarding against the possibility of over-training; be able to modify programs as needed.

Standard 20   Demonstrate knowledge of proper nutrition and educate athletes about the effects of nutrition upon health and physical performance.

(continued)

Standard 21   Demonstrate knowledge of the use and abuse of drugs and promote sound chemical health.

Social/Psychological Aspects of Coaching

Standard 22   Subscribe to a philosophy that acknowledges the role of athletics in developing the complete person.

Standard 23   Identify and interpret to co-coaches, athletes, concerned others, and the general public the values that are to be developed from participation in sports programs.

Standard 24   Identify and apply ethical conduct in sport by maintaining emotional control and demonstrating respect for athletes, officials, and other coaches.

Standard 25   Demonstrate effective motivational skills and provide positive, appropriate feedback.

Standard 26   Conduct practices and competitions to enhance the physical, social, and emotional growth of athletes.

Standard 27   Be sufficiently familiar with the basic principles of goal setting to motivate athletes toward immediate and long range goals.

Standard 28   Treat each athlete as an individual while recognizing the dynamic relationship of personality and socio-cultural variables such as gender, race, and socio-economic differences.

Standard 29   Identify desirable behaviors (self-discipline, support of teammates, following directions, etc.) and structure experiences to develop such behaviors in each athlete.

Skills, Tactics, and Strategies

Standard 30   Identify and apply specific competitive tactics and strategies appropriate for the age and skill levels involved.

Standard 31   Organize and implement materials for scouting, planning practices, and analysis of games.

Standard 32   Understand and enforce the rules and regulations of appropriate bodies that govern sport and education.

Standard 33   Organize, conduct, and evaluate practice sessions with regard to established program goals that are appropriate for different stages of the season.

Teaching and Administration

Standard 34   Know the key elements of sport principles and technical skills as well as the various teaching methods that can be used to introduce and refine them.

Standard 35   Demonstrate objective and effective procedures for the evaluation and selection of personnel involved in the athletic program and for periodic program reviews.

(continued)

Professional Preparation and Development

Standard 36	Demonstrate organizational and administrative efficiency in implementing sports programs, e.g., event management, budgetary procedures, facility maintenance, and participation in public relations activities.
Standard 37	Acquire sufficient practical field experience and supervision in the essential coaching areas to ensure an adequate level of coaching competence for the level of athlete coached. This would include a variety of knowledge, skills, and experiences.

intercollegiate athletics (and the rewards that accrue to the victorious). Seldom is there an off-season or free time. While most college coaches have earned master's degrees, this is not a prerequisite, and the major field does not have to be physical education, although it often is. Ways of gaining entrance into college coaching vary. For example, you may volunteer to serve as an assistant or to serve as a graduate student assistant coach, you may earn an assistant coach's position after a successful high school coaching career, or you may win a job because of outstanding achievements as a collegiate or professional athlete. In most cases, future head coaches, even those at small institutions and for nonrevenue-producing sports, must get experience serving as successful assistant coaches.

Once jobs are obtained, most coaches, although not guaranteed tenure, retain them as long as they abide by the rules, keep their athletes happy, maintain their own desire to coach, and develop successful programs. In larger institutions, most football and basketball coaches have job security only when they win and show that they can handle the pressures of the job without violating institutional, NCAA, or other rules. For these coaches, the long hours and pressures are compensated for by the material benefits and the prestige. Most coaches take satisfaction in helping their athletes improve their skills and in seeing them mature as individuals.

Coaches' salaries are dependent on the sport, the competitive divisions in which their teams play, whether their sports are revenue-producing or not, their years of experience, their past won-lost records, and additional benefits such as sport camp revenues, shoe contracts, and radio and television shows. Assistant coaches may receive no salaries, only tuition and fee waivers as graduate students, or may receive starting salaries around $30,000. Part-time coaches, who teach or hold other jobs, can expect stipends ranging from $1000 to $10,000 depending on the factors listed above. Full-time, head coaches' salaries can range from $20,000 to over $100,000. Entire salary packages for a few coaches with winning records at large universities can exceed a million dollars.

At small colleges, coaches are often the directors of athletics. As larger universities' athletic programs grew, however, they entered the entertainment business and required administrators to direct them. Athletic directors, associate and assistant directors, fund-raisers, and ticket managers often have earned master's degrees in sport management to prepare them for these careers. Financial and people management skills are crucial, as is expertise in public relations, since skyrocketing budgets have made fund-raising vital. When skillfully achieved, all of these factors mesh into a successful athletic program that brings prestige and lucrative benefits to their directors. Security is based on the institution's overall program rather than on one team's performance, although the successes of the revenue-producing sports are certainly most important.

Associated with intercollegiate athletics and vital to their programs are numerous career options. Assistant and associate athletic directors assume responsibility for facility management, NCAA compliance, grants-in-aid, business affairs, fund-raising, and coordination of nonrevenue-producing sports. These positions may be filled by coaches, former athletes, or people trained in sport management. Job security is not guaranteed; continuation is based on successful completion of assigned duties. A major benefit is the association with a successful athletic program and its reflected glamour. Individuals in these management positions earn from $30,000 to over $100,000 depending on level of responsibility, experience, and the institution served.

For individuals who wish to combine writing skills with athletics, sports information is an applicable career choice. This vital component of the athletic program is responsible for compiling statistics and personal information about the athletes and teams to publicize upcoming events and to provide postgame data. Press releases and team brochures further publicize the intercollegiate program. A degree in journalism or sport communication would be appropriate, but volunteer experience and the willingness to start at the lowest level and work upward may be necessary to gain entrance into this athletic career. Travel, personal contacts with players and coaches, and contributing to the success of a program are among the benefits.

Sports promotions specialists are responsible for filling the stadium through advertising and various promotional strategies. At a small college, one person may handle both sports information and sports promotions, or each coach may have to accept these additional responsibilities for his or her team. Large institutions have promotions specialists who frequently share in activities to raise funds for grants-in-aid and facilities. Public relations skills are usually more important than a particular educational degree. These persons' primary efforts are directed toward bringing money into the athletic department through gifts and donations. Salaries for these individuals are directly linked with their abilities to market their teams, resulting in increased ticket sales and donations.

Strength and conditioning coaches design and implement training programs for all athletes. Frequently, these positions are filled by exercise scientists with strong exercise physiology and biomechanics backgrounds and those who hold certifications from the National Strength and Conditioning Association. Helping athletes reach their athletic potentials is a significant reward for these individuals.

Many professional teams and a few colleges hire sport psychologists to work individually with athletes. Because the athletic skills of all elite athletes are

Sports promotions specialists work to attract fans to intercollegiate competitions. (Photo courtesy Lisa Sense.)

superior, many believe that the key to athletes achieving optimal performances is mental. Sport and exercise psychologists use biofeedback, relaxation, imagery, and various coping mechanisms to help athletes handle the pressures of competition, achieve their potential, and enjoy their experiences.

Nonschool

More than 20 million children participate on youth sports teams sponsored by recreation departments, private clubs, community service organizations, national sport associations, and churches as well as in after-school physical activity programs. In most cases, the coaches are volunteers; the officials and the league, program, and association directors are usually paid. Many of these same groups also provide athletic competitions for adults, such as softball and basketball leagues, master's swimming events, and road races. Experience gained as a volunteer coach, program administrator or assistant, or official may lead to a full-time job in a recreation-related career.

Professional

Prior playing experience in college and as a professional is an asset for coaches of professional teams, although not necessarily a prerequisite. Coaches are hired on the basis of demonstrated success with high school, college, or professional teams and are fired for not producing winning teams. Lucrative salaries, some in excess of a million dollars, help compensate for the pressures to win and constant media bombardment.

Professional sports require hundreds of people working behind the scenes to ensure that events take place as scheduled. A commonality of many of these positions is the need for experience in business and marketing. Responsibilities of the ticket sales staff include season ticket packaging, selling tickets for individual events, and arranging for complimentary seating. Correspondence and direct contacts with fans are extensive, with the greatest challenge always remaining that of

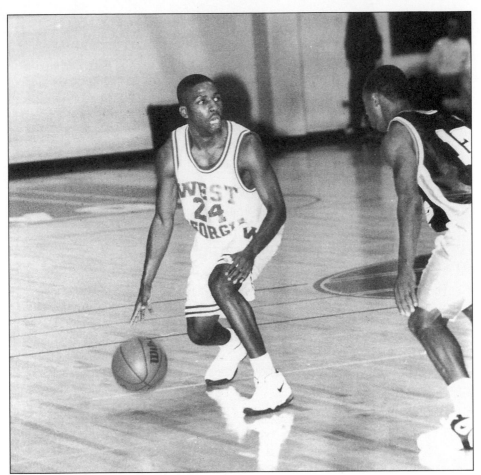

The hours of practice and competition necessary for highly skilled athletes to develop and refine their talents may help qualify them for coaching careers later in life. (Photo courtesy of the State University of West Georgia Sports Information Office.)

trying to satisfy as many fans as possible. Customer satisfaction is essential. No formal educational background is required, but a sport management degree is highly desirable.

Business managers are responsible for planning budgets and administering the expenditures to support the program. Although accountants and secretaries may actually handle the daily transactions, business managers oversee multimillion-dollar budgets and the many personnel who work in this area. A business background is helpful, but on-the-job training in a small program or as an intern may be equally valuable in obtaining a job in this field.

Marketing directors serve various functions, depending on the situation. With teams needing to maintain or increase fan support, their primary responsibility focuses on public relations efforts to increase ticket sales. Radio or television

WEB CONNECTIONS

1. www.womensportscareers.com/network/feature_articles.htm
   Female students interested in careers in sports will find a plethora of
   information about alternatives at this site.

2. www.ncaa.org
   Check out the official site of the National Collegiate Athletic
   Association for employment opportunities in college sports.

3. http://WomenSportsJobs.com
   Even though the sports industry is a tough industry to break into,
   Women'Sports Services™ can assist you; it has helped over 100,000
   individuals in their pursuit of sports careers.

4. www. onlinesports.com/pages/CareerCenter.html
   Visit the online Sports Career Center to learn more about sports-
   related career opportunities and a resumé bank for potential
   employers in sports and recreation.

5. www.sgma.com
   Find out more about sport-related careers in the sporting goods
   industry.

6. www.feminist.org/research/sports2.html
   Learn more about the barriers women face in pursuing athletic careers,
   women in the media, and much more information of interest to
   enhancing women's opportunities in sports.

commercials, newspaper advertisements, exciting upcoming events or opponents, or winning records may be used to generate greater spectator interest. Season ticket sales are the next promotional effort, since these stabilize income and
indicate increased and consistent fan support. Marketing directors may also help
promote team emblems or merchandise. These marketing specialists are hired for
their proven abilities to fulfill job responsibilities rather than for any educational
degree.

Professional sport officiating provides many part-time and some full-time
careers (mostly in baseball and basketball). No specific educational background
is required, but years of experience are necessary. As early as possible, such as in
recreational youth leagues, anyone interested in officiating should start learning
the rules and the techniques while gaining experience and expertise. There may
be some reflective glamour and prestige, but officials often are the villains and are

only begrudgingly accepted as vital to professional games. After years of success in the high school and college ranks and completion of training programs, the best-qualified officials may get opportunities to officiate in the professional leagues. Most officials, however, hold other jobs and officiate as a hobby or as a second career. Unusual hours and travel are inherent characteristics, although salaries for professional officials are quite good.

SPORT MANAGEMENT

Business and Industry

Golf courses, bowling lanes, gymnastics schools, tennis camps, swimming centers, racquetball clubs, and health spas all require managers who have administrative skills in addition to knowledge about physical skills. Directors in each of these settings must possess budgetary skills, personnel management abilities, planning knowledge, and supervisory capabilities. Although these organizations are primarily interested in producing profits and thus maintaining high enrollments or large attendance, they must hire qualified instructional staff. These sport managers may earn $30,000 to $50,000 a year.

Corporate fitness programs also demand management, motivational, and supervisory skills. Exercise and sport science and fitness specialists who possess knowledge in public relations and marketing can advance more easily into management positions within corporate fitness programs. Since employers want the dollars spent for fitness programs to result in enhanced worker productivity, the goals are to motivate workers to adhere to fitness programs and to increase their active participation.

Theme parks and resorts have become multimillion-dollar ventures providing leisure for people of all ages. Recreation administration and sport management backgrounds are essential for handling the massive budgetary, facility management, and personnel aspects of these businesses.

More than 150 sport halls of fame and museums each year host millions of people who view sports memorabilia and photographs and recall stars of the past. These tourist attractions highlight the achievements of former heroes and heroines and periodically elect new enshrinees; some host events to promote their respective sports. Sport historians and administrative curators are needed for these careers.

Facility managers are associated with arenas and stadiums at universities, in communities, and with professional teams. To be cost-efficient, large facilities must be multipurpose because audiences must be attracted to several different sporting events as well as to concerts, other types of entertainments, and conventions. There are some specialized facilities, such as aquatic or ice arenas, that are limited to competitive and recreational uses. Facility managers must have planning and organizational abilities as well as personnel management skills. Facility managers either work for a university, governmental agency, private corporation, or a professional team. They schedule events around the major team(s) or work for a municipality that rents time to teams. Depending on the size of the facility and the number of scheduled events, the individuals managing them may earn salaries of $40,000 to $80,000.

Schools and Colleges

Administration is another career possibility for physical educators in the schools. This position may be as a department head who accepts management responsibilities, resulting in a reduced teaching load, or as a principal, headmaster, or superintendent. Advancement can result from successful service to the school, advanced education, or interest in and demonstrated competence for these positions. In these jobs, increased salaries parallel longer hours and greater responsibilities.

Colleges and universities have many administrative positions, ranging from program director to department head to college dean. These careers are open to individuals with doctoral degrees, years of experience, expertise in working with people, and management skills. Competition for these positions is strong. Administrative hassles, such as personnel problems, tight budgets, and day-to-day operational demands are offset by opportunities to affect program change, to lead faculty in the attainment of professional goals, and to positively impact students' education.

Intramural recreational sports and campus recreation programs are popular components of collegiate life. Directors, assistant directors, facility supervisors, and program coordinators constitute the staff. Job responsibilities vary from publicity to facility management and from personnel to programming. These intramural and recreational programs are administered through either the physical education department or the office of student affairs. In the first context, the staff may also teach; in the second, they seldom do. Most intramural recreational sports or campus recreation professionals have earned at least master's degrees in physical education, exercise science, sport studies, or recreation. Increasingly, the trend is to make these positions nonfaculty, with job security based solely on fulfillment of assigned responsibilities. Rather than the usual school-day hours, these programs operate in the afternoons, evenings, and weekends, the leisure hours of the students they serve. Student interactions in nonacademic activities and the opportunities to administer fun-filled programs attract people to these positions. Entry-level program coordinators may earn $25,000 to $30,000; assistant directors' salaries range from $30,000 to $50,000; directors are paid between $50,000 and $100,000.

SPORT MARKETING

Sporting attire is popular for everyone, whether the wearer is exercising, going out on the town, or working. From cross-training shoes to designer warm-up suits to team logo jackets, everybody is wearing sports clothing. Billions of dollars of athletic and sports clothing and shoes are sold annually. Regardless of skill level,

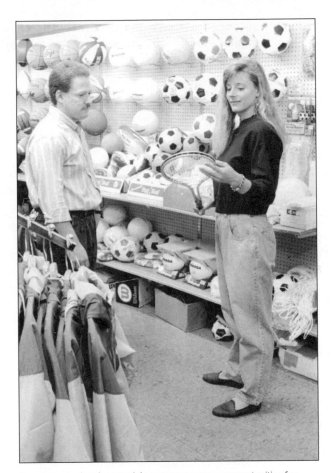

Sporting goods sales provide numerous career opportunities for individuals interested in combining business skills with knowledge about sports equipment and clothing.

seemingly only oversized tennis rackets, custom-made golf clubs, and auto-graphed baseball gloves are good enough for aspiring athletes. Therefore, jobs are and will continue to be plentiful in the sales and marketing of sporting goods. Expertise in sports is an advantage for people in sales, marketing, and manage-ment. Individuals choosing sales may enjoy flexible hours, travel, rapid advance-ment, and job security if they are good at what they do.

Most administrators and many instructors in health and sports clubs are expected to sell memberships. Those who are especially adept at this task frequently advance into management positions with increased marketing respon-sibilities, such as initiating special promotions.

The design of new equipment and improved facilities requires a great deal of research. Safety and improved performance motivate these efforts to produce the best ball or surface. Inventors or innovative designers may reap financial benefits, if their products gain the same kind of wide acceptance that the makers of over-sized tennis rackets, for example, have seen.

SPORT COMMUNICATION

The interdependence of the media and sports has created numerous opportunities in the glamour careers of sport broadcasting, sport journalism, and sport photography. Broadcasting opportunities vary from prime-time, national telecasts to special events coverage to sports reporting for a local network. On-the-air experience, expertise in play-by-play announcing, an aptitude for interviewing, and a smooth delivery in reading sports news overshadow an educational degree. Willingness to start in small markets at a salary just above minimum wage is a key to advancement. Cable networks provide another avenue for aspiring sport broadcasters.

Since sports sell newspapers and magazines and increase television ratings, thereby selling commercial time, professional and college teams are especially sensitive to the media. The sportswriting field attracts a large number of people, although the percentage who succeed in it is small. Many sportswriters have earned college degrees in journalism, but some secure newspaper or magazine jobs because of their past experiences in college sports information offices, their own sports careers, or their background in physical education, exercise science, or sport studies. A sportswriter must possess an inquiring mind, a desire to talk with people, the ability to listen, and the willingness to work unusual hours while under the pressures of deadlines and space limitations.

A sport photographer may start by taking pictures for a college newspaper or yearbook and then progress to assignments with a major publication. A thorough understanding of the intricacies of various sports provides a photographer with the insight necessary to capture the essence and meaning of sports as well as the outcome of a particular event. Long hours, low compensation, and little glamour may eventually be rewarded with extensive travel for a national publication.

OTHER RELATED CAREERS

In addition to the aforementioned broad categories of jobs open to physical education, exercise science, and sport studies majors, several other specific careers are available. Many of these, however, require specialized education, training, or certification. For the medical doctor with an interest in sports, there are specializations in exercise physiology, orthopedic surgery, and sports podiatry as well as the option to serve as a team physician. Sport nutrition and sport and exercise psychology are growing fields for both private practice and consultation with college and professional athletes. Lawyers may choose to emphasize the ever-expanding area of sport law.

Dance careers include not only those of performing artists with national and regional companies but also those of artistic directors, managing directors, development officers, public relations agents, booking agents, dance journalists, and dance photographers. Limited jobs and long hours, though, deter some people from pursuing careers as dancers or in dance-related jobs. No educational degree is required for these positions or for those of studio teachers, yet all who pursue them have spent years developing their expertise.

Rather than viewing the sky as falling, a young professional should view the sky as the limit. The box on page 154 provides an overview of some potential careers and lists the necessary preparation. Knowing these alternatives should help you focus on one or more broad areas of interest as you choose a career pathway.

Individuals choosing to enter a career in physical education, exercise science, and sport have the additional challenge of serving as positive role models for fitness and healthy lifestyles. The overweight, unfit person, who also may smoke, use other tobacco products, or abuse alcohol or other drugs, is a poor representative of the principles valued by those in physical education, exercise science, and sport careers. Rather, teachers, coaches, fitness specialists, recreation directors, exercise science professionals, athletic trainers, and sport managers should participate in sports and activities to maintain their fitness lifestyles.

See the box on page 157 for suggestions about how to locate more information about careers.

SUMMARY

In this rapidly changing, technological world, career changes as often as every 10 years or less have become the norm rather than the exception. Instead of looking at one specialty, you need to become a multispecialist who can make different applications of your knowledge. Young people entering the work force need to bring creativity and imaginative reasoning to their jobs as well as an adventuresome willingness to accept risks and failures while bouncing back to try again. Your first challenge is to assess your preferences and interests. Factors that influence your career choice(s) include family, role models, knowledge about career alternatives, opportunities to work with certain age groups, ease of entry, salary range, career advancement, time compatibility, job security, and location. Career opportunities abound in physical education, exercise science, and sport in teaching, inside and outside of educational institutions, in developmental and rehabilitative fitness, in school and college athletics, and in sport management, marketing, and communication. After matching your aspirations and abilities with career characteristics, you can select one or more as the focus for your college preparation and initial and subsequent careers.

JOB OPPORTUNITIES MATCHED WITH PREREQUISITE BACKGROUNDS

Undergraduate Degree and Certification in Physical Education Required
Public school teacher (K–12)
Public school coach (some states only)

Undergraduate Degree in Physical Education, Exercise Science, Sport Studies, or Recreation Preferred
Sports instructor in a private club, camp, resort, or military installation
Recreation department program director
Leader in a corporate or industry fitness program

Specialized Course Work, Internship, or Certification Required
Athletic trainer
Corporate or commercial fitness exercise specialist
Health or fitness clinic leader
Sport official
Strength and conditioning coach

Master's or Doctor's Degree Required
College or university professor
Intramural/campus recreation director or staff
Sport psychologist

Sport Management Course Work Preferred
Athletic director or athletic administrator
Corporate fitness director
Facility manager
Recreation department director

Experience or Internship Preferred
College coach
Sports broadcaster
Sports information director
Sport journalist
Sport marketer

INTERVIEW OUTLINE

Name: _____
Title: _____
Company or Institution: _____

JOB RESPONSIBILITIES AND HOURS

What are your primary job responsibilities?

_____
_____
_____
_____
_____
_____

What are your normal work hours? Are these typical?

_____

Is overtime or extra work required? If so, how often and for how long?

_____

What is the salary range for people in your career?

_____

SPECIALIZED COURSE WORK, DEGREES, AND WORK EXPERIENCES NEEDED FOR THIS CAREER

What specialized experiences were necessary as a prerequisite to being qualified for this career?

_____
_____
_____

What academic degrees, certifications, or licenses are required to do your job?

_____
_____
_____
_____

What course work that you completed is most useful in fulfilling your job responsibilities?

_____
_____
_____

FIGURE 5.1   **(continued)**

Interview Outline-Sample questions about potential careers.

SATISFYING ASPECTS OF YOUR CAREER

What are the most satisfying aspects of your career?

_____

_____

_____

_____

_____

Are there any aspects of your career that you dislike?

_____

_____

_____

_____

_____

JOB POTENTIAL

What are the opportunities for advancement (salary, responsibility, and promotion) in this career?

_____

_____

_____

_____

_____

SUGGESTIONS FOR STUDENTS

What suggestions and advice can you give students considering a career like yours?

_____

_____

_____

_____

_____

FIGURE 5.1

Teachers in all settings should serve as role models for healthy lifestyles.

INFORMATION ON CAREERS IN SPORT

See *The Guide to Careers in Sports,* by Len Karlin, 1995 for information on:

- Professional leagues
- Sport facilities management
- Sport marketing and management industry
- College sport management .
- Golf industry
- Turf management
- Tennis industry
- Sports broadcasting
- Athletic training
- Recreational management

Contact the American Alliance for Health, Physical Education, Recreation and Dance at 1-800-213-7193 for information about careers in these and related areas. Colleges and universities, school counselors, and state departments of education also have information about careers in these areas. Check out the certifying organizations listed in Appendix B for information about careers in exercise science, fitness, and sports medicine.

CAREER PERSPECTIVE

PATRICIA ANN HIELSCHER
President
P.H. Enterprises of Apex, Inc.
Apex, North Carolina

EDUCATION
B.S., Physical Education, University of North Carolina at Greensboro
M.S., Physical Education, University of North Carolina at Greensboro

JOB RESPONSIBILITIES AND HOURS

Developing your own sports business permits absolute freedom to design it in any way. Based on her interests and expertise, Pat's business initially offered five related, yet different, services and products. While developing her business, Pat conducted volleyball camps and clinics, marketed and sold volleyball uniforms and equipment, exhibited at professional conferences, contracted for screen printing of T-shirts sold to various groups, and offered a consignment program for summer sport camps. Once the business grew sufficiently to become self-sustaining, she discontinued the volleyball camps and clinics to focus on sales. Ordering, billing, selling, and stocking her product lines are vital parts of her responsibilities. Generally Pat works from 8:00 A.M. to 5:00 P.M. and some evenings, typical hours for this type of career. The amount of time worked determines the salary or income. Pat has chosen to stay a one-person business because she wants to be able to guarantee quality to her customers, most of whom she knows; getting rich is not her goal.

SPECIALIZED COURSE WORK, DEGREES, AND WORK EXPERIENCES NEEDED FOR THIS CAREER

Pat recommends that students interested in forming their own sports products and services businesses take physical education courses (with a coaching emphasis), psychology, and business courses (such as marketing and accounting). Although no degree is absolutely necessary, based on her experiences, a bachelor's degree in physical education combined with a business minor and coaching experience would be ideal. Pat has found her background in coaching, including administrative duties such as managing a team, ordering equipment, and fund raising, and her master's degree in physical education most helpful. Coaching, developing personal contacts with people in athletics, having a general background in sales, and having some work experience in business are important prerequisites for this career.

SATISFYING ASPECTS

The popularity of sports and leisure activities provides a bountiful market for services and products that anyone may wish to furnish as a career. Satisfaction comes both from helping others select the equipment, shoes, and clothing that will enhance their pleasure in sports participation and from teaching skills that can motivate people to start or to continue participating in a sport. Pat designed her business so she could enjoy a continued association with female athletes and coaches and could maintain involvement with the promotion of women's sports.

JOB POTENTIAL

There are many jobs for men and women in athletic sales and services throughout the country, especially in urban areas. These opportunities include running one's own business or working for others. For Pat specifically, as owner of her own business, there is no security except that which comes from her belief in herself. While working for others may lead to greater job security, self-employment guarantees maximal freedom to design a custom-made career. Pat adds that her business is successful because 75 percent of it is with people she knows, her products are good quality and priced fairly, and she maintains a pleasant, trusting relationship with her customers.

SUGGESTIONS FOR STUDENTS

First, Pat suggests talking with people in this career and considering their advice. Second, she advocates working for someone else before starting a business, to get vital training and experience, especially in marketing, sales, and accounting. Third, she recommends getting experience in athletics as a player, coach, and official to learn the needs and preferences of future customers as well as to learn to communicate with them. Last, she cautions not to become discouraged by people who say that women's sports or a particular sport cannot provide a viable career.

REVIEW QUESTIONS

1. What are several factors that may influence one's career choice?
2. What factors may outweigh the importance of one's salary?
3. What are several noneducational careers that involve teaching?
4. What are several careers in professional sports?
5. What are the responsibilities of the sport marketing specialist?
6. What are three careers related to the media and sports?
7. What is the job potential for careers in recreational services for senior citizens?
8. What are several types of careers in which a sport management background would be beneficial?
9. What are typical entry-level positions in coaching that may lead to becoming a college coach?
10. What are the major differences between the responsibilities of athletic directors at small colleges and large universities?

STUDENT ACTIVITIES

1. Complete the self-assessment inventories in the boxes on pages 127–128.
2. Write a three- to five-page essay describing your professional and personal career goals.

3. Compile a list of the abilities and characteristics needed for success in your prospective career.
4. Talk with one person in each of the following careers: (a) one that you think you definitely would like to pursue; (b) one that you think you might like to pursue; (c) one that you know little or nothing about.
5. Read any two of the suggested readings, and relate each article's concepts to your career choice.
6. Using the outline of Figure 5.1 on pages 155–156, conduct a formal interview of a person in a career that you are considering.
7. Using the Internet, find and briefly describe five career options discussed in this chapter or identify five emerging physical education, exercise science, and sport careers.

SUGGESTED READINGS

Aldana SG, Stone WJ: Report to fitness professionals—changing physical activity preferences of American adults, *JOPERD* 62(4):67, 1991. According to this survey of Arizona adults, more engage in regular, vigorous physical activity than in the past two decades. Walking surpassed jogging/running, aerobics, swimming, weight lifting, dance, basketball, and calisthenics in popularity for males and females of all age groups.

Anderson SC (ed.): Therapeutic recreation—meeting the challenge of new demands, *JOPERD* 62(4):25, 1991. This nine-article "Leisure Today" feature suggests alternative approaches to meeting the needs of Americans with disabilities. These approaches include integration into community-based programs, social skills training, use of computers to link providers, enhanced professional preparation programs, creative play environments, a model for improving clients' self-esteem, use of volunteers, and music therapy.

Green K: Leading the fit life: jobs in health clubs, *Occup Outlook* 39(2):14, 1995. This article describes the various types of positions available in health clubs and provides information about how to acquire credentials in this field.

Hofacre S, et al.: Demographic changes in the U.S. Into the twenty-first century: their impact on sport, *Sp Mkt Q* 1(1):31, 1992. Sport marketers must identify changing demographics, such as an older and more ethnically diverse population and a society characterized by changes in family makeup, in order to properly target their potential customers in sports.

Mathes SA, McGivern AT, Schneider CM: The influence of participation and gender on employee's motives for involvement in a corporate exercise program, *J of Sp Mgmt* 6:1, 1992. In one selected corporate fitness program, males and females were surveyed to determine their reasons for participation. Enhancing fitness, reducing stress, and learning to relax were most important as was having structured programs.

Mustain WC: Are you the best teacher you can be? *JOPERD* 61(2):69, 1990. The author suggests eight components that contribute to teaching effectiveness:

goals and objectives, planning, lesson presentation, student engagement, management, student activity, feedback, and teacher assessment.

Parks and Recreation and Promoting the Physical Activity Objectives in the Surgeon General's Report, *JOPERD* 70(1):21, 70(2):66, 70(3):36, 1999. This six-article series in the January, February, and March issues provides suggestions for how individuals in the leisure services area can provide opportunities for people of all ages, ability levels, ethnicities, and genders to participate in physical activities. Recreation professionals can help all of their clients develop and benefit from physically active lives through enjoyable leisure pursuits.

Rowe PJ, Miller LK: Treating high school sports injuries—are coaches/trainers competent? *JOPERD,* 62(1):49, 1991. Due to the large number of injuries experienced by high school athletes, the question is raised about the quality of care they receive. The risk of negligent first aid and the associated legal ramifications indicate the importance of employing a certified athletic trainer in each school.

Rupp JC, Campbell K, Thompson WR, Terbizan D: Professional preparation of personal trainers, *JOPERD* 70(1): 54, 1999. In this article, the authors describe the qualifications of the personal trainer, legal liability issues, and employment opportunities in this field.

Smith DS, Smith SH: Investigating the meaning of play and recreation for families, *J of Rec & Leisure* 13(1):1, 1993. The most important human institution, the family, can use play and recreation to improve relationships, the sense of being connected, and enjoyment.

CHAPTER

6

PREPARATION FOR A CAREER

KEY CONCEPTS

- Establishing short- and long-term goals helps in the process of career development.
- Course work required for a liberal arts education combined with a major in physical education, exercise science, or sport studies varies by institution and career choice.
- Extracurricular activities, internships, and volunteer work in physical education, exercise science, and sport offer important learning experiences and preparation for careers.
- Certifications in officiating, aquatics, first aid, exercise testing, athletic training, coaching, and other areas improve professional credentials for employment.
- Graduate programs provide opportunities for advanced study in various specialties.

Professionalism is based on knowledge. Thus far, you have learned about the objectives, disciplinary content, and professional structure of physical education, exercise science, and sport. You have begun to learn more about various careers through the career perspectives in each chapter. Now, with a career targeted, you are getting ready to learn more about your intended work. The information in this chapter should help you get the most out of your college years. As you grow in your knowledge of physical education, exercise science, and sport, take advantage of various activities in the field, and obtain certifications. You are not just joining a profession, you are becoming a professional. This professionalism will demonstrate itself by your commitment to learning and your desire to develop your capabilities to the fullest.

While this chapter introduces you to various alternative careers, at this point you will want to focus on learning more about each one and as much as you can about those of greatest interest to you. At the end of this chapter, you will be provided information about writing application letters, developing a resumé, and preparing for interviews.

THE CHALLENGE

Everyone's existence depends on self-worth. All of us have varying degrees of this basic need that relate directly to our personal levels of happiness. Self-worth is developed by participating and achieving success in different activities. This may include feeling confident with one's sports skills as well as how a person has enhanced his or her leadership skills as a volunteer youth coach, a camp counselor, or an intern in a health and fitness club. An enhanced feeling of competency comes from taking on and completing responsible roles like team manager, lab assistant, Special Olympics or Senior Games volunteer, and sports reporter for a school newspaper. Most people want to feel satisfied with and successful in their lives. Each person, however, defines these concepts uniquely. Many factors contribute to this "satisfaction factor" in our lives. Listed below are some characteristics that people value personally. Select any of these that can help you establish a sense of direction for the personal, social, and professional goals that you will be setting. It may help if you can identify one or more individuals who you think personify those traits that you wish to emulate.

Analytical	Loyal	Respectful
Assertive	Organized	Responsible
Benevolent	Outgoing	Sensitive
Cautious	Patient	Serious
Competent	Persevering	Sincere
Considerate	Poised	Sociable
Cooperative	Polite	Spontaneous
Creative	Practical	Tactful
Determined	Progressive	Tenacious
Energetic	Prudent	Thorough
Enthusiastic	Quiet	Thoughtful
Friendly	Rational	Tolerant
Fun	Reflective	Trustworthy
Helpful	Reliable	Understanding
Honest	Resourceful	Versatile

Once you have observed some of these traits in others, you are encouraged to learn how you can adopt these characteristics. Others who have been praised for being good role models are usually willing to share how they developed their unique abilities. These same individuals are often eager to share strategies that have worked to make them more successful.

Goal setting helps us assess abilities and interests and establish immediate and future expectations. Goal setting helps individuals establish their personal philosophies as described in Chapter 4. Short-term goals are accomplishments that can occur within a day, week, month, or another not-too-distant time period. Such goals could include attending a weekend workshop, starting a personal exercise program, or joining a professional association. It is important that short-term goals be readily achievable, positively reinforcing, and related to or leading to the attainment of long-term goals. Long-term goals are larger in scope and are often comprised of numerous short-term goals. Continual self-assessment and the reestablishment of goals are essential since interests and aspirations change. Before establishing some professional goals, it might be easier to start with personal and performance goals. To facilitate this process, respond to the questions in the box below.

Associated with developing positive character traits and goal setting is the skill of networking. As you decide what you want to do and determine the type of person you want to be, you can be helped by others who have experienced the same process through which you are progressing. Associating yourself with others who can serve as your mentors and who can introduce you to others in

PERSONAL AND PERFORMANCE GOAL SETTING

Personal

1. What is your personal long-term career goal or dream?
2. Is it possible to achieve this goal if you work hard and motivate yourself the next few years?
3. What intermediate goals must you fulfill in the next few months to progress toward your dream?
4. What are immediate (today/this week) goals that you can accomplish that will help you advance toward your long-term career goal?

Performance

5. What is one academic goal that you can achieve this semester?
6. How can you improve your academic performance during the following semester?
7. If you fail to meet this academic performance goal, how will you feel about yourself?
8. What is one athletic or fitness goal that you can achieve this semester?
9. How can you improve your athletic or fitness performance during the following semester?
10. If you fail to meet this athletic or fitness performance goal, how will you feel about yourself?
11. What is one leadership goal that you can achieve this semester?
12. How can you improve your leadership performance during the following semester?

your chosen career can be valuable. These individuals can help you obtain internship experiences and possibly get an entry-level job. They are tremendous resources for information, guidance, and personal development.

EDUCATIONAL BACKGROUND

Academic success in college can greatly facilitate the achievement of your goals. Try to benefit as much as possible from these educational opportunities to learn and develop your skills and abilities. This does not mean that all you need to do is to study, but lifelong learning certainly is vital.

Everyone needs to develop basic academic competencies in reading, writing, speaking, listening, mathematics, reasoning, studying, and computer literacy. Basic academic competencies and general education course work constitute most liberal arts programs through which institutions provide students the broad knowledge base for their lives and careers. Advocates of a liberal arts education think that all students should be educated to function effectively in a culturally diverse world, regardless of their career choices. Such an education potentially helps the research scientist interact with the practitioner, assists the coach in understanding family backgrounds and pressures on their athletes, provides insights about other people and their languages in our multicultural society, and develops appreciation for the arts, history, and philosophy.

Some students may fulfill these core requirements by taking a conglomeration of courses without much thought or direction. Whether general education courses are taken during the first two years at a junior or community college or throughout a four-year collegiate program, you should seriously consider your selection and sequence of course work to maximize career preparation. Your major or specialized studies normally hold greater interest because they seem to relate more directly to your chosen career. Nevertheless, you still need to make a serious commitment to learning the most that you can from each class.

Internships and fieldwork are valuable for career preparation. Some majors' programs require students to observe in the schools each week, to complete an internship, to design practicum experiences for their career choices through independent study courses, or to take a laboratory course that offers practical experiences. Usually, education courses for the prospective teacher require observation and mini-teaching experiences, some as early as the first year in college.

Several curricula allow students to earn college credit for paying jobs, such as recreation leader for a community, camp counselor, sport club instructor, or personal trainer, that provide learning experiences. An independent study option allows students to earn college credit for developing research projects or for work experiences specific to their areas of interest. Other curricula have experiential courses as a part of their requirements. Each of these options allows students

Maintaining personal fitness is one vital aspect of preparing for a career in physical education, exercise science, and sport.

opportunities to gain valuable experiences while they are selecting and preparing for their careers.

RELATED EXPERIENCES

Some people suggest that during the college years considerable career-relevant learning occurs outside the classroom. It is certainly true that experiential learning is important. For example, by serving as a team manager, sport official, or event coordinator in intramural recreational sports, you can learn about personnel management, scheduling, and rules. Working with a club sport, like karate or rugby, you may get an opportunity to coach and to manage the club's financial affairs. Of course, you can learn many things just by participating in various college activities or as a varsity athlete.

Volunteer Activities

While the knowledge gained in college courses introduces content and provides the foundation for a career choice, experiences and practical applications solidify learning. Volunteer activities, while a student, offer valuable opportunities to

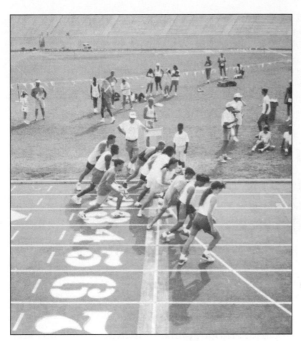

Volunteer assistance with a track meet may provide valuable experience in learning how to manage sporting events. (Photo courtesy Barry Pennell.)

gain experience. If athletic training interests you, volunteer to serve as a student trainer to learn more about this potential career. If a career in fitness appeals to you, you may start by attending aerobics classes or joining a health club before volunteering to assist instructors in these classes or clubs. Later, you may progress in your skills to become an instructor. Other volunteer possibilities in this field include conducting fitness classes for children in after-school programs, for senior citizens at retirement centers, or for students in your residence hall.

Exercise science majors often choose volunteer work in commercial or corporate fitness programs or a clinic setting. You could help exercise physiologists, fitness leaders, and physicians assess the fitness levels of clients, prescribe exercise programs, and monitor progress. You could observe and learn how to measure various fitness parameters and help participants adhere to their prescribed programs.

Exercise science students who aspire to achieve graduate degrees should volunteer to serve as subjects in research studies. As undergraduate or graduate laboratory assistants working with your professors, you can gain tremendous experience using exercise physiology, biomechanical, and other scientific instrumentation. You will quickly learn whether the research process—hypothesis, design, data collection, statistical analysis, and interpretation—appeals to you.

Through volunteer officiating students can gain experience and prepare for possible careers or part-time jobs. (Photo courtesy Maggie McGlynn.)

The sport management major can seek out volunteer activities both on- and off-campus. Your college's intramural recreational sports program needs students to serve as team managers for residence units, club sports officers, and facility and activity supervisors. Opportunities may also be available to organize special events such as fun runs, orientation sessions, or all-night activities. Volunteers provide valuable assistance working with the Special Olympics, family recreational centers, Senior Games, church sports leagues, and State Games. After successfully completing minor tasks, you may qualify for the responsibility of coordinating sports competitions during these events. Volunteer coaches are needed in youth sport leagues and recreation programs. Experiences gained in these settings may lead to opportunities to serve as an assistant coach in a junior or senior high school.

Officiating

Officiating opportunities abound in intramurals, within recreational leagues, and in the junior high schools; some colleges offer classes in officiating. These learning experiences may result in advancement into the high school, college, and professional ranks. The National Federation of State High School Associations, through its state associations, requires interested individuals to attend clinics and take written examinations to become certified as a sports official. Following successful completion of these requirements, individuals earn ratings that qualify them to officiate high school athletic contests. The most proficient officials receive the top rankings, earn the honor of working in championships, and may

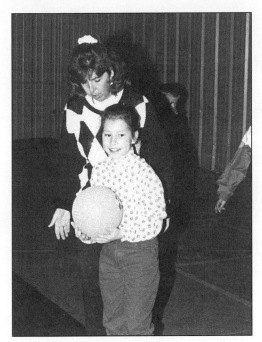

Volunteering to work with children in an after-school
program can help develop teaching skills.
(Photo courtesy Bob Hilliard.)

get an opportunity to advance to the next competitive level. Several single-sport organizations, such as the United States Volleyball Association, have their own programs to train and certify officials for their sports.

Internship Opportunities

Many experiences as a volunteer provide greater knowledge and expertise to assist the aspiring teacher, exercise scientist, and sport manager in their internships. Most fields associated with physical activity require one or more internships, where students enhance their skills and abilities and link the theory from their course work with the actual practice of their future career. For example, the NATA requires work in this field under the guidance of a certified athletic trainer in addition to completion of a required course of study. The aspiring sport manager has to participate in on-the-job experiences such as in sport marketing and facility and event management in order to help prepare for future jobs. Exercise scientists who aspire to prescribe exercise programs in a variety of settings need to experience through internships how to administer fitness assessments and to assist individuals with their personal programs in order to gain the knowledge

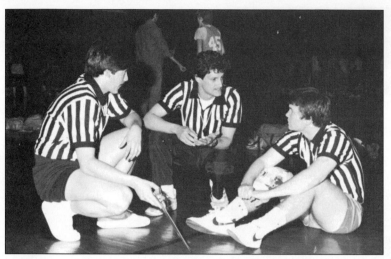

Officiating is a popular part-time job for both students and physical education, exercise science, and sport professionals.

and skills needed to succeed. In most programs, these internships are a part of the degree requirements, with associated academic expectations. In some cases, students are permitted to receive pay for these; in others, these must be completed without pay.

• • •

These experiences associated with your potential career choice may help confirm your interests or indicate that another field might be preferable. Another valuable learning experience is shadowing a person who agrees to mentor you as you learn more about a potential career. As a volunteer or intern, you will help others while developing your abilities. Each time you participate in one of these activities, add this to a list of your extracurricular experiences. Later, when you apply for a job, you can include these activities on your resumé. Volunteer and internship experiences help differentiate you from the other applicants.

BEGINNING YOUR CAREER INVOLVEMENT

While you are a student, get involved in career-related activities. Most colleges and universities have majors' clubs in physical education, exercise science, and sport studies. Majors' clubs often sponsor faculty-student colloquia, invite leaders in the profession to give presentations, and interact academically and socially. These organizations also frequently organize trips to state, district, and national

⌕ RESEARCH VIEW

Questions to Respond to in Preparing for Potential Careers

1. What would I like to do immediately following graduation? After five years? Ten years? Twenty years?
2. What experiences and learning opportunities can I take advantage of while in college to help prepare me for immediate, short- and long-term career goals?
3. What resource people can I have access to while in college who will help prepare me for immediate, short- and long-term career goals?
4. What objectives and action plans have I established to help me explore various aspects of my career development while in college?
5. How will the development of a portfolio (describing work experiences, internships, volunteer experiences, and class activities) help demonstrate what I have learned in my career preparation?
6. How will what I am learning help me make better decisions in my career?
7. How are my personal, academic, and social strengths matched to the potential career for which I am preparing?
8. How can others help me evaluate and understand my abilities and develop strategies to work on areas in need of strengthening?
9. How will I use feedback from experiences and from others to better prepare myself to make decisions relative to my career choice?
10. How motivated am I to devote the time and effort needed to be successful in and satisfied with my career choice?

---

conferences or workshops where students learn about the profession, hear about current developments, and listen to research reports. Service projects, such as working with Special Olympics, holding Jump Rope for Heart programs, and officiating at sporting events to raise money for charities, are also popular ways for young professionals to help others by sharing their expertise; at the same time, you gain valuable experience. (See the Research View box for some questions to assist you in your career development.)

Certifications

An important aspect of professional growth is obtaining one or more certifications. (See Appendix B for addresses of several certifying organizations.) For

A certified personal trainer can help individuals of all ages develop physically. (Photo courtesy Bob Hilliard.)

those who choose a career in athletic training, certification by the NATA is strongly recommended, if not required. (Chapter 3 describes these requirements.)

The American Red Cross offers certifications for lifeguards and instructors in water safety, first aid, cardiopulmonary resuscitation, and other health and safety services courses. The YMCA of the USA also certifies lifeguards and swimming instructors. These certifications can lead to employment as pool and beach lifeguards and as swimming teachers.

The American College of Sports Medicine (ACSM) offers certifications in a health and fitness track and a clinical track as well as certifications of enhanced qualification. The health and fitness track is designed for leaders of preventive programs in corporate, commercial, and community settings (see box on pages 173–175 for information on these and other certifications). The three certifications in this track include:

- ACSM Health/Fitness Director
- ACSM Health/Fitness Instructor
- ACSM Exercise Leader

CERTIFICATIONS

American College of Sports Medicine

Certification	Description
Exercise Leader	Designed for the person proficient in leading and demonstrating safe and effective methods of exercise, such as aerobics, step aerobics, slide aerobics, stationary indoor cycling; interval, circuit, water, muscle conditioning; and flexibility classes; by applying the fundamental principles of exercise science
Health and Fitness Instructor	For leaders who can prescribe and conduct safe and effective individual exercise programs, fitness testing, and health education for apparently healthy individuals
Health and Fitness Director	For persons who can demonstrate administrative leadership skills for health and fitness programs based on a strong understanding of exercise science principles
Exercise Specialist	Designed for persons who can demonstrate competence in graded exercise testing, exercise prescription, exercise leadership, emergency procedures, patient counseling, and health education programs for individuals with cardiovascular, cardiopulmonary, and metabolic diseases
Program Director	For persons who have demonstrated the ability to organize and administer preventive and rehabilitative exercise programs for healthy and diseased populations
Advanced Personal Trainer	Designed to enhance the understanding and knowledge of the professional for prescribing the safest and most effective exercise programs and for enhancing one's skills for training an apparently healthy population that possesses varied health and medical conditions
Exercise and the Older Adult	To enhance the knowledge and skills of the fitness instructor and exercise specialist for safely and effectively training an older adult population in an exercise setting designed to delay the onset of disease and restore functional mobility
Nutrition and Exercise: From Health to Physical Performance	To provide ACSM certified individuals with the knowledge to clarify misconceptions regarding nutrition and ergogenic aids, recognize unhealthy eating behaviors, and refer their clientele to appropriate allied health personnel
Scientific and Applied Aspects of Resistance Exercise Training	To provide health/fitness instructors and exercise specialists with advanced knowledge about the optimal strategies for improving the muscular strength of their clients and patients

(continued)

CERTIFICATIONS (CONTINUED)

The Cooper Institute for Aerobics Research

Certification	Description
Physical Fitness Specialist	Provides personal trainers and health and fitness professionals with the leadership and technical skills necessary for the implementation of individualized, safe, and effective physical fitness programs
Physical Fitness Specialist—Law Enforcement	For training officers, physical fitness instructors, coordinators, supervisors, training specialists, technicians, and fitness officers to learn the leadership and technical skills necessary for the implementation of individualized physical fitness programs within public safety agencies
Master Fitness Specialist	Provides advanced and in-depth information and up-to-date research regarding the implementation of individualized fitness programs to fitness professionals with previous certifications
Biomechanics of Resistance Training Specialty	For personal trainers and health and fitness professionals to learn fitness leadership and technical skills necessary for the implementation of individualized, safe, and effective strength training programs
Group Exercise Leadership	Provides exercise instructors with leadership and technical skills to offer group exercise programs that are safe, effective, and motivational
Health Promotion Director	For leaders of wellness programs in a variety of settings to learn the skills and strategies for implementing health promotion programs
Providing Dietary Guidance: Nutrition Speciality	Provides fitness specialists, personal trainers, aerobics instructors, coaches, worksite health promoters, health club staff, and hospital-based personnel with information about important dietary principles and strategies necessary to assess clients' general dietary practices
Indoor Cycling Specialty	For exercise instructors to learn what is needed to implement safe, effective and enjoyable indoor group cycle classes
Fitness Specialist for Older Adults Specialty	Provides personal trainers, exercise leaders, fitness specialists, recreational leaders, and health promotion directors in health clubs, retirement centers, and other wellness program sites with information about physical fitness programming to meet the needs of older individuals
Special Populations Specialty	For fitness professionals in recreation centers, health clubs, worksite programs, rehabilitation programs, and hospital-based programs to address the needs of populations who require special fitness programming
Aquatics Specialty	For health and fitness professionals who work with people exercising in water
Martial Arts Specialist	Provides martial arts instructors the opportunity to learn fitness concepts and terminology and effective teaching techniques

National Strength and Conditioning Association

Certified Personal Trainer	Designed for professionals who work one-on-one with their clients in a variety of environments, including schools, health/fitness clubs, and clients' homes, to provide the knowledge and skills to design and implement safe and effective strength and conditioning programs

(continued)

CERTIFICATIONS (CONTINUED)

Certified Strength and Conditioning Specialist	Designed to encourage a higher level of competence among fitness practitioners and raise the quality of strength training and conditioning programs

Other Certifications

Aerobics and Fitness Association of America

- Kickboxing
- Primary Aerobic Instructor
- Step Aerobic Instructor
- Personal Trainer/Fitness Counselor
- Weight Training
- Emergency Response
- AFAA Fitness Practitioner

American Council on Exercise

- Personal Trainer
- Clinical Exercise Specialist
- Group Fitness Instructor
- Lifestyle and Weight Management Consultant

Young Men's/Women's Christian Association

- Aquatics
- Camping
- Health and Fitness
- Scuba Diving
- Youth Sports

American Sport Education Program

Youth Sport
- Coaching Youth Sport
- Youth Sport Director

High School and Club Sports
- Coaching Principles
- Sport First Aid
- Drugs and Sport
- Citizenship through Sports

Advanced Education for Coaches
- Sport Physiology
- Sport Psychology
- Sport Rehabilitation
- Teaching Sport Skills
- Sport Administration
- Mechanics

The clinical track is designed for professionals who work with high-risk or diseased individuals as well as healthy individuals. The two certifications in this track include:

- ACSM Program Director
- ACSM Exercise Specialist

ACSM also offers certificates of enhanced qualification in:

- ACSM Advanced Personal Trainer
- ACSM Exercise and the Older Adult
- ACSM Nutrition and Exercise
- ACSM Scientific and Applied Aspects of Resistance Exercise Training

These programs are only open to those individuals who already have extensive experience and health and fitness or clinical certificates.

The American Sport Education Program (ASEP) offers educational and certification courses for coaches, sport directors, and parents. Its beginning level is designed for volunteers who work with youth sports. The Coaching Youth Sport course, a three-hour clinic, introduces the basic principles and techniques of coaching various youth sports. ASEP, in conjunction with the National Federation Interscholastic Coaches Education Program, offers a curriculum specifically designed to meet the needs of high school coaches. In partnership with the National Federation of State High School Associations, this program has been adopted by over half of the state high school athletic associations. It includes courses in coaching principles, sport first aid, drugs and sport, and citizenship through sport. The advanced education for coaches program includes courses in sport physiology, sport psychology, sport rehabilitation, teaching sport skills, sport administration, and biomechanics.

Some institutions offer students the option to complete course work in tracks, specializations, concentrations, or minors in addition to their major. For example, students majoring in exercise science might choose to use their electives to specialize in a corporate fitness track. Or a student in physical education might choose to take a coaching minor in order to better prepare for a teaching/coaching position in a school. Another student might choose to major in sport management while completing a concentration in marketing through the business school. Although each institution uses its own terminology for these programs, each allows students to take undergraduate courses in areas directly relevant to their particular careers or as preparation for a graduate program for which both areas of emphasis would be beneficial.

GRADUATE EDUCATION

Your career objective may require advanced study in physical education, exercise science, or sport studies at an accredited institution. Master's degree programs usually take one to two years to complete; doctoral degree programs require

WEB CONNECTIONS

1. www.cooperinst.org
   At this site, you can learn more about the certification programs of the Cooper Institute for Aerobics Research, health promotion products and services, the FITNESSGRAM, and internship opportunities.

2. www.acsm.org
   Learn more about the American College of Sports Medicine, including its certification programs. The ACSM promotes scientific research and application of sports medicine and exercise science to enhance physical performance, fitness, health, and the quality of life.

3. www.acefitness.org
   Check out this site for more information about fitness certifications, programs, and fitness facts.

4. www.nsca-lift.org/menu.asp
   Learn more about certifications, programs, and services offered by the National Strength and Conditioning Association.

5. www.awhp.org/pages/info_top.cgi
   This site describes the work of the Association for Worksite Health Promotion, which encourages worksite health by supporting health promotion professionals through education and resources.

6. www.nfshsa.org
   Go to this site to learn more about internship opportunities as well as job openings in high school sports.

two to four years beyond the master's degree. Master of Science (M.S.), Master of Arts (M.A.), Master of Education (M.Ed.), and Master of Arts in Teaching (M.A.T.) are the typical offerings. They normally require 30 to 36 semester hours for completion, although the actual course work taken varies from institution to institution. The M.S. and M.A. degrees generally emphasize more discipline-oriented study and may allow for specialization in athletic training, exercise science, sport management, or sport psychology, as shown in the box on page 178. Completion of these degrees usually requires a thesis, an original research project, or an internship in addition to a comprehensive examination or other summative assessment. Oriented toward education and teaching, the M.Ed. and the M.A.T. degrees lead to advanced certification for individuals

EXAMPLES OF MASTER'S DEGREE SPECIALIZATIONS

Athletic Training
Clinical methods in athletic training
Exercise physiology
Human anatomy for athletic trainers
Management and rehabilitation of athletic injuries
Research
Therapeutic analyses and modalities

Sport Management
Financial accounting
Organizational behavior
Personnel management
Research
Social issues in sport
Sport law
Sport marketing

Exercise Science
Cardiac rehabilitation
Nutrition for exercise and sport
Physiological functions in exercise
Research
Exercise prescription
Statistics

Sport and Exercise Psychology
Advanced sport psychology
Applied sport psychology
Motor learning
Research
Social issues in sport
Statistics

working in the schools and usually require a practicum experience (see the box on page 179). Many institutions offer certifications in advanced study beyond the master's degree in special education, supervision, counseling, and administration as well as educational specialist degrees. Increasingly, schools expect teachers to obtain master's degrees or higher in order to continue their lifelong learning.

The highest academic degrees are the Doctor of Philosophy (Ph.D.) and the Doctor of Education (Ed.D.). The Ph.D. is oriented toward research in a specialty such as exercise physiology, sport history, sport management, motor learning, or sport and exercise psychology. The focus of most Ed.D. programs is advanced study in education, with physical education comprising one portion of the program.

Before deciding whether to enroll in a prospective graduate program, determine whether advanced education is needed for your career. If so, then you may want to find out which accredited universities offer the type of program that meets your needs. For example, only a few institutions offer a specialization in athletic training at the master's degree level. Although some institutions require an area of specialization for a master's degree, others offer a general physical education program.

Most admission requirements include an undergraduate degree in physical education or related applied science emphasis, a minimum of a 3.0 (on a 4.0 scale) grade point average, and a better-than-average score on the Graduate Record Examination (GRE) or the Miller Analogies Test (MAT). Since institutions are free to set their own admissions standards, review the institutions that offer

TYPICAL COURSE WORK FOR MASTER'S DEGREE EMPHASIZING PHYSICAL EDUCATION

Curriculum
Educational psychology
Educational research
Educational statistics
Issues and trends in physical education
Legal issues in education
Motor learning in physical education
Internship or field work experience
School and program management
Scientific foundations of physical education

One important component of graduate education is participation in research projects.

the program desired. Libraries house catalogs of most leading institutions, or you may write for information. Another way to check out multiple institutions and their programs is to visit their web sites. Applications should be completed during the middle of the senior year or at least six months prior to the expected entrance date. Required admissions materials include college transcript(s), letters of recommendation, application forms, and test scores (such as GRE or MAT results).

For careers that do not require advanced degrees, additional and ongoing education is beneficial. Employers sometimes provide this on the job; otherwise, employees need to attend workshops, conferences, or continuing education classes. Keep current with and stimulated by career changes and developments. These often result in greater job productivity and can lead to career advancement. Career development is a lifelong process.

GAINING EXPERIENCE

While you are still a first- or second-year college student, it is important to investigate the job market by talking with older students, faculty members, or individuals in the career(s) you are considering, maybe by asking them the questions listed in the box below. Reflect on their responses as you continue to narrow or to broaden your career possibilities and make the most of your education. By carefully selecting your elective courses, you may be able to obtain a double major or specialize in some area, such as corporate fitness. Through certain courses you may qualify for an internship, a summer field work experience, or a

POSSIBLE QUESTIONS TO ASK ABOUT YOUR PROSPECTIVE CAREER

1. What is the educational background required?
2. How much prior experience is needed?
3. What are the typical hours?
4. What is the daily routine and the average time spent on each part?
5. What is the salary range?
6. How much vacation time is provided?
7. What are the fringe benefits?
8. To what extent will this job affect my personal life?
9. What are the requisite skills and knowledge for this job?
10. What personal characteristics, such as creativity, problem-solving ability, or enthusiasm, are necessary for this job?
11. What is the potential for employment in this career?
12. In what regions or states is this job available?
13. What is the potential for advancement in this career?
14. Is on-the-job training or advanced education required to maintain employment or to advance in this career?
15. What are the specific work responsibilities of this type of job? How much time is spent doing each?
16. What criteria are used to evaluate job performance?
17. What are the most satisfying or advantageous aspects of this job?
18. What are the most frustrating or disadvantageous aspects of this job?
19. What has been your biggest disillusionment?
20. What has been your most rewarding or enjoyable experience?

part-time job, or you may have an opportunity to gain valuable experience as a volunteer in intramurals or intercollegiate athletics.

During your college years be sure to take advantage of your institution's resources. Most college libraries have materials on market trends, career guidance, and opportunities for advanced education. Counseling or guidance personnel offer career aptitude testing, assistance in resumé writing, and hints for interviews. (The boxes on pages 181–185 show sample resumés, sample application letters [for full-time or part-time positions], and a portfolio outline that can help you prepare your job search materials.) You should visit your college's placement

SAMPLE RESUMÉ FOR A PROSPECTIVE TEACHER

LEWIS RAY KNIGHT

School Address:
1234 Drake Lane
Columbus, FL 38281
Phone: (915) 437-4921

Permanent Address:
567 Swinging Bridge Boulevard
Norlina, TX 72802
Phone: (173) 548-2183

Career Objective: To teach physical education in a junior high school and to coach basketball

Education: University of Miami, Miami, Florida, May, 2001
Bachelor of Arts in Physical Education
Major GPA: 3.7; Overall GPA: 3.1

Experience: Student Teacher, East Junior High School, Miami, Florida (Spring 2001)
Teacher's Aide, West Junior High School, Miami, Florida (Fall 2000)
Miami Boys' Club volunteer basketball coach (1997–2001)
Counselor at Norlina, Texas, summer sports camp (1998–2000)

Honors and Awards: Residence Hall Intramural Manager of the Year (2000)
Dean's List (1998–2000)

College Activities: Chairperson of the Physical Education Majors' Club Social Committee (1999–2000)
Intramural and Boys' Club basketball official (1997–2001)
Intramural participant in basketball, touch football, softball, and tennis (1997–2001)

Personal Data: Student member of the American Alliance for Health, Physical Education, Recreation and Dance
Available for employment, August, 2001

References: Will be furnished upon request

SAMPLE RESUMÉ FOR A PROSPECTIVE CORPORATE FITNESS LEADER

MARY ANN SMITH

School Address:
8923 Amigo Drive
Northridge, CA 90324
Phone: (412) 901-4413

Permanent Address:
7421 Langley Road
San Antonia, CA 97181
Phone: (433) 821-0431

Career Objective:
To develop and implement a corporate executive fitness program utilizing skills in exercise prescription

Education:
California State University, Northridge, California, May, 2001
Bachelor of Science in Physical Education (with an emphasis in exercise and sport science)
Major GPA: 3.8; Overall GPA: 3.5

Experience:
Intern exercise leader with Jones & Jones Company in Newark, New Jersey (summer 2000)

- Designed an aerobics program for 125 employees
- Organized a family-oriented fun run
- Initiated a company-wide incentive program for weight reduction

Volunteer at Redwood Convalescent Center, Northwest, California (1998–1999)

- Developed a recreation program for non-ambulatory patients

Sales person, The Sports Shop, Northwest, California (1996–1998)

College Activities:
Vice President of the university's Racquetball Club (2000–2001)
Member of Physical Education Majors' Club (1998–2001)
Volunteer assistant in department's exercise physiology laboratory (1999–2001)

Special Skills:
Certified as a Health and Fitness Instructor (American College of Sports Medicine)
Certified in first aid and cardiopulmonary resuscitation

Affiliations:
Student member of the American College of Sports Medicine
Student member of the American Alliance for Health, Physical Education, Recreation and Dance

References:
Will be furnished upon request

SAMPLE APPLICATION LETTER FOR A PART-TIME JOB

Ms. Terry Ann Cowan
Manager, Sports Unlimited
1902 Smithfield Road
Helena, MO 61102

Dear Ms. Cowan:

As a sophomore at Western State University majoring in physical education with an emphasis in sport management, I am interested in finding a part-time job related to my prospective career in sport management. Specifically, I would like to learn about retail sporting goods sales by working 10 to 12 hours per week, in the evenings and on weekends.

My previous work experience includes three summers as a church camp counselor, teaching racket sports to boys and girls ages 6 to 16, and 9 months as a clerk in a fast-food restaurant. My immediate supervisors for these two jobs have agreed to provide you with an evaluation of my work.

At the university, I am a member of a social sorority, the jazz dance club, and the Sport Management Majors Club. My commitments to these would not interfere with whatever hours you might assign me to work. I have enclosed my resumé, which provides you with additional information about my work experiences and campus activities.

If you have an opening for a sales clerk or anticipate one in the near future, I would appreciate your calling me at 371-9882. In the event that you cannot reach me within one week, I will call you to follow up on this inquiry. Thank you for your consideration.

Sincerely,

Mary Sue Markam

---

center to learn about the services they offer. They can help you get a summer job as well as your first job after graduation.

It has been said that "it's not what you can do, but who you know," that determines whether or not you get certain jobs. Many good jobs are obtained through personal contacts. Why not let this work for you? Notify friends, relatives, former employers, and other people whom you have met that you are looking for a part-time or summer job or an internship. Follow up on all leads, because sometimes getting a good job results from "being in the right place at the right time." Initiate contact with anyone you think can help you. Networking is vitally important. You can begin to establish a network of acquaintances in physical education, exercise science, and sport careers through your extracurricular

SAMPLE APPLICATION LETTER FOR A TEACHING/COACHING POSITION

1742 Maple Avenue
Cary, FL, 37938

March 1, 2001

Dr. Raymond C. Van Meter
Personnel Director
Guilford City Schools
Guilford, FL 37941

Dear Dr. Van Meter:

In May, 2001, I will graduate from the University of Miami with a bachelor's degree in physical education and probably with a 3.22 G.P.A. (out of a possible 4.0). I am writing to inquire about current or potential vacancies for a physical education teacher and coach in Guilford.

I have benefited from a strong liberal arts and in-depth professional education at Miami. With the completion of my current student teaching experiences, conducted under the supervision of John R. Williams, at East Junior High School in Miami, I will be eager to continue to enjoy helping students learn. I am committed to and enthusiastic about teaching as a career.

As a volunteer coach, an intramural and Boys' Club official, and an intramural participant for four years and a former varsity player in high school, I believe that I have both the technical knowledge and the personal qualities to coach basketball at the junior high school level. I would also welcome the opportunity to serve as an assistant coach in football, baseball, or softball because of my past experiences in these sports.

Other items on my enclosed resumé indicate my potential to be involved professionally and to contribute as a faculty member at a school in Guilford. If a vacancy currently exists, I would appreciate being considered a candidate. If no positions are available at this time, please keep my application on file in the event one becomes available. I may be contacted at my school address through May 7 and thereafter at my permanent address.

Thank you very much for considering my application. I hope that we will meet someday to discuss the possibility of my teaching in the Guilford City Schools.

Sincerely,

Randy Smith

Enclosure

activities, internships, volunteer experiences, summer jobs, and attending workshops and conferences. The people whom you meet, interact with, and impress can help you get your initial or a subsequent job. Networking includes expanding your number of friends in the field and building positive relationships with them.

OUTLINE FOR A TEACHING PORTFOLIO

Teaching Philosophy
- Describes the what, how, and why of my teaching

Teaching Experiences
- Volunteer teaching or tutoring
- Field experiences and internships in schools
- Employment as a teacher, such as in a club or camp

Instructional Methods and Strategies
- Explaining the context of classes taught
- How you teach
- How is instruction diversified to meet the needs of a variety of learners

Activities Completed to Enhance Teaching Effectiveness
- Professional workshops and conferences attended
- Journals and books read
- Sharing of instructional expertise with others

Examples of Instruction and Instructional Materials
- Videotaped lessons
- Self-reflection journals
- Peer evaluations of teaching
- Lesson plans
- Technology-enhanced learning aids
- Innovative hand-outs, classroom activities, and student projects

Products of Good Teaching
- Students' work and your assessment of this work
- Collaborations with colleagues

Annual Goals to Enhance Teaching

SUMMARY

As you prepare for your career, you need to begin to set short- and long-term goals. These will help you make incremental progress toward the achievement of your career aspirations. As an undergraduate, your choices of courses to fulfill requirements, your selection of a major, and your use of electives will determine the quality of your education and career preparation. The quantity, quality, and diversity of your extracurricular activities will enrich your college years and possibly assist in your career choice. Internships and volunteer activities, especially those that enable you to gain invaluable experiences related to your interest area, are important additions to your undergraduate years. Obtain certifications prior to seeking your first job since many positions require these for employment. In addition, completing advanced degrees in an area of specialization will enhance your knowledge and marketability. The process of getting a job begins with the courses you take, the experiences you gain, and the abilities you demonstrate as a young professional. Build upon this base of knowledge and experience by examining various career options, developing a resumé, writing application letters, and interviewing for a part-time or summer job.

CAREER PERSPECTIVE

SUSAN B. JOHNSON

Director of the Division of Continuing
Education and Certification
Cooper Institute
Dallas, Texas

EDUCATION

B.S., Physical Education, Memphis State University
M.Ed., Physical Education, Memphis State University
Ed.D., Teacher Behavior in Physical Education, University of
North Carolina at Greensboro

JOB RESPONSIBILITIES AND HOURS

Susan and her staff develop and conduct certification workshops for exercise instructors, law enforcement agencies, military instructors, and a variety of other health and fitness professionals such as physicians, fitness specialists, and personal trainers. Her division provides products, consulting services, and training for Health Promotion, particularly at the worksite. She also writes articles, initiates research, develops new materials, teaches workshops, and consults with agencies, businesses, and organizations in regard to physical fitness programs. Susan works from 7:00 A.M. to 5:00 P.M. Monday through Friday and 10:00 A.M. to 2.00 P.M. most Saturdays, typical hours for this career.

SPECIALIZED COURSE WORK, DEGREES, AND WORK EXPERIENCES NEEDED FOR THIS CAREER

Management is a major function of this job, so administrative courses are important. Also, teaching is a primary responsibility, so education courses are critical. It is highly recommended that individuals wishing to pursue this career possess specialized knowledge in health promotion, exercise physiology, psychology, kinesiology, nutrition, and sociology. Susan states that her doctorate has provided a vital background for her specific responsibilities, although other corporate fitness careers may require only master's degrees. In addition, a medical background, statistical skills, and research methodology complement this work. Computer knowledge and skills are a necessity, particularly as distance learning and web-based courses are gaining prominence. Other abilities needed include competence in speaking before groups, writing skills, leadership abilities, and administrative skills. Jobs that involve teaching and research will best prepare students for this type of career. Also, administrative jobs could help students acquire the necessary organizational and management skills they need.

SATISFYING ASPECTS

One reason health and fitness professionals are needed is the growth in corporate fitness programs. Leaders in business and industry are realizing that taking care of their number one asset, their employees, is cost-efficient as well as an excellent fringe benefit for the participants. Many physical educators are attracted to working with adults in the fitness field, where the major challenges are developing motivational and adherence strategies. Susan especially enjoys training fitness leaders to implement safe, effective, and enjoyable programs. She also takes pleasure in seeing individuals make lifestyle changes that lead to healthier and happier lives.

JOB POTENTIAL

Susan predicts that the fitness boom will continue to expand and will affect all phases of life—work, home, school, business, and church. In the twenty-first century, the availability of jobs for training health and fitness professionals will expand dramatically. Businesses and industries will continue to provide fitness programs for executives, and they will offer more programs for blue-collar workers, too. Urban areas with larger companies will have more jobs, although businesses in small cities may jointly offer programs for their employees. Occupational groups, such as police officers, will begin to set health and fitness standards for their members, and the general public will seek out qualified professionals to help them regain and maintain health. The salary range is $90,000–$100,000 a year for this type of fitness management position.

SUGGESTIONS FOR STUDENTS

Susan suggests that students study the field and all its related subdisciplines and acquire as much knowledge as possible from current leaders in the field and from their writings. Students should become involved in professional organizations and develop professional networks and contacts. On an emotional level, she recommends that students find a special area of interest or study that appeals to their sense of commitment. In the field of physical fitness, Susan stresses the importance of functioning as a role model. Credibility is lost if fitness leaders smoke, are overweight, use drugs, or practice unhealthy habits. Susan believes that working as a team player and being willing to do a variety of tasks to reach an ultimate goal are important. She also recommends that physical educators learn to think futuristically and to act progressively and productively to make valid plans come to life.

REVIEW QUESTIONS

1. What are the values of establishing long- and short-term goals?
2. Why is an internship important?
3. Give four examples of internship possibilities for an exercise science or sport management major.
4. Give four examples of volunteer experiences that can enhance your undergraduate years and make you more marketable in your job search.
5. What are the various types of graduate degree programs? What is the emphasis of each?
6. What are five important questions that you should ask about your prospective career?
7. Name several types of certificates that you can obtain to prepare you for working in the health and fitness industry.
8. What should be included in a resumé?

STUDENT ACTIVITIES

1. Talk with other students who have completed internships in intramurals, in athletics, with a community group, in a corporate fitness program, or with a sports business. Ask them about the positive and negative aspects of their experiences.

2. Get involved in one professionally related extracurricular activity for at least one semester. Evaluate your experiences to determine what you learned and how they could help you in the future.
3. Find out about your institution's majors' club in your field of study and become actively involved with it.
4. Select a certification, such as one in health and fitness, and set short- and long-term goals for achieving it.
5. Interview individuals in a career that interests you. Ask their advice about how best to prepare to enter that career.
6. Write a letter of application for a position in your chosen career. In one paragraph, highlight your most significant qualities.
7. Using the Internet or library resources, find out information about three graduate programs that you might be interested in attending.
8. Conduct a debate in class about the pros and cons of doing volunteer activities.
9. Find three articles about the value of either networking, volunteering, or internships. Write a one-page paper reporting on your choice.

SUGGESTED READINGS

Ammon R, Ming L, Delpy L: Careers in sport management: part II, *Strategies* 11(5):13, 1998. The article provides information about various career possibilities in the field of sport management.

Campbell K, Kovar SK: Fitness/exercise science internships: how to ensure success, *JOPERD* 65(2):69, 1994. The authors identify four potential areas associated with an internship—academic preparation, intern accountability, supervisor's skills, and appropriateness of the internship site. They suggest possible solutions.

Cuneen J, Sidwell MJ: Sport management interns—selection qualifications, *JOPERD* 64(1):91, 1993. This article examines and rates the qualities and qualifications that sport managers are looking for in candidates for internships.

Field N: Your A to Z guide to sports careers, *Women's Sp & Fit* 16(6):48, 1994. Various sports careers are described along with brief job descriptions, salary ranges, employment outlooks, and suggested contact people.

Field S: *Career Opportunities in the Sports Industry,* 2nd ed., 1998. Checkmark Books. This comprehensive guide to over 70 careers in sports includes entries ranging from coaching to selling sporting goods.

Focus on careers in sports: what does it take to stay in the game? *Career World* 21(6):6, 1993. A good education and a strong interest in sport can prepare you for an exciting future in one of the sports-related careers described in this article.

For the love of coaching, *Palaestra* 6(3):26, 1990 (Special Issue). The keys to Special Olympics are the volunteers who give of their time and energy so that individuals with mental retardation can participate in sport and recreational activities.

Helitzer M: *The dream job: $port$ publicity, promotion and marketing,* 3rd ed., Athens, OH, 2000, University Sports Press. This easy-to-read book describes effective strategies for marketing, publicizing, and promoting college and professional sports.

Michno D: Gotta get a plan: setting and reaching goals, *Career World,* 25(3):14, 1996. This special feature focuses on setting goals and working to achieve those goals to establish the direction of your career.

Pollock ML: Exercise prescription for physical fitness, *Quest* 47(3):320, 1995. The current guidelines for physical fitness are described along with the differences between these and the physical activity guidelines for health.

HISTORY AND DEVELOPMENT OF PHYSICAL EDUCATION, EXERCISE SCIENCE, AND SPORT

7

SPORT IN THE ANCIENT WORLD AND OUR EUROPEAN HERITAGE

KEY CONCEPTS

- Early civilizations, including the Greeks, valued physical development to varying degrees.
- The Greek Ideal stressed the unity of the "man of action" with "the man of wisdom."
- Training to become a knight was the primary physical development valued during the Middle Ages.
- A search for knowledge and an emphasis on "a sound mind in a sound body" emerged during the Renaissance.
- Naturalism focused on teaching children when they were ready to learn and on meeting their individual needs.
- European gymnastics programs developed to train soldiers for nationalistic purposes and later influenced school curricula.
- The British popularized and spread their love of sports and games.

Throughout history, people have participated in various physical activities. Integral to the early civilizations' survival tasks of seeking food, clothing, shelter, and protection were the utilitarian skills of running, jumping, throwing, wrestling, climbing, and swimming. Before formal educational programs, tribal leaders and parents mandated that children learn and practice survival skills through imitation. Communal requirements stressed physical prowess for both aggressive and defensive purposes.

Modern programs of physical education in the United States borrowed primarily from the philosophies, activities, and developments of Europeans from prehistoric times through the 1800s. The Greeks revered optimal physical prowess, and Greek athletics laid the foundation for subsequent physical education and sport programs. Military training in many countries served utilitarian purposes and sometimes supplanted religious ideals. After social conditions stabilized, the philosophy of naturalism stressed development of the body to help educate the whole child. Gymnastics that stressed nationalistic goals borrowed the apparatus and activities of the earlier naturalistic programs. Sports and games in England offered an alternative to these formalized gymnastics systems.

EARLY CULTURES

The Egyptians (2000 to 30 B.C.) have been recognized more for their alphabet and their scientific, agricultural, and engineering prowess than for their educational achievements. Although the Egyptians did not have health objectives related to physical activity, they showed interest in physical development if it achieved a vocational, recreational, or religious objective. The warrior class physically trained for hunting, charioteering, warfare, and wrestling. For recreation, the people of all classes swam, hunted, and played ball games. Dancing, like wrestling, was a form of entertainment. Dancing was also important in religious rituals.

Between 2500 B.C. and A.D. 1200, the Chinese adhered to an entrenched social system based on reverence for the aged scholar. Although in earlier eras physical training was somewhat valued, the religions of Taoism, Buddhism, and Confucianism emphasized the contemplative life. The defense-minded Chinese maintained a military class, who participated in archery, boxing, chariot racing, football, and wrestling, but these activities were never popularized for the masses. Many Chinese flew kites, played chess, practiced light exercises called Ku fu, hunted, and fished. For the Chinese, literary studies and moral and religious training were valued most.

In India (2500 B.C. to A.D. 500), the Hindu religion imposed an unchanging social caste system upon the people. This dogma renounced pleasure and individualism and advocated asceticism in preparation for the next life. Spiritual well-being led to healthful practices and to participation in physical exercises such as yoga, a system of meditation and regulated breathing. Buddhism sought to reform the excesses of the Indian caste system, yet it, too, deemphasized physical activities.

For various reasons, the Egyptians, Chinese, and Indians engaged minimally in physical activities. Not until the Greeks did a civilization openly stress physical prowess and prescribe organized methods for its development.

Greece, regarded as the birthplace of Western civilization, produced a rich heritage of art, drama, history, mathematics, oratory, philosophy, poetry, science, and sculpture as well as the earliest recorded athletic or sports activities. This dynamic, progressive society, which recognized the importance of educating the whole individual, evolved through four eras: (1) the Homeric era from prehistoric times until the first recorded Olympic Games, in 776 B.C.; (2) the era of the totalitarian city-state of Sparta, in the period from 776 B.C. to 371 B.C.; (3) Simultaneously the early Athenian era emphasized democracy and individual freedom, from 776 B.C. to the end of the Persian Wars in 480 B.C; and (4) the later Athenian era, in the period from 480 B.C. until 338 B.C., which grew out of heightened intellectual curiosity (Van Dalen & Bennett, 1971).

THE HOMERIC GREEKS (BEFORE 776 B.C.)

The Homeric era was named for the Greek poet Homer, who is credited with writing the *Iliad* and the *Odyssey,* which include the earliest records of athletic competitions. Book XXIII of the *Iliad* describes the funeral games held in honor of Patroclus, Achilles' friend who had been killed in the Trojan War. The contests included a chariot race, boxing, wrestling, a footrace, a duel with spears, a discus throw, archery, and a javelin throw. Athletes of the period competing in individual events fought fiercely to win. In the *Odyssey,* Homer chronicled the wanderings and return of Odysseus from the Trojan War. Illustrative of these adventures was one episode in Book VIII in which Odysseus, taunted by the Phaeacians, responded by throwing the discus beyond the distances achieved by their athletes.

The predominant philosophy that developed during the Homeric era became known as the **Greek Ideal,** which stressed the unity of the "man of action" and the "man of wisdom." This all-around mental, moral, and physical excellence was called **arete** and was personified by the Greek gods. Revered as part deity and part human, the 12 major gods of the Olympic Council were worshipped as the personifications of the Greek Ideal, with superior intellectual and physical capacities, such as strength, endurance, agility, and bravery. In funeral games held in honor of both respected soldiers killed in battle and the gods, Greek warrior-athletes competed to prove their arete. But success was valued more highly than prizes. Prior to competing, many sought the favor of the gods.

THE SPARTANS (776 B.C. TO 371 B.C.)

The Greeks organized themselves into small governmental units known as city-states. The two dominant, though dramatically contrasting, city-states were Sparta and Athens. By the eighth century B.C., Sparta had begun its military conquests. As Sparta conquered land and took captives, a strict code of discipline, not adherence to the Greek Ideal, was imposed on its people. The **agoge,** an educational system that ensured the singular goal of serving the state, evolved. Mandating complete submission, the Spartan civilization became static because everything, including education, was controlled exclusively by the government.

At birth, a child was examined by a council of elders. If healthy and strong, the child was spared. Weak or sickly children were exposed to the elements to die. The mothers' roles in raising children resembled those of state nurses; they had to suppress all tender and maternalistic feelings. While sons were taught to value their roles as obedient soldiers, daughters learned about their responsibility to bear healthy children.

To prepare themselves physically for this duty, girls participated in state-prescribed gymnastics in addition to wrestling, swimming, and horseback riding.

Dancing was also important in the education of girls and boys as a means of physical conditioning and of honoring the gods.

The boys' educational system, the agoge, was highly structured and formalized. Boys were conscripted by the state at seven years of age and remained in military service until death. Spartan boys began their military training with running and jumping for conditioning. They progressed to swimming, hunting, wrestling, boxing, playing ball, riding horses bareback, throwing the discus and the javelin, and competing in the **pancratium,** a contest combining wrestling and boxing skills. Young boys were trained to endure hardships and pain. Discipline reigned supreme; youths who failed to develop valor, devotion to the state, and military skill were punished.

Beginning at 20 years of age, youths engaged in intensive military maneuvers and actual warfare. These Spartan soldiers, who had been conditioned to fight until death, repeatedly demonstrated their superiority over neighboring city-states and other foes. Not only did the Spartans dominate militarily during this time, but they also won more Olympic victories than athletes from any other city-state. Spartan men, at the age of 30 years, qualified for citizenship and were expected to marry; however, their obligation to the state continued as they trained youth in the public barracks. The Spartan military machine, with its singular focus on physical prowess and disregard for intellectual development, contributed to its inability to rule its innumerable captives and lands. Although they made excellent soldiers, the people were not trained to think for themselves, but rather to perform on command. The Spartans were also few in number due to their strict practices. These factors led to the end of their domination as a city-state in 371 B.C.

THE EARLY ATHENIANS (776 B.C. TO 480 B.C.)

Athens differed sharply from Sparta. The Greek Ideal became the Athenian Ideal as this city-state sought to provide an educational system that encouraged boys to develop their physical and mental abilities. Within this framework of democracy, liberalism, and the popularization of various philosophies, physical prowess flourished as an integral part of the preparation of boys for war and as a means through which beauty and harmony could be depicted.

Girls remained at home under the care of their mothers and received little or no education. Once married, they lived secluded lives. Unlike the physically trained women in Sparta, the Athenian women's social role, quite typical for that time, was very different from the men's role. Boys in the lower classes, though, were as uneducated as girls.

The Athenian educational system, which valued the all-around citizen, dominated the life of upper-class boys who, under the guidance of their fathers, learned about their future responsibilities. Usually beginning at seven years of age and lasting until 14 to 18 years of age, young boys were formally educated at privately owned schools. The time when each boy started, the length of time he attended, and the time when he ended this phase of his education were determined solely by the father, since no governmental regulations existed. Not all boys could attend these schools since fathers had to pay for their sons' education.

The importance attached to the all-around development ideal was evident in each boy's attendance at two schools. A music school provided instruction in arithmetic, literature, and music, while at a **palaestra,** or wrestling school, the boys trained physically. Both schools were equally valued, as the unity concept prevailed. Palaestras were owned and directed by **paidotribes,** the first physical education teachers. They were not elaborate athletic facilities but varied from sparse rooms to simple buildings. There, the boys practiced wrestling, boxing, jumping, and dancing. Some palaestras also included playing fields and a place for swimming.

At the age of 18 years, Athenian boys became eligible for citizenship. For two years thereafter they were subject to military service, if the state needed them, although no mandatory conscription existed. From 20 years of age onward, upper-class Athenian men did not work but instead spent their days at government-furnished **gymnasiums.** There they practiced athletics to maintain their readiness as warriors in case they were needed by the state. Intellectual discussions, governmental decisions, and social interactions were equally important facets of life at the gymnasium.

Greek dancing provided one means of honoring the gods as part of religious worship. It also enhanced physical conditioning and demonstrated the symmetry and beauty adored by the Athenians. Athletics played a similar role, as festivals honoring the gods gave Greek men the opportunity to display their physical prowess and aesthetically pleasing bodies. The importance of honoring the gods eventually led to a proliferation of festivals throughout Greece.

THE LATE ATHENIANS (480 B.C. TO 338 B.C.)

The Athenian-led victory over the Persians in 480 B.C. set the stage for several cultural changes. Economic expansion, self-confidence, increased leisure time, intellectual curiosity, and expansion of political power combined to shift educational goals away from devotion to the state and toward a heightened pursuit of individual happiness. This rampant individualism led to a deemphasis of the physical aspects of education, because, as members of the dominant city-state, citizens no longer saw the need to train as soldiers. The Athenian warrior-athletes were replaced by mercenaries and professional athletes.

The gymnasiums became more like pleasure resorts than exercise areas. They provided sites for philosophical discussions and the training of professional athletes. The Golden Age of Athens (443 B.C. to 429 B.C.) was highlighted by a flowering of democracy and intellectual curiosity led by the Sophists, a class of teachers of rhetoric, philosophy, and the art of successful living, and by philosophers such as Plato. Warning cries from some philosophers about the undermining of the Athenian society went largely unheeded. As a result, the Athenians were militarily unprepared and fell to the Macedonians in 338 B.C.

WEB CONNECTIONS

1. http://devlab.cs.dartmouth.edu/olympic
   This site provides historical facts and interesting information about the history and events of the ancient Olympic Games.

2. www.perseus.tufts.edu/olympics
   Students visiting this site can learn more about ancient Olympic sports, tour ancient Olympia, gain an understanding of the context and spirit of the ancient Olympic Games, and read stories from Olympic athletes of that time.

3. http://ivory.trentu.ca/www/cl/ahb/ahb11/ahb-11-2-3g.html
   Learn more about the gladiators of Rome in reading this review article of three books that describe activities in the arena.

4. www.learner.org/exhibits/renaissance/middleages.html
   After visiting this site, you will know more about the major aspects of the rebirth of knowledge as Europe emerged from the Dark Ages.

5. www.2.cybernex.net/~mhodges/movers/renaiss-reform.htm
   This site provides a wealth of information about the leading "movers and shakers" of the 1400s through the 1600s. It also provides links to biographical information about individuals from Ancient Greece, the Hellenistic and Roman periods, the Middle Ages, and the Enlightenment.

6. http://members.aol.com/Heraklit1/rousseau.htm
   Log on to this site to investigate Jean-Jacques Rousseau's life and leadership in the philosophy of naturalism.

THE PANHELLENIC FESTIVALS (776 B.C. TO A.D. 400)

Festivals honoring the gods during the Homeric period led to the establishment of regular celebrations, which expanded dramatically in the fifth century B.C. The warrior-athletes, who were expected to perfect their skills for warfare, used these religious festivals to demonstrate their physical prowess, especially since this proved their allegiance to the Greek Ideal as personified by the gods. Some of these **Panhellenic** (meaning for all Greeks) festivals also included musical events and aquatic displays. The Panhellenic festivals were exclusively for men. One exception, the Heraean Games, were held for maiden women, who competed in a footrace.

The ancient Olympic Games were unmatched in prestige among these festivals. They were held every four years at Olympia, in honor of Zeus, the chief Greek god. These events began at least by 776 B.C. (the date of the earliest existing artifact of a victory at Olympia), but probably started much earlier. The sacrifices to Zeus, feasting, and athletic contests lasted five days in August and attained such prestige that the perennially warring city-states would guarantee safe passage to travelers to the games. The box on page 199 lists when each event became a part of the games at Olympia and provides an outline of how events were organized during the five days. This sequence of events, with sacrifices and other tributes to Zeus, reinforced the link between religious service and athletic competition.

To be eligible for the games at Olympia, prospective athletes had to be male, Greek-born, free (not a slave), and had to train for 10 months before the contests (with the last month of training at Olympia, under the guidance of the judges). Although the games were open to men from all social classes, the training requirement precluded participation by most poor Greeks, who had to work. Athletes were required to take an oath of fair play. Victors received a wreath of olive branches to symbolize their highly respected victory. Accorded a hero's welcome when returning home, a victor reveled in triumphal processions and banquets, special privileges, and monetary rewards. Initially, Olympia provided no accommodations for either spectators or athletes, as neither a stadium nor a site for the contests existed. The games were scheduled in open spaces with spectators sitting wherever they could. Later, construction of a stadium (for footraces) and the hippodrome (for horse and chariot races) provided space for about 40,000 spectators.

The stade race, so named because it was a footrace the length of the stadium (about 200 meters), was probably the only event in the first games at Olympia. A two-stade race, a long race of about 12 laps, and a race in armor were later added to this phase of the athletic contests. Marble slabs with toe grooves may have served as starting blocks, and a trumpet blast or starting gate was used to start these events. In the longer distance races, the athletes rounded posts at the opposite end of the stadium.

Hand-to-hand combat events included boxing, wrestling, and the pancratium. Since no weight categories existed, boxing pitted two athletes of any size against each other, until one raised a hand to admit defeat. No gloves were worn; the boxers' hands were wrapped with pieces of leather. Blows were confined primarily to the head, often resulting in severe injuries. Wrestling was one of the most popular events because its competitors displayed agility, gracefulness, and strength. The objective was to throw the opponent to the ground three times. The **pancratium** borrowed from boxing and wrestling to become an "almost anything goes" combat. Except for biting and gouging, an athlete could employ any maneuver, such as tripping, breaking fingers, and strangle holds, to force an opponent's admission of defeat.

Chariots, two-wheeled vehicles pulled by four horses, raced, as did horses, at the hippodrome, a narrow field about 500 meters long. These races were limited to the wealthy who could afford to maintain the horses and to hire the charioteers. The victors were the owners, not the charioteers or jockeys. The chariot race consisted of 12 laps.

ANCIENT OLYMPIC GAMES

Chronology

776 B.C.	Stade race
724 B.C.	Added the two-stade race
720 B.C.	Added the longer distance race
708 B.C.	Added pentathlon and wrestling
688 B.C.	Added boxing
680 B.C.	Added chariot race
648 B.C.	Added pancratium and horse race
632 B.C.	Added events for boys
580 B.C.	Added the race in armor
472 B.C.	Festival set as a five-day event and the sequence of events set as follows:

First Day

Oath-taking ceremony
Contests for heralds and trumpeters
Contests for boys
Sacrifices, prayers, singing of hymns, and other religious observances

Second Day

Chariot race
Horse race
Pentathlon (discus, javelin, long jump, stade race, and wrestling)

Third Day

Main sacrifice to Zeus
Footraces

Fourth Day

Wrestling
Boxing
Pancratium
Race in armor

Fifth Day

Prize-giving ceremony
Service of thanksgiving to Zeus
Banquet

The winner of the **pentathlon** was recognized as the best all-around athlete. Although the order of events and the method of determining the victor have been lost in antiquity, the discus throw, the javelin throw, the long jump, the stade race, and wrestling constituted the pentathlon. Like the long jump and the javelin throw, the discus throw existed only as a pentathlon event. In the discus throw,

Greek sprinters in the stade race—one of the five events in the pentathlon as well as an individual event.

Javelin throw—one of the five events in the pentathlon.

a circular piece of stone or bronze about one foot in diameter and weighing four to five pounds was hurled by the athlete. In the long jump, probably similar to today's triple jump, legend recorded that one athlete jumped a distance of more than 55 feet. Jumpers were aided by handheld weights, called **halteres,** which were swung to enhance their performances. The javelin was thrown for both distance and form as a test of skill and strength. A leather thong was wrapped around the 8- to 10-foot javelin, giving it a rotary motion upon release, thereby increasing accuracy. The stade race and the wrestling match probably concluded

Long jump—one of the five events in the pentathlon.

Discus throw—one of the five events in the pentathlon.

the pentathlon, although they may not have been held if one athlete had already won the first three events.

Two developments ushered in a change in attitude toward the Panhellenic festivals. Beginning in Athens, intellectual curiosity and a search for knowledge replaced the Greek Ideal and, hence, lessened interest in physical development. Within the games themselves, lucrative prizes increasingly overshadowed the

Wrestling—one of the five events in the pentathlon as well as an individual event.

The ancient stadium at Delphi, site of the Pythian Games.

earlier motive of honoring the gods through displays of athletic prowess (see box on page 203). Professional athletes who trained under coaches at the gymnasiums and who specialized in certain events became prominent in the contests. Expensive prizes led to cheating, corruption, and bribery. Although officially ended by Roman decree around A.D. 400, the Olympics had much earlier lost association with their former values.

Pancratium.

PANHELLENIC FESTIVALS				
Name	*Frequency*	*Honoring*	*Location*	*Wreath for Victor*
Olympic Games	Every four years	Zeus	Olympia	Olive leaves
Pythian Games	Every four years (third year of each Olympiad)	Apollo	Delphi	Bay leaves
Isthmian Games	Every two years (second and fourth years of each Olympiad)	Poseidon	Corinth	Dry parsley leaves or pine
Nemean Games	Every two years	Zeus	Argolis	Fresh parsley
Panathenaean Games	Most prominent local festival	Athena	Athens	None

THE ROMAN REPUBLIC (500 B.C. TO 27 B.C.)

Roman civilization began as a small tribal community near the Tiber River during the height of the Greek civilization. By extending its rule over neighboring tribes, the Roman nobles, who were landowners, succeeded in establishing a republic around 500 B.C. Soon the common people, who had been given land for their military service, demanded and received greater voice in the government. Thus, many Romans, through this democratization process, attained a higher degree of political and economic freedom.

Roman life during this era focused singularly on serving the state, even though the home provided education for youths without government involvement. Fathers and mothers taught their sons to become citizen-soldiers, including in their education a mental and physical readiness for war, respect for the law, and reverence for the gods. Accompanying their fathers to the Campus Martius or other military camps, boys learned military skills such as archery, fencing, javelin throwing, marching, riding, running, swimming, and wrestling; they developed bodily strength, courage, and obedience to commands as they trained. Conscripted into the military at 17 years of age, men were available for active duty, if needed, until the age of 47. During these 30 years, men were expected to fulfill their business and political duties as well.

Daughters were educated to assume a vital role in raising children and were expected to instill in their sons the importance of fighting, and even dying, for the state. Roman women were more highly respected and socially active than Athenian women.

Religious festivals honoring the gods held as prominent a place in the Roman society as they had during Greek times, yet the Romans did not participate in athletic contests or dance. Rather, they offered sacrifices to their gods and then watched horse and chariot races or gladiatorial contests. These festivals provided leisure-time relief from strenuous military training, but served no educational purposes. (Table 7-1 compares Greek and Roman athletic programs.)

THE ROMAN EMPIRE (27 B.C. TO A.D. 476)

The economic and political freedoms gained by citizens during the Republic were rapidly undermined during the century before the Empire was established in 27 B.C. under Augustus Caesar. The hardy peasants, who had received land in exchange for military service, were ravaged by years of war and subsequent debts and mortgages. Powerful landowners seized this opportunity to expand their estates and to gain greater political influence. The poorer citizens, who were forced off their land, migrated to Rome, where they lived off the public dole. Replaced by a professional army and denied political freedoms and personal dignity, the common people spent their days attending the festivals and games sponsored by corrupt, upper-class senators or the emperors. Gambling on the outcomes of these contests became a favorite pastime.

At least 200 days per year were public holidays and provided opportunities for festivals. Up to 260,000 spectators watched chariot races at the Circus Maximus, attesting to the popularity of these contests. Professional charioteers hired by the teams (the blues, the greens, the reds, and the whites) raced their low, lightweight chariots drawn by four horses in seven-lap races around a **spina,** for a distance of about three miles. The Colosseum became the favorite site for the gladiatorial contests, where, to the pleasure of as many as 90,000 spectators, animal fights featured

TABLE 7-1			
COMPARISON OF ATHLETIC PROGRAMS			
Early Athens	**Late Athens**	**Roman Republic**	**Roman Empire**
Participants			
Aristocratic citizens	Professional athletes	Citizen-soldiers	Professional gladiators and charioteers
Motivation			
All-around development	Profit	Preparation for war	Profit
Training			
Gymnasiums and palaestras	Gymnasiums under trainers	Military camps and fathers	Specialized schools
Events			
Archery, boxing, chariot races, discus, footraces, javelin, and wrestling	Boxing, chariot races, footraces, horse races, pancratium, pentathlon, and wrestling	Archery, fencing, javelin, marching, riding, running, swimming, and wrestling	Chariot races and gladiatorial contests
Organization			
Festivals	Scheduled games and festivals	Festivals	Frequent, organized festivals
Number of Stadiums or Arenas			
Few	Many	Few	Many
Number of Spectators			
Limited	Thousands	Limited	Thousands
Professionals or Amateurs			
Amateurs	Professionals	Amateurs	Professionals
Awards			
Some, but not most important	Lucrative benefits	Limited awards	Lucrative prizes

elephants, bulls, tigers, lions, panthers, and bears. Condemned criminals, social undesirables, and Christians were forced to combat lions, tigers, and panthers. Massive sea battles in the Colosseum provided additional bloody, gory entertainment. Gladiators armed with shield and sword, buckle and dagger, or net and spear, fought each other for freedom or for money.

Gladiators and charioteers trained physically, but most other Romans lost interest in developing their own bodies because they were no longer expected to serve as soldiers. Instead, **thermae,** or baths of varying water temperatures provided leisure for both men and women (with separate hours reserved for the women). At the numerous thermae, Roman men participated in health gymnastics or ball play to overcome indolent lifestyles that featured gluttonous feasts and drinking bouts.

Claudius Galen, born in Pergamum in Greece and educated in Alexandria in Egypt when it was the greatest medical center in the ancient world, became a physician to emperors and gladiators. His public demonstrations of anatomy enhanced his stature as a physician, despite the prevailing taboo against human dissection that resulted in his conducting most of his anatomical studies using animals. Galen's writings were circulated widely during his lifetime with translations of his original Greek manuscripts forming the basis of medical education in medieval universities.

The moral fabric and physical abilities of the Romans dissipated rapidly during an era characterized by governmental upheavals, power struggles, and an apathetic and dependent populace. In A.D. 476, with the deposition of the last Roman emperor by the Visigoths under Odoacer, the domination of the Roman Empire came to an ignoble end. As was true of the demise of the city-state of Athens, a lack of emphasis on physical development contributed to the decline of a once-powerful civilization.

MEDIEVAL EUROPE (500 TO 1500)

The years following the fall of the Roman Empire represented a low point physically and intellectually. Many church leaders during the Middle Ages, such as St. Augustine, spoke against dancing because it had degenerated from its earlier religious purpose. Church leaders also opposed frivolous activities that might detract from piety, proper commitment to worship, and godly living. The Catholic church, in seeking a higher level of morality than displayed by most Romans, regarded the body and anything that benefited it as sinful. **Asceticism,** a doctrine that renounces the comforts of society and espouses austere self-discipline, especially as an act of religious devotion, was practiced by many monks during medieval times.

The only schools that existed during this time were at the monasteries, which restricted intellectual education to those who served the church. The common people were dominated by concerns for survival rather than education. The monks, however, preserved the Greek philosophies. Later, these philosophies would again be studied and valued by a broad range of people.

European society in the eleventh to the sixteenth centuries was feudalistic. The economic, political, and social aspects of life centered around ownership of land and the military power to maintain or expand territory. The monarch, at least theoretically, owned the land. Unable to rule diverse properties successfully, the king divided the territory among nobles who, in turn, promised military service. As **vassals** to the king, they similarly divided their holdings among lesser vassals, with the same reciprocal protection guarantees. At the bottom of this pyramidal

Medieval knights prepared for battle.

structure were the serfs, or peasants, who toiled in the fields. Their labors were meagerly rewarded with protection provided by those they served.

The vassal landowners, who were **knights**, were the only ones in feudal society to value physical training, although the peasants engaged in various recreational pursuits. At seven years of age, the sons of nobles left their homes to go to the manors of other knights. Under the guidance of the ladies of the castles for the next seven years, these **pages** were educated through stories about chivalry, with its code of moral and social duties of knighthood. **Squires**, beginning at 14 years of age, learned the arts of archery, climbing, dancing, fencing, jousting, riding, swimming, tourneying, and wrestling. As a valet for a knight, the squire served meals, cleaned armor, cared for the knight's horse, played chess and backgammon, and accompanied the knight into battle. Following seven years of extensive training as a squire, the youth became eligible for knighthood. Once knighted, these nobles engaged in hunting and hawking and continued their training for battle.

In the isolation of the manorial system of the Middle Ages, few opportunities existed for social interaction and entertainment, so tournaments grew in popularity to fill this void. Although festive occasions, these **tournaments** focused on combats between knights, who divided into two teams and fought under conditions similar to war in the **grand tourney,** or **melee.** Although strict rules and blunt weapons supposedly limited the injuries, fatalities frequently occurred in the melee, leading to its demise. Another event at the tournaments was **jousting,** which pitted two mounted knights armed with lances in a head-on attempt to unseat each other. Since weapons were blunt and the objective was not to kill the opponent, the joust gradually became the primary event of the tournaments.

Because war served as an adventurous solution to boredom, and because service to God was required of the knights, many willingly volunteered for the eight Crusades between 1096 and 1270. Instigated by the church, these military expeditions attempted to expel Moslems and Turks from the Holy Lands and to establish papal control in that region. The knights profited from the captured spoils of war, and some took part mainly for this reason.

Interaction with people from other civilizations through the Crusades contrasted markedly with the isolated lifestyle of the feudalistic period, which peaked between 1250 and 1350. As the importance of the knights lessened because of the invention of gunpowder, towns became established as trade centers. The emergence of a strong merchant class in these towns started the transition to a period of intellectual, cultural, and social reawakening.

THE RENAISSANCE AND THE REFORMATION (1450 TO 1650)

A renewed appreciation for classical culture grew out of the intellectual void of the Middle Ages. Intellectual curiosity and creativity were encouraged rather than stymied as education came to be highly valued by people of all social classes. During the Middle Ages, several allied, yet diverse, philosophies developed; these blossomed during the **Renaissance** period. They directly influenced attitudes toward physical education, although most often the mind and the body were viewed as two separate entities. Scholasticism, based on the authority of church leaders and the writings of the Greek philosopher Aristotle, placed intellectual development in a revered position alongside a fixed religious dogma.

Humanistic education in Italy stressed the harmonious and wholistic development of human beings, embracing the Greek Ideal of unity. "A sound mind in a sound body" described this philosophy, which implemented the principles of humanism and emphasized the physical as well as the intellectual development of students. Humanists stressed the importance of a healthy body as preparation for intellectual endeavors rather than stressing a dichotomous relationship between mind and body.

Realism, which grew out of humanism, emphasized the importance of understanding the Greek classics and of educating for life. The development of health (through exercise and play) and scientific thinking became critical educational outcomes for the realists. Realism and the other philosophies of this era directly or indirectly influenced the philosophies discussed in Chapter 4.

Educational moralism developed during the Protestant Reformation of the 1500s and 1600s as religious fervor combined with nationalism. Although initially wanting only to purify the Catholic church, reformers such as Martin Luther and John Calvin became catalysts for widespread religious and cultural change. Their doctrines stressed personal salvation, moral responsibilities, and state duties. Most of the Protestant sects deemphasized physical development as a distraction from these objectives. One religious group, the Puritans, was especially vehement in its opposition to frivolous activities and tried to enforce its strict doctrines on others. While humanism and realism furthered the Renaissance theme of "a sound mind in a sound body," moralism hindered its acceptance as an educational goal.

Throughout the Renaissance, the 1700s, and most of the 1800s, education was valued for boys, especially those from the upper class, who attended boarding schools or were taught privately by tutors. Seldom was education provided for girls.

THE AGE OF ENLIGHTENMENT (1700s)

The Renaissance set the stage for the Age of Enlightenment, during which two additional philosophies influenced physical education. Englishman John Locke wrote about educational disciplinarianism. He said that character, especially valued for upper-class boys, required "a sound mind in a sound body," and developed best through moral and physical discipline. Jean-Jacques Rousseau, a French philosopher, led the rebellion against the devaluation of the individual. In his book *Emile,* Rousseau described the ideal way to educate a boy, stressing **naturalism,** or "everything according to nature." That is, each child possessed a unique readiness to learn in a natural developmental process that should dictate when a child was exposed to various types of knowledge. The child, free to explore nature while recreating, would thus prepare physically for later intellectual pursuits and would, therefore, learn optimally. The Age of Enlightenment provided additional insights into how to educate a child, thereby laying the foundation for European gymnastics programs. Before examining these programs, however, it is important to frame the 1400s to 1800s into an educational context by describing some of the leaders in education.

EDUCATIONAL PROTAGONISTS (1400s TO 1800s)

Vittorino da Feltre (1378–1446) has been acclaimed as the greatest humanist schoolmaster and teacher of the Renaissance. As a teacher in the Italian "court" (or private) schools supported by wealthy patrons, as well as in his school La Giocosa, da Feltre stressed the importance of intellectual, moral, and physical development, elevating physical education to a place of prominence. In his curriculum, he used archery, fencing, riding, and martial exercises to help create the complete citizen.

François Rabelais (1490–1553) helped provide a bridge between Renaissance humanists and seventeenth-century realists. He believed that physical education should focus on teaching skills to prepare young gentlemen for war. Especially valuable were the knightly exercises of the medieval era.

Michel de Montaigne (1533–1592) held that the body and soul were equal and inseparable. Thus, the mind and body were to be educated simultaneously,

EDUCATIONAL PROTAGONISTS

Individual	Philosophy	Focus	Program/Setting
Vittorino da Feltre	Humanism	Physically sound youth with alert intellect	Ball games; riding; running; fencing; dancing
François Rabelais	Verbal realism	Prepare gentlemen for war	Horsemanship; swordsmanship; swimming
Michel de Montaigne	Social humanism	Shape aristocratic youth for integrated life as a gentleman	Running; wrestling; dancing; hunting; riding
John Comenius	Sense realism	Play is essential to the natural educational process	Children's games; play with toys
John Locke	Educational disciplinarianism	A sound mind in a sound body	Swimming; dancing; riding; fencing
Jean-Jacques Rousseau	Educational naturalism	Everything in education according to nature	Jumping; leaping; climbing; ball play
Johann Pestalozzi	Educational developmentalism	Children learn progressively and in harmony with the body and mind	Games; gymnastics; outdoor activities
Friedrich Froebel	Educational developmentalism	Connect interest in learning with pleasure	Games in the open air; play

as the Greek philosopher Plato had stated centuries earlier. Montaigne's plan for education stressed thinking, learning by doing, developing the whole person, and preparing students for life. His *Essays* advocated a human-centered morality.

John Comenius (1592–1670) in *The Great Didactic* set forth a comprehensive methodology for teaching. A body/mind dualist, like John Locke, he regarded play as essential for children's development, especially for ensuring healthy, vigorous bodies.

John Locke (1632–1704) despite his preoccupation with the education of gentlemen, valued physical exercise for its health benefits for all. His phrase "a sound mind in a sound body," taken from *Some Thoughts Concerning Education* (1693), became the motto for physical educators who supported his belief in the development of the healthy body as a primary function of education.

Jean-Jacques Rousseau (1712–1788) in *Emile* (1762) described an ideal education that continues throughout life. Physical activity within a natural setting should occur when the child is ready to learn.

Johann Pestalozzi's (1746–1827) ideas, as expressed in his book *Leonard and Gertrude,* established the foundation of modern educational theory. He advocated empirical education whereby children became adept at using their senses to make accurate observations. He also stressed the progression of learning from the simple to the complex, the importance of developmental readiness to learn, and the use of children's interest as an indicator of ability to understand. Daily physical exercise aided his students in achieving full unity and harmony between the body and intellect.

Friedrich Froebel (1782–1852) believed in play as the highest phase of child development. The efficacy of play could bring children to a realization of the internal and external unity of the world.

These educational protagonists are compared in the box on page 210.

NATURALISM (1770 TO 1830)

Although the French were not receptive to Rousseau's educational theories, Johann Basedow, a German teacher, was. In establishing a school for boys called the Philanthropinum in 1774, Basedow sought to implement naturalistic principles that focused on meeting individual needs; he also stressed the importance of readiness to learn. At his school, he allotted three hours each day to instructional and recreational activities, such as gymnastics, sports, and games, and two hours to manual labor. While Basedow advocated dancing, fencing, riding, and vaulting, the teacher hired to direct the program, Johann Simon, introduced Greek gymnastics, consisting of jumping, running, throwing, and wrestling. Simon utilized natural settings to provide the needed apparatus, such as balance beams, high-jumping poles, jumping ditches, and tree swings. Johann Du Toit, Simon's successor, added archery, skating, swimming, marching, gardening, and woodworking to Basedow's original curriculum.

In 1785, Christian Salzmann patterned the program at Schnepfenthal Educational Institute after Basedow's naturalistic lessons in games and gymnastics. Johann GutsMuths, who taught at Schnepfenthal for 50 years, was strongly influenced by Basedow's writings and provided similar activities and pieces of apparatus. GutsMuths' three- to four-hour daily program consisted of natural activities, such as jumping and running; Greek gymnastics, such as throwing and wrestling; military exercises, such as fencing and marching; knightly activities, such as climbing and vaulting; and manual labor, such as gardening and woodworking. GutsMuths influenced many people with two significant books: *Gymnastics for the Young* (1793), which not only described Schnepfenthal's program but also laid the theoretical foundation for modern programs, and *Games for Exercise and Recreation of the Body and Spirit* (1796), which described the skills developed in 105 games or activities and provided illustrations of the apparatus used, such as climbing masts, hanging ladders, rope ladders, and wooden horses.

NATIONALISM (1800s)

Friedrich Jahn, a German educator and an ardent patriot, visited the Schnepfenthal Educational Institute and borrowed many aspects of GutsMuths' program. Jahn's purpose in promoting physical development was nationalistic rather than naturalistic. He sought to develop fitness and strength in German youth for the eventual unification of all German people. After encouraging his students to climb trees, jump over ditches, run, and throw stones on half-holiday excursions from classes, he established the first **turnplatz** near Berlin in 1811. A turnplatz was an outdoor exercise area where boys, who became known as **turners,** trained using balance beams, ropes and ladders for climbing, high-jumping standards, horizontal bars, parallel bars, pole-vaulting standards, broad-jumping pits, vaulting horses, a figure-eight-shaped track, and a wrestling ring. Jahn also promoted **nationalism** through patriotic speeches and stories and group singing of patriotic songs. First boys and then, as this turner system of gymnastics expanded, males of all ages and social classes participated in the increasingly

German gymnastics on the horse.

popular gymnastic exercises. Jahn explained his program in his book, *German Gymnastics* (1816).

The turners vigorously advocated for a unified Germany, and many local turnplatz sites initially received government subsidies. After the Congress of Vienna realigned Germany into a confederation of 38 independent states in 1815, the turners' single-minded goal of a unified nation was viewed as threatening. Finally, in 1819, government leaders succeeded in banning turner gymnastics. Not until 1840 was it again legal to participate in turner gymnastics, although underground programs continued during the intervening years. Turner gymnastics never gained widespread popularity in other nations because of the nationalistic appeal and emphasis on strength.

Adolph Spiess borrowed from his training in turner gymnastics to devise a system of German school gymnastics in the 1840s. Approval of his program in the public schools hinged on his defense of gymnastics as a subject equal to all others, one that had progressions for various ages, for boys and girls, for all ability levels, and one that required trained teachers and equipped indoor and outdoor facilities. Although influenced somewhat by Jahn's and GutsMuths' programs, Spiess devised a school system that stressed discipline and obedience and

COMPARISON OF EUROPEAN GYMNASTICS SYSTEMS

System	Theme(s)	Participants	Program	Apparatus
German	National regeneration; physical activities used to develop strong, sturdy fearless youth	Working and lower-middle classes; first boys, then men, too	Individualized under Jahn and vorturners (teachers)	Vaulting horses; parallel bars; ropes and ladders for climbing; balance beams; running track
Danish	Nationalism	Soldiers; teachers	Formalized exercises on command; no individual expression	Hanging ladders; rope ladders; masts and poles for climbing; balance beams; vaulting horses
Swedish	National preparedness; therapeutic healing; pedagogical; aesthetics	Soldiers; teachers	Movement on command; posture correcting	Stall bars; vaulting boxes; climbing poles; oblique ropes; Swedish boom

Class of female students at the Royal Gymnastics Central Institute.

included diverse activities, such as marching, free exercises, and gymnastics with musical accompaniment.

Nationalism dominated Danish gymnastics in the early 1800s, too. Fitness, strength, and military competence emerged as the goals of Franz Nachtegall. In 1799, he established a private gymnasium in Copenhagen, the first of its kind. Nachtegall's curriculum, which borrowed extensively from the apparatus and exercises of GutsMuths, gained popularity and helped Denmark initiate the first European school program in physical education for boys, in 1809. His *Manual of Gymnastics,* published in 1828, provided the curriculum for the schools. Teachers for the schools were initially educated alongside military men at the Military Gymnastic Institute, founded in 1804 by the king of Denmark, with Nachtegall as its director. Danish gymnastics in the military and in the schools was based totally on command-response exercises, with rigid, mass drills associated with the nationalistic theme.

Patriotism raged in Sweden in the late 1700s and early 1800s due to Sweden's loss of territory to Russian and Napoleonic forces. This nationalistic fervor initially influenced Per Henrik Ling to study and write about the Scandinavian heritage. While pursuing this objective in Denmark for five years, he learned gymnastics from Franz Nachtegall and engaged in fencing, through which he improved an arthritic arm. The personal therapeutic benefits that Ling experienced led him to promote gymnastics throughout his career. Returning to his homeland in 1804, Ling became a fencing master and an instructor of literature and history, while also teaching gymnastics.

Ling's theory that the knowledge of Norse literature and history combined with gymnastics training could make Sweden a stronger nation influenced the king. As a result, the Royal Gymnastics Central Institute was established in Stockholm in 1814, under Ling's direction. As a training program for military men, this program

Swedish school gymnastics.

allowed Swedes to stress precise execution of movements on command, mass drills, posture-correcting movements, and specific exercises on specially-designed exercise apparatus. England, Denmark, Belgium, Greece, and other countries adopted Swedish gymnastics for military training. Ling initiated therapeutic, or medical, gymnastics to restore health through exercises, and is credited with devising a system of massage to treat ailments involving joints and muscles. He also promoted gymnastics for pedagogical (educational) and aesthetic pur-poses. Swedish apparatus, such as stall bars, booms, vaulting boxes, and oblique ropes, as developed by Ling, were always subordinated to the exercises and to stu-dents' needs. (The box on page 213 compares the three major gymnastics systems in Europe.)

When Hjalmar Ling, Per Henrik Ling's son, began teaching at the Royal Gym-nastics Central Institute, he initiated the development of Swedish school gymnas-tics. Borrowing from his father's program the principles of progression and pre-cise execution of movements on command, Hjalmar Ling devised the **Day's Order**, systematized, daily exercises that progressed through the whole body from head to toe. These lessons were appropriately graded for the age, ability, and gender of each child and used apparatus designed for children. Mass drills under a teacher's direction remained paramount.

The timeline in the box on page 217 lists the various activities that people of each era participated in, along with the primary purpose of each activity. Figure 7.1 illustrates how European philosophies and innovators influenced subsequent programs.

SPORTS IN GREAT BRITAIN (1800s)

The nationalistic fervor for European gymnastics never gained prominence in Great Britain, other than through minimal usage of Ling's program by the British military. As the dominant world power, Great Britain had not faced

FIGURE 7.1

Origins of modern physical education.

territorial decimation as so many other nations had, so nationalism failed to undergird a gymnastics program in that country. Instead, the British legacy to both European and worldwide physical education has undoubtedly been its sports and games.

The Greek Ideal paralleled Englishman John Locke's "sound mind and sound body" concept. The Greek love for athletic supremacy, rather than lucrative benefits, in the Panhellenic festivals is remarkably similar to the **British**

ANCIENT WORLD AND EUROPEAN HERITAGE TIMELINE

Dates	People	Popular Activities	Purpose
Pre-776 B.C.	Homeric Greeks	Chariot racing; boxing; wrestling; footracing; throwing the discus and javelin	Preparation for war; honoring the gods
776 B.C. to 371 B.C.	Spartans	Running; jumping; wrestling; boxing; horseback riding; throwing the discus and javelin; pancratium; hunting; swimming	Military supremacy
776 B.C. to 480 B.C.	Early Athenians	Wrestling; boxing; jumping; throwing the discus and javelin; dancing	Preparation for war; honoring the gods
500 B.C. to 27 B.C.	Romans during the Republic	Archery; fencing; throwing the javelin; marching; riding; running; swimming; wrestling	Preparation for war
A.D. 500 to 1500	Knights	Archery; climbing; dancing; fencing; jousting; riding; swimming; wrestling; hunting; hawking	Preparation for war
1450 to 1650	Educational protagonists	Archery; fencing; riding; games; play; gymnastics	Education of the whole child
1770 to 1830	Naturalists (Germans)	Dancing; fencing; riding; vaulting; jumping; running; throwing; wrestling; manual labor; gymnastics; games	Meeting individual needs
1800s	German turners	Climbing; vaulting; jumping; wrestling; running	National regeneration
1800s	Danish	Vaulting; climbing; jumping; gymnastics exercises	Nationalism
1800s	Swedish	Vaulting; climbing; gymnastics exercises	Nationalism; therapy

Amateur Sport Ideal of "playing the game for the game's sake." The Greek Ideal as displayed by upper-class males in Great Britain dramatically influenced Frenchman Pierre de Coubertin, who founded the modern Olympic Games.

Sports and recreational pastimes have traditionally been divided along class or socioeconomic lines in Great Britain. Given few alternatives due to their socioeconomic status, working-class males were especially attracted to pugilism

The British popularized rugby in boys' boarding schools in the 1800s.

(bare-knuckle boxing), blood sports (such as cockfighting), and varieties of football (soccer). These "poor man's sports" required little equipment, usually encouraged gambling, and were often banned by the church.

British upper-class sports, such as cricket and rugby, were popularized at private boys' boarding schools, called public schools, in the 1800s. Thomas Arnold, headmaster at Rugby School, praised the role of sport according to Thomas Hughes in *Tom Brown's Schooldays*. Arnold regularly advocated sports participation as a means for boys to learn moral virtues, such as cooperation, leadership, loyalty, self-discipline, and sportsmanship. Sport within these public schools stressed participation in a variety of sports, rather than specialization in one; playing the game, rather than training in skills and fitness; and competition between the boys in various residences. Public school boys often demonstrated greater learning through sport than in their scholastic efforts. Since graduates of these public schools were the future leaders of the nation, lessons learned in sports were acclaimed for preparing better citizens.

Cricket, rowing, association football (soccer), track and field athletics, rugby, and field hockey became the most popular sports at Oxford and Cambridge Universities despite faculty disfavor. The British Amateur Sport Ideal of playing the game for the game's sake, rather than for remuneration, prevailed in these sports competitions, especially since these upper-class men did not need to play for money.

The emergence of the philosophy of **muscular Christianity,** that is, the teaching of values through sport, impacted British sports and subsequently those in the United States. Most Protestants, viewed participation in sports and games as sinful. However, when people refused to conform to rigid prohibitions, attitudes gradually softened to permit sporting diversions as long as moral values could be taught and reinforced. Religion and sport peacefully coexisted whenever ethical virtues remained foremost. Fair play, honorable victories, respect for the opponent, and sports for fun rather than winning at all costs, characterized British upper-class and schoolboy sports (see "Selected Sports and Their Origins" box).

SELECTED SPORTS AND THEIR ORIGINS

Wrestling	China	1788 B.C.
Boxing	China	850 B.C.
Track and Field	Greece	776 B.C.
Rugby	Great Britain	900 A.D.
Golf	Scotland	1457
Cricket	Great Britain	1679
Gymnastics	Germany	1816
Baseball (Rounders)	Great Britain	1846
Soccer	Great Britain	1859
Badminton	India	1870
Tennis	Great Britain	1873
Water Polo	Great Britain	1885
Field Hockey	Great Britain	1886
Table Tennis	Great Britain	1889

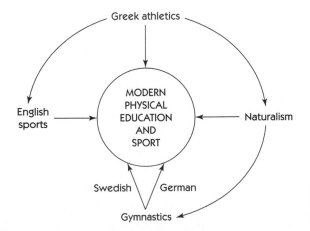

FIGURE 7.2

European contributions to modern physical education and sport.

Many sports started in Great Britain were spread throughout the world during their years of colonization. Sometimes these sports were welcomed by indigenous people; at other times they were rejected outright. Horse racing, tennis, golf, soccer, badminton, field hockey, and rugby are a few of the most prominent of these sports. Most sports in the United States were introduced by British colonists.

SUMMARY

The European legacy of athletics, gymnastics, and sports laid the foundation for physical education and sport programs in the United States (as depicted in Figure 7.2). The Greeks provided a rich heritage of mind/body unity and glorified the aesthetically-developed, all-around athlete. Varying dramatically from this ideal were the Spartan soldiers and the specialized, professional athletes of the later Athenian era. The Roman Republic illustrated the utilitarian goal of a fit military force. During the next thousand years, only the knights developed their bodies, but they did so primarily for military conquest rather than for any inherent value. Church leaders discouraged frivolous activities. Philosophers and educators, during the Renaissance, emphasized physical development for overall education, and grappled with whether the mind and body should be educated separately or simultaneously. Naturalism and nationalism directly influenced the development of gymnastics systems in Germany, Denmark, and Sweden. British sports and games, with their associated emphasis on values, laid the foundation for physical education and sport programs in the United States.

CAREER PERSPECTIVE

JOHANN CHRISTOPH FRIEDRICH GUTSMUTHS
(1759–1839)

BACKGROUND

Johann GutsMuths taught gymnastics at the Schnepfenthal Educational Institute for 50 years. His program, based on naturalistic principles, provided the model for subsequent European and American programs. And, his many writings added a philosophical framework to his various activities. Historians have acclaimed him as the "grandfather of physical education" for his monumental contributions.

In 1786, GutsMuths ended his years as a private tutor to accept a teaching position at Schnepfenthal, where he continued the gymnastics program started by Christian Andre. Throughout his work there, GutsMuths experimented with new exercises and apparatus as Christian Salzmann, the founder of Schnepfenthal, provided him with bountiful opportunities to offer activities for the students. Gymnastics was taught between 11:00 and 12:00 daily. After the noon meal and in the evening, time was set aside for recreation. Games and outdoor excursions filled Sunday afternoons under GutsMuths' guidance.

ACCOMPLISHMENTS

GutsMuths opposed the traditional European methods of education, promoting naturalistic principles, instead. He stressed that health, strength, and overall physical development were essential. The influence of naturalism on the program at Schnepfenthal was readily evident. Andre instituted walking on the balance beam, jumping standards, pole-vaulting across ditches, vaulting (jumping over an apparatus), and other outdoor activities. GutsMuths introduced seesaws, rope ladders, vertical ropes for swinging, and climbing masts. In addition to activities using the above apparatus, the students engaged in leaping, jumping, running, throwing, wrestling, climbing, skipping, dancing, walking, swimming, and military exercises. GutsMuths' and Salzmann's belief that manual labor was important led to instruction in woodworking and gardening. GutsMuths' program integrated naturalistic, Greek, and knightly heritages with military exercises and manual labor. He divided his gymnastic exercises into three categories: for bodily improvement, for manual labor, and for social games.

CONTRIBUTIONS TO PHYSICAL EDUCATION

Although people throughout Europe visited Schnepfenthal and observed his program and teaching, GutsMuths' greatest impact came from his writings. His two greatest works were *Gymnastics for the Young* (1793) and *Games for Exercise and Recreation of the*

Body and Spirit (1796). The first of these was 700 pages in length; it was the first modern book about physical education. In exhaustive fashion, he explained exactly how and why physical education activities developed the body. Published in Denmark, Great Britain, the United States, Holland, Bavaria, France, Sweden, and Austria, *Gymnastics for the Young* went through several revisions. *Games for Exercise and Recreation of the Body and Spirit,* published in three editions, provided detailed descriptions of 105 games. GutsMuths classified these according to the function and the skills each should develop. GutsMuths also wrote the *Small Manual of the Art of Swimming for Self-Teaching, Mechanical Avocations for Youths and Men, Book of Gymnastics for the Sons of the Fatherland,* and *Catechism of Gymnastics: A Manual for Teachers and Pupils.* Several of these also underwent revision.

Health and strength were the goals of GutsMuths' gymnastics program. Naturalism provided the methodology through which it could be achieved. His mammoth legacy is demonstrated by the number of subsequent physical educators who to varying degrees have borrowed from his philosophy, his ideas regarding apparatus, or his exercises.

REVIEW QUESTIONS

1. What is the Greek Ideal?
2. How did the education of girls and boys in Sparta differ from that in Athens?
3. What took place at an Athenian gymnasium during both the early and the later eras?
4. Why did the Olympic Games start, and how did they attain such a prestigious status?
5. Why were the Romans a nation of spectators?
6. How and why did the Renaissance serve as a transitional period between the Middle Ages and the Age of Enlightenment?
7. How did naturalism influence the early development of European gymnastics?
8. How did nationalism influence the development of European gymnastics?
9. What were the similarities and differences among the school gymnastics programs of Adolph Spiess in Germany, Franz Nachtegall in Denmark, and Hjalmar Ling in Sweden?
10. What outcomes were stressed to justify sports and games for boys in the public schools in Great Britain?

STUDENT ACTIVITIES

1. As a class project, reenact the ancient Olympic Games by having each student participate in an appropriate athletic contest. Each student will be expected to research the specifics about the assigned or selected event before "competing" against classmates.
2. Select one activity or area of training for a page or squire during medieval times. Prepare a five-minute oral report and demonstration of how the boys were taught and how they practiced the necessary skills.

3. Along with several classmates, prepare a demonstration of German, Swedish, or Danish gymnastics, and then lead the rest of the class in a five-minute lesson.

4. Write a five-page paper about the early history and development of any sport that is associated with the British Amateur Sport Ideal or was founded in Great Britain.

5. Challenge yourself to find 16 people, ideas, or terms from the medieval era forward in the history puzzle below. Define or describe each one found.

```
E R H S I L B U F J A H N E H T M O R F N O I T N I R W G O R O E S I W N G R
T H A V S T E S W I N L E T A R P U Y O S B N Y L A O L A Z C X U D E S U E U
D H E T A R K A G E S E S D I C S O M S T Y P O L Q E N Z V B K S A J M U B G
S F E I R B S M E T I A I D E M H E G D E L W O N K T A N R H C E A Q O S L B
P R F R U T C E L D S A S P I R T I D N I F H L C R I C K E T U T I W O P L Y
I Z X C V T U R N V E R I E N S O L V J U Z X P R E W Z S D H I Y O P C V B U
E N M B V C X Z L K J H G F D S A B N A E W Q A T Y L R O U S S E A U O P U X
S F N A T U R A L I S M E S Y T E I R A L E W Q J I O P L M Y H N R F L S C U
S Q P O I U T R E W L K J H G F D S U I O R E W Q J I O P L M Y H N R Y S X C
Y U I O P T Y B A S E D O W Q W E R T Y I F Y O P L K J H G F D S A M M B V P
P C V X B N M J I K L A G Y T F D E S G U T S M U T H S L M H Y I A U P U R E
S Z G H S W C D C R U S A D E S S B G T N H M Y J U K I P O Z A G W S I Y I O
C B V X J I F O N O S D F G H J O Q O N A C H T E G A L L O L U P T R C O E B
O Z P X A O C I V U B Y N A T W E R E N A I S S A N C E O K L Y U G C S V B A
P E R H E N R I K L I N G A M S N A T I O N A L I S M C H X J Z L Q E J H R G
```

6. Conduct a class debate about the similarities and differences between the early and later Athenians, the Roman Republic and Empire, and modern-day sporting activities and competitions.

7. Identify 20 contributions to or influences on American physical education and sport as described in this chapter.

REFERENCE

Van Dalen DB, Bennett BL: *A world history of physical education,* 2nd ed., Englewood Cliffs, N.J., 1971, Prentice-Hall.

SUGGESTED READINGS

Broekhoff J: Physical education, sport, and the ideals of chivalry, in Bennett BL, editor: *History of physical education and sport,* Chicago, 1972, The Athletic Institute. During the Middle Ages, chevaliers learned about courtly love; the ideals of chivalry, and, especially, the knightly arts of riding, swimming, shooting, climbing, jousting and tourneying, wrestling, fencing and fighting; courtly manners and behavior; and playing board games.

Crowther NB: Qualifying for the Olympic Games in ancient Greece, *J of Sp Hist* 23 (Spring):34, 1996. This article explains the requirements for eligibility in the most popular of the Panhellenic Festivals.

Finkelberg M: Time and arete in Homer, *Classical Quar* 48(1):14, 1998. This article presents information about the all-around mental, moral, and physical excellence valued by the ancient Greeks.

Gerber EW: *Innovators and institutions in physical education,* Philadelphia, 1971, Lea & Febiger. Fifty outstanding leaders in European and American physical education along with 10 significant institutions are described in this comprehensive history.

Golden M: *Sport and society in ancient Greece,* Cambridge, 1998, Cambridge University Press. The author draws distinctions among social classes, genders, and ages in this examination of the role of sport in ancient society.

Harris HA: *Sport in Greece and Rome,* Ithaca, 1972, Cornell University Press. This classical scholar comprehensively examines athletics, ball games, and chariot racing in both Greece and Rome and helps the reader understand the role of each in the cultures of these early civilizations.

Kennell NM: *The gymnasium of virtue: education and culture in ancient Sparta,* Chapel Hill, NC, 1995, University of North Carolina Press. This book expounds the unique characteristics of the city-state of Sparta, with an emphasis on education.

Kyle DG: Winning and watching the Greek pentathlon, *J of Sp Hist* 17:291, 1990. Based on a reexamination of the archaeological evidence, the author suggests how the winner of the Greek pentathlon was determined. Some comments on Greek sport and spectating are offered.

Thompson-Noel M: Not so far from Mount Olympus: comparison of modern and ancient Olympics, *New Statesman* 125:31, 1996. This article compares the corruption and crass commercialization of the ancient and modern games, concluding that the ancient Greeks would have felt at home in Atlanta in 1996.

Ueberhorst H: *Friedrich Ludwig Jahn,* Bonn-Bad Godesberg, 1978, InterNations. This biography of the controversial "father of gymnastics" describes his achievements in promoting nationalism through turner gymnastics.

EARLY AMERICAN PHYSICAL EDUCATION AND SPORT

KEY CONCEPTS

- Participation in sporting activities was a valued part of Native Americans' lives.
- Colonists coming to the New World, especially those from Great Britain, brought with them a love for sports and games.
- Early physical education programs in the United States promoted calisthenics, light gymnastics, hygiene, and strength development.
- German and Swedish gymnastics formed the basis for many early physical education programs.
- Teacher training institutes and a professional organization provided the educational foundation and a forum for the future development of physical education and sport programs.
- Play became recognized as an essential aspect of healthy child development.
- Amateur sports in clubs and on college campuses were organized and became competitive.

Individuals arriving in the New World found Native Americans playing sports. The early colonists brought with them a love for sporting pastimes. Once survival was assured, time was spent bowling, racing horses, skating, wrestling, and playing various ball games. Formalized exercises comprising the German gymnastics and Swedish gymnastics systems appealed to a few, but neither won full acceptance as a unified, national approach to physical education appropriate for people in the United States. People from Great Britain, through worldwide colonization (including North America), spread their love of sports and games. **Hygiene,** the science of preserving one's health, was the focus of many early school programs in the United States. These programs were often called physical culture or physical training because of the beneficial effects of exercise. Emphasizing health, strength, and bodily measurements, physical training programs in the 1800s were added to school and college curricula primarily under the direction of physicians. Leaders established teacher training institutes that offered course work in the theoretical aspects of the emerging profession of physical education. Sports and play activities drawn from a European heritage continued to grow in popularity as college students and upper-class clubs sponsored contests. Many towns also provided playgrounds, further stimulating interest in physical education and sport.

Before examining the major programs and developments that contributed to early American physical education programs, it is important to explain their significance. The emerging field of physical education was built upon a heritage of hygiene, medicine, strength development, formalized exercises, play, and sports. Early leaders in physical education developed organizations to govern their myriad activities. Many individuals contributed to the sound foundation laid prior to the twentieth century that led to subsequent developments in physical education, exercise science, and sport described more fully in Chapter 9.

PHYSICAL ACTIVITIES IN THE COLONIES

Sports, physical activities, and dance occupied a prominent role in the traditional life of most Native Americans when colonists from other countries arrived in North America. These events were associated with religious ceremonies, festive celebrations, and social relaxation. However, differences in language, lifestyles, geographic regions, livelihoods, and overall cultures verify that one cohesive image did not exist. Most tribes' outlook on life contributed to the popularity of their preferred sporting pastimes.

According to Oxendine (1988), some of the most important factors characterizing traditional Native American sports include the following:

- a strong connection between sport and other social, spiritual, and economic aspects of daily life;
- the serious preparation of mind, body, and spirit of both participants and the community as a whole prior to major competition;
- the assumption that rigid adherence to standardized rules and technical precision was unimportant in sport;
- strong allegiance to high standards of sportsmanship and fair play;
- the prominence of both males and females in sport activity, but with different expectations;
- a special perspective on team membership, interaction, and leadership styles;
- the role of gambling as a widespread and vital component in all sports;
- the importance of art as an expression of identity and aesthetics (pages 3–4).

The most popular Native American sport was lacrosse, also called baggataway, meaning ball game, or the game of ball. The competitors displayed grace, adroitness, and dexterity, often in honor of their gods. The courage, ruggedness, skill, speed, and endurance required to play this game helped train males for war. The rules, size of the playing field, equipment, and clothing varied by tribe.

Native Americans, including many females, played shinny, a ball and stick game similar to modern field hockey. Women also actively participated in double ball, in which a stick was used to propel two balls attached by a string.

Footraces, especially among Native Americans, served as a source of motivation and pride. Besides children's play and ceremonial uses by adults, running skills benefitted tribes in war, the pursuit of game animals, and the delivery of messages. The sacred ball race combined kicking a ball along a prescribed 25-mile course and running after it each time.

Other sports of major interest to Native Americans included archery, swimming, fishing, canoeing, and snow snake, which involved sliding a pole a great distance across a frozen path. Ritualistic dances and games of chance were also popular.

The first colonists came to the New World in the late 1500s in search of a new life, adventure, and religious freedom. During that century, the prime motivator for physical activity was survival: men hunted, fished, and grew crops while women performed domestic chores. What little time existed for relaxation was frequently spent in work-related recreation, such as barn raisings, corn huskings, or quilting bees. Dancing and games were often a part of these gatherings, although some religions forbade dancing.

The sporting heritage brought to this country by Europeans became increasingly popular in the 1700s. In spite of Puritan-initiated laws forbidding gambling, card playing, and mixed dancing, New Englanders relaxed by bowling, fishing, fowling, or playing cricket, rugby fives (a game similar to handball), or marbles.

Led by the Dutch in New York, the settlers in the middle colonies, without many of the religious prohibitions imposed on their northern neighbors, eagerly engaged in merriments such as pulling the goose (snapping off the head of a greased goose while riding horseback or while standing in a moving boat); played games, such as skittles (in which a ball or flat disk is thrown down an alley at nine skittles, or pins); and participated in outdoor amusements, such as boating, fishing, hunting, horse racing, and sleighing. These activities were enthusiastically pursued by the upper class. Interestingly, when nine-pin bowling was prohibited by law because of its association with gambling, a tenth pin was added to allow bowlers, and hence gamblers, to participate legally in their favorite pastime. The Quakers of Pennsylvania favored fishing, hunting, and swimming as diversions while banning many other leisure pursuits.

Virginia, strongly influenced by the British, emerged as the leading Southern colony. Emulating the gentry across the ocean, the Southern plantation owners sought to acquire all the trappings befitting their aristocratic status, including sporting pastimes. Cockfighting, bowling, card playing, and horse racing were pursued vigorously at taverns, which initially were exclusively for men. Fox hunting, hawking, and watching boxing matches found many enthusiasts.

Participation in various physical activities increased throughout the 1770s, as an emerging nationalism placed emphasis on the development of health and strength. Benjamin Franklin, Noah Webster, and Thomas Jefferson were among those who supported physical activities for healthful benefits. At the same time, sports involvement continued to win new adherents because sports offered competition, freedom, and fun.

In the late 1700s, as the colonists prepared for a confrontation with the British, military days provided opportunities for marching and drilling with weapons, yet they also offered opportunities for social interaction and game playing. The military training was utilitarian in purpose, though, and did not lead to an emphasis on physical fitness in the post-Revolutionary War years. This trend repeated itself throughout the history of the United States as each war signaled a need to have trained soldiers; aside from these times of emergency, there was little emphasis by the military on physical fitness programs.

Many immigrants traveled to the New World in search of religious freedom. Mostly Protestants, they valued labor and education, as long as the latter contributed to the development of the highest type of Christian manhood. Latin grammar schools, and a few universities, educated the intellectually and financially elite. Dame schools offered mostly boys the basics of reading, writing, and arithmetic (the three Rs).

Following the War of 1812, nationalism burst into popularity, setting the stage for a gradual extension of democratic rights to more people and for the provision of education to more children. Free, public education for boys and girls, beginning in the 1800s, consisted primarily of the three Rs. These public schools initially showed little interest in physical education, although in 1853 Boston became the first city to require daily exercise for children. In private academies and schools in the early 1800s, though, the belief that physical activities contributed to health led to children's participation in sports. Prior to the Civil War, few colleges provided for their students' physical development; yet academies and private schools for boys and occasionally for girls (such as Mt. Holyoke Female Seminary beginning in 1837) included physical exercises in their curricula.

Early American physical education and sport was influenced by European systems of exercises (called gymnastics), the development of normal schools and a national organization, the provision of play for children, and amateur sports for men and women. Each of these contributed to the content and structure of twentieth century physical education and sport programs, which are an amalgamation of a variety of exercises, gymnastics, formalized educational curricula, play, and sports.

EARLY GERMAN GYMNASTICS IN THE UNITED STATES

The most significant private school to initiate required physical education in the United States was the Round Hill School, founded in 1823 in Northampton, Massachusetts. The box on pages 229–230 lists this school's establishment along with other highlights in the development of physical education in the nineteenth century. The founders of Round Hill School scheduled time each day for sports and games even before they employed Charles Beck, a German turner, to instruct the boys in the German system of gymnastics. Beck established an

SIGNIFICANT EVENTS IN EARLY AMERICAN PHYSICAL EDUCATION

1823	Round Hill School established with physical education in its curriculum
1824	Hartford Female Seminary, directed by Catharine Beecher, included calisthenics in its curriculum
1825	Charles Beck became an instructor of German gymnastics at Round Hill School
1825	New York City high schools offered gymnastics
1826	Charles Follen organized gymnastics classes for students at Harvard University
1831	John C. Warren's *The Importance of Physical Education* published
1832	Catharine Beecher's *Course of Calisthenics for Young Ladies* published
1837	Mount Holyoke Female Seminary opened, with calisthenics listed as part of its school program
1837	Western Female Institute founded by Catharine Beecher
1848	Friedrich Hecker organized the first American turnverein in Cincinnati
1851	First national turnfest held in Philadelphia
1853	Boston became the first city to require daily exercise for school children
1855	Cincinnati, Ohio, first offered physical education using German gymnastics in its public schools
1856	Catharine Beecher's *A Manual of Physiology and Calisthenics for Schools and Families* published
1859	A. Molineaux Hewlitt, an African-American, appointed gymnasium instructor at Harvard University
1861	Normal Institute for Physical Education founded by Dioclesian Lewis
1861	Edward Hitchcock, M.D., became director of physical education at Amherst College
1862	Dioclesian Lewis's *New Gymnastics for Men, Women, and Children* published
1865	First women's physical education program started at Vassar College
1866	California passed the first state physical education law
1866	Normal School of the North American Gymnastic Union established
1869	First YMCA gymnasiums opened in New York City, San Francisco, and Washington, D.C.
1872	Brookline, Massachusetts, became the first community in America to vote for the establishment of a playground using public funds
1879	Harvard University's Hemenway Gymnasium opened under the direction of Dudley Sargent, M.D.
1883	Hartvig Nissen started teaching Swedish gymnastics in Washington, D.C.
1885	Nils Posse started teaching Swedish gymnastics in Boston, Massachusetts
1885	Association for the Advancement of Physical Education founded in Brooklyn, New York
1885	YMCA Training School established in Springfield, Massachusetts
1886	Brooklyn Normal School established by William Anderson, M.D.
1886	Chautauqua Summer School of Physical Education established
1887	Harvard Summer School established
1889	Boston Normal School of Gymnastics established
1889	Boston Conference on Physical Training held
1890	Posse Normal School founded
1890	Edward Hartwell, M.D., became director of physical education for the Boston public schools
1892	Ohio became the second state to pass a physical education law
1893	Harvard became the first college to confer an academic degree in physical education

(continued)

SIGNIFICANT EVENTS IN EARLY AMERICAN PHYSICAL EDUCATION (CONTINUED)

1894   American Association for the Advancement of Physical Education established departments of interest including the Department of Anthropometry and Statistics under the leadership of Edward Hitchcock, M.D.

1896   American Association for the Advancement of Physical Education began publication of *American Physical Education Review*

1897   American Association for the Advancement of Physical Education established a committee on School Anthropometry with Henry Bowditch, M.D., of Harvard Medical School as chairman.

1897   Society of College Gymnasium Directors founded

German gymnastics in the United States in the late 1800s.

outdoor gymnasium, taught the first turner exercises on apparatus in this country, and translated Friedrich Jahn's treatise on gymnastics into English. In addition, Harvard students and Bostonians were also taught turner gymnastics by German immigrants in the 1820s. The interest in turner gymnastics dissipated when these Germans ceased to teach and because this system's emphasis on strength-developing work on apparatus failed to appeal to sports-minded Americans.

When a second wave of political refugees fled Germany beginning in 1848, they, too, brought their love of gymnastics to the United States, where they established turner societies (beginning in 1848 in Cincinnati) and turner festivals (in 1851). These **turnfests** featured thousands of turners who exhibited their physical prowess on German apparatus and through running and jumping activities. In 1866, they founded the Normal School of the North American Gymnastic Union in New York City to prepare teachers of German gymnastics. When most German immigrants migrated to the Midwest, they settled in isolated communities and maintained their national identity, including their gymnastics programs. Gradually, these turner societies broadened their programs to include social functions and exercises appropriate for the entire family. Later in the 1800s they introduced the turner system into several schools, although it was modified with Adolph Spiess' school gymnastics principles. The influence of German gymnastics on programs in the United States was limited because of its regional nature and because of the emphasis on strength development and nationalism. However, during the late 1800s and early 1900s, many schools and colleges incorporated exercises on German apparatus into their programs. Some of these apparatus, such as the parallel bars, rings, and balance beam, remain vital parts of the sport of gymnastics.

EARLY AMERICANS WHO INFLUENCED PHYSICAL EDUCATION PROGRAMS

Catharine Beecher, the first American to design a program of exercises for American children, tried to get daily physical activity into the public schools. As director of the Hartford (Connecticut) Female Seminary beginning in 1824, and later, when she founded the Western Female Institute in Cincinnati in 1837, she introduced girls to **calisthenics.** At the latter school, she set aside 30 minutes per half day for this program of exercises, which was designed to promote health, beauty, and strength. Beecher's objective was to aid girls in improving their vitality so that they could better fulfill their missions in life as wives and mothers. She expanded her concepts from a *Course of Calisthenics for Young Ladies,* which she wrote in 1832 primarily for girls, to *A Manual of Physiology and Calisthenics for Schools and Families,* published in 1856. In this book, Beecher advocated the introduction of physical training in the American schools for all children. Borrowing from the therapeutic concepts of Swedish gymnastics as developed by Per Henrik Ling, Beecher, through her writings and school programs, emphasized exercises that could be executed at home without a teacher, using diagrams from her books as guides.

Although Beecher's efforts did not achieve widespread results, she did influence another American. Dioclesian Lewis was a promulgator of causes for the day, including the abolition of slavery, temperance, women's rights, and health. In 1860 at the convention of the American Institute of Instruction, Lewis had the opportunity to bring his concept of **light gymnastics** to the attention of educators from around the country and especially, Boston. For his program, Lewis borrowed from Beecher's calisthenics, adding light apparatus such as bean bags, dumbbells, Indian clubs, and wands. He also borrowed from Swedish gymnastics their special emphasis on treatment of curvature of the spine and other chronic maladies. As a result of his promotional efforts, Boston adopted his system in their elementary schools. To prepare teachers to instruct children in light gymnastics, he founded the Normal Institute for Physical Education in 1861, the first institute of its kind. A **normal school** was a specialized institution for preparing students to become teachers in one or more subjects.

The 10-week program of study at the Normal Institute for Physical Education included instruction in anatomy, physiology, hygiene, and gymnastics. Seemingly ahead of his time, Lewis believed in equity among the genders, cardiovascular

Lewis' light gymnastics.

conditioning, and anthropometric measurements to demonstrate the success of his program in improving the health of students. He also emphasized that exercises done to the accompaniment of music would result in more activity and more enjoyment.

The first required college physical education program was begun, in 1860, at Amherst College because its president was concerned about the health of the students. This paramount concern led to the hiring of Edward Hitchcock, a physician. As director of the Department of Hygiene and Physical Education, Hitchcock gave health lectures, served as college physician, and supervised the required physical exercises for all students. As was true of most of the early physical educators, Hitchcock's primary credential for the job was a medical degree. Borrowing from Lewis' light gymnastics, Hitchcock's program, led by squad captains, included class exercises to the accompaniment of music. Students had class four days per week, and were allowed to use a portion of their class time to practice sports skills or to exercise on the horizontal bars, rings, ropes, and vaulting horses. Hitchcock also administered a battery of bodily, or **anthropometric,** measurements, such as height, weight, chest girth, and lung capacity, to evaluate the effects of the program on students and to compare their progress from year to year.

A second noteworthy college physical education program was developed by Dudley Sargent at Harvard University beginning in 1879, when he was hired to direct the newly opened Hemenway Gymnasium. Since no required physical education program existed at Harvard, Sargent, who was also a physician, used an individualized approach to encourage students to exercise. Based on numerous anthropometric measurements, Sargent prescribed a series of exercises to meet each student's physical needs, using chest expanders and developers, leg

Class exercises at Amherst College.

machines, rowing machines, and other apparatus that he had designed. Opposed to strict German gymnastics and to light gymnastics programs, Sargent encouraged students to participate in baseball, bowling, boxing, fencing, rowing, and running in addition to their individual conditioning programs.

A brief summary of the contributions of the early leaders in physical education in the United States is provided in the box on pages 234–235.

EARLY SWEDISH GYMNASTICS IN THE UNITED STATES

The first American introduction to Swedish gymnastics as a complete system occurred in 1883, when a Norwegian, Hartvig Nissen, opened a Swedish Health Institute in Washington, D.C. Two years later Nils Posse, a graduate of the Royal Gymnastics Central Institute in Stockholm, introduced Swedish gymnastics in Boston. Impressed by Posse's program, philanthropist Mary Hemenway volunteered to furnish the Boston School Committee free teacher training in Swedish gymnastics, if the schools would offer this program to children. This led Hemenway to finance the establishment of the Boston Normal School of Gymnastics in 1889. Hemenway selected Amy Morris Homans for its director; Nils Posse became the first instructor. The graduates of this school taught in the Boston schools and nationally, especially in women's colleges, spreading Swedish gymnastics. Edward Hartwell, Director of Physical Training for the Boston public schools beginning in 1890, was also a strong supporter of Swedish gymnastics. Previously, he had directed the Johns Hopkins University gymnasium, where he experimented with many of the principles that Dudley Sargent advocated.

EARLY LEADERS IN PHYSICAL EDUCATION IN THE UNITED STATES

Charles Follen (1796–1840)
Established gymnasium in Boston (1826)
Taught German gymnastics to Harvard University students (1826–1828)

Charles Beck (1798–1866)
Hired as first physical education teacher in the United States (1825)
Taught at Round Hill School (1825–1830)

Catharine Beecher (1800–1878)
Taught at the Hartford Female Seminary (1824)
Started the Western Female Institute (1837)
Promoted calisthenics in American schools for boys and girls

Dioclesian Lewis (1823–1888)
Developed light gymnastics with handheld apparatus
Started the Normal Institute for Physical Education (1861)

Edward Hitchcock, M.D. (1828–1911)
Served as Professor of Hygiene and Physical Education at Amherst College (1861–1911)
Elected first president of the Association for the Advancement of Physical Education (1885)
Led in development of anthropometric measurements of males

Amy Morris Homans (1848–1933)
Directed the Boston Normal School of Gymnastics (1889–1909)
Directed the Department of Hygiene and Physical Education at Wellesley College (1909–1918)
Founded the Association of Directors of Physical Education for Women (1915)

Dudley Sargent, M.D. (1849–1924)
Directed the Hemenway Gymnasium at Harvard University (1879–1919)
Led in development of anthropometric measurements of males
Founded the Sargent Normal School (1881)
Founded the Harvard Summer School (1887)

Edward Hartwell, M.D. (1850–1922)
Instructed (1882) and directed (1885–1890) the gymnasium at Johns Hopkins University
Directed physical training for the Boston public schools (1890–1897)

William Anderson, M.D. (1860–1947)
Initiated the meeting that led to the formation of the Association for the Advancement of
    Physical Education (1885)
Founded the Chautauqua Summer School of Physical Education (1886)
Founded the Brooklyn (Anderson) Normal School (1886)

(continued)

EARLY LEADERS IN PHYSICAL EDUCATION IN THE UNITED STATES (CONTINUED)

Hartvig Nissen
Introduced Swedish gymnastics at the Swedish Health Institute in Washington, D.C. (1883)
Served as assistant director (1891–1897) and then director (1897–1900) of physical training for the Boston public schools
Taught at the Harvard Summer School and the Sargent Normal School and directed the Posse-Nissen School

Nils Posse (1862–1895)
Graduated from the Royal Gymnastics Central Institute
Led in instruction of Swedish gymnastics in the United States (1885–1895)
Taught at the Boston Normal School of Gymnastics (1889)
Started the Posse Normal School (1890)

Delphine Hanna (1854–1941)
Taught at Oberlin College (1885–1920)
Became the first female professor of physical education (1903)
Initiated anthropometric measurements of females
Taught Luther Gulick, Thomas Wood, Jay Nash, and Jesse Williams

THE BATTLE OF THE SYSTEMS

Between 1885 and 1900, a leading topic for discussion among physical educators was which system of gymnastics could provide a unified, national program for the United States. This raging controversy became known as the **Battle of the Systems.** Although there was some overlap between programs, in general the German and Swedish systems and those advanced by various Americans developed and vied for supporters (see Figure 8.1 and the box on page 237).

In an attempt to introduce Swedish gymnastics to the general public and to leaders in physical training and thus gain its acceptance as *the* program for American schools, Mary Hemenway financed the Boston Conference on Physical Training in 1889. Under the capable direction of Amy Morris Homans, this conference was highly successful and was one of the most important conferences in physical education ever held in the United States. Its significance can be attributed to the exposure given to the various programs existing at that time. German gymnastics, Swedish gymnastics, Hitchcock's program, Sargent's system, and others were explained and the merits of each was discussed. Sargent, after explaining his program, proposed an answer to the search for an American system:

> What America most needs is the happy combination which the European nations are trying to effect: the strength-giving qualities of the German gymnasium, the active and energetic properties of the English sports, the grace and suppleness acquired from French calisthenics, and the beautiful poise and mechanical precision of the Swedish free movement, all regulated, systematized, and adapted to our peculiar needs and institutions. (Barrows, 1899, page 76)

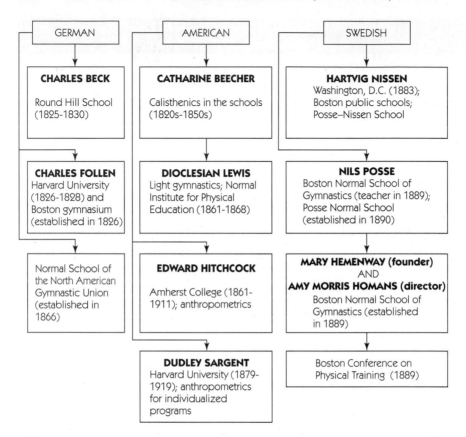

FIGURE 8.1

Leaders in early American physical education.

Although the leaders in physical education at this conference were exposed to the various systems, no one system was found to meet completely the needs of American programs because each seemed to have its weaknesses. Still, the Boston Conference provided an opportunity for leaders to learn about the various systems and to exchange ideas for the future promotion of American physical education.

Although German gymnastics in the Midwest and Swedish gymnastics in the Northeast were widely accepted, few states mandated physical education. In 1866, California passed a law providing for twice-a-day exercises for a minimum of five minutes to promote health and bodily vigor, but it was short-lived. Ohio's 1892 law was the first lasting physical education law. Louisiana (in 1894), Wisconsin (in 1897), North Dakota (in 1899), and Pennsylvania (in 1901) passed similar legislation. In the late 1800s most colleges included German and Swedish gymnastics in their physical education programs, but they also borrowed from Hitchcock's program and Sargent's principles and apparatus.

BATTLE OF THE SYSTEMS

System	Purpose	Advocates
German gymnastics	Developed individual abilities and healthy, strong youth for war or emergencies using apparatus	German turners including Carl Betz, C.G. Rathman, George Brosius, and William Stecher
Swedish gymnastics	Promoted health, correct expression, and beauty of performance using exact movement patterns	Hartvig Nissen; Nils Posse; Amy Morris Homans; Edward Hartwell; and women's colleges
Hitchcock's system	Emphasized hygiene through required exercises with light apparatus	Edward Hitchcock
Sargent's system	Advocated hygienic, educative, recreative, and remedial aims through individualized exercises on apparatus	Dudley Sargent; Delphine Hanna; women's colleges
Association gymnastics	Contributed to the development of the all-around man	YMCA directors

ESTABLISHMENT OF NORMAL SCHOOLS FOR PHYSICAL EDUCATION

One means by which the various programs were promoted was the development of normal, or teacher training, schools. The 1880s were especially noteworthy: six institutions were established to prepare physical education teachers either in a specific system or in an eclectic program that borrowed from several systems. In 1881, Dudley Sargent began teaching women from Harvard Annex and other women and men who were interested in his apparatus and methodology. At the resultant Sargent Normal School, he provided a general curriculum based on a theoretical, scientific foundation along with various activities of a practical nature.

Delphine Hanna took courses from Dioclesian Lewis, Nils Posse, and Dudley Sargent; she attended both the Sargent Normal School and the Harvard Summer School of Physical Education. The program she initiated at coeducational Oberlin College in 1885 closely resembled Sargent's. Besides using many of the pieces of apparatus that he designed, Hanna emphasized anthropometric measurements of female students to assess their individual development. The scope of her work included teaching a class to train men to instruct their fellow male students. Among her first students were Thomas Wood and Luther Gulick, later luminaries in physical education.

Harvard University's Hemenway Gymnasium was equipped with
exercise apparatus designed by Dudley Sargent.

The box on page 239 summarizes the early teacher training institutions in the
United States and their curricula.

A unique normal school established in 1885 in Springfield, Massachusetts,
was the Young Men's Christian Association (YMCA) Training School. The YMCA's
goal, through its association gymnastics, was to develop the all-around man and
to send him out as a physical director to the increasing number of YMCAs, both
nationally and internationally. (The first YMCA gymnasiums had opened in 1869
in New York City, San Francisco, and Washington, D.C.)

In 1886, William Anderson established two additional institutions. While teaching in New York, he started the Brooklyn Normal School; later, when he became the
director of the Yale University gymnasium, he moved this school to New Haven,
Connecticut, and renamed it the Anderson Normal School. Anderson, along with
Jay Seaver, also worked with leaders in the Chautauqua movement to set up the
Chautauqua Summer School of Physical Education. The curricula at both schools focused on a generalized approach with theoretical and practical course work.

In 1887, Dudley Sargent succeeded in gaining approval to open the Harvard
Summer School of Physical Education, which provided opportunities for teachers
already in the field to start or to continue their professional training in physical

A class at the Sargent Normal School performing an Indian club routine.

EARLY PROFESSIONAL PREPARATION INSTITUTIONS OR NORMAL SCHOOLS IN THE UNITED STATES

Years	Founder	Name	Program
1861–1868	Dioclesian Lewis	Normal Institute for Physical Education	Light gymnastics
1866–1951	Turners	Normal School of the North American Gymnastic Union	German gymnastics
1881–1929	Dudley Sargent	Sargent Normal School	Theoretical and practical curriculum
1885–today	Young Men's Christian Association	YMCA Training School	Association gymnastics
1886–1920s	William Anderson	Chautauqua Summer School of Physical Education	Advanced theoretical and practical curriculum
1886–1953	William Anderson	Brooklyn (Anderson) Normal School	Theoretical and practical curriculum
1887–1932	Dudley Sargent	Harvard Summer School of Physical Education	Advanced theoretical and practical curriculum
1889–1909	Mary Hemenway and Amy Morris Homans	Boston Normal School of Gymnastics	Swedish gymnastics
1890–1942	Nils Posse	Posse Normal School	Swedish gymnastics

WEB CONNECTIONS

1. www.ymca.com
   Check out this site for more information about the Young Men's
   Christian Association and its heritage in the promotion of sports.

2. www.ncaa.org
   In addition to extensive information about the rules and governance of
   intercollegiate athletics, this site provides some historical information
   with a virtual tour of the NCAA's Hall of Champions.

3. www.aausports.org/ysnim/home/aau_index.jsp
   This site provides information about one of the largest, multisport,
   volunteer sports organizations in the United States. The organization
   promotes amateur sports and physical fitness programs.

4. www.northnet.org/stlawrenceaauw/timeline.htm
   Check out this site for an extensive timeline of the significant events in
   women's sports.

5. http://longago.com/sports.html
   Examine some of the sports costumes worn by males and females in
   the 1800s.

6. www.hickoksports.com/history/collfhof.shtml
   This site provides historical information aplenty about men's college
   sports.

education. This summer school was particularly important to the expansion of
knowledge in physical education since at this time no graduate programs existed.
The diversity and breadth of the offerings, along with its outstanding faculty,
made attendance at the Harvard Summer School prestigious; and a certificate
from the school was highly respected.

Swedish gymnastics was initially taught at the Boston Normal School of Gymnastics in 1889 and continued to be taught following the school's affiliation with
Wellesley College beginning in 1909. Amy Morris Homans directed the programs
at both of these institutions. In 1890, Nils Posse established the Posse Normal
School, which also promoted Swedish gymnastics.

Beginning in the late 1800s, normal schools were replaced with teacher
preparation programs that offered undergraduate college degrees. At Oberlin
College, in 1885, Delphine Hanna initiated a physical education teacher curriculum for women students; it became a four-year degree program in 1900. Only
programs at Stanford University, the University of California, the University of
Nebraska, and Harvard University preceded it.

This country's first degree program in physical education (a Bachelor of Science in Anatomy, Physiology, and Physical Training) was established in 1891 at Harvard University. Carl Fitz, a physician, worked with Dudley Sargent in the development and delivery of this program, which was designed to prepare gymnasium directors to teach, and to provide general preparation for individuals wishing to pursue the study of medicine. Working at the Physiological Laboratory, which was associated with the Lawrence Scientific School, Fitz focused on the importance of research in the relatively new field of physical education and was one of the foremost researchers in the experimental study of physiology of exercise in the 1890s.

FOUNDING OF THE NATIONAL ASSOCIATION

In the late 1800s, physical education programs offered a potpourri of activities reflecting the philosophies and interests of their leaders. As a young teacher, William Anderson recognized this diversity and the fact that few opportunities existed for the exchange of curricula and philosophical ideas among individuals interested in physical development. After seeking support from two recognized leaders in the field, Edward Hitchcock and Dudley Sargent, Anderson invited gymnastics teachers, ministers, journalists, school principals, college presidents, and others engaged in the promotion of physical training to meet at Adelphi Academy in Brooklyn, New York, on November 27, 1885, to discuss their various programs and to decide whether sufficient interest existed to regularly provide a forum for professional interchange. Of the 60 people who attended, 49 responded positively, resulting in the formation of the Association for the Advancement of Physical Education, today's American Alliance for Health, Physical Education, Recreation and Dance. (The box below traces its various name changes.)

Edward Hitchcock of Amherst College was elected the first president. Dudley Sargent, who was selected as the first vice president, later served as the third, fifth, and eighth president. William Anderson agreed to serve as the first secretary. Other recognized leaders in attendance included Dioclesian Lewis; Henry Ward Beecher, clergyman and brother of Catharine Beecher; Helen Putnam, head of the Vassar College Gymnasium, who was elected as one of the vice presidents; and William Blaikie, author of the acclaimed book *How to Get Strong and How to Stay So* and the second president of the Association. This organization's objectives,

THE CHANGING NAMES OF THE NATIONAL ORGANIZATION

1885	Association for the Advancement of Physical Education
1886	American Association for the Advancement of Physical Education
1903	American Physical Education Association
1937	American Association for Health and Physical Education
1938	American Association for Health, Physical Education and Recreation
1974	American Alliance for Health, Physical Education and Recreation
1979	American Alliance for Health, Physical Education, Recreation and Dance

established in 1886, were "to disseminate knowledge concerning physical education, to improve the methods, and by meetings of the members to bring those interested in the subject into closer relation to each other" (Lee & Bennett, 1960,
page 27). Discussions in the early meetings focused on the strengths and attributes of the various programs or systems, methods of teaching, anthropometric
measurements, military drills, athletics, and hygiene. To provide another forum to
share professional knowledge and experiences, the *American Physical Education
Review* was published, beginning in 1896.

The American Association for the Advancement of Physical Education's
(AAAPE) first contact with the National Education Association (NEA) occurred
in 1893. The NEA asked Edward Hartwell, 1891–92 AAAPE President, to chair a
departmental conference on physical education and hygiene at the International
Congress on Education held in connection with the 1893 Chicago World's Fair.
Two years later the NEA established a permanent Department of Physical Education; in 1924, this became the Department of School Health and Physical
Education. The American Association for Health and Physical Education merged
with this department when it became affiliated with the NEA in 1937.

PROMOTION OF PLAY FOR CHILDREN

While organized school programs were being established, the play movement
outside the schools gained support and momentum. The industrialization of the
United States directly influenced this development. Immigration and the massive

Play is a child's favorite activity.

influx of Americans into urban areas, resulted in overcrowded cities with miles and miles of brick tenements. In an effort to provide suitable play space for children in this environment, sand boxes were first built in Boston in 1885. In 1888, New York passed the first state legislation that led to an organized play area for children. By 1899, the Massachusetts Emergency and Hygiene Association sponsored 21 playgrounds.

Boston constructed the Charlesbank outdoor gymnasium in 1889. Jane Addams' Hull House, a Chicago settlement house started in 1894, included a model playground. Religious leaders, school administrators, philanthropists, and social workers worked together or alone in the late 1800s to ensure that children were provided both places and opportunities to play. In part, these efforts demonstrated a genuine concern for the welfare of children and for society as a whole, and in part these playgrounds were used as a method of social control. That is, the early leaders in the playground movement sought to use play to "Americanize" the myriad immigrants pouring into the cities.

DEVELOPMENT OF AMATEUR SPORTS

Americans' love for sports preceded the founding of the United States but really blossomed after the Civil War, as baseball became the national sport for men of all ages and for amateurs as well as professionals. Races between cyclists, horses, runners, and yachts, with associated gambling, were especially attractive to the upper class. Normally these races, as well as sports such as cricket, golf, and tennis, were organized or played by members of elite social clubs. The New York Athletic Club, founded in 1868, led in the formation of the Amateur Athletic Union (AAU) in 1879. This organization sought to promote amateur sports for upper-class males, similar to the British ideal of the pure amateur who played sports for the love of the game. Paid, professional athletes were distained because they played for the money; hence, the AAU sought to check the evils associated with professionals playing sports. In 1853, Scottish immigrants, through their Caledonian games, began to promote their native sports, such as hammer throwing, putting stones, and tossing the caber (lifting a large wooden pole and flipping it end over end). The Czechoslovakian Sokols also promoted physical activities through mass displays in national festivals, such as that first held in 1879 in New York City. The box on the next page lists many of the sports organizations that helped promote amateur sports during the late 1800s.

Frenchman Pierre de Coubertin, through persistent efforts, revived the Olympic Games and the spirit of amateurism that honored the integration of mind, body, and spirit. The classical restoration of the Panathenaic Stadium, in pure white marble, provided an awe-inspiring setting for the opening of the Athens Olympic Games on April 5, 1896. Male athletes (311) representing 13 countries competed. While track and field athletics occupied center stage, athletes also competed in cycling, fencing, gymnastics, lawn tennis, shooting, swimming, weight lifting, and wrestling.

Jim Connolly, one of the 13 athletes representing the United States, captured the first victory in the hop, step, and jump (triple jump) and was honored by the

AMATEUR SPORTS ORGANIZATIONS

1871	National Rifle Association
1875	National Bowling League
1878	Cricketer's Association of the United States
1879	National Archery Association
1879	Amateur Athletic Union
1880	League of American Wheelmen (cycling)
1880	National Canoe Association
1881	United States National Lawn Tennis Association
1882	National Croquet Association
1884	United States Skating Association
1887	American Trotting Association
1892	United States Golf Association

hoisting of an American flag while the national anthem played. Athletes from the United States dominated the track and field events, with silver first-place medals in the 100-meters, 400-meters, 110-meters, hurdles, broad jump, high jump, pole vault, shot put, and discus throw. Greek athletes placed in swimming, cycling, fencing, gymnastics, and shooting and won the marathon. Germans captured most of the gymnastics medals.

Two sports were developed in the YMCA and promoted by this association. In 1891, at the YMCA Training School, Canadian James Naismith developed the rules for and initiated the first game of basketball. This game was designed as an indoor sport to fill the void between football and baseball seasons. Five years later, William Morgan, at a YMCA in Holyoke, Massachusetts, originated volleyball as a less vigorous indoor game for businessmen. Both sports met a need and found more of their early adherents in the YMCAs than in the private clubs and colleges. The YMCA promoted both sports internationally and especially urged American youth to play basketball.

Gambling had been associated with sports since colonial times when owners and spectators bet on the outcome of horse races. Americans, from all levels of society, wagered on cockfights, wrestling bouts, boxing matches, walking contests, and baseball games throughout the 1800s. One of the evils the AAU sought to eliminate in its promotion of amateur athletics was gambling. Baseball promoters had to overcome the perception that all players and fans bet on the outcome of professional games. Nevertheless, college students enthusiastically gambled on their sports competitions, especially football.

COLLEGIATE SPORTS FOR MEN

Sports on college campuses were initially organized by students as extracurricular activities, to the displeasure of administrators and faculty, who viewed them as extraneous to the mission of higher education. The first intercollegiate event,

Men's intercollegiate basketball was a slower-paced game years ago when a center jump followed each basket scored.

in 1852, matched Harvard and Yale in rowing. The two early favorites in collegiate sports were baseball, which first matched Amherst against Williams in 1859, and football, which actually began as a soccer-like game between Princeton and Rutgers in 1869. Students founded organizations to standardize rules for competitions in rowing, baseball, football, and track.

College faculties paid little attention to sports until they began to infringe on students' academic work. Missed classes, decreased academic performance, injuries, gambling, property damage on campus and in nearby towns during victory celebrations, playing against professional teams, commercialization, and a general overemphasis on athletics compelled faculties to take action. In 1882, a group of Harvard University faculty members recommended that a committee of three faculty members should oversee athletics. Three years later this committee was expanded to include two students and one alumnus. In 1888, it again expanded to an equal representation of three faculty, three students, and three alumni. Representatives of nine eastern colleges met in 1883 as the Intercollegiate Athletic Conference and proposed that colleges should not compete against professional teams, no professional athletes should coach college teams, students should be permitted only four years of participation in athletics, contests should take place only on campuses, and faculties should control athletics. Because only three colleges ratified them, these regulations failed to take effect.

In 1895, the Intercollegiate Conference of Faculty Representatives (today's Big Ten Conference), which was comprised of one faculty member from each of seven midwestern institutions, adopted rules requiring all players to be enrolled in college, all transfer students to wait six months before being eligible to play on a team, and all athletes to maintain the required academic standards in order to be eligible to play. These few efforts, however, did not control the overwhelming

The University of Virginia versus the University of North Carolina in baseball in 1895.
(Photo courtesy North Carolina Collection, UNC Library at Chapel Hill.)

growth of student-initiated and student-administered intercollegiate athletics in the late 1800s. The box on page 247 chronicles the initiation of collegiate sports organizations and competitions, primarily for men.

COLLEGIATE SPORTS FOR WOMEN

In the late 1800s, archery, croquet, and tennis were among the first sports to attract women as participants because these activities did not require revealing clothing and were nonvigorous. Male and female attitudes about proper feminine behavior and medical opinion that vigorous activity would irreparably harm women's reproductive capabilities combined to prevent women from engaging in aggressive and highly competitive sports. Bicycling introduced a radical change in attire with the bloomer costume, or divided skirt, which allowed freedom from the appropriate attire of the day, which included voluminous skirts and petticoats and tightly laced corsets. Bloomers and middy blouses became the accepted costume for gymnastics and other physical activities, with students at the Sargent Normal School among the first to wear them.

Societal attitudes toward women in the 1800s closely paralleled the Victorian perception that females were weak, objects to be placed on pedestals for admiration, but not to be taken seriously because they were incapable of mental achievements. Females who sought schooling, and especially college attendance, encountered ridicule and suspicions about their femininity. Their roles as wives and mothers were viewed as contradictory to the development of their minds.

DEVELOPMENT OF COLLEGIATE SPORTS FOR MEN AND WOMEN

1843	First collegiate rowing club started at Yale
1844	Harvard forms a rowing club
1852	First intercollegiate sports competition in rowing occurs as Harvard defeats Yale by four lengths
1859	College Union Regatta Association established by Harvard, Yale, Brown, and Trinity
1864	Haverford beats Penn 89–60 in first intercollegiate cricket competition
1869	Rutgers outscores Princeton (6–4) in the first intercollegiate football game
1871	Rowing Association of American Colleges formed
1873	First intercollegiate track and field competition held in conjunction with the intercollegiate rowing regatta
1876	Intercollegiate Football Association established
1876	Intercollegiate Association of Amateur Athletes of America formed to govern track and field
1877	Harvard shoots 20 points better than Yale in the first intercollegiate rifle competition
1877	New York University defeats Manhattan (2–0) in the first intercollegiate lacrosse contest
1883	Intercollegiate Lawn Tennis Association founded
1883	Harvard's J. S. Clark wins the singles and the doubles (with P. E. Presbrey) events during the first intercollegiate tennis tournament
1883	Intercollegiate Athletic Conference established by Harvard, Princeton, and Cornell
1884	Penn defeats Wesleyan (16–10) in the first intercollegiate polo contest
1890	First intercollegiate cross country saw Penn beat Cornell
1894	Harvard outscores Columbia (5–4) in the first intercollegiate fencing meet
1895	Brown beats Harvard (4–2) in the first intercollegiate ice hockey game
1895	Intercollegiate Conference of Faculty Representatives formed by midwestern colleges
1896	Yale beats Columbia by 35 holes in the first intercollegiate golf event with six-man teams
1896	First intercollegiate swimming meet held with Penn defeating Columbia and Yale
1896	First intercollegiate sports competition for women in basketball occurs as Stanford defeats California (2–1)
1899	Penn surpasses Columbia (2–0) in the first intercollegiate water polo contest
1899	Intercollegiate Cross Country Association of Amateur Athletes of America established
1899	Yale's gymnastics team defeats competitors from 19 institutions in the first intercollegiate gymnastics meet

Catharine Beecher's calisthenics and Swedish gymnastics with their therapeutic emphasis became acceptable because they complemented the feminine role. When college women enthusiastically participated in baseball, basketball, and rowing, many physicians and some women strongly opposed such vigorous exertion. They argued that although mild activity such as walking, gardening, or moderate exercise could benefit women, an overexpenditure of energy might leave them infertile, hopelessly depleted of the energy needed to survive childbirth or motherhood. Not until medical opinions gradually changed in the twentieth century did these restrictive opinions dissipate as women began to be viewed as capable of physical and mental achievement.

Female archers in 1890s attire.

Women in the upper socioeconomic strata shared their husbands' and fathers' desires to engage in conspicuous consumption. The rich, in flaunting their wealth, popularized sports such as archery, golf, tennis, and yachting. In each case, these sports were organized at private clubs or in settings where social interaction between the sexes usually was a desired outcome. Following the lead of men, upper-class women began to compete nationally in archery (1879), tennis (1887), and golf (1896). Because of societal expectations, they always dressed in the latest fashions, many of which severely limited their mobility and skill development.

Women eagerly adopted basketball but adapted and modified its rules to make the game less strenuous and not as rough. A Committee on Women's Basketball was established by the American Association for the Advancement of Physical Education to standardize these rules. In 1896 the first intercollegiate contest between women from the University of California and Stanford University occurred. In addition to basketball, field days for track events and a few other sports became popular in the women's colleges in the 1890s.

SUMMARY

Early physical education in the United States evolved from recreational sports and games into organized school and college programs that either emphasized one system of gymnastics or combined exercises from various systems. Swedish and German gymnastics had their advocates, but neither found widespread national acceptance. Health and strength were favored outcomes, but even these did not seem to fully satisfy Americans' needs. Prior to 1900, teachers of physical education had completed programs in normal schools, and a fledgling national

Senda Berenson, in the long skirt, with Smith College students in Northampton, Massachusetts, where women played in their first public basketball game on March 22, 1893. (Photo courtesy Basketball Hall of Fame.)

association existed, but a unified, national program had not yet emerged. With the popularization in the late 1800s of children's play and of sports in amateur clubs and on college campuses, the stage was set for the development in the 1900s of an American program based primarily on playing sports and games.

CAREER PERSPECTIVE

DUDLEY ALLEN SARGENT
(1849–1924)

EDUCATION
B.A., Bowdoin College
M.D., Yale Medical School

BACKGROUND

Dudley Sargent, one of the most influential leaders in physical education in the United States, contributed significantly in the areas of individualized programs, measurements of the dimensions and the capacities of the body, and teacher training. He also accepted leadership positions in professional organizations, wrote numerous papers, and made scholarly presentations.

After an early career as a professional acrobat, Sargent obtained a bachelor's degree from Bowdoin College and a medical degree from Yale Medical School. While a student at these institutions for nine years, he worked as Director of Gymnastics (at Bowdoin) and Director of the Gymnasium (at Yale). In 1879, he began his 40-year tenure at Harvard University after being named Director of the Hemenway Gymnasium and Assistant Professor of Physical Training.

ACCOMPLISHMENTS

Sargent immediately implemented an individualized program that focused on meeting the needs of the Harvard students who were physically underdeveloped. Sargent took a series of anthropometric measurements and, based on these, prescribed an individual exercise program for each student. Measurements of each student's progress were taken periodically and followed by changes in the prescribed program. Sargent opposed the heavy German apparatus as well as Dioclesian Lewis' light apparatus and instead designed or improved devices adaptable to students' various abilities. In addition to chest weights and pulleys, he provided chest expanders and developers, leg machines, inclined planes, and hydraulic rowing machines—about 80 developing machines in all.

Athletes' abilities were also measured through various tests. Rather than opposing athletics, as some detractors have accused, Sargent encouraged students to engage in boxing, rowing, fencing, bowling, running, and baseball. Sargent's anthropometric measurement procedures and charts for athletes and all other students were widely used and contributed to physical education's entry into the scientific world.

Also a pioneer in the realm of teacher training, Sargent in 1881 opened the Sanatory Gymnasium to students at Harvard Annex and to women and men who wanted to become teachers of physical education. Although the resultant Sargent Normal School was coeducational between 1904 and 1914, few men enrolled. The significant female enrollment made it the largest normal school in the United States as its more than 3000 graduates spread the Sargent system throughout the country. The school's eclectic curriculum consisted of theoretical courses emphasizing the sciences and practical exercises as varied as free movements, light gymnastics using dumbbells and Indian clubs, marching, sports, and heavy gymnastics.

The Harvard Summer School of Physical Education, established by Sargent in 1887, became the most significant source of professional education in the United States during physical education's early years. During a time when teachers had minimal or no training in physical education, Harvard Summer School met teachers' needs in an exemplary manner. An eminent faculty, often the recognized authorities in their subjects or activities, provided both theoretical and practical instruction, resulting in school administrators highly regarding a certificate from Harvard Summer School. Most of the students were teachers, but physicians, army officers, and other professionals attended, too. During its 46 summers of operation, more than 5000 students attended.

REVIEW QUESTIONS

1. What types of physical activities were considered recreation by the colonists in the 1700s? How did these differ by region of the country?
2. Why did German gymnastics not gain wide acceptance in the United States in the 1820s and between the 1850s and 1880s?
3. What constituted the program of hygiene and physical education at Amherst College?
4. What were the basic principles of Dudley Sargent's program for Harvard University students?
5. Why was the Boston Conference on Physical Training in 1889 significant?
6. Why were normal schools for physical education established, especially in the 1880s?
7. Why was the Association for the Advancement of Physical Education founded?
8. What events or developments led to the playground movement?
9. Why did the faculty get involved in men's intercollegiate athletics?
10. What types of physical activities were considered appropriate for females in the 1800s and why?

STUDENT ACTIVITIES

1. As a class, reenact a portion of the Boston Conference on Physical Training (1889) by having each student report on one of the following systems: Swedish, German, Edward Hitchcock's, or Dudley Sargent's.
2. Read about the founding of the first professional organization in physical education (today's American Alliance for Health, Physical Education, Recreation and Dance), and report your findings orally to the class or in a three-page paper.
3. By examining histories of your state or region, find the most popular sport or recreational activity for one of the following groups:

    Native American adult males
    Native American adult females

Native American children
Early male colonists
Early female colonists
Children of early colonists
Upper-class males in the 1800s
Upper-class females in the 1800s
Upper-class children in the 1800s
Middle-class males in the 1800s
Middle-class females in the 1800s
Middle-class children in the 1800s
Lower-class males in the 1800s
Lower-class females in the 1800s
Lower-class children in the 1800s

4. Research the name(s) and the starting date(s) of the oldest normal school(s) for physical education for males and for females in your state.
5. Investigate which college(s) in your state offered the first intercollegiate athletic competitions for men and for women. In which sports did these competitions occur?
6. Research any one of the individuals, events, or topics discussed in this chapter. Write a five-page paper about the major contributions of this individual, event, or topic to the history and growth of physical education and sport.

REFERENCES

Barrows IC: *Physical training,* Boston, 1899, George H. Ellis Press.

Lee M, Bennett BL: This is our heritage, *JOHPER* 31(4):27, 1960.

Oxendine JB: *American Indian sports heritage,* Champaign, Ill., 1988, Human Kinetics.

SUGGESTED READINGS

Borish LJ: The sporting past in American history, *OAH Mag of Hist* 7(1):3, 1992. This article reviews the role of sports from the Puritans to today and suggests how primary sources and scholarly articles about sport can be integrated into history courses.

Cazers G, Miller GA: The German contribution to American physical education: a historical perspective, *JOPERD* 71(6):44, 2000. This article recounts the origins of German gymnastics and its impact on programs in this country.

Daniels BC: *Puritans at play: leisure and recreation in colonial New England,* New York, 1995, St. Martin's Press. The author provides a balanced perspective about New England Puritan colonial life that included both somber attitudes and lighthearted fun.

Davenport J (ed.): The normal schools: exploring our heritage, *JOPERD* 65(3):25, 1994. This seven-part feature describes the contributions made by seven normal schools to the profession. Those described included Dioclesian Lewis' Normal Institute for Physical Education, the Sargent School for Physical Education, William Anderson's Brooklyn Normal School, the Harvard Summer School of Physical Education, the Boston Normal School of Gymnastics, the Posse Gymnasium, and the H. Sophie Newcomb Memorial College.

Hult JS, Trekell M: *A century of women's basketball: from frailty to final four,* Reston, VA, 1991, American Alliance for Health, Physical Education, Recreation and Dance. This book contains numerous articles that chronicle the rich history of girls' and women's basketball.

Lee M, Bennett B: Alliance centennial: 100 years of health, physical education, recreation and dance, *JOPERD* 56(4):17, 1985. This article reprints the "This Is Our Heritage" historical series in 15-year thematic sections that highlight significant occurrences related to the activities of today's American Alliance for Health, Physical Education, Recreation and Dance. It also chronicles the profession's major developments between 1960 and 1985.

Oxendine JB: *American Indian sports heritage,* Champaign, Ill., 1988, Human Kinetics. This book chronicles the sports and games in traditional Native American life with emphasis on ball games, footracing, children's play, and games of chance. The roles of leading Native American schools and the achievements of prominent athletes are acclaimed.

Park RJ: Physiology and anatomy are destiny!?: brains, bodies and exercise in nineteenth century American thought, *J of Sp Hist* 18:31, 1991. Using the biomedical literature of that period, the author concluded that one's physiology and anatomy—that is, the body as icon for gender—dictated athletics for men and modest exercise for women.

Smith RA: History of amateurism in men's intercollegiate athletics: the continuance of a 19th century anachronism in America, *Quest* 45:430, 1993. The myth of amateurism in intercollegiate athletics is analyzed and dispelled in this comprehensive history.

Struna NL: *People of prowess: sport, leisure, and labor,* Champaign, Ill., 1996, University of Illinois Press. This book tells the story of sporting pastimes during the colonial era.

9

TWENTIETH CENTURY PHYSICAL EDUCATION AND SPORT

KEY CONCEPTS

- The new physical education emphasized play, sport, games, outdoor activities, and educational developmentalism.
- Programs developing from the play movement, the rise of teacher training, the growth of women's physical education, the growing emphasis on fitness, the focus on physical movement, principles of the scientific movement, educational developmentalism, and social education contributed to twentieth century physical education and sport.
- Leadership from the national association and efforts to establish standards for teachers led to the recognition of physical education as a profession.
- Men's intercollegiate sports expanded from their interclass origins into commercialized businesses.
- Women's intercollegiate sports featured mass participation until the early 1970s, when competition, aided by Title IX legislation, became a primary goal.
- The children's play movement began with a recreational emphasis and revolved into a focus on fitness.
- Starting in the 1950s, youth sports expanded from value-oriented programs to adult-controlled leagues.
- The federal government mandated equal educational opportunities (including physical education), for individuals with disabilities and special needs.

Professional discussions concerning which system of gymnastics would best meet the needs of students in the United States continued into the early years of the twentieth century. Beginning in the 1920s, school physical education moved away from formalized exercise programs to curricula that included sports, games, aquatics, and outdoor activities with educational outcomes foremost. Two themes emerged in the middle of the twentieth century; education "through" the physical and education "of" the physical vied for advocates and influenced school physical education and sport curricula. Since the turn of the century, the popularity of athletics at all levels and for both sexes has expanded tremendously. Nonschool programs from mid-century until today offer sports competitions for individuals of all ages and skill levels, lifetime recreational activities, and fitness alternatives. Federal legislation mandating equal opportunity for participation in sports and physical activities for females and disabled individuals led to dramatic changes in school and nonschool programs. Today, people participate in physical activities to develop and maintain fitness and in lifetime sports for fun, fitness, and competition.

THE NEW PHYSICAL EDUCATION

By the end of the nineteenth century, no one gymnastics system had been adopted. The formal nature of the alternatives had failed to appeal to a broad base of physical educators and their students, who were seeking activities that offered competition, fun, and more freedom of expression.

Speaking at the International Congress on Education sponsored by the National Education Association in 1893, Thomas Wood articulated his vision for a new physical education.

> The great thought in physical education is not the education of the physical nature, but the relation of physical training to complete education, and then the effort to make the physical contribute its full share to the life of the individual, in environment, training, and culture. (page 621)

The **new physical education** focused on developing the whole individual through participation in play, sports, games, and natural, outdoor activities. The curriculum and philosophy of this new physical education was heavily influenced by and consistent with educational and psychological theories that were developing at that time.

Psychologist G. Stanley Hall made Clark University a center for child study after publishing his landmark book, *Adolescence* (1904), in which he defined the educational significance of children's developmental stages. Other leaders in the study of the individual, many of whom influenced each other's work, included William James, Edward Thorndike, William Kilpatrick, and John Dewey. They successfully integrated scientific education, educational developmentalism, and social education. Educational developmentalism, also known as the psychological movement, used children's play and other natural activities for learning. Teachers College of Columbia University nurtured the development and popularization of the latter two educational themes through faculty members Thorndike and Dewey, who were close associates of Hall.

Teachers College also contributed to the integration of educational developmentalism and social education into the new physical education. Thomas Wood taught there for 31 years. Rosalind Cassidy took a Teachers College degree, as did hundreds of physical educators in the middle decades of the 1900s. For 27 years Jesse Williams influenced Teachers College students to advocate for education through the physical as proposed by Wood and Cassidy. Williams was the primary advocate for seeking to achieve social outcomes through physical education and sport.

LEADERS IN THE NEW PHYSICAL EDUCATION

Luther Gulick and his roommate Thomas Wood discussed their mutual interest in physical education while at Oberlin College, where they were influenced by Delphine Hanna. In 1887 Luther Gulick became an instructor at the YMCA Training School in Springfield, Massachusetts, and, two years later, was named superintendent. While at the YMCA Training School, he emphasized sports in the physical directors' curriculum and started the YMCA's Athletic League to promote amateur sports. Stressing unity in the development of body, mind, and spirit, he designed the YMCA triangle (Figure 9.1), emblematic of the all-around man. He then moved to New York and taught before accepting the position of Director of Physical Training for the New York City public schools. Although Gulick supported gymnastics as the basis of school curricula, he founded the Public Schools Athletic League to provide after-school sports opportunities for boys, especially in track and field activities.

Another Gulick legacy was his promotion of play. In 1906, he helped establish the Playground Association of America and served as its first president. He also advocated for the provision of playgrounds and public recreation in this country, initiated (with his wife) the Campfire Girls in 1913, and led in the camping movement. In *A Philosophy of Play,* he powerfully articulated the importance of play as an educational force and helped begin the play movement within physical education.

For two years Thomas Wood directed the gymnasium work for men at Oberlin College. After receiving a medical degree at Columbia, he developed the undergraduate teacher training curriculum in physical education at Stanford University (beginning in 1891). Ten years later, he joined the faculty of Teachers College of Columbia University, where he led in the establishment of the first master's (1910) and doctor's (1924) degree programs in physical education. He was also instrumental in the development of health education as a

FIGURE 9.1
YMCA emblem designed by Luther Gulick.

separate field of study. *The New Physical Education,* which he co-authored with Rosalind Cassidy in 1927, provided the philosophical foundation for refocusing school programs from gymnastics to sports, games, dance, aquatics, and natural activities.

Rosalind Cassidy helped broaden and clarify the tenets of the new physical education during her professional career at Mills College in California. She helped develop and promote education through the physical, a leading theme for understanding physical education as the field that could uniquely contribute to the education of the whole person through physical activities. Through her voluminous writings, she also redefined physical education as the study of human movement.

Clark Hetherington was taught and greatly influenced by Wood at Stanford University. This influence is evident from Hetherington's coining of the term "new physical education" and from his advocacy of organic, psychomotor, character, and intellectual development as descriptive of physical education's objectives. G. Stanley Hall, a second mentor for Hetherington, also emphasized educational developmentalism, which paralleled Hetherington's philosophy that play was a child's chief business in life. At the University of Missouri, the University of Wisconsin, New York University, and Stanford University, Hetherington helped establish undergraduate physical education programs. At New York University he led in the development of graduate degree programs.

One of the first graduates of New York University's Ph.D. program in physical education was Jay Nash. Nash had served as the California Assistant Supervisor of Physical Education under Hetherington before joining the faculty at New York University in 1926 as Hetherington's replacement. Nash stressed that recreational skills should be learned early in life and could provide enjoyment throughout life. Fearing an overemphasis on spectating in the United States, Nash stated that school programs should teach carry-over, or lifetime, sports to encourage people to adopt active lifestyles; that is, people should be educated for leisure.

Influenced by Wood and Cassidy's concept of complete education through the physical and John Dewey's social education theories, Jesse Williams believed that the development of physical skills in the schools could only be justified if such activities helped to educate the total child. Williams' theories of **education through the physical,** which prompted educating a child to live in a democratic society through social and intellectual interactions within physical education, became a part of the standard curriculum in the schools. Through his 41 books and the students he influenced in the highly regarded graduate physical education programs at Teachers College of Columbia University, Williams became one of the most influential leaders in physical education, especially between 1930 and 1960.

Figure 9.2 summarizes the influence of these new physical educators on each other. It is interesting that Nash signaled a change in the professional training of physical educators. Whereas Gulick, Wood, and Williams held medical degrees, Nash earned a Ph.D. in physical education.

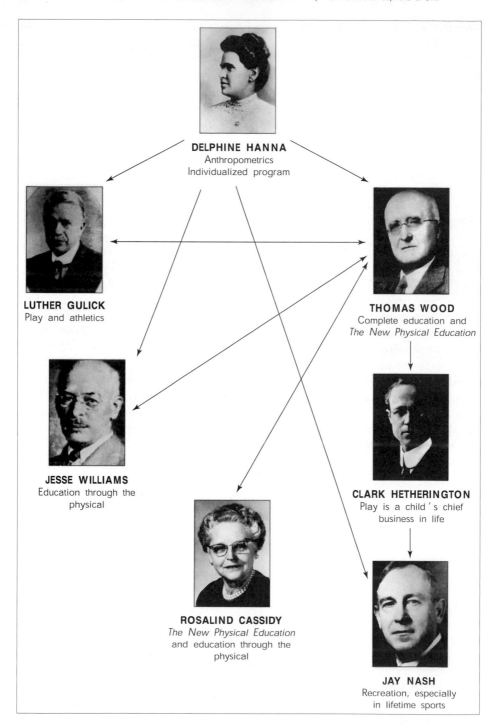

FIGURE 9.2

New physical educators.

MAJOR DEVELOPMENTS IN PHYSICAL EDUCATION

Several parallel movements built on the advances of the new physical education, expanding the educational curriculum even further. These developments included the play movement, the rise of teacher training, the growth of women's physical education, the education of the physical movement, the growing emphasis on fitness, the focus on human movement, and the influence of the scientific movement, educational developmentalism, and social education in the schools. Many of the leaders in these developments are highlighted in the box on pages 261–262.

The Play Movement

Luther Gulick proclaimed the importance of play for children, especially outside of the schools. In New York, he established the Public Schools Athletic League's (PSAL) sports competitions for boys and the Girls' Branch of the PSAL, which provided opportunities for girls to participate in folk dancing. Elizabeth Burchenal directed the Girls' Branch of the PSAL before founding and presiding over the American Folk-Dance Society.

As Supervisor of Physical Culture in the Detroit public schools for 14 years, Ethel Perrin stressed informal, coeducational classes that emphasized play, rather than formalized gymnastics. Under her leadership, Detroit led the nation in the provision of specially trained physical educators at all levels of instruction.

The play movement also influenced nonschool programs. Following the passage of child labor laws, children were taken out of the sweat shops and returned to their neighborhoods where playgrounds and parks were provided for them. There, many children of immigrants were assimilated into the American culture. There, they made friends, learned social skills, and learned how to win and lose. There, they perfected their baseball, basketball, football, softball, and ice hockey skills. Cities and towns prioritized offering sports competitions and recreational activities, first for children and later for adults, to meet this inherent need to play.

Teacher Training

When physical education gained stature as a recognized subject by the National Education Association in 1891, it began to move from its association with medicine to allegiance with educational philosophies and curricula. Whereas many early physical educators, like Hitchcock, Sargent, Wood, and Williams, held medical degrees, after 1900 several universities offered professional preparation courses in physical education. Oberlin College, the Universities of Nebraska, Missouri, and California, and Stanford University developed the initial programs.

Most states established teacher training institutes, or normal colleges, to replace the private schools that had predominated in the late 1800s. While the state normal colleges became comprehensive regional universities, most retained their commitment to teacher education, including physical education.

TWENTIETH-CENTURY LEADERS IN PHYSICAL EDUCATION IN THE UNITED STATES

Luther Gulick, M.D. (1865–1918)

Served as instructor (1887–1900) and superintendent (1889–1900) of the Department of Physical Training at the YMCA Training School

Directed physical training for the New York City public schools (1903–1908)

Established the Public Schools Athletic League in New York City (1903)

Helped establish the Playground Association of America (1906)

Influenced by Delphine Hanna and Thomas Wood

Thomas Wood, M.D. (1864–1951)

Taught at Stanford University (1891–1901)

Taught at Teachers College of Columbia University (1901–1932)

Helped formulate the philosophical cornerstone for the new physical education

Appointed first Professor of Health Education at Teachers College of Columbia University

Influenced by Delphine Hanna, Luther Gulick, and Rosalind Cassidy

Clark Hetherington (1870–1942)

Directed physical training and athletics at the University of Missouri (1900–1910)

Established a Demonstration Play School at the University of California, Berkeley (1913–1917)

Taught at the University of Wisconsin (1913–1918)

Served as state supervisor of physical education for California (1918–1921)

Taught at New York University (1923–1929)

Taught at Stanford University (1929–1938)

Influenced by Thomas Wood and G. Stanley Hall

Jay Nash (1886–1965)

Taught at New York University (1926–1953)

Promoted recreation and carry-over sports

Influenced by Clark Hetherington and extended his theories as well as those of Luther Gulick and Thomas Wood

Jesse Williams, M.D. (1886–1966)

Taught at Teachers College of Columbia University (1911–1916; 1919–1941)

Stressed educational values, social education, and education through the physical

Became a dominant influence in physical education (1930–1960)

Influenced by John Dewey

Rosalind Cassidy (1895–1980)

Taught at Mills College, California (1918–1947)

Taught at the University of California at Los Angeles (1947–1962)

Led in writing about and promotion of the new physical education, education through the physical, and physical education as human movement

Influenced by Thomas Wood

(continued)

TWENTIETH-CENTURY LEADERS IN PHYSICAL EDUCATION IN THE UNITED STATES (CONTINUED)

Elizabeth Burchenal (1876–1959)
Served as Executive Secretary of the Girls' Branch of the Public Schools Athletic League (1906–1916)
Founded and served as first president of the American Folk-Dance Society (1916–1929)
Became first chairperson of the Committee on Women's Athletics of the American Physical Education Association (1917)
Influenced by Luther Gulick and Melvin Gilbert (in dance)

Ethel Perrin (1871–1962)
Supervised physical culture in the Detroit public schools (1909–1923)
Provided leadership with the executive committee of the Women's Division of the National Amateur Athletic Federation (1923–1932)
Served as assistant/associate director of health education for the American Child Health Association (1923–1936)
Influenced by Amy Morris Homans

Tait McKenzie, M.D. (1867–1938)
Taught (1891–1904) and served as Medical Director of Physical Education (1896–1904) at University Medical College (Canada)
Taught as professor on medical faculty and directed physical education (1904–1931) and served as professor of physical therapy (1907–1931) at the University of Pennsylvania
Depicted hundreds of athletic events in works of sculpture that showed the aesthetic harmony of bodily proportion and expression

Mabel Lee (1886–1985)
Directed physical education for women at the University of Nebraska (1924–1952)
Elected first woman president of the American Physical Education Association (1931)
Led the profession as a proponent of wholesome sport for women and, as an author, was
Influenced by Amy Morris Homans

Charles McCloy (1886–1959)
Worked for the YMCA in the United States and internationally (1908–1930)
Served as a research professor in physical education at the State University of Iowa (1930–1954)
Stressed the development of skills and organic vigor as the primary objectives of physical education (education of the physical)

Eleanor Metheny (1908–1982)
Taught at Wellesley College and at the Harvard Fatigue Laboratory (1940–1942)
Taught at the University of Southern California (1942–1971)
Led in the study of meaningful movement experiences
Influenced by Charles McCloy

The impact of teacher training has extended to nonschool settings as well. Physical educators, who were educated to use physical activities to teach sports skills and physical fitness, have moved into other careers. For example, physical educators have been leaders in training military personnel during wartime and times of peace. Physical educators have directed public and private recreational programs, coached sports teams for youth and adults, taught lessons in swimming, tennis, and golf at private clubs, and managed commercial and professional sporting events. Most of these individuals received their education at one of the physical education teacher education institutions.

Women's Physical Education

Not until the 1970s did most college physical education programs lose their separation by gender. Throughout most of the 1900s, women's physical education focused on preparing teachers with strict disassociation from competitive athletics. Curricula remained somewhat formalized; centered on minimal skill development for all, rather than on enhancement of the abilities of the highly skilled; and focused on value development, not winning, through sport.

Only gradually did women gain acceptance as equals within the physical education profession, possibly because most early male leaders were physicians and few females had the opportunity to pursue medical degrees in those early years. Eliza Mosher and Helen Putnam were exceptions and served as vice presidents in the national organization. Mabel Lee was elected the first woman president of the American Physical Education Association (APEA) 46 years after it was established. Within the APEA, Lee, Burchenal, and other women fought to preserve an educational model for women's participation in sport.

Education of the Physical

Charles McCloy led the campaign against a primary emphasis on educational outcomes as advocated by Wood, Cassidy, and Williams. Instead of supporting Williams' claim that physical education merited inclusion in the schools because

Mabel Lee, the first female president of the American Physical Education Association.

it helped attain social, emotional, and intellectual goals, McCloy affirmed his belief in **education of the physical.** This referred to a belief that physical education's unique contribution within education should be to develop individuals' physical fitness and sport skills. During his more than 20 years with the YMCA and especially during his tenure at the State University of Iowa, McCloy stressed organic and psychomotor development as the most important objectives for physical education. He stated that the uniqueness of physical education depended on the development of physical skills. And he encouraged the teaching of sports skills and the measurement of progress through standardized tests.

An extension of this philosophical approach to physical education was the growth in the use of tests and measurements, which paralleled the scientific movement in education. Built on the importance of anthropometric measurements in the late 1800s, early twentieth-century physical educators developed numerous physical tests. The Public Schools Athletic League initiated achievement tests to reward boys' successful performances. College achievement tests measured cognitive knowledge, motor ability, endurance, and sports skills. David Brace's Motor Ability Test, Frederick Cozens's test of general athletic ability, Frederick Rogers' Strength Index and Physical Fitness Index, and Charles McCloy's Motor Quotient were among the most notable measures developed.

Fitness

Historically, fitness as a curricular emphasis surfaced during wartime or times when peace was threatened. Certainly this characterized physical education during the years surrounding World Wars I and II. One of the greatest advocates

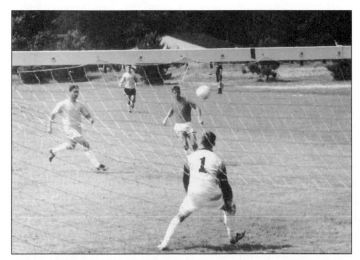

Fitness activities, such as soccer leagues, are offered by recreation departments, YMCAs and YWCAs, corporate recreation programs, and school intramural programs.

for the importance of physical training for the war effort was Tait McKenzie. Although recognized more for his outstanding sports sculptures, McKenzie used his training as a physical educator and physician in England, his native Canada, and the United States to rehabilitate soldiers who had been injured during World War I. Many male and female physical educators served as physical training instructors or consultants to the Armed Forces.

During World Wars I and II in schools and colleges, mass calisthenics and the development of fitness formed the basis of the curricula. In peacetime, fitness was seldom emphasized in the educational curriculum.

However, during the Cold War years of the late 1950s, that all changed. First, many felt threatened by the rising prominence of the Union of Soviet Socialist Republics (USSR). Second, the United States was embarrassed by the 1953 results of the Kraus-Weber Test that showed American children inferior to European children. This minimal muscular fitness test included six items:

- In supine position, execute one straight leg sit-up;
- In supine position, do one bent-knee sit-up;
- In supine position, hold extended legs above the floor for ten seconds;
- In prone position, pull the head, shoulders, and chest off the mat and hold for ten seconds;
- In prone position, raise the extended legs off the mat and hold for ten seconds; and
- From a standing position, bend until fingertips touch the floor without bouncing or bending the knees and hold this contact for three seconds.

As an immediate response to this report and following a national conference on the topic, President Dwight Eisenhower established the President's Council on Youth Fitness. This Council promoted a minimum of 15 minutes a day of vigorous activity for all children and distributed thousands of copies of *Youth Physical Fitness: Suggested Elements of a School-Centered Program*. The American Association for Health, Physical Education and Recreation (AAHPER) stimulated fitness through its 1958 Operation Fitness project that included the AAHPER Youth Fitness Test.

Human Movement

Rosalind Cassidy and Eleanor Metheny helped revolutionize the conceptual base of physical education. Metheny, a student of Charles McCloy, was acclaimed for her insightful writings and her inspirational speeches on this topic.

Movement education, especially as influenced by Rudolf Laban from England, significantly impacted elementary school curricula. Movement education, a child-centered curriculum, emphasized presenting movement challenges to students and encouraging them to use problem solving and guided discovery to learn fundamental skills. To some, the developmentally appropriate subject matter for children should focus on their free expression of movements in response to challenges or problems. Advocates favored individualized learning of locomotor, nonlocomotor, and perceptual-motor skills.

Other Influencing Factors

Public school physical education in the 1900s was directly influenced by the scientific movement, educational developmentalism, and by social education. Athletic and motor ability achievement tests, measurements of posture, and the use of statistical analyses are three examples of techniques resulting from the scientific movement. The justification of play for children led the way for the playground and recreation movement that carried over into the schools. Educational developmentalism influenced the passage of state laws requiring physical education as an integral part of each child's school experiences. The popularity of sports within physical education curricula contributed to achievement of social education outcomes, including development of cooperation, good citizenship, and ethical conduct.

In more recent years, however, school physical education programs have experienced numerous attacks, partially as a result of administrators with limited resources attempting to cut any programs viewed as nonessential. Such attacks increased when physical educators were unable to demonstrate the achievement of educational standards. Another causal factor was the national call to improve and reform education in response to the belief that the economic predominance of this country was threatened. An examination of *AMERICA 2000: An Education Strategy,* released in 1991, verified the lack of centrality of physical education. The health and physical well-being of children was not valued enough to receive mention.

Throughout the decade of the 1990s, politicians and parents consistently advocated raising academic standards for all students and demanded that educators be held accountable for improved student learning. Despite significant increases in the diversity of student populations and the guaranteeing of the educational rights of children with special needs, educators are increasingly being judged on how their students perform on norm-referenced, high-stakes tests. In the 1990s the National Standards for Physical Education were developed to articulate what students should know and be able to do in terms of physical education. The challenge, however, was how to achieve the seven content standards in physical education in the wake of decreased funding, reduced programs and personnel, and renewed emphasis on so-called academic subjects.

Understanding the history of physical education, exercise science, and sport as a field can help professionals respond to such difficulties. Certainly these major developments in school physical education have shaped today's programs.

LEADERSHIP FROM THE NATIONAL ASSOCIATION

In the early 1900s, the American Physical Education Association (APEA) was dominated by Easterners who attempted to build a strong profession through the exchange of ideas and shared projects. James McCurdy, who served as editor of

WEB CONNECTIONS

1. www.aahperd.org/index.html
   Students can visit the home page of the American Alliance for Health, Physical Education, Recreation and Dance to learn about the organizational structure and services, order publications, review the latest news, and join.

2. www.activeparks.org
   The homepage of the National Recreation and Park Association provides information about the activities of this organization, which promotes active lifestyles for everyone.

3. www.womenssportsfoundation.org/wosport/stage/interact
   This site provides links to sports and fitness information for women.

4. www.americanfitness.net/fitnessgram
   At this site, you will find comprehensive information about the FITNESSGRAM and Physical Best educational materials.

5. www.ed.gov/offices/osers/osep/osep98anlrpt
   Learn more about the implementation of the Individuals with Disabilities Education Act through a review of annual reports to Congress.

6. http://bailiwick.lib.uiowa.edu/ge
   This site at the University of Iowa focuses on the latest information about gender equity issues in intercollegiate sports.

7. http://infosports.net/index.html
   Parents, coaches, and sports enthusiasts can check out this site for information about all aspects of youth sports.

the APEA's *American Physical Education Review* for 23 years, was one outstanding leader during the early years.

In the early 1900s, dancing and athletics were frequently added to school and college programs, challenging the former supremacy of gymnastics. Besides these two, frequently discussed topics at the annual meetings of the APEA included school hygiene, the value of gymnastics, skill and fitness testing, and standards for teacher preparation and graduate education. There was a proliferation of professional preparation in physical education between 1920 and 1927, during which 70 new college programs were begun.

Following the merger of the Midwest Society (a regional group of physical educators) into the national APEA in 1930, Elmer Mitchell assumed the editorship of the profession's two major publications, the *Journal of Health and Physical Education* and the *Research Quarterly;* he served in this capacity for 13 years. The Department of School Health and Physical Education of the National Education Association merged with the APEA in 1937, to become the American Association for Health and Physical Education (*recreation* was added to its name in 1938). The national organization was subsequently configured into six geographical districts.

After World War II, the AAHPER sponsored numerous conferences focusing on facilities, undergraduate professional preparation, graduate professional preparation, fitness, and other interest areas. In 1974, it was restructured into an alliance composed of seven (now six) associations (see Chapter 3) to allow greater autonomy in providing leadership and programs for the diverse interests of its members. The addition of dance and to its current acronym AAHPERD occurred in 1979.

In 1985, AAHPERD'S centennial celebration focused on recalling its service and leadership in health, physical education, recreation, dance, and sports. The April 1985 issue of the *Journal of Physical Education, Recreation and Dance* traced 100 years of the profession by highlighting special events and notable leaders. The message conveyed in this publication and through the centennial convention was that the AAHPERD, through its membership, had enriched programs for diverse populations. In the twentieth century, the six national associations focusing on health, leisure and recreation, dance, active lifestyles, physical education, and sport have gained greater autonomy within the Alliance, thus enabling each specialized area to serve the unique needs of its members more effectively.

TEACHER PREPARATION

A perennial concern of AAHPERD and its preceding organizations has been the inconsistencies among professional preparation programs for teachers. Each normal school, as it developed, was free to pursue its own course of study, with little relationship to what was being taught at the others. When four-year degree programs were developed in colleges and universities, each institution had the latitude to design and implement its own curriculum. Since, in the early 1900s, there were no **accreditation** procedures or standards, great program diversity resulted. In the 1930s, the Department of School Health and Physical Education of the National Education Association established a committee to evaluate teacher education curricula and to establish standards. In 1948, the National Conference on Undergraduate Professional Preparation in Health Education, Physical Education, and Recreation recommended standards and programs in teacher preparation. In 1960, the AAHPER voted to accept the National Council for Accreditation of Teacher Education (NCATE) as the official accrediting agency in its fields of study. This led to many state departments of education certifying only teachers who graduated from NCATE-approved institutions. In the 1970s, many state departments began to require that certain competencies be met in professional course work before future teachers would be certified. Each of these developments enhanced the quality of the graduates of teacher education programs.

In the 1980s, many people expressed concern about the lack of standards for and credentials of individuals engaged in various sports and fitness programs. For example, there was no national certification for aerobic dance instructors. Seemingly anyone with a leotard and coordinated tights and leg warmers who could enthusiastically motivate people to exercise to the resounding beat of the latest hit tunes could teach. Knowledge about human anatomy, exercise physiology, first aid, cardiopulmonary resuscitation, psychology, and teaching progressions was not a prerequisite. This lack of standards led to repeated injuries, some serious; high dropout rates; and a general lack of accountability on the part of the instructors and the sponsoring groups. Certification programs for fitness instructors and leaders, such as through the American College of Sports Medicine, have filled the gap in this area, but still such training is often optional rather than mandatory. Unless sports like scuba diving, weight training, karate, and racquetball regulate their own instructors' training, anyone is free to teach these or other activities outside the schools.

AMATEUR AND COLLEGIATE SPORTS

The popularization of sports in the twentieth and twenty-first centuries has been phenomenal. In addition to becoming the nucleus of physical education programs, sports are organized for competition both inside and outside the schools.

Intramurals

Most college athletic teams and some physical education programs in the late 1800s and early 1900s evolved out of interclass competitions organized by male students. As athletics and physical education developed their own separate programs, a need still existed for recreational activities for students. In 1913, the University of Michigan and The Ohio State University appointed the first intramural directors. At Michigan, beginning in 1919, Elmer Mitchell led in the development of sports opportunities for students who were not varsity athletes but who wanted more competition than was available in physical education classes. Originally in the colleges and after the mid-1920s in the schools, **intramurals** offered league and class (or homeroom) competition in individual and team sports. In the 1940s, the introduction of coeducational activities became popular. The greatest expansion in combined male and female activities occurred in the 1970s.

Today, many intramural programs operate as campus recreation programs, having greatly expanded the scope of their activities. In addition to competitive leagues and coeducational recreation, club sports, extramural competitions, faculty/staff programs, instructional clinics, fitness classes, special events and tournaments, and free-play opportunities have been offered. Over the years, many of these intramural recreational sports programs have moved from receiving funds first from athletic departments and then from physical education departments to being supported by students' fees. At the school level, where intramural activities vary from traditional competitions to a variety of leisure-time events and where these events are scheduled throughout the day and night, physical educators normally provide the expertise while school budgets provide the equipment.

Outside of the schools, this same concept of intramurals, or sports competition within the walls, has provided innumerable opportunities for physical activity. Many corporations offer sports leagues and competitions in volleyball, bowling, softball, and many other sports for their employees at all levels of the organization. These leisure-time activities help build camaraderie among employees as well as help them live healthier lifestyles.

Collegiate Sports for Men

In the early 1900s, concerns in collegiate sports focused on football, primarily because of the injuries and deaths that occurred with shocking regularity. While President Theodore Roosevelt expressed concern, college presidents threatened to ban intercollegiate football. As a direct result of football injuries and deaths, the National Collegiate Athletic Association (NCAA) was formed in 1906. Although composed of a small group of faculty representatives with power only to make recommendations, the NCAA attempted to control the roughness and brutality of football by revising its rules. Gradually, football overcame these problems and emerged as the major collegiate sport. Baseball in colleges, though rivalled by the professional major leagues, retained a degree of popularity secondary to the pros

College football in the 1930s. (Photo courtesy North Carolina Collection, UNC Library at Chapel Hill.)

SPORT GOVERNANCE ORGANIZATIONS

Boys and Men
1888   Amateur Athletic Union (AAU)
     *1879—National Association of Amateur Athletes of America
1910   National Collegiate Athletic Association (NCAA)
     *1906—Intercollegiate Athletic Association of the United States
1922   National Federation of State High School Associations (NFSHSA)
1938   National Junior College Athletic Association (NJCAA)
1952   National Association of Intercollegiate Athletics (NAIA)
     *1940—National Association of Intercollegiate Basketball

Girls and Women
1974   National Association for Girls and Women in Sports (NAGWS)
     *1917—Committee on Women's Athletics
     *1927—Women's Athletic Section
     *1932—National Section on Women's Athletics
     *1953—National Section on Girls and Women's Sports
     *1958—Division of Girls and Women's Sports
1971   Association for Intercollegiate Athletics for Women (AIAW) (ceased in 1982)
     *1966—Commission on Intercollegiate Athletics for Women

First Championships Offered for Girls and Women:
1916   Amateur Athletic Union
1976   National Junior College Athletic Association
1980   National Association of Intercollegiate Athletics
1981   National Collegiate Athletic Association

*Earlier name of the same organization.

and to football, while intercollegiate competitions in boxing, golf, tennis, track and field, and wrestling have never seriously challenged the supremacy of football. Basketball did emerge as the second leading collegiate sport, but not until the 1950s.

The NCAA continued as the sole voice of and controlling organization for college athletes until 1938, when the National Junior College Athletic Association (NJCAA) was founded to provide competitive opportunities for students in two-year institutions. Then in 1952, the National Association of Intercollegiate Athletics (NAIA) began to sponsor championships for small colleges (it sponsored an annual basketball tournament for men starting in 1940). (The box above lists these and other major sports organizations for men and women.)

Today, collegiate athletics for men are very different from what they were in the 1940s. Under faculty control by representative vote, the NCAA remained primarily an advisory organization during its first 40 years. Control rested with each institution, where most frequently athletic councils composed of alumni, faculty, and students exercised authority over athletics. Institutions that held membership in conferences agreed to follow additional regulations and guidelines. Other than standardizing the rules and providing championships, the NCAA had not been granted power by the institutions to legislate or to mandate rules. Beginning with the national acceptance of athletic grants-in-aid in 1952 and throughout the decade following, the role of the NCAA changed dramatically because institutions were willing to relinquish some of their autonomy to the NCAA to ensure that other institutions would comply with the regulations governing grants-in-aid and recruiting. A second development began with the first negotiation of a television contract in 1951, thus providing the NCAA with enforcement leverage. Subsequently, the NCAA could penalize an institution economically by disallowing television appearances. The NCAA, with a budget in the hundreds of millions of dollars, has become the most powerful amateur sports organization in the United States and possibly the world.

During the last quarter of the twentieth century, the NCAA once again experienced dramatic change. In its Division III programs, students without grants-in-aid continued to compete for the love of the sport, cheered on by a handful of friends and family, and with minimal hope of continuing their athletic careers beyond graduation. While students competing in Division II programs received grants-in-aid, most realized that their talents were limited and, therefore, focused more on the educational opportunities provided them. It was at the Division I level, though, that highly commercialized sport emerged. Corporate sponsorships, donations from enthusiastic fans (in return for priority seating and other perks), and television contracts became essential to funding the multi-million dollar budgets needed to support athletic programs at the highest level. Athletic administrators at the approximately 100 "big-time" football and basketball programs finally admitted to being in the entertainment, rather the education, business. Coaches with multi-million dollar contracts were hired to win and fired for losing. Athletes received an educational opportunity that was too often discounted while universities reaped millions for their performances in bowl games or for coming away with a win during a Final Four game. Gamblers increasingly influenced the outcomes of games; the media exploited every angle; athletes, coaches, and others associated with intercollegiate athletics sought ways to gain personal advancement and financial benefits. The NCAA seemingly made every attempt to solidify its control over intercollegiate sports with apparent disregard of the raging controversies such as gambling, drug abuse, commercialization, and professionalism.

Collegiate Sports for Women

During the early 1900s, sports for women were strictly controlled by women physical educators, who consistently followed the societal expectations for their gender. Caution about a potential overemphasis on competition or on unladylike behavior led to modified rules in several sports. Mass participation in class exercises, field days, play days, and sports days, rather than competitive athletics, became the norm. Physical education, because of its healthful benefits, was stressed

1890s.

1890s to early 1900s (Photo courtesy Basketball Hall of Fame.)

Photos on pages 272–274 show the changes in women's sports attire.

1920s to 1930s.

1940s.

for girls in schools and for women who attended colleges. Outfitted in middy blouses and bloomers, the traditional gymnasium costume of the day, these women exercised in mass drills, engaged in therapeutic Swedish gymnastics, and enjoyed sports such as archery, basketball, field hockey, rowing, and tennis. It should be noted, however, that some girls and women competed on teams, especially in basketball, until these teams were eliminated by physical educators who believed that competitive sports were harmful to females physically, emotionally, and mentally.

Late 1940s to early 1950s.

In women's colleges, field days were normally conducted once or twice a year on campus, and all students were urged to participate. Play days, beginning in the 1920s, provided for social interaction as women students met and formed teams composed of representatives from several institutions. These teams played one or more sports before reassembling for a picnic or other social event. Evolving from these play days were sports days, during which college teams competed, frequently in only one sport, but still with the emphasis on social interaction and fun.

In 1917, a Committee on Women's Athletics was established by the American Physical Education Association (today's AAHPERD) to establish standards and policies that advocated mass participation while vigorously opposing varsity competition. Between 1923 and 1942, the Women's Division of the National Amateur Athletic Federation also opposed highly competitive sports, including those in the Olympic Games, claiming they were inappropriate for women.

In the late 1960s, a gradual change in societal attitudes regarding women in sports paralleled a liberalized philosophy displayed by women leaders in physical education. As long as the welfare of the athletes was guaranteed and high standards were maintained, competitions were permitted and even encouraged, especially beginning in 1969, when the Commission on Intercollegiate Athletics for Women began sponsoring national tournaments. Two years later, the Association for Intercollegiate Athletics for Women (AIAW), an institutional membership organization, assumed this responsibility. During the next 11 years, the AIAW sponsored championships and established standards and policies governing women's intercollegiate athletics. With equal opportunity mandated by Title IX of the 1972 Education Amendments, colleges and schools financed increased sports competitions for girls and women. In 1976, the NJCAA and, in 1980, the NAIA began offering championships for college women; smaller institutions benefited financially from having one membership fee, one governance structure and set of rules, and similar sport schedules for all athletes.

The NCAA initially opposed Title IX of the 1972 Education Amendments claiming that its requirement for equal opportunity in all educational programs would end men's intercollegiate athletics. The NCAA lobbied the Department of Health, Education and Welfare for exclusion of athletics from Title IX, they campaigned in support of the Tower Amendment in the Senate to exclude revenue sports from Title IX jurisdiction, and they turned to the courts, arguing the inapplicability of Title IX to athletics on constitutional grounds. Each of these approaches were unsuccessful (see A Brief History of Title IX on page 276).

Claiming that Title IX mandated the NCAA govern both men's and women's athletics, the NCAA began in 1981 to offer championships for women, in what amounted to a hostile takeover of women's intercollegiate athletics. The AIAW in the previous decade had grown to 960 members and sponsored 42 championships, in three competitive divisions, in 19 sports. But the AIAW could not match the NCAA's large financial base, out of which they covered the expenses for women's teams participating in NCAA championships. The NCAA also waived its membership dues for women's athletic teams if their men's programs were already NCAA members, and it contracted to televise the women's basketball finals (directly opposite the AIAW's title game). Despite the AIAW's educational model for athletics, which was specifically designed to avoid the problems associated with the male sports model, the AIAW ceased to exist in June, 1982. Although a few women have gained some status in NCAA, such as Judith Sweet, the first female to serve as president, the NCAA is predominantly governed by men. They hold most coaching and administrative positions in women's athletics within the NCAA as well as in the NAIA and NJCAA.

Amateur Sports

The amateur sports scene in the United States outside the colleges remained largely under the direction of the AAU through the 1970s, since this organization sponsored a diversity of sports competitions for people of all ages. Basketball, boxing, swimming, and track and field especially attracted thousands of participants. Because championships in these sports were offered by NCAA institutions, the two organizations frequently clashed. Repeatedly, when the time arrived for the selection of Olympic teams, controversies raged. In 1922, the National Amateur Athletic Federation was formed to mediate this dispute, with few positive results. The conflicts inevitably affected the athletes because the two associations often refused to sanction events, to certify records, or to permit athletes to participate in each other's events. The Amateur Sports Act, passed in 1978, resolved some of these problems by requiring that each Olympic sport have its own governing body and by establishing guidelines governing the selection of these organizations.

A BRIEF HISTORY OF TITLE IX

"No person in the United States shall, on the basis of sex, be excluded from participation in, be denied the benefits of, or be subjected to discrimination under any education program or activity receiving Federal financial assistance."

1972	Congress enacts Title IX of the Education Amendments of 1972	Prohibits sex discrimination in any education program or activity in an institution receiving Federal financial assistance
1974	Attempt to exclude revenue-producing sports from Title IX	Senator Tower introduces an amendment (which was not adopted) to exempt revenue-producing sports from inclusion in determining whether an institution was in compliance with Title IX; other similar attempts fail in 1975 and 1977
1974	Javits' Amendment	Senator Javits' amendment (which was adopted) requires the Department of Health, Education, and Welfare (HEW) to issue Title IX regulations that include specific reference to particular sports
1975	HEW issues final Title IX regulations	Higher education institutions and secondary schools have three years to comply with Title IX
1979	HEW issues final policy interpretation on Title IX and intercollegiate athletics	This policy interpretation requires institutions to provide equal opportunity and specifies three areas required for compliance: financial assistance (athletic grants-in-aid); programs areas such as coaching, facilities, travel and per diem, and tutoring); meeting the interests and abilities of male and female students
1980	Department of Education (DOE) is established	DOE is given oversight of Title IX through the Office for Civil Rights (OCR)
1984	*Grove City vs. Bell*	The Supreme Court rules that the applicability of Title IX in athletics programs is limited to only those programs or activities that receive direct Federal financial assistance
1988	Civil Rights Restoration Act	This Congressional Act overrides *Grove City vs. Bell* and mandates that all educational institutions receiving Federal financial assistance, whether direct or indirect, must comply with Title IX
1992	*Franklin vs. Gwinnett County Public Schools*	The Supreme Court rules that under Title IX plaintiffs may receive punitive damages when noncompliance with Title IX is intentional
1992	Gender Equity Study	National Collegiate Athletic Association publishes its Gender Equity Study
1996	Policy Clarification	OCR issues clarifications about how institutions can provide effective accommodations in intercollegiate athletics
1996	First EADA Report Due	The Equity in Athletics Disclosure Act requires all institutions to have specific information about their intercollegiate athletics programs available

Jim Thorpe, a Native American, won gold medals in the 1912 Stockholm Olympic Games in the pentathlon and decathlon.

For the most part, the spirit of the Olympics promoted by Pierre de Coubertin, founder of the modern games, and perpetuated by the governing International Olympic Committee, prevailed during the first half of the twentieth century. The five interlocking rings symbolized friendship among the athletes of the world. Competitive superiority remained the ideal until the Olympic Games became the stage for displaying the supremacy of one's national ideology. This was certainly the case in the 1952 Helsinki Games, where professionally trained athletes from the USSR entered Olympic competition. It would seem that nationalism's intrusion into Olympic competition, where winning demonstrates the superiority of one's political or ideological system, has signaled the beginning of the end for amateurism as the foundation of the Olympic Games. The boycotts of 1980 and 1984 certainly confirmed the power of politics in international sports competition.

Commercialism, with its product displays and lucrative television contracts, has forever changed the image of these competitions. Media attention and the potential of leveraging medals into endorsements have also played significant roles in the demise of amateur competition in the Olympics. While the 1984 Los Angeles Games were the first to be commercially successful, the 1996 Atlanta Games hosted mostly professional athletes who were also paid by their countries when they won medals. Scandals associated with site selection and perks for International Olympic Committee members substantiated the influence of money on these games.

Mildred (Babe) Didrikson in the 1932 Los Angeles Olympic Games
won gold medals in the 800-meter hurdles and the javelin throw
and a silver medal in the high jump.

The original events of the modern Olympic Games paralleled the popular activities of the turn of the century such as track and field, gymnastics, fencing, and tennis. These and other Olympic sports had minimal impact on school curricula. While many Olympic sports were associated with elitist clubs for men, including shooting, rowing, yachting, and equestrian clubs, the entry of college males in track and field, swimming, and wrestling broadened the composition of the teams from the United States and thus may have attracted participants from throughout society. A few women, primarily in swimming (starting in 1912) and track and field (starting in 1928), competed in the Olympics, until the number of sports opened to them increased. The popularity of gymnastics, basketball, and other women's sports certainly has been enhanced through the showcasing of Olympic competitions. However, only the growth in gymnastics can probably be linked specifically to the Olympics.

PLAY TO RECREATION TO FITNESS

Play

The playground movement continued apace in the early 1900s, as the Playground Association of America (PAA), founded in 1906 by Luther Gulick and Henry Curtis, provided the necessary leadership. Gulick served as its first president and

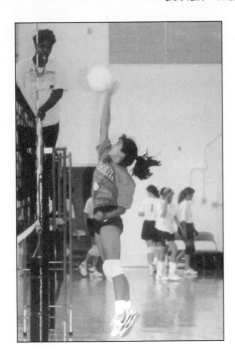

Many states offer amateurs competitive opportunities through State Games. (Photo courtesy Maggie McGlynn.)

was instrumental in the publication of its monthly magazine, *The Playground.* The provision of adequate playgrounds throughout the country was also enhanced by the support of President Theodore Roosevelt. Clark Hetherington supervised the writing of *The Normal Course in Play* in 1910, the book used to prepare recreation leaders. Joseph Lee, as president of the PAA, helped expand the play concept to include the value of play and recreation for all ages, leading to the reorganization of the PAA in 1911 and its new name, the Playground and Recreation Association of America (PRAA).

Recreation

In 1930, the PRAA became the National Recreation Association (which became the National Recreation and Park Association in 1965), verifying the importance and worth of leisure time for people of all ages. The Depression years suddenly gave people large amounts of leisure time, but many had limited financial resources. The federal government helped in two ways. Federal agencies, such as the Works Progress Administration, provided jobs by funding construction of camping sites, golf courses, gymnasiums, playing fields, and swimming pools. Once completed, these were opened for mass recreational use. Especially popular sports during the 1930s were bowling and softball.

Wartime production brought the United States out of the Depression. At the same time, sports competitions and recreational programs were initiated to revive the spirits and bodies of soldiers and factory workers. While the armed services

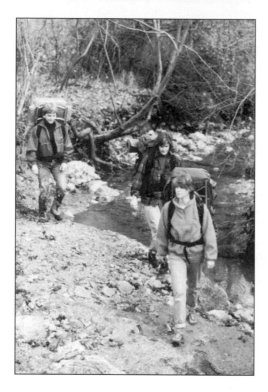

Backpacking is one of several popular outdoor activities. (Photo courtesy Jim Kirby.)

used sports for training and conditioning soldiers, industries began to provide sports teams and competitive opportunities for employees, realizing that such activities positively affected productivity and morale. Industrial recreation continued to expand even after the war crisis ended.

Outdoor education emerged as the recreational thrust of the 1950s. As the country became more mechanized and technological, the appeal of camping, hiking, and similar back-to-nature activities provided people with the chance to get away from daily routines and stress. Some schools and colleges began to offer backpacking, rock climbing, spelunking, winter survival, ropes courses, and orienteering, all of which have maintained their popularity.

As early as the 1930s, Jay Nash promoted carry-over, or lifetime, sports within the curriculum. By the 1960s, this philosophy gained numerous supporters and affected programs. Led by the Lifetime Sports Foundation with joint sponsorship of AAHPER, archery, badminton, bowling, golf, and tennis were introduced into many schools. Slowly, programs expanded from offering only team sports to the inclusion of these and other lifetime sports.

Fitness

Fitness mania began in the 1970s, with joggers leading the craze. In 1970, the lonely runner was suddenly joined by thousands of marathoners and road racers of all ages and both genders, while tennis participants multiplied and swimming became more popular. The pervasiveness of this fitness mania could be verified by observing not only the sport paraphernalia that enthusiasts used and wore but also the popularity of sporting attire for everyone. This fitness phenomenon has continued as verified by the sharp rise in health club memberships. However, the people most involved in getting and keeping in shape have come from the middle and upper classes, rather than being drawn equally from all economic levels. Also, many school-age children, rather than becoming fitness advocates, have preferred to watch television, play video and computer games, surf the web, or become sports spectators.

Fitness for Children   When the results of the Kraus-Weber Minimal Muscular Fitness Test were published in 1953, European children demonstrated greater fitness (only 9% failed) than children in the United States (57.8% failed). Since the six-item Kraus-Weber Test primarily measured flexibility and abdominal strength (and thus received criticism that it inaccurately assessed overall fitness), the physical education profession developed the AAHPER Youth Fitness Test. To the dismay of professionals, the 1958 results of this eight-item test battery showed that children in the United States had low levels of fitness. This test included pull-ups (for boys), flexed-arm hang (for girls), straight-leg sit-ups, the shuttle run, the standing broad jump, the softball throw, the 50-yard dash, and the 600-yard run/walk. Between 1958 and the second national administration of this test in 1965,

Body composition is an excellent indicator of overall fitness. (Photo courtesy Diane Victorson).

teachers promoted fitness through daily physical education classes, periodic testing, and an increased consciousness of the importance of fitness. These efforts were rewarded with improvement by all age groups in all skills, except for 17-year-old girls in the softball throw. Unfortunately, these vigorous efforts lapsed, so poor fitness levels of school-age children were once again reported in national studies in 1985 and 1987.

In response to widespread criticism that the AAHPER Youth Fitness Test failed to measure the major components of fitness, in 1981 the AAHPERD introduced the Health-Related Lifetime Physical Fitness Test. Its items measured strength with sit-ups, flexibility using a sit-and-reach, cardiovascular endurance in a 1.5-mile or 12-minute run, and body composition by taking skinfold measurements. While more accurately measuring the recognized components of fitness, these test norms only reconfirmed the lack of fitness among school-age children in the 1980s.

In 1994, AAHPERD joined with the Cooper Institute for Aerobics Research (CIAR) in a collaborative physical fitness education and testing program. AAHPERD's educational approach to fitness helps motivate students to change their behaviors and commit themselves to lifetime fitness. Physical Best provides comprehensive health-related physical fitness educational materials for students to use in setting individualized fitness goals. By monitoring progress, reporting to parents, and recognizing achievement, this program helps students incorporate the cognitive, affective, and psychomotor components of fitness into their lives. FITNESSGRAM is the health-related fitness test component of this program. It is designed to assess aerobic capacity (1-mile walk/run), body composition, muscular strength, and endurance (through curl-ups, push-ups, pull-ups, modified pull-ups, flexed-arm hang, and trunk lift), and flexibility (back saver sit-and-reach). The ACTIVITYGRAM module asks students to assess their own activity levels. The Physical Best recognition system reinforces the importance of attaining individual goals and participation in extracurricular physical activities. The latest data on the fitness of American youth come from the National Children and Youth Fitness Study I (1985) and II (1987). These studies revealed that the fitness levels of American youth still need improvement. The need for improvement in youth fitness comprise a part of *Healthy People 2010* goals as discussed in Chapter 1.

Although some local and state assessments of the fitness levels of children have been conducted, there has not been a replication of the national study since the 1980s. Available data, however, show that the youth fitness goals in *Healthy People 2010* have not been achieved. In the wake of the 1996 publication of the Surgeon General's *Report on Physical Activity and Health* and the identification of physical inactivity as a primary risk factor contributing to coronary heart disease, the nation's interest in the physical well-being of parents and children alike has never been stronger. Schools, public recreation programs, and private businesses need to combine their efforts in providing greater opportunities for physical education and sport activities for children. Increased funding is needed to provide daily physical education classes for all children as well as to purchase equipment such as aerobic machines and heart rate monitors.

Fitness for All Ages   The emphasis on aerobic fitness for individuals of all ages was aided by the 1968 publication of Kenneth Cooper's *Aerobics*. This book outlined a program for helping every individual attain and maintain physical fitness by compiling a certain number of points each week while participating in favorite activities. Since the 1970s, many Americans have renewed regular physical activity by playing tennis, racquetball, and golf, running road races and marathons, skating, wind surfing, and skiing, as well as purchasing millions of dollars of home exercise equipment. Women, many for the first time ever, have joined classes in aerobic dance, step aerobics, water aerobics, and several other variations of exercise combined with music. Health and fitness clubs now offer aerobics classes, individualized weight training programs, aerobic machines such as stair climbers, treadmills, stationary bikes, and rowing machines, and instruction in tennis, racquetball, and golf. Many clubs also offer various sports leagues and tournaments, massage, sports medicine consultation, and nutritional counseling. Some people have suggested that these clubs have replaced social events and bars as the preferred places for meeting and interacting with others. The appearance of fitness is certainly vogue when looking at fashions—so many Americans are trying to achieve a level of fitness that both looks and feels good. Unfortunately, this glamorizing of ideal body images may be pushing females into unhealthy exercise and diet habits that can lead to amenorrhea, anorexia, and osteoporosis.

YOUTH SPORTS PROGRAMS

In the 1920s, the popularity of sports in the United States led many people to expect the schools to provide competitive sports for children. Some junior and most senior high schools assumed this responsibility because physical educators believed that students in these age groups were physiologically and psychologically prepared for competition. For elementary-age children, educators widely believed that the negative outcomes from competitive sports outweighed the positive benefits. This belief did not prevent the development of youth sports programs, however. Communities, private associations, and civic organizations stepped in to fill the void, seeing sports as a deterrent to delinquency, a tool for social control, a means of developing self-discipline and cooperation, and as an outlet for exercise and fun. Local as well as national programs such as Little League Baseball, Pop Warner Football, and Biddy Basketball expanded to the point that today they involve millions of young athletes and adult organizers and billions of dollars.

Although many physical educators philosophically disagree with highly competitive youth leagues, these sports enterprises are deeply entrenched in American society. Parents have favored youth sports programs for several reasons:

- Their children have fun through participation;
- These programs offer opportunities for learning sports skills;

- These experiences enhance socialization abilities like cooperation and teamwork and development of values;
- Sports involvement contributes to physical development and fitness; and
- Youth sports programs provide children wholesome alternatives for the use of their time, thus lessening misbehavior or unattended hours at home watching television or surfing the web. Additionally, many value youth sports because the whole family can participate together—as players, coaches, cheerleaders, and in various other volunteer capacities.

Children have varying reasons for participating in youth sports. Mostly, they want to have fun, learn or improve sports skills, stay in shape or get exercise, associate with friends, or merely have something to do. Unfortunately, some youth join a team or participate in individual youth sports just to please their parents. After years of success as a young athlete winning, seeking valued rewards or awards, maintaining popularity, or even qualifying for college grants-in-aid or professional careers may become the primary motivations for participating in sports.

When youth sports programs remain focused on the aspirations of the children, and when parents' attitudes and behaviors are kept in perspective, millions benefit. When winning surpasses all other goals, exploitation of the children and an erosion of values reign. For example, exposure to the media, such as the televising of the Little League World Series, has only served to intensify the pressures on young competitors as well as raise the expected levels of performance to adult, and even professional, levels. As a result, children are no longer allowed to be children or to play just for the fun of it. When adults rudely dispute officials' calls and berate their athletes, they become part of the problem. These adults rob children of the many benefits of playful participation in sport. Adult domination also prevents children from learning in and through sport the art of negotiation, how to make decisions, communication skills, and how to lead and follow.

Numerous occurrences in youth sports call attention to the prevalence of exploitation. Pressures to win, commercialization, elimination of less competitive players, injuries resulting from excessive play or practice, violence, overspecialization, cheating, and lack of value development are but a few examples. As more and more educators promote and provide coaching education programs, these problems may be reduced. Parent orientation sessions are also important deterrents to adult misbehavior and the placing of excessive pressures on children.

FEDERAL LEGISLATION

Although early leaders of this country, such as Benjamin Franklin and Thomas Jefferson, were promoters of physical education, the federal government has not, until recent years, become involved in physical education issues. Legislation that directly influences physical education includes mandates for equal opportunity for both genders and for students with special needs.

Coeducational Physical Education

Title IX of the 1972 Education Amendments required equal opportunity in all educational programs and stated as its basic principle that "no person in the United States shall, on the basis of sex, be excluded from participation in, be denied the benefits of, or be subjected to discrimination under any education program or activity receiving federal financial assistance." In relation to physical education, this statement meant it was illegal to discriminate against either gender in curricula content, equipment and facility usage, teacher quality, or other program areas.

Although equitable treatment, which mandated mixed classes (except in sex education and contact sports), was the law, some schools and colleges resisted

An increasingly popular school elective in physical education is weight training. (Photo courtesy Bob Hilliard.)

change. Often this resistance was due to teachers' refusal to instruct students of the opposite gender or to the administration's lack of insistence on compliance. Many institutions maintained class rolls of boys and girls but offered gender-segregated instruction and activity. As attitudes and behaviors gradually changed, some teachers instructed mixed classes but refused to allow girls and boys to compete with and against each other.

Despite such resistance, Title IX has led to substantial changes. Elementary school children accept classes composed of both girls and boys as the norm. As they participate with and against each other during the developmental years, the differences in their levels of performance lessen. Teachers assess abilities and evaluate performances to ensure fair standards and groupings. Increasingly, students in the secondary schools accept combined classes, learning respect for the capabilities of those of the opposite gender. Gradually acceptance and appreciation of girls and women actively participating in sports have led to recreation and fitness programs that welcome all who seek to enjoy activity and develop their physical capabilities.

Adapted Physical Education Programs

Historically, students with disabilities were not given opportunities to participate in activity classes or were assigned to corrective or remedial classes, with a resulting social stigma. The development of adapted programs led to a more individualized approach. **Adapted physical education** is for excep-

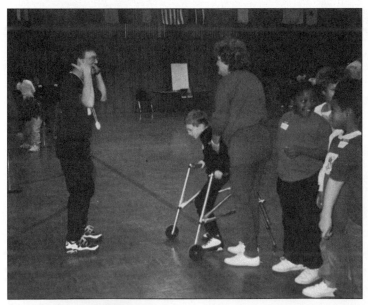

Inclusion places physically-challenged children into regular education classes. (Photo courtesy Bob Hilliard.)

tional students who are so different in mental, physical, emotional, or behavioral characteristics that, in the interest of quality of educational opportunity, special provisions must be made for their proper education. Yet not all schools made such provisions for students' special needs; therefore, the federal government became involved.

Section 504 of the Rehabilitation Act of 1973 specified that "no otherwise qualified handicapped person shall, on the basis of handicap, be excluded from participation in, be denied the benefits of, or otherwise be subjected to discrimination under any program which receives or benefits from Federal financial assistance." Thus every student was guaranteed access to the entire school program, including physical education. The Education Amendment Act of 1974 mandated that all children must be placed in the least restrictive environment (LRE), or the setting in which their optimal learning and development could occur.

The Education for All Handicapped Children Act of 1975 (Public Law 94-142) was the first law to specifically mandate physical education in its guidelines. Generally, it required that physical education, specially designed if necessary, must be provided for every child with a disability in the public schools within regular physical education classes, unless the student has unusual restrictions; any unusual restrictions are to be provided for through the development of an Individualized Education Program (IEP).

The basic tenets of the Individuals with Disabilities Education Act (IDEA) have remained intact since the original passage of the law in 1975, even though each set of amendments has strengthened the original law. This legislation has fostered significant changes in the lives of children with disabilities, their families, and in the roles of schools and teachers who educate children with disabilities. The six principles of IDEA include: free, appropriate public education; appropriate evaluation; an individualized education program; the least restrictive environment for each child; parent and student participation in decision making; and procedural safeguards. Special education and related services, including the initial evaluation, must be provided at public expense, under public supervision and direction, and be delivered by appropriately trained personnel. (In addition, the Americans with Disabilities Act [passed in 1990] sought to eliminate barriers that have prevented individuals with special needs from fully participating in society.)

The IEP must be a written plan that has been designed by a representative of the public agency (school) who is qualified to provide or to supervise special education, and may include the input of the child's teacher, one or both of the child's parents, the child (when appropriate), and other individuals selected at the discretion of the parent or school. One problem in the development of IEPs has been the frequent failure to involve physical educators, even though Public Law 94-142 specifies that the children's physical needs must be met.

Each IEP must contain the following:

- A statement of the child's present levels of educational performance;

INDIVIDUALIZED EDUCATION PROGRAM

Student: <u>Chris Miller</u>　　　　　　Age: <u>9</u>　　　　　　　　Grade: <u>3</u>
School: <u>Eastwood Elementary</u>　　Height: <u>42"</u>　　　　　　Weight: <u>62</u>
Placement: <u>Least Restrictive Environment</u>　　Date of annual review: <u>August, 2001</u>
Present level of performance: Chris is mildly mentally retarded and lacks balance and eye-hand coordination skills; prefers sedentary to vigorous activity; can toss and catch a rubber ball thrown from 12 feet, 3 times out of 10; can do two bent-knee sit-ups and comes within 6 inches of touching toes with legs slightly flexed.

Annual goals:

1. Increase abdominal strength
2. Increase flexibility
3. Increase eye-hand coordination
4. Increase balance

Sample Performance Objectives	Sample Activities	Evaluation Measure	Completion Date
1. Perform 10 bent-knee sit-ups without stopping	1. Teacher-assisted sit-ups daily; leg lifts held for 1 to 10 seconds	1. Observation	1. December, 2001
2. Touch toes with fingers without bending knees and hold for 2 seconds	2. Lower and upper leg stretches; teacher-assisted toe touches	2. Observation	2. December, 2001
3. Toss and catch a 20-inch rubber ball, at 20 feet, 6 times out of 10 times	3. Self-toss, wall toss, and partner toss from 10, 15, and 20 feet	3. Observation	3. March, 2002
4. Walk 6 feet on a 4-inch balance beam placed 6 inches off the floor	4. Walk on a 4-inch line on the floor; teacher assistance while on balance beam	4. Observation	4. March, 2002

Date: _____　　Teacher: _____

- A statement of measurable annual goals, including benchmark short-term objectives;

- A statement of the specific special education and related services to be provided to the child;

- A statement of any individual modifications in the administration of statewide or districtwide assessment of student achievement;

- Projected dates, frequency, location and duration of services; and
- Transition services.

The box on page 288 provides a sample IEP.

Inclusion refers to the integration of children with disabilities into classes with nondisabled students. Full inclusion means that regardless of whether a child can do the appropriate classwork or keep up with the achievements of other students, a child with a disability is placed in a regular educational setting. Advocates of full inclusion emphasize that being near and interacting with nondisabled peers, primarily to foster social skills and to build self-esteem or self-image, far outweigh any liabilities. The principles of full inclusion rest upon the rights of children to attend their local schools, instead of being isolated in special programs. Critical to the success of inclusion classrooms are well-prepared teachers, supplementary aids and services, and support personnel.

Another approach that complies with federal legislation is the use of the least restrictive environment. Each child is placed into the educational setting most appropriate for his or her learning and development. Placement and curricular decisions are based on individuals' abilities and needs, with a continuum of alternatives available from full inclusion to one-on-one instruction. Special classes, such as adaptive physical education, should be provided, if needed, to enhance the learning of each child. Although students may learn from one another, students with disabilities may also negatively affect the academic environment of other students by increasing class sizes or by making the teacher's job more difficult. Rather than automatically including all children with special needs in a regular classroom, each child should be placed in the setting where optimal learning can occur. This least restrictive environment varies from child to child. Whether mentally retarded, learning disabled, emotionally disturbed, or physically handicapped, all children can benefit from having programs that are appropriate for their developmental levels.

SUMMARY

Curricula in physical education today provide a blend of gymnastics, play, fitness, health, intramurals, recreation, and sports. The new physical education, beginning in the 1920s, led in this transition, demonstrating that physical education contributed to the complete education of students. The box on pages 290–291 highlights many of the significant occurrences in physical education and sport in the twentieth century, including the play movement, the rise of teacher training, the growth of women's physical education, the education of the physical movement, the growing emphasis on fitness, the focus on human movement, and the influence of the scientific movement, educational developmentalism, and social education as well as the establishment of standards, and accountability. Intramural programs developed to meet the needs of students desiring sports competition outside of physical education classes yet

SIGNIFICANT EVENTS IN TWENTIETH CENTURY PHYSICAL EDUCATION AND SPORT

1900	Grammar School Athletic League of Philadelphia created
1903	Public Schools Athletic League formed in New York by Luther Gulick (Girls' Branch began in 1905)
1906	Playground Association of America founded
1909	Publication of Jesse Bancroft's *Games for School, Home, Playground, and Gymnasium,* Clark Hetherington's *The Normal Course in Play,* and R. Tait McKenzie's *Exercise in Education and Medicine*
1910	Teachers College of Columbia University offered the first master's degree with a specialization in physical education
1913	First departments of intramural sports started at the University of Michigan and The Ohio State University
1916	New York became the first state to appoint a Director of Physical Education, Thomas Storey
1919	Fred Leonard published *Pioneers of Modern Physical Training*
1919	Eastern District of the APEA founded
1924	National Association of Physical Education of College Women started
1924	James McCurdy's *Physiology of Exercise* and Elmer Mitchell's *Intramural Athletics* became the first books published on both subjects
1924	Teachers College of Columbia University conferred the first Ph.D. with a specialization in physical education
1926	American Academy of Physical Education founded
1927	*The New Physical Education: A Program of Naturalized Activities for Education toward Citizenship* authored by Thomas Wood and Rosalind Cassidy
1928	Southern District of the APEA founded
1930	First publication of the *Journal of Health and Physical Education* and the *Research Quarterly*
1931	Mabel Lee elected first woman president of the American Physical Education Association
1931	Northwest District of the APEA founded
1934	Central District and Midwest District of the APEA established from the former Middle West District
1935	Southwest District of the APEA founded
1937	American Physical Education Association merged with the Department of School Health and Physical Education of the National Education Association to form the American Association for Health and Physical Education
1938	The AAHPER established a national headquarters at the National Education Association in Washington, D.C.
1947	The AAHPER published *A Guide on Planning Facilities for Athletics, Recreation, Physical and Health Education*
1948	National Conference on Undergraduate Professional Preparation in Health Education, Physical Education, and Recreation held
1950	National Conference of Graduate Study in Health Education, Physical Education, and Recreation held
1953	Results of the Kraus-Weber Minimal Muscular Fitness Test published
1955	AAHPER began an Outdoor Education Project
1955	*Physical Education for High School Students* published by AAHPER

(continued)

SIGNIFICANT EVENTS IN TWENTIETH-CENTURY PHYSICAL EDUCATION AND SPORT (CONTINUED)

1956	President's Council on Youth Fitness established
1956	AAHPER Fitness Conference held
1958	Administration of the AAHPER Youth Fitness Test began
1959	The International Council on Health, Physical Education, and Recreation established
1965	Lifetime Sports Foundation established
1971	Association for Intercollegiate Athletics for Women established
1972	Title IX of the Education Amendments passed
1972	National Conference on Professional Preparation of the Elementary Specialist held
1974	National association restructured into the American Alliance for Health, Physical Education and Recreation, comprised of seven associations
1975	The Education of All Handicapped Children Act passed
1978	Amateur Sports Act passed
1980	AAHPERD moved into its headquarters in Reston, Virginia
1980	AAHPERD initiated the Lifetime Health-Related Physical Fitness Test
1984	Second National Conference on Preparing the Physical Education Specialist for Children held
1985	Centennial convention of the American Alliance for Health, Physical Education, Recreation and Dance held
1988	AAHPERD introduced Physical Best, physical fitness assessment and education program
1996	Surgeon General's *Report on Physical Activity and Health* published

at a lower level than varsity athletics. Leadership from the national association, such as through professional journals or at conferences, and standards for teacher preparation helped solidify physical education into a recognized profession.

Collegiate sports for men expanded from their student-organized status into multimillion-dollar business enterprises with extensive regulations and media exposure. Women's sports in the colleges focused on a philosophy of mass participation until the 1970s when the AIAW encouraged competition and Title IX mandated equality of opportunity. The most visible amateur sports competitions were the Olympic Games. The play movement for children expanded into recreational activities and then fitness for families and workers.

Despite sporadic emphasis on fitness, throughout the twentieth century many American children have not achieved optimal fitness. Yet, instilling in children a commitment to health-related fitness remains a primary goal of education. Youth sports programs can also potentially benefit the participants, although adult-controlled leagues may threaten the intended outcomes. The federal government has attempted to ensure that all Americans have equal educational opportunities by legislating that all school children, including those with disabilities, have the right to physical education.

CAREER PERSPECTIVE

JESSE FEIRING WILLIAMS
(1886–1966)

EDUCATION
A.B., Oberlin College
M.D., Columbia University

BACKGROUND

Jesse Feiring Williams has been called the dominant physical educator between 1930 and 1960. He emphasized that the development of the individual was physical education's *raison d'être* and that physical education was obligated to equip students to live in and to contribute to society. Through his voluminous writings and the students he taught, his philosophical influence spread throughout the country.

Williams obtained his bachelor's degree at Oberlin College. While an undergraduate, he served as Director of Athletics and as a coach and a tutor at Oberlin Academy. For the majority of his career (1911–1916; 1919–1941), he taught at Teachers College of Columbia University; after 1923, he also served as head of the department. Teachers College was one of the foremost institutions for graduate study in physical education in the United States at that time. Numerous students were directly influenced by Williams' philosophy. The most significant of his 41 books was *The Principles of Physical Education,* which was published in eight editions between 1927 and 1965. In addition, Williams authored numerous articles, which were published in the *Journal of Health and Physical Education, Journal of Higher Education, School and Society, Teachers College Record,* and other professional journals.

ACCOMPLISHMENTS

Throughout his writings, Williams maintained that the role of education, and hence physical education, should be to prepare children to live in a democratic society. He stressed that physical education merited inclusion in the educational process because it provided opportunities for equality of learning opportunity, for developing personal worth and individual responsibility, and for realizing self-fulfillment. The development of social values, such as a sense of belonging, working together as a member of a group, and group responsibility, reinforced Williams' belief that physical education should help individuals adjust to and serve in society.

Programmatically, Williams opposed formalized gymnastics because they thwarted, rather than enhanced, the learning of moral and social values. In contrast, sports and games provided the mechanism through which values such as initiative and self-discipline were learned. In his advocacy of this change in curricular content, he paralleled the ideas of Thomas Wood, who also taught at Teachers College.

Williams constantly reiterated that humans were unified beings. To overemphasize physical development distorted harmony and acknowledged a mind/body dualism. He insisted that physical education must concern itself with developing proper emotional responses, personal relationships, group behavior, mental learning, and other related outcomes. To achieve these objectives, he advocated that more time be devoted to class discussions, even at the expense of activity.

CONTRIBUTIONS TO PHYSICAL EDUCATION

Heavily influenced by the social and educational theories of John Dewey, Williams' philosophy answered an especially timely concern. Namely, he stated that the objectives of education and physical education were inextricably interwoven. Education's mission must rest on inculcating students with society's values, and physical education provided a vital laboratory for learning these lessons. So forceful were his writings that he convinced the profession that it should afford opportunities for individuals and groups to learn mentally and socially as well as physically.

REVIEW QUESTIONS

1. What were the philosophies of the new physical educators of the 1920s? How are these philosophies different from or similar to those of your teachers?
2. What was the significance of any two developments in physical education, other than the new physical education, during the 1900s? Who were the key leaders in these developments?
3. What is the difference between Jesse Williams' education *through* the physical and Charles McCloy's education *of* the physical?
4. What are several programs for which the American Alliance for Health, Physical Education, Recreation and Dance has provided leadership?
5. Why were intramural programs begun? Why did they flourish in the colleges?
6. How is the National Collegiate Athletic Association's power different today from what it was in its earlier years?
7. Why were the sports opportunities provided for girls and women from the 1920s to the late 1960s different from those provided for boys and men?
8. What recreational developments have highlighted each decade since the 1930s? How popular has each been?
9. What have been the major developments in the promotion of youth fitness since the 1950s?
10. What were the major changes that resulted from passage of the following federal legislation: Title IX of the Education Amendments of 1972, Section 504 of the Rehabilitation Act of 1973, and the Education for All Handicapped Children Act of 1975 (IDEA, today)?

STUDENT ACTIVITIES

1. Interview someone in the sports information office, athletic department, library, or news bureau who can help you learn about the earliest intercollegiate men's and women's sports at your institution. Based on this and on

information that you can obtain from other sources, write a two-page description of each of these two programs.

2. Write a three-page comparison of the philosophies and major contributions of the "new physical educators."

3. Learn about the test items of the FITNESSGRAM. Divide into groups and administer these test items to each other.

4. Ask your professors who they think have been the most important physical educators of the twentieth century. Based on their responses and your reading, summarize the career and contributions of one of these persons in a two-minute class presentation.

5. Select one personality from a decade of the twentieth century. Write a three-page description of his or her contributions to physical education, exercise science, and sport.

6. Conduct a class debate about whether the most appropriate theme for physical education should be "education *through* the physical" or "education *of* the physical."

7. Select one theme each for school and for nonschool physical activity programs for the first half and second half of this century. Develop a position statement to explain the value and impact of each on the field of physical education and sport in the twenty-first century.

8. Write a five-page paper comparing the major developments in men's and women's intercollegiate sports in the twentieth century.

REFERENCE

NEA Proceedings, 32:621, 1893, National Education Association.

SUGGESTED READINGS

Bandy S: Clark Wilson Hetherington: a pioneering spirit in physical education, *JOPERD* 56(1):20, 1985. Throughout his many years of service at Missouri, Wisconsin, New York University, and Stanford and in other professional positions, Clark Hetherington stressed achieving educational objectives and reinforced his advocacy of play.

Davenport J: Thomas Denison Wood: physical educator and father of health education, *JOPERD* 55(8):63, 1984. Stressing educational outcomes, Thomas Wood, at Stanford and Teachers College, initiated bachelor's degree programs in physical education. At the latter institution, he also started master's and doctor's degree programs in physical education and undergraduate health education programs.

English EB: Charles H. McCloy: the research professor of physical education, *JOPERD* 54(4):16, 1983. Charles McCloy led in producing a scientific body of knowledge for physical education, especially in the area of strength tests, cardiovascular measures, classification indices, anthropometric scores, and character/social traits.

French R, Henderson H, Kinnison L, Sherrill C: Revisiting Section 504, physical education, and sport, *JOPERD* 69(7):57, 1998. The authors provide an overview of the implications of IDEA for physical education and sport programs.

Hardy D (ed.): Girls' and women's sports—it is our season, *JOPERD*, 61(3):45, 1990. This nine-article feature emphasizes that the time is now for females to get involved in sports—at the grassroots level, in leadership positions, as coaches, in networking, in marketing and promotions, and in public relations.

Massengale J, Swanson R: *History of exercise and sport,* Champaign, 1996, Human Kinetics. This book provides a comprehensive history of the development of exercise and sport programs.

Miller SE: Inclusion of children with disabilities: can we meet the challenge?, *Phy Educ* 51(1):47, 1994. The impact of the Education for All Handicapped Children Act on physical education classes is presented along with the challenges that are presented in inclusion classrooms.

NAGWS Title IX toolbox, I and II, Reston, VA., 1992, 1997, American Alliance for Health, Physical Education, Recreation and Dance. These materials include reprints of legislation, litigation reports, articles, quotation from physical education leaders, and recent gender equity litigation for use in the fight against sex discrimination in education-related athletics.

Sack AL, Staurowsky EJ: *College athletics for hire: the evolution and legacy of the NCAA's amateur myth,* Westport, Conn., 1998, Praeger. This critique exposes the failures, excesses, and hypocrises of the NCAA in its attempts to protect its turf and economic interest.

Stein JU: Total inclusion or least restrictive environment? *JOPERD* 65(9):21, 1994. This article describes the principles of total inclusion and the least restrictive environment (LRE). It includes an explanation of the basic legislative requirements relevant to the LRE.

Thorngren CM (ed.).: Women in sport leadership, *JOPERD*, 64(3):33, 1993. This seven-article feature emphasizes the leadership roles women physical educators have had and continue to have in coaching, sports officiating, conducting research, and changing societal attitudes.

The Changing Nature of Physical Education, Exercise Science, and Sport

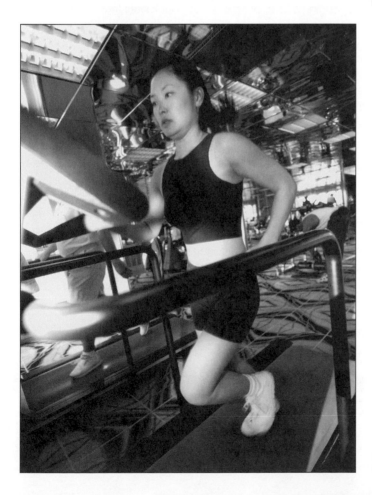

© PhotoDisk
website

10

OPPORTUNITIES AND CHALLENGES IN PHYSICAL EDUCATION AND EXERCISE SCIENCE

KEY CONCEPTS

- A major health need facing Americans of all ages is the importance of attaining and maintaining a level of fitness that contributes to a positive quality of life.
- The expansion of research by specialists in physical education and exercise science, along with the technological advances in research methods and measurements, have contributed to a broader and deeper knowledge base.
- School programs include the concepts of movement education, a renewed emphasis on fitness, and a focus on the development of lifelong fitness behaviors.
- Increasingly, professionals are being held accountable for their students' and clients' learning through a variety of assessments.
- Greater competencies expected of professionals have led to significant changes in certification requirements and accreditation standards.
- Teachers of physical activity in all settings must understand and meet their legal obligations.
- Career burnout can be alleviated by recognizing the signs, counteracting the causes, and by providing appropriate rewards for excellent performance.
- Several instructional challenges face physical educators, but these can be overcome through a comprehensive and relevant curriculum, excellent instruction, varied assessments, lifelong learning, and leadership.

Being physically active is an important key to an enhanced quality of life for individuals of all ages. Providers of recreational and leisure services must adapt to changing demographics, family structures and schedules, work patterns, and economic realities, while enhancing the quality of their programs. Fitness specialists and exercise scientists in various settings work with adults to help them establish and maintain lifelong activity programs. Specialization, research, technology, and the scholarly pursuit of knowledge are significant factors in the expansion and recognition of careers associated with physical activity. Changes in school programs should guarantee opportunities for all persons to meet their unique needs while engaged in progressively challenging experiences. Daily physical education for students, changes in certification requirements, increased teacher competencies, and accreditation standards are all related efforts to improve the quality of education for students. The threat of lawsuits and the high risk of injuries mandate that individuals working in physical activity settings avoid negligent behavior by acting responsibly. Challenges confronting school physical educators include limited equipment and facilities, lack of parental support for education, and discipline problems.

THE VALUE OF PHYSICAL ACTIVITY FOR EVERYONE

Physical activity is for everyone. But convincing people of this fact remains a major challenge. However, as listed in the box on page 301, there are significant and lasting values that result from participating regularly in physical activity.

The objectives of physical education in the schools include: learning and applying fitness concepts, learning motor and fundamental sports skills, encouraging lifetime fitness, gaining knowledge about sports rules and strategies, and enhancing social and emotional development. As discussed in Chapter 1, teachers can only meet these objectives by making them a central focus of their work and teaching them consistently, to ensure their achievement. Teachers must provide quality programs and promote the value of these programs to school administrators, legislators, and parents.

Children and youth must learn healthful living habits while in the school because many will not attend college or be able to afford sports club memberships or expensive private exercise equipment. During the critical elementary years, students need to learn how to develop cardiovascular endurance, with a focus on the frequency, intensity, and duration of exercise. They need to learn to walk, jog, swim, cycle, and jump rope as alternative ways of developing aerobic endurance. They need to learn how to attain and maintain muscular strength, endurance, and flexibility because these health-related fitness components will enhance not only how they feel but also their ability to study, work, and play more easily and productively. Closely aligned with these needs is the importance of teaching children sports skills that they can use throughout life. Basic throwing, catching, striking, and locomotor movements are easily transferable to tennis, golf, bowling, dance, and other lifetime activities. Teachers should demonstrate and positively reinforce development of cooperative behavior, teamwork, fair play, and the ability to be

Tennis is a favorite lifetime physical activity. (Photo courtesy Department of Physical Education and Recreation, State University of West Georgia.)

a follower and a leader. Individually, students will nurture self-confidence and self-worth by being successful in achieving personal goals. Concurrent with these psychomotor and affective outcomes, teachers should ensure that children are provided information about nutrition, diseases, environmental concerns, and the harmful effects of drugs.

After ensuring that quality experiences are offered to their students, teachers should invite school administrators, legislators, and parents to observe what physical education really is. Hosting PTA/PTO programs, parents' nights, mall demonstrations, and other special events show that physical education is vital to the health and well-being of students. In addition, parents should be encouraged to participate more fully in the education of their children.

VALUES OF PHYSICAL ACTIVITY

- Reduces risk of premature death
- Reduces risk of coronary heart disease
- Reduces risk of stroke
- Reduces risk of high blood pressure
- Reduces risk of obesity
- Reduces risk of osteoporosis
- Reduces risk of colon cancer
- Reduces risk of diabetes
- Reduces risk of high cholesterol
- Reduces risk of feelings of depression and anxiety
- Reduces risk of sedentary behaviors such as television viewing and playing computer games
- Increases functioning of the metabolic, endocrine, and immune systems
- Increases maintenance of healthy bones, muscles, and joints
- Increases self-efficacy
- Increases alertness and ability to learn
- Increases emotional and mental health
- Increases energy level and feeling of well-being
- Increases enjoyment of life

To achieve these values, everyone should participate in at least 30 minutes of moderately intense activity on most days of the week and a minimum of 30 minutes of vigorous physical activity at least three days a week

Other Recommendations

- Require quality physical education classes every day for students in grades K-12
- Ensure that every child becomes proficient in one lifetime sport or fitness activity
- Provide publicly-funded physical activity programs for individuals of all ability levels and ages

At the high school level, there should be a continuation of the emphasis on fitness development, lifetime sports, and health issues such as smoking, drugs, sex education, and nutrition. At this level, it is especially important to give students some options in what sports and activities they want to learn. Although some consumer information may be relevant at an earlier age, the teen years lend themselves well to consumer education. Adolescents need to learn how to differentiate between the facts and fallacies of fitness ads. Although some home exercise equipment, such as rowing machines or exercise bicycles, can improve one's fitness if used properly, machines that supposedly help a person lose weight without effort blatantly misrepresent the truth. What are the caloric and nutritional components of the average fast-food meal? Are any diet centers or diet programs safe or worth the money? Should a high school athlete take drugs to enhance performance? Should a person smoke cigarettes or marijuana? What are the effects of alcohol on the body and its fitness? Where can a person find a qualified aerobics instructor? Given the need for answers to these questions and the potential benefits of school physical education, it is imperative that schools fund physical education and health curricula.

Those who are opposed to this funding claim that physical education is nonessential. But the poor fitness levels of American school-age children, which may currently be the worst ever, say otherwise. Others argue that community programs and interscholastic athletics can provide students with adequate sports opportunities. However, due to the cost and the additional time, many students (especially those who tend to drop out of school), will never participate in these programs. And in most community-sponsored programs, competition rather than instruction is stressed.

Parents who realize the importance of living fit lifestyles can demand that the schools help their children learn these habits. But they must be convinced of the importance of developing the fitness parameters themselves; by making lifestyle changes at home, they can reinforce their child's learning in school. Again, the involvement of parents in the education of their children is vitally important.

Less than half of the colleges and universities have retained their required physical education programs. Many other colleges and universities have reduced their requirements because of budget limitations and an increasing emphasis on general education and major course requirements. In many of the programs at institutions where physical education is an elective, these programs have had to become entirely self-supporting. Students elect any activity course available, but they pay instructional, facility usage, and equipment rental fees. On other campuses, this pay-as-you-participate approach applies only to certain off-campus or nontraditional courses. This type of program is limited to those who are genuinely interested in a particular activity or sport and who can afford to enroll in it. Unfortunately, at universities with elective programs, those who need physical education the most may not choose to enroll.

In 1992, the American Heart Association added physical inactivity to high blood pressure, smoking, and high blood cholesterol as one of the significant contributors to heart disease. To counteract the effects of these, many inactive, overweight adults are changing their habits. As middle-aged and senior citizens join the millions of others who are walking to stay fit, these segments of the population reinforce being physically active. To help prevent their becoming the next coronary statistics, older Americans are quitting smoking, reducing alcohol consumption, ridding their diets of many sources of cholesterol, and exercising. Popular exercise and recreational activities include walking, swimming, fishing, camping, aerobics, and bowling. For those with physical limitations, many retirement homes, recreation departments, churches, and hospitals are providing appropriate opportunities for movement, sports, and recreational pastimes. Providing for the leisure needs of older Americans may become the largest segment of new physical activity-related jobs in this century.

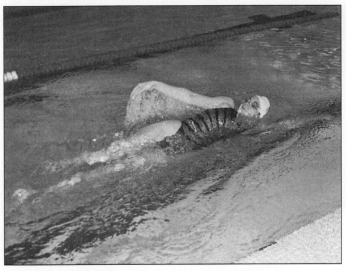

Exercise and sport scientists may prescribe swimming as part of an aerobic conditioning program for clients. (Photo courtesy Bob Hilliard.)

PROGRAM ADHERENCE FACTORS

- Set realistic goals
- Implement an individualized and progressive program that is safe
- Ensure proper supervision that includes education and motivation
- Be patient—developing fitness takes time
- Ensure convenient access to facilities
- Provide periodic assessments and feedback
- Provide family and peer group encouragement and reinforcement
- Participate in fun and satisfying activities

Once people are convinced that regular exercise is not only important, but essential, the next challenge is how to get those who have begun exercise programs to continue them. Adherence is a pervasive problem for everyone who prescribes exercises and activities. Whether a corporation or the individual is paying for the exercise program, the goal is positive, lasting outcomes. The box above lists several factors that contribute to activity adherence. Most adult exercise programs emphasize similar strategies to enhance lasting and positive lifestyle changes. Most importantly, all people need appropriately designed programs that they can understand, goals that are feasible, measureable, and monitored, and positive experiences that will encourage them to adhere to the program.

PHYSICAL ACTIVITY TIPS

- Schedule a time for daily physical activity of at least 30 minutes
- Vary your physical activities to maintain enthusiasm and interest
- Find a partner to join you in your physical activity program so you can help each other adhere to your physical activity program
- Set realistic goals so that you can achieve success
- Include physical activities that contribute to all around physical fitness, such as cardiovascular endurance, muscular strength and endurance, and flexibility
- Use time while engaged in physical activity to socialize with others
- Use time while riding a stationary bicycle or using other aerobic equipment to read (intellectual benefits)
- Make sure that your equipment and exercise areas are safe
- Combine physical activity with healthier eating patterns
- Have fun and enjoy

Physical activity should be a part of everyone's life regardless of age or capability. Some physical activity suggestions are provided in the box above. The earlier you can teach others the value of being physically fit, the greater the quality of their lives. You are challenged to serve as advocates who never cease to proclaim and demonstrate through your lives the value of physical activity.

RECREATION AND LEISURE SERVICES

Demographic changes, altered family and work patterns, environmental concerns, and shifts in the economy have transformed contemporary recreation and leisure services. An increasingly diverse ethnic mix in the population of the United States makes business as usual no longer acceptable. African Americans, Native Americans, Asian Americans, Hispanics, and other ethnic groups are demanding recreational and artistic programs that appeal to their unique cultural backgrounds. The former melting pot concept has given way to an appreciation and promotion of diversity throughout society, which means these changes must be reflected in leisure programming.

Demographics indicate a graying of America. This segment of the population possesses considerable political clout and financial resources. As life expectancies increase, older adults are expecting to have their recreational needs met along with those of younger groups. Senior citizens are often physically vigorous. While some may require only passive activities in a retirement center, other retirees robustly play golf and tennis, walk and hike, travel and tour, and swim and cycle. In this century, serving the recreational and leisure needs of this population will become more widespread and demanding. Seniors want more opportunities for:

- Masters competitions in sports like tennis, swimming, golf, and running
- Senior Games in numerous sports
- Age-and ability-appropriate activity classes at health and fitness clubs
- Age-and ability-appropriate activity programs sponsored by recreation departments
- Walking clubs
- Sport leagues such as in bowling, golf, and softball
- Therapeutic programs sponsored by senior citizen programs, retirement centers, and hospitals
- Intergenerational after-school activity programs for kids and grandparents

The traditional 1950s family of a working father, a homemaking mother, and two or three children characterizes less than half of today's families with school-age children. Divorced parents, broken homes, and absent fathers leave approximately one out of every two children in single-parent homes before they reach adulthood. The cost and quality of childcare have become major issues for these parents. Meeting the developmental play needs of preschool children challenges those who offer in-house or commercialized childcare services. Currently, schools, churches, and public centers offer after-school care for children, which may or may not include developmentally appropriate play opportunities.

Many adolescents (and some preadolescents) have become latchkey kids—children who come home from school to empty houses. These unattended children often have to lock themselves in their houses because playing outside is considered unsafe. This setting seems to foster unending hours of watching television and eating junk food. Lack of supervision may also permit youthful experimentation with alcohol, tobacco, illegal drugs, sex, and law-breaking activities.

In most cities and towns, the schools, recreation departments and private clubs provide numerous alternatives to unsafe, inactive, and delinquent behaviors. Competitive youth sports teams, children's fitness clubs and programs, adventure activities, cooperative games, and creative playground opportunities are just a few of the options available. While some parents can afford to enroll their children in private dance, gymnastics, swimming, or tennis lessons, many rely on public programs for facilities, equipment, and instruction.

Threats to the environment also threaten the resources available for recreation and leisure. Outdoor enthusiasts are increasing their efforts to protect natural resources and open spaces from abusive individuals and encroaching real estate developers. Rock climbers, hikers, and campers are expected to leave nature exactly as they found it. Industries are expected to stop polluting the air, water, and land. Despite limited resources, cities and states continue to acquire land to meet the recreational needs of present and future generations.

Like many public programs, recreation and leisure services have experienced increased budgetary constraints. Although people are taxed for municipal services, including recreation, there never seems to be enough money, space, or programs. To meet their budgets, many recreation departments must charge entry or participation fees, which excludes those unable to pay. In addition to the rising cost of programing, these agencies have increased expenses due to vandalism, lawsuits, and security. And, bringing programs and facilities into compliance with the Americans with Disabilities Act is costly. To adequately serve individuals with limitations, facilities must be handicapped accessible, have specialized recreational equipment, and qualified, trained personnel.

Outdoor education activities, such as rock climbing can be practiced in safe situations. (Photo courtesy Department of Physical Education and Recreation, State University of West Georgia.)

Recreation and leisure services are among the human services industries that have proliferated in recent decades. Everyone pursuing careers in national and state parks, boys' and girls' clubs, commercial and corporate fitness, sports clubs, and recreation must focus on customer or client satisfaction. In order to accomplish this, you must determine the personal goals of those you serve. For example, those who choose careers in backpacking, rock climbing, and canoeing may have the following goals in mind for program participants:

- To learn outdoor skills
- To challenge the limits of one's ability
- To enjoy risk-taking achievements
- To develop cooperative or self-reliant behavior
- To appreciate nature

Knowing these goals, you can propose suitable programs to meet their goals or help them design a customized individual or group program.

Recreation and leisure services professionals may choose to seek national certification through the National Recreation and Park Association. To be certified, one has to meet educational and experience requirements as well as demonstrate a high level of professionalism in their work. As with other certifications, the Certified Park and Recreational Professional has enhanced credibility and contributes to the status of the field. The challenge for recreation and leisure services specialists is to create programs with activities that match each person's interests and needs.

EXERCISE SCIENCE

More and more students are pursuing careers related to physical activity that are outside educational settings. Many prepare for these noneducational careers by studying exercise science where one studies human movement along with the body's adaptations to movement. The exercise scientist seeks to understand the scientific foundations of exercise's physiological responses. This field has grown more specialized as the quantity and quality of knowledge has expanded.

In the 1970s and 1980s, colleges and universities responded to the decrease in physical education majors preparing to teach by offering specializations. Students were attracted to these majors because they sought careers in the emerging fields of athletic training, corporate and commercial fitness, and sport management. Most of these graduates were attracted to positions that allowed them to work with adults participating in fitness and sports programs. The diversity of career options and opportunities for advancement, travel, economic security, research, and management also appealed to many.

Career options in exercise science have increased in recent years due to the media-reinforced appeal of cosmetic fitness, concern about health conditions related to lifestyle such as coronary heart disease and obesity, and skyrocketing health care costs. Those most likely to participate in fitness programs are the upper class, young adults, males, whites, suburban residents, and the more highly educated, although fitness enthusiasts occupy every demographic stratum. Fitness specialists find their greatest challenge in trying to motivate individuals to initiate and maintain activity programs through self-discipline. The two most frequent explanations for not exercising are lack of time and poor motivation or self-discipline.

Fitness programs have expanded in private and public health and sports clubs, recreation departments, retirement homes, work sites, rehabilitation clinics, hotels, and resorts. Many people have joined clubs specifically to receive instruction and encouragement from fitness leaders in aerobics and weight training. Besides teaching, individuals in these careers are expected to prescribe safe exercise programs, monitor members' progress, provide nutritional guidance, manage the facility, and sometimes supervise other personnel. Many fitness specialists and exercise scientists are expected to conduct smoking cessation classes, provide information about injury prevention and care, and teach exercises for the reduction of low back pain. Undergraduate students need to be prepared to handle these diverse responsibilities. Increasingly, graduates of exercise science curricula are working with adults (and sometimes children) in health and fitness programs. As described in previous chapters, these professionals are challenged to direct and manage programs that help unfit Americans develop and maintain personal fitness, to provide recreational opportunities in a wide variety of sports and games,

Exercise scientists can help athletic teams improve their flexibility, strength, and endurance, which in turn can help improve performance. (Photo courtesy State University of West Georgia Sports Information Office.)

and to offer leisure-time activities that may include spectator events, cruises, and trips to theme parks.

College graduates may need to obtain certifications and licensure in order to work in exercise science positions. More and more health and fitness clubs are expecting their employees to hold certifications as personal trainers, aerobics leaders, and fitness program directors. Almost all individuals responsible for providing emergency care to athletes in sports competitions are expected to have training in basic first aid and cardiopulmonary resuscitation. Persons serving as athletic trainers *must* hold such certifications. States and employers will increasingly require higher levels of expertise to ensure that only qualified individuals work in physical activity situations. Exercise scientists need to demonstrate competencies in areas such as the following:

- The structure and function of the human body and its systems
- The operation of muscles and joints through various movements, such as supination, pronation, flexion, extension, adduction, and rotation
- The major components of motor fitness, including agility, speed, balance, coordination, and power, and the biomechanical principles underlying these
- The biomechanical principles associated with striking, throwing, catching, running, walking, and jumping
- The ability to accurately measure body fat, blood pressure, heart rate, and oxygen consumption during exercise
- The ability to explain, demonstrate, and prescribe the physiological principles associated with warm-ups and cool-downs
- The ability to explain, demonstrate, and prescribe appropriate cardiovascular endurance activities
- The ability to explain, demonstrate, and prescribe exercises designed to increase muscular strength and endurance
- The ability to explain, demonstrate, and prescribe appropriate flexibility exercises
- The care and prevention of common exercise injuries

Most people who solicit the services of an exercise scientist want to develop all-around wellness. Physical activity is only one component of all around wellness. Increasingly, people are also seeking emotional, spiritual, intellectual, and social benefits along with fitness. Many want to find balance through their workouts leading to the management of stress reduction, increased self-esteem, friendships, and peace of mind. This means that program and exercise leaders must prepare themselves to address the whole person, not just their bodies. The expansion in program offerings in health and fitness clubs to include massage, yoga, nutrition counseling, stress management workshops, and musical and artistic outings along with personal fitness plans reflects this broadening focus.

GENERALISTS REPLACED BY SPECIALISTS

Traditionally, physical educators were generalists who could teach a dozen or more sports, coach two or three teams, and still make time to sweep the gymnasium floor. They proudly considered themselves generalists who focused on the practical field of teaching. Students majoring in physical education in previous generations were exposed to such breadth. Today, students are more likely to specialize in one of the exercise sciences.

The knowledge explosion in recent years has influenced all subject areas. Expanded research efforts, technological advances, and computer-assisted data analyses have aided this proliferation. The quality and quantity of information have led to increasing specializations for two primary reasons. First, the sheer volume of books, research, reports, and scholarly papers makes it difficult for individuals to gain a comprehension of knowledge in any one discipline, let alone several. Second, a greater understanding of a sub-discipline encourages people to specialize in an area of particular interest. For example, the coach who prefers treating athletic injuries and helping to rehabilitate athletes could become a full-time athletic trainer. The physical education generalist who teaches a wide spectrum of courses, but really enjoys teaching weight training, might choose to become a personal trainer. Or a person who wants to help highly skilled individuals enhance their performances may become a sport psychologist, biomechanist, or exercise physiologist.

Exercise physiologists measure oxygen consumption to help prescribe appropriate fitness programs.

The popularity of physical activity and sport throughout society has created numerous, diverse career options. Colleges and universities have responded by broadening the types of majors offered. Most students today choose to specialize in athletic training, sport management, fitness, or exercise science because these areas interest them and because of the availability of jobs. When hired, they will be expected to remain knowledgeable in their specialty.

Graduate degree programs at the master's and doctor's levels are increasingly specialized. For example, graduate students with career goals of becoming exercise physiologists or sport psychologists study specific content areas, like biochemistry and experimental psychology. Corporate fitness directors, club managers, athletic trainers at universities or on staff with professional teams, and facility managers are often required to have master's degrees because of the scope of their responsibilities.

College faculty are required to have the minimum of a master's degree, while university professors must have earned doctorates. Both groups are usually expected to teach in their areas of specialization. Most universities also require scholarly productivity of faculty including research-based presentations at professional conferences and publications in peer-reviewed journals. Most of this scholarship is narrowly focused, reflecting areas of specialization, faculty interests, and current research.

PROLIFERATION OF RESEARCH

Within the past decade, the quantity of scholarly publications and presentations in physical education and exercise science has been increasing. Responding to university mandates, specialists with Ph.Ds are dedicating themselves to expanding knowledge in their areas of specialization. They pursue research questions such as how to improve athletic performance, how to enhance the process of teaching and learning movement skills, and how to maximize muscle mass and flexibility using certain types of exercise equipment. Physical education and exercise science professionals in corporate fitness centers, recreation programs, and fitness and health clubs are also conducting research on their various fitness programs, training regimens, and success rates among their clientele.

A growing area of research in physical education focuses on pedagogy. Pedagogical studies include teaching observations such as analyses of time-on-task and academic learning time, student performance, and teacher expectations, and how these are interrelated. Research in this specialization has the potential to dramatically affect the quality of instructional classes in all settings.

Technology has also contributed to the proliferation of research in physical education and exercise science. Athletes can now recover from injuries faster through advanced surgical techniques and computer-monitored rehabilitation programs. Data collection on the incidence and cause of injuries has been used to redesign conditioning and practice drills to both reduce injury and enhance rehabilitation. Sport psychologists use biofeedback and relaxation techniques to positively impact performance. Biomechanists apply computer technology to skill

Computers can be used for word processing and data analysis.

execution in order to both improve technique and reduce the risk of injury. Computer analyses of blood lactates, oxygen exchange, workloads, and drug effects are invaluable to the exercise physiologist's understanding of how the body functions under the stress of exercise.

Library retrieval systems and CD-ROMS help researches in all disciplines keep abreast of current research, trends, and experimental data. Access to such information allows researchers to attempt to replicate studies or build upon the findings of their colleagues. Electronic mail also assists researchers collaborate in a timely manner. Without the use of personal computers for word processing, data analyses, and information retrieval through the Internet, the productivity of today's university, corporate, and community researchers would be tremendously hampered. Increasingly, physicians, sport psychologists, sport biomechanists, exercise physiologists, and athletic trainers will share their expertise and research electronically, to the benefit of students, world-class athletes, and the general public.

Physical education and exercise science researchers are frequently criticized for their failure to apply their findings. Technology can help alleviate at least part of this problem by emphasizing practical as well as theoretical studies, disseminating new information more widely, and focusing on specific situations in need of change. For example, those participating in various weight-loss programs could be outfitted with heart rate monitors to ensure that they are exercising within their target heart rate zones. By careful record-keeping with regard to heart rates, diets, frequency and duration of exercises, types of exercises, and so forth, exercise scientists along with athletic trainers, aerobics instructors, and fitness program directors would not only add to the base of knowledge concerning weight loss, they would also have one more scientific measure by which to compare various weight loss

WEB CONNECTIONS

1. www.kidsrunning.com

    This innovative site sponsored by *Runner's World* includes ideas about recreational and competitive running activities for children, including news events, writings by kids, advice on setting up programs, and school curricular suggestions.

2. www.acsm-msse.org

    This site for *Medicine and Science in Sports and Exercise* lists the full-text position stands of the American College of Sports Medicine that have been published in this professional journal. Among these are "The Recommended Quantity and Quality of Exercise for Developing and Maintaining Cardiorespiratory and Muscular Fitness," "Flexibility in Healthy Adults," "Exercise and Physical Activity for Older Adults," and "Recommendations for Cardiovascular Screening, Staffing, and Emergency Policies at Health/Fitness Facilities."

3. www.aoa.dhhs.gov/aoa/pages/agepages/exercise.html

    At this site, the National Institute on Aging provides information about exercise as well as helpful links to other sites that focus on physical activity and health issues.

4. http://chid.nih.gov/welcome/welcome.html

    The Combined Health Information Database provides a comprehensive bibliography of health-related agencies of the Federal Government with links to titles, abstracts, and availability of health information and health education resources.

5. www.ncate.org

    This site of the National Council for Accreditation of Teacher Education describes the performance-based standards for teacher education programs and provides links to the content standards in all fields.

6. www.ncbi.nlm.nih.gov/pubmed

    Check out the PubMed site of the National Library of Medicine to gain access to over 11 million citations in MEDLINE, PreMEDLINE, and other related databases, with links to participating online journals.

7. http://pe.central.vt.edu/websites/websitesmenu.html

    This site provides a plethora of links to sites of instructional value to physical education teachers.

8. www.acsm.org/pdf/careers.pdf

    Go to this site to learn about the variety of careers in sports medicine and exercise science.

programs. Physical educators and exercise scientists who could benefit from such findings also have a responsibility to work with researchers in applying new information in a timely fashion. This will help close the research-to-practice gap.

It is incumbent on fitness and exercise professionals to remain current with the latest research. Regardless of the position held, the knowledge explosion has made the "half-life" of information learned in college, graduate school, or certification courses short-lived. That is, the relevancy and even accuracy of information that you learn while obtaining your physical education or exercise science degree may be wrong, dangerous, or of questionable validity a decade after you graduate. A few examples follow. Once-popular exercises such as squat thrusts are now contraindicated. Withholding fluid replacement from athletes, which was once thought to build stamina or toughness, is very dangerous. Such an action today would be the basis for a wrongful death lawsuit if an athlete died after being denied fluids. Drugs taken to enhance performance or build muscular strength may be legal today but tomorrow might be banned if new research determined that they were harmful to the body. Thus, lifelong learning is imperative, particularly with regard to research in your specialty.

ELEMENTARY SCHOOL PROGRAMS

Since the early 1900s, elementary school physical education programs have focused on teaching fundamental skills that lead directly to the ability to play sports and games (see Chapter 9). As the curricula evolved, greater stress was placed on a balanced and varied range of activities that progressed from the simple to the complex (in keeping with developmental skills to the various grade levels). These activities included stunts, tumbling, simple games and relays, rhythmic activities, basic sport skills, lead-up games, and game play. Professional preparation courses and textbooks suggested the importance of progressions, certain allotments of time for each major category of activity, and instructional methodology.

In the 1960s, an alternative elementary physical education curriculum, called **movement education,** was introduced in the United States. It was based on the concepts of spatial and body awareness, movement qualities of flow, force, space, and time, and relationships to others or to objects. Students learned about their own space—relative to body size, movement task, and equipment—thereby gaining insights into their own capabilities and becoming more skilled movers. Movement education stressed the following:

- Lessons were to be both activity and student centered.
- Specific movement patterns were to be determined by each child within parameters established by teachers, emphasizing experimentation through movement, not following instructions.
- Children were encouraged to explore and analyze space, their bodies, and various uses for pieces of equipment, with a focus on self-directed or individualized learning.

- Problem solving and guided discovery were incorporated into fun and games, using open-ended challenges and goals.
- The teacher was to guide students through movement experiences by imaginatively and creatively involving both their minds and their bodies.
- Independently and at their own rates of development, children were to be given time to think about the challenges and then move in response.
- Each child was to be evaluated on an individual basis.
- Informality in class structure allowed children to create freely and to learn at their own levels of achievement.

Today, in addition to selecting elementary physical education curricula that match their own philosophies, teachers must be aware of national standards and state curriculum requirements. Each elementary school child should gain competency in several movement forms, learn to express and communicate through movement, and be able to demonstrate movement principles while learning motor skills. In addition, they can begin to achieve a high level of physical and health-related fitness, gain greater self understanding and acceptance of themselves and others, and learn how to handle winning and losing.

Each elementary physical education program should be centered on the concept that movement is a child's first expressive opportunity. Since it is through movement experiences and challenges that the world is discovered, these must be developmentally appropriate for the age, size, and maturational level of each child. For example, parallel and cooperative activities are developmentally

Elementary school students should be encouraged to learn fundamental movement skills. (Photo courtesy Bob Hilliard.)

DEVELOPMENTALLY APPROPRIATE PHYSICAL EDUCATION PRACTICES FOR CHILDREN

Appropriate Practice
Curricular Decisions

The physical education curriculum has an obvious scope and sequence based on goals and objectives that are appropriate for all children. The curriculum includes a balance of skills and concepts in the areas of games, educational gymnastics, and rhythmical activities and dance. Teachers design experiences and select benchmarks to enhance the psychomotor, cognitive, and affective development of all children.

Physical Fitness Testing

Teachers use fitness assessment as part of the ongoing process of helping children understand, enjoy, improve, and/or maintain their physical fitness and well-being. Test results are shared privately with children and their parents as a tool for developing personal goals and strategies for maintaining and increasing the respective fitness parameters. As part of an ongoing program of physical education, children are physically prepared in each fitness component so they can safely complete the assessments.

Forming Groups/Partners

Groups/partners are formed in ways that preserve the dignity and self-respect of every child. For example, a teacher privately forms groups or teams by using knowledge of children's skill abilities in ways that will facilitate learning. Groups or teams may also be formed by grouping clothing colors, birthdays, and favorite activities.

Inappropriate Practice
Curricular Decisions

The physical education curriculum lacks age appropriate, developmental goals and objectives and is based primarily on the teacher's interests, preferences, and background rather than those of the children. For example, the curriculum consists primarily of large group and competitive team games. Activities are the same for all grade levels.

Physical Fitness Testing

Teachers administer the physical fitness test once or twice each year for the purpose of identifying children to receive awards or to meet a school district or state development requirement. Children complete physical fitness test batteries without understanding why they are performing the tests or how the tests or the relationship to their activity level and individuals goals. Results are interpreted based on comparison to norms rather than in terms of how they apply to children's future health and well-being. Individuals scores are publicly posted, comparisons are made between student scores, and/or grades are based on fitness scores. Children are required to take fitness tests without adequate conditioning.

Forming Groups/Partners

Groups or teams are formed by student "captains" publicly selecting one child at a time, sometimes with a system of alternating gender, and always exposing the lower skilled children to peer ridicule or embarrassment. Groups/teams are formed by pitting "boys against the girls" emphasizing gender differences rather than cooperation and working together. Students are regularly asked to select partners without strategies to assure that no children are left out.

(continued)

DEVELOPMENTALLY APPROPRIATE PHYSICAL EDUCATION PRACTICES FOR CHILDREN (CONTINUED)

Appropriate Practice	*Inappropriate Practice*
Facilitating Maximum Participation	*Facilitating Maximum Participation*
Teachers organize small games, e.g., 2–3 per team that allow numerous practice opportunities for children while also allowing them to learn the various aspects of the game being taught. Equipment is provided to permit active participation and practice for every child. A variety of equipment is selected to accommodate the size, confidence, and skill levels of the children. Teachers make sure that equipment is kept up-to-date and routinely inspected for safety.	Teachers organize full-sided or large-sided games (e.g., the class of 30 is split into two groups of 15 that play against each other), thereby limiting practice opportunities for individual students. An insufficient amount of equipment is available to maximize practice repetitions. "Adult-size" equipment is used, which may inhibit skill development, injure, and/or intimidate the children. Teachers use outdated and potentially unsafe equipment.

appropriate for five- to seven-year-olds, whereas team sports are not. Dodge ball, relays, musical chairs, and kickball are contraindicated games for this age group because they emphasize hitting classmates with balls, stress speed over technique, involve too little activity, and eliminate, rather than include, student participation. NASPE's document, "Developmentally Appropriate Physical Education Practices for Children," describes these concepts in greater detail (see the box on pages 316–317 for some examples).

MIDDLE SCHOOL PROGRAMS

The emergence of middle schools occurred in response to the unique developmental needs of students during this transitional period of physical, social, emotional, and intellectual growth. Students between the ages of 10 and 14 should have already been taught fundamental movement skills and basic fitness concepts. If they have, they are ready to learn lead-up games, specific sports skills, and cooperative and competitive games and sports. Interest and ability grouping, rather than gender-role stereotyping, are essential during these pivotal years.

At the middle school level, time should be spent on developing responsible personal and social behavior, respecting differences among people, and using physical activity for enjoyment, challenge, self-expression, and social interaction. Although seasonal team sports like volleyball, basketball, and softball may comprise a portion of the curriculum, these young people need instruction in the skills of throwing, catching, striking, and running independently and within lead-up games. Inclusion of various dance forms, tumbling, outdoor adventure activities, and games chosen by students will enrich the curriculum. Despite limited facilities and equipment, skill heterogeneity, and large class sizes, physical educators need to creatively design and implement broad curricula that meet the interests and needs of their students.

Girls and boys in middle school physical education often participate in games to develop their sports skills. (Photo courtesy Maggie McGlynn.)

Vital components of middle school curricula are health-related physical fitness and sport-skill-related fitness. Students in this age group are capable of taking greater responsibility for establishing personal goals to enhance their cardiovascular endurance, muscular strength and endurance, and flexibility, as well as skill-related fitness. School programs should creatively reinforce the achievement of these goals using honor rolls on bulletin boards, school-wide announcements, newsletter features, assembly recognitions, "I'm Fit" t-shirts, or opportunities to lead or select class fitness activities.

Motor skill, fitness, and cognitive standards should guide the development of sequential and progressive instruction. Periodic assessments should be made to ensure the attainment of these standards. Whenever possible, the physical education specialist, who is a certified physical education teacher, should integrate instructional material with other subjects. With these standards in place, middle school students, their parents, and school administrators will value physical education programs of quality. Other important characteristics of middle school physical education include:

- ensuring that the physical education's program goals are consistent with the overall goals of the school;
- collaborating with other educators in interdisciplinary courses or units;
- planning the curriculum to include a scope and sequence of instruction that is appropriate to the needs and diversities of middle school learners;
- adapting instructional approaches to the developmental needs and learning styles of all students;
- providing opportunities for remediation and practice to ensure that all students enjoy success in their movement experiences.

SECONDARY SCHOOL PROGRAMS

In the high school grades, students would prefer to work at achieving and maintaining a health-enhancing level of physical fitness rather than be placed in classes where they are again taught volleyball, basketball, and softball. Most students want to receive instruction in lifetime sports like bowling, golf, and tennis and in fitness activities such as aerobics or weight training. Facility and equipment limitations can be overcome by using community lanes, courses, and courts and by getting students to use personal sports equipment. School gymnasiums

In secondary school physical education, students can be introduced to activities that they may participate in during their leisure hours and later in life. (Photo courtesy Maggie McGlynn.)

Traditional sports such as softball may be offered in secondary physical education. (Photo courtesy Bob Hilliard.)

In addition to traditional sports, lifetime activities such as dancing, tennis, and bowling should be offered in secondary physical education programs.

can be used for a variety of activities including aerobics, badminton, rock climbing and rappelling, dance, one-wall racquetball, martial arts, and target archery. Community recreation centers with weight training equipment and aerobics machines, such as stationary bicycles, stair climbers, and treadmills, might be able to be used by students during the school day. States and local educational agencies might be more likely to offer a wider range of elective courses to secondary school students if these broadened curricula were available. Learning skills in sports that they can enjoyably participate in throughout their lives should be a primary focus of secondary physical education programs.

Another area of emphasis should be creating opportunities to develop and implement individualized physical fitness programs. While these may be incorporated into aerobic or weight training classes, students should be encouraged to establish fitness goals using activities that they find personally satisfying. Secondary school students are capable of learning how to initiate and sustain fitness programs that they enjoy and are likely to continue throughout their adult lives.

Secondary school physical education classes should meet daily and be equal in length and class size to those for other subjects. Most states, however, have reduced (or are reducing) the requirements for physical education for high school graduation. And physical educators face the same issues challenging other secondary school programs: insufficient instructional time, large classes, discipline problems, apathetic students, and meeting the needs of heterogeneous students by gender, race, and disability. Relevant curricula, committed professionals backed by supportive administrators and parents, and instructional quality can alleviate, or at least reduce, many of these problems.

At all levels of education, it is essential that teachers help their students achieve high standards. If the programmatic characteristics described above are implemented, school-aged children will be able to demonstrate proficiency in various movement and motor skills, maintain a physically active lifestyle, and interact positively with others in physical activity settings.

CHANGES IN CERTIFICATION REQUIREMENTS

State control of education has resulted in the establishment of certification standards for public school teachers. Most state departments of education (or the equivalent) specify the standards or competencies that must be completed before a person can teach. This requirement often includes specific courses in instructional methodologies and educational and developmental psychology as well as a period of supervised student teaching. Physical education programs include disciplinary content, a specialized methodology of teaching, and the application of knowledge to student learning.

More and more states are requiring that students in all disciplines, including physical education, take the *Praxis Series: Professional Assessments for Beginning Teachers* to ensure that they possess both the general and specialized knowledge necessary to teach. Praxis includes assessments of academic skills (general for all teachers), subject matter, and classroom performance. Some states have developed their own competency tests. Many states have reciprocity agreements with other states so that certification in one is equivalent to certification in the other. Certification in a nonreciprocating state requires a teacher to complete one or more courses.

The most common requirement for interscholastic coaches is a teaching certificate (required for all coaches in about half of the states). For those states with no established standards (and for those that commonly grant exceptions to the state regulations), liability concerns are paramount. The recent trend of hiring nonteachers to coach has developed because a number of coaching jobs do not have corresponding teaching positions. Those who want to be well-prepared professionals should consult the National Standards for Athletic Coaches (see Chapter 5).

ACCREDITATION

Although not under the jurisdiction of state or federal governments, **accreditation** helps ensure quality in education. Based on established criteria or standards, accreditation in teacher education, as provided by the National Council for Accreditation of Teacher Education (NCATE), makes institutions accountable for program content. Although compliance is voluntary, many schools require that prospective teachers graduate from NCATE-accredited programs. Some institutions, however, choose not to seek NCATE accreditation believing that they can best monitor the quality of their programs.

For physical education, NASPE has been given the responsibility for ensuring that physical education undergraduate and graduate programs meet the minimal disciplinary standards. Each college or university must submit its curricula (with accompanying explanatory documents) to NASPE on a periodic basis. A national panel of reviewers assesses whether that program is in compliance. If it is not, changes are mandated.

The two phases comprising accreditation are the institutional self-study and the peer evaluation. Nationally established standards and an institution's stated purposes and goals provide the characteristics and criteria for the self-study. After a comprehensive examination of each institution's governance, curricula, faculty, students, physical resources, self-evaluation, program review, and long-range planning, the accreditation committee documents the degree of adherence to the standards. Next, a visiting team of evaluators conducts an objective study to determine the accuracy of the report. Its judgments are submitted in writing to the accrediting agency, which decides to grant or to deny accreditation for a five-year period. Thereafter, continuing accreditation is granted every five years if a visiting team positively evaluates the program quality.

Accreditation standards apply in nonschool physical activity settings as well. As described in Chapter 6, certifications are offered by several organizations because employers are requiring that fitness and exercise leaders attain a specified

Competence as a teacher may include assessing whether students learn proper movement skills such as throwing. (Photo courtesy Lisa Sense.)

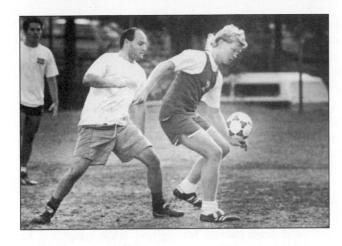

Standards are important for instructional programs at all levels. (Photo courtesy Lisa Sense.)

level of competence. Whether leading group exercises, serving as a personal trainer, teaching aquatics activities, providing athletic training, or coaching youth sports, certifications are increasingly being mandated. People want to participate in programs that are conducted according to standards so they can be confident that the information they receive is accurate and up-to-date information and the activities they take part in are safe, effective, and appropriate.

ACCOUNTABILITY

Accountability demands that an individual or institution be held responsible to achieve a specified action. For example, schools are held accountable for increasing students' test scores because it is believed that these are indicators of student achievement, and, hence, inextricably linked with America's economic competitiveness. Accountability matters significantly when incentives and punishments await those who do or do not achieve the performance levels expected by politicians or special interest groups. While accountability sounds good, this term may gloss over the political agendas of those who believe that public schools are failing to meet national academic standards. Some argue that reliance on high-stakes testing fails to address serious fallacies in psychometrics, especially when many of the tests violate construct validity, consequential validity, and fairness. That is, most of these tests distort or misrepresent what students have actually learned because they do not accurately reflect the content of the curriculum or the typical context in which the curriculum is taught. Huge pressures to raise test scores, however, have led to inordinate amounts of time being devoted to test preparation, instruction being geared to the test, and even cheating.

A **standard** is a uniform criterion or foundational guide used to measure quality. Educational standards determine what children at each grade level should know and be able to do. Schools are increasingly being expected to ensure that every child can achieve these standards of performance. Most states have adopted national tests and/or developed their own tests to measure student progress and achievement. State appropriations often depend on the test scores achieved, regardless of the socioeconomic context, the racial and ethnic composition of the student body, or the transient nature of the population. Sometimes, the tests used to measure educational achievement bear little relationship to the state or local mandates regarding curriculum. In most cases, these achievement tests tend to measure and reward memorization of facts rather than critical thinking skills.

An **assessment** is a measure of knowledge, skills, and abilities. Assessments are tools used by those considered competent to judge student achievement, such as teachers and specialists. It is incumbent upon educators to incorporate a wide range of authentic assessments throughout their programs in order to deflect an overemphasis on high-stakes test scores. That is, a variety of evaluative measures that reflect the curriculum should be implemented to

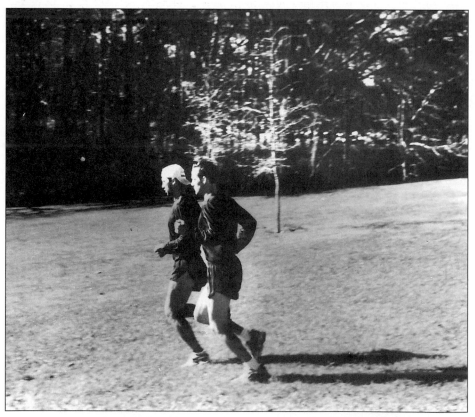

Assessments of program quality may include monitoring heart rates during and following a jogging session. (Photo courtesy Department of Physical Education and Recreation at State University of West Georgia.)

FIGURE 10.1

Assessment model for physical education.

determine student progress as well as those areas that need more work. Formative assessments are particularly useful for giving students constructive feedback and for determining how to provide individualized remediation. The Assessment Model in Figure 10.1 illustrates the comprehensiveness of the assessment process in a university setting.

Every physical education class should be designed and taught by a competent and certified physical education teacher (see the box on pages 326 to 328 for the characteristics of competent physical educators). Like every other school subject, physical education should include sequential learning activities characterized by objectives, instructional strategies, developmental levels, content standards, and assessments (see the box on page 328 for the components of performance-based assessments). Objectives should be identified by grade level, and specified outcomes should be assessed at each level by valid and reliable measurements. High quality physical education programs will help students of all abilities develop

COMPETENCIES REQUIRED OF PHYSICAL EDUCATION TEACHERS

General

- Understand the scientific and philosophical bases of physical education and sport
- Develop a comprehensive knowledge for analyzing movement
- Develop a wide range of motor skills, especially those related to the area of teaching
- Study the teaching/learning processes specifically related to the area of physical education and sport
- Become knowledgeable about planning, organizing, administering, supervising, evaluating, and interpreting various aspects of a balanced physical education and sport program

Elementary School Physical Education Teacher

We believe that:

- Professional preparation for the elementary school physical education teacher should focus on the child in preschool through grade six. The curricula should result in the prospective teacher being competent in:
  - Understanding child growth and development, with an emphasis on motor development
  - A knowledge of and appreciation for the structure function of human movement
  - Observing and assessing children and their movement
  - The knowledge and assessment of health-related and skill-related aspects of physical fitness
  - A knowledge of learning processes, teaching strategies, and factors that affect motor learning
  - Developing curriculum with emphasis on curriculum designs and strategies appropriate for elementary school programs
  - Assessing and working with children who have special needs
  - Personal skills and teaching skills in the content areas of fundamental movement patterns, games/sports, dance, gymnastics, and, aquatics to meet the needs and interests of children
  - In addition, teacher preparation/staff development will provide:
    - Laboratory and field experiences that are directed and supervised throughout the teacher preparation program
    - Opportunities to become acquainted with a variety of elementary school organizational structures and the administration physical education within those settings. The professional preparation curricula should culminate in certification specific for teaching children in the elementary grades
- Preparation for the classroom teacher should include an understanding of the relationship of physical growth and motor development to the total development and learning experience of the child. Course work in movement skills, methods, and content of elementary school physical education programs should be required. Laboratory assignments which provide for experiences with children in physical education are essential

(continued)

COMPETENCIES REQUIRED OF PHYSICAL EDUCATION TEACHERS (CONTINUED)

- Continuous staff development opportunities should be provided to meet the individual needs of educators concerned with physical education programs for children. Teachers in the field should be involved in the planning of such programs
- Personnel concerned with teacher preparation and staff development in physical education should have continuous interaction with children. They also need to be aware of current research and legislation, and be able to interpret and apply these to the teaching context

Middle School Physical Education Teacher

Preparation of teachers should include courses and teaching experiences that pertain to the education of middle school students. The in-service education program for physical education teachers is imperative to assure skilled and knowledgeable teachers to administer the varied programs required for middle schools. Administrators should provide opportunities for teachers to attend workshops, meetings, and conventions which keep physical education personnel current on materials and information.

Educational programs should prepare teachers who:

- Have an understanding of the middle school concept
- Possess teaching certification in physical education
- Avoid gender-role discrimination and gender stereotyping by grouping students according to interest and ability levels
- Understand the physical, social, emotional, and intellectual characteristics that are unique to middle school students
- Possess a positive self-concept and demonstrate respect for the dignity and worth of all individuals
- Have developmentally appropriate knowledge and skills for working with students on a one-to-one basis
- Are familiar with a wide variety of skills and activities in order to implement the exploratory qualities of the program
- Apply various teaching styles and modify rules, equipment, and instructional stations to conform to the needs of the learner
- Continually strive to increase their knowledge and understanding to meet the changing needs of middle school students and their learning environment
- Can interact with students and fellow teachers in a way that is supportive of the special needs of the middle school student
- Will assume leadership in providing for the expanding physical experiences for all students in the school
- Are able to interpret the goals and objectives of the activity programs to students and their parents
- Use instructional strategies based upon the developmental and skill level of the student as well as the nature of the activity
- Are able to maintain and manage record-keeping systems for planning sequential instruction

(continued)

COMPETENCIES REQUIRED OF PHYSICAL EDUCATION TEACHERS (CONTINUED)

Secondary School Physical Education Teacher

Educational programs should be conducted by certified physical education teachers who:

- Serve as positive role models of personal health, fitness, skill, and enjoyment of participating in physical activities
- Are knowledgeable in curriculum and instruction, demonstrate sportsmanship and sensitivity to students' needs
- Know and apply teaching strategies that provide maximum student time on task
- Apply various teaching methods and instructional strategies that personalize physical education classes and allow students to attain optimum personal growth
- Provide for equitable instruction and participation with regard to the individual needs of the student
- Demonstrate professional commitment through involvement in professional organizations and other enrichment experiences
- Plan program activities that promote understanding of cultural diversity
- Accommodate the needs of exceptional students in regular physical education classes
- Understand that the instructional program and athletics are separate and distinct; they strive to keep a balanced perspective between the dual role of the teaching and coaching
- Use recognized assessment and evaluation instruments in planning for accountability of the instructional program
- Apply technology in their teaching on a regular and continuing basis

PERFORMANCE-BASED ASSESSMENT

- Define content standards and learning outcomes
- Develop and implement a variety of assessments for measuring student performance
- Design curriculum to ensure that students achieve content standards and learning outcomes
- Plan and deliver instruction to ensure that all students achieve content standards and learning outcomes

physical fitness and motor skills, gain a thorough understanding of fitness, nutritional, and health concepts, enact appropriate social behavior, and value a healthy lifestyle.

Educators cannot achieve these objectives if children and adolescents take part in physical education only one or two days per week. The National Association for Sport and Physical Education recommends that children from kindergarten through grade 5 receive at least 30 minutes of physical education instruction per day; students in grades 6 through 12 should receive at least 50 minutes per day.

Experiences in sport and physical activity programs outside of the classroom are also important for children's overall intellectual, social, emotional, and physical development. Whether a recreational youth sport league, individual sports lessons, or a commercial fitness program, appropriate objectives, standards, and assessments will help ensure fun, program adherence, and maintenance of a healthy lifestyle.

LEGAL LIABILITY

One challenge facing professionals working in physical-activity-related careers is dealing with the legal issues surrounding injury to participants. The risk of injury mandates that teachers, leaders, supervisors, and administrators understand and comply with their legal obligations to those they serve. Because so many in our society are predisposed to seek legal redress for any real or perceived mistreatment, physical educators must be especially prudent. **Negligence,** the most frequent claim, occurs when a teacher or director's failure to act in a reasonable or prudent manner results in injury to another person. Four factors must exist for negligence to be proven:

- Presence of a duty (such as providing supervision of a class)
- A breach of that duty (failure to act as a reasonable and prudent person would under similar circumstances)
- Proximate cause of the injury (the action or failure to act caused the subsequent injury)
- The substantial nature of the injuries (the extent of the injuries)

There are two legal defenses against negligence:

- **Assumption of risk** by program participants (however, they must know, understand, and appreciate these risks).
- Contributory or comparative negligence by the person injured. Some states have adopted contributory negligence; others use comparative negligence.
  - **Contributory negligence** refers to behavior by the plaintiff that contributed to the injury. Sometimes contributory negligence can bar recovery for the injury.
  - **Comparative negligence** apportions damages between a negligent plaintiff and a negligent defendant.

In order to avoid liability for negligence, you must act reasonably by recognizing potentially hazardous conditions or situations and by protecting your students and clients from them. First, **general supervision** is always required when class

One liability issue is what sports activities are appropriate for school and college curricula. (Photo courtesy Lisa Sense.)

is in session. This responsibility includes knowing what to look and listen for, where to stand, how to move around, and what to do when a problem arises. The more dangerous the activity, such as a gymnastics class or a stress test, the closer the **specific supervision** is mandated. Second, not only do you have a responsibility to eliminate known hazards (those about which you had **actual notice**), but also those that constitute **constructive notice,** hazards that any reasonable and responsible person should have noticed, such as broken glass on a floor. Instructors bear the responsibility of informing those in charge of necessary repairs or of situations that might lead to injury. Third, the person in charge should make regular inspections, involve participants in taking responsibility for their own safety, do preventive maintenance, and post warnings about using facilities. Fourth, every participant should be warned about potential risks; specifically, each person should understand and appreciate the risks and potential for injuries involved in the particular activity. In order to understand the extent of your obligations to students or clients served, consider the questions for reflection in the Research View box on the next page.

Whether dealing with an athlete, a client, or a subject in a research project, **an agreement to participate** helps each participant understand and appreciate the risks involved and any related safety rules. This is not a waiver of responsibility or a guarantee against lawsuits. However, an agreement to participate may help instructors defend themselves against negligence because it articulates what assumption of risk means. An agreement to participate, written specifically for each activity, should describe the necessary skills required for safe participation, the possible injuries, and the important rules for safe participation. On this form, the participant should be questioned about any preexisting physical condition and/or limitations. These agreements should include a statement suggesting that at any time a participant experiences discomfort or stress that they discontinue the activity. The final statement signed by the participant should specify that they understand and appreciate the risks involved in the activity. In preparing an agreement to participate, the professional should ensure that it is

RESEARCH VIEW

1. Under what circumstances, if any, should you as a coach permit your athletes to warm-up prior to practice when you cannot be present?
2. What are your obligations to a person who will be participating in a research project that involves a sub-maximal treadmill run?
3. What is your obligation to an injured athlete who may have a head or neck injury?
4. As a personal trainer, what are your legal responsibilities for the welfare of your client who is participating in a strength training program?
5. Under what conditions should the athlete, coach, trainer, or a physician decide when the athlete could return to practice or competition?
6. What legal obligations does the facility manager owe to fans?
7. What legal responsibilities does a recreation department owe to parents relative to the hiring of personnel to work with children in its programs?
8. Under what conditions, if any, does an owner or manager of a fitness club have legal responsibilities to provide members with equipment that is in safe condition?
9. What should the exercise scientist require of a subject in a research study before administering a treadmill test?
10. What health and safety responsibilities must the person responsible for a community fun run meet?

consistent with the legal defense of assumption of risk. Several other steps can also be taken to avoid liability.

- Provide instruction in the proper techniques for skill execution. Meeting this responsibility requires preparation of and adherence to sequential and progressive instructional plans that clearly show that no one is expected to attempt skills beyond their ability to safely execute them.

- Ensure that each participant's fitness, conditioning, and ability levels are appropriate to the expectations. Failure to ascertain limitations or apprehensions may lead to injuries for which you will be liable.

- Enforce safety rules and regulations. Strict compliance with school, club, or corporate policies, including those governing the reporting of accidents and injuries, is critical.

- When injuries occur, you must respond appropriately. It is assumed that you will hold current cardiopulmonary resuscitation and first aid certifications and thus will know how to respond properly to various injuries. For example, any person suffering from a possible neck, head, or back injury should not be moved without supervision from emergency responders.

MANAGEMENT STRATEGIES TO AVOID THE CHARGE OF NEGLIGENCE

- Follow the guidelines established by the school, employers, and state for safe programs.
- Prepare a statement of safety procedures and distribute it to the program director and to parents, if appropriate.
- Establish an operational system of emergency care in the event of a serious injury.
- Establish a system for identifying, treating, reporting, and recording all injuries.
- Purchase from reputable dealers the best equipment that the budget will allow.
- Make sure that all facilities are safe and free of hazards.
- Follow sound practices and program-approved activities that specify appropriate skill progressions.
- Learn and teach using the latest and the best instructional techniques.
- Closely supervise all activities.
- Carry liability insurance with broad coverage.

- Do not use inadequate, ill-fitting, or defective equipment. The instructor must regularly inspect all equipment, removing any in need of repair or replacement.
- Only qualified persons should supervise physical activity.

Closely adhering to each of these suggestions and the risk management strategies listed in the box above will not only help you meet your legal obligation to those you instruct, but it will also greatly reduce the likelihood of your becoming a defendant in a negligence lawsuit. You should also make sure your employer provides adequate insurance protection for you. If such insurance is lacking or inadequate, you should purchase personal liability insurance.

COMMERCIALIZATION OF PHYSICAL FITNESS

When people choose to become physically fit, they are faced with a multitude of choices about how to best achieve that goal. Making a well-informed, wise choice is made more difficult in our media-saturated culture. Multimillion-dollar advertisements dominate television, the web, and print media. Sporting goods manufacturers market their products through highly paid professional athletes. Every imaginable fitness fad is foisted upon an often naive public who seek a quick fix to a lack of physical fitness. The latest fitness gadget guaranteed to "take off pounds quickly," "with no effort" soon becomes an unused or broken relic in the basement. Commercialization in physical fitness has extended to health and sports clubs that promise fitness results if you join. Sometimes, the prospective member is not told about additional charges for aerobics classes, swimming lessons, and personal trainers because these clubs exist to make a profit more than to provide a service.

One additional concern about the commercialization of physical fitness is the subliminal, and sometimes overt, message of sex appeal associated with muscular males and sexy females who look like models. In response, many males have chosen to take drugs such as creatine to build muscle mass and enhance their appearance of masculinity. Many females, in an unending attempt to enhance their appearance of femininity through weight loss, succumb to the dangerous—and at times deadly—triad of anorexia, amenorrhea, and osteoporosis.

Any piece of fitness equipment, program, or drug that is guaranteed to provide immediate and substantial results should automatically be suspected. Research has proven time and again that the only way to safely and effectively reduce body weight is to increase caloric expenditure and decrease caloric intake. Some highly touted devices, such as rubber suits, can be dangerous because they can lead to dehydration. The only safe and effective approach to developing and maintaining physical fitness is regular physical activity combined with a healthy diet.

CAREER BURNOUT

A combination of discipline problems, apathetic students, inadequate facilities, equipment, and other resources, and minimal administrative support, often leads to teacher burnout. Many physical education teachers feel isolated from other teachers, lack professional mobility, and face the constant threat of spending cuts. Thus, many individuals display the signs and symptoms of burnout listed in the box below. Persons in physical-activity-related careers other than teaching may also find their jobs unrewarding or frustrating due to a lack of change or too much change too fast, unchallenging routines, work overload, or lack of advancement potential.

SIGNS AND SYMPTOMS OF BURNOUT

- Chronic stress
- Emotional exhaustion
- Depersonalization
- Reduced sense of mastery
- Less enjoyment of work and leisure activities
- Bodily changes such as fatigue, high blood pressure, insomnia, digestive disorders, or increased heart rate
- Overeating or under eating
- Excessive drinking or abuse of drugs
- Frustration with job-related factors such as task repetitiveness, lack of recognition, overwork, and lack of advancement
- Anxiety and depression

Often burnout occurs as a result of role conflict. A physical education teacher is often hired to teach a full load of classes and to coach one to three sports. Lesson plans, grades, reports, student monitoring responsibilities, and associated teaching duties combine with year round planning, practices, competitions, and administration of the teams to fill most days and nights. One of four patterns then usually develops:

- A tenured teacher/coach decides that the small coaching supplement is not worth the time demands, so he or she resigns from coaching but keeps teaching.
- The teacher/coach concentrates on coaching, putting little effort into teaching because it is viewed as repetitive and unrewarding.
- The teacher/coach becomes apathetic about both jobs, and just goes through the motions instead of being committed.
- The teacher/coach changes careers.

A teacher/coach who resigns may be burned out in part because of the inordinate pressures that parents and school administrators place on them to win. This teacher/coach conflict is aggravated by the higher recognition and rewards for coaching as compared with those for teaching. The chronic, job-related stress resulting from role conflict or role ambiguity can be reduced, but probably not

Teacher/coach conflict is often associated with the time required to fulfill practice and game responsibilities. (Photo courtesy Maggie McGlynn.)

eliminated, since the teacher/coach holds two somewhat incompatible positions simultaneously.

Combating burnout has become essential to career survival. Job satisfaction necessitates taking a positive approach toward work responsibilities. Financial rewards, job challenges, recognition, promotion, variety in responsibilities, and professional development all contribute to job satisfaction. Positive feedback is essential. If people are constantly bombarded by negative comments, they cannot continue to function effectively. Recognition and praise for completing responsibilities often lead to positive changes and enhanced self-motivation.

When individuals are given the opportunity to take part in the planning process, a greater allegiance to the resultant programs or goals is readily evident. Finally, physical education and exercise science professionals should interact with others on the job by attending seminars, workshops, and conferences. At least once a year, everyone needs to rejuvenate their commitment to and enthusiasm for job responsibilities.

Work-related stress probably cannot be avoided. Yet each of us should understand what causes stress and how to eliminate or cope with stress. Physical educators and exercise scientists have a definite advantage in the latter case because they know that exercise reduces stress. We need to attain and maintain a personal level of fitness that not only positively affects our productivity and quality of life but also allows us to serve as role models for others.

Participation in physical activity, like volleyball, can help relieve stress and lessen the possibility of career burnout. (Photo courtesy Lisa Sense.)

INSTRUCTIONAL CHALLENGES FACING SCHOOL PHYSICAL EDUCATORS

School teachers, including those in physical education, face many challenges. Among these are insufficient resources for facilities and equipment, apathetic students, drug abuse, lack of family support, heterogeneous students in large classes, and discipline and behavioral problems. Despite these factors that negatively affect the instructional environment, teachers are held accountable for student learning.

Limited facilities and equipment need not dissuade physical educators from expanding their programs. The gymnasium can be used for rock climbing, badminton, and aerobics as well as traditional team sports. Community courts, driving ranges, and lanes are often available for tennis, golf, and bowling. Additional equipment can be brought by students, borrowed from recreational departments, leased from companies, and even obtained free from organizations seeking to promote certain sports. Ask students and parents to help construct goals, net supports, weights, and playground apparatus.

Apathetic students who do not want to dress out, participate, or behave, present an even greater challenge to teachers. Since each student is unique, teachers need to use whatever resources or referrals they can to determine the causes for this apathy. Only then can the physical educator appeal to these students' interests and needs. Replacing dodge ball or unpopular activities with weight training or aerobics may be the only change needed. Rewarding appropriate behavior, rather than simply punishing misbehavior, encourages positive change. Teaching relevant content, ensuring equal opportunity for all students, and making classes enjoyable may not engage every student, but the number of apathetic ones will certainly diminish. Keeping students busy is not education. Teaching must result in learning.

When students attend school under the influence of alcohol or purchase and use drugs on school grounds, the learning process is severely hampered. Drug education classes and enforcement of school policies for drug-free campuses are two ways to help reduce the incidence of these problems. The physical educator should use every opportunity to discourage drug use by showing how it adversely affects physical performance and well-being.

Dramatic demographic and socioeconomic changes are partly to blame for the lack of parental and family support for education in this country. Over half of the children in the U.S. will spend a portion of their school years in single-parent homes. Most children with two parents will find no one at home after school because both parents work. About a quarter of today's children live in households with incomes below the poverty level. Children of minorities already exceed the number of whites in some schools; this population shift will continue. Teachers must overcome a lack of parental support by helping students learn the value of education. Teachers need to help students take greater responsibility for their own education. The physical educator can help by creating an after-school fitness club that can instill self-worth, confidence, discipline, and responsibility in students. Physical education can have a significant role to play in helping to overcome some of these problems. Educators need to engage these problems

ADVOCACY EFFORTS

- Write letters to parents that describe your physical education program and invite them to come to their child's class and observe.
- Develop a physical education program web site where you describe the curriculum, announce special events, and share physical activity tips.
- Publish a physical education program newsletter.
- Share position statements developed by professional organizations.
- Distribute press releases about recent research studies that influence the welfare of youth and impact your physical education program.
- Invite other teachers, school administrators, Board of Education members, and politicians to your classes so they can learn more about your innovative and engaging curriculum.
- Send news stories to the local media about the exciting activities in your program.
- Work with the PTA/PTO or local service organizations to obtain funds to establish a wellness center for students and the general public.
- Distribute public service announcements to the broadcast media.
- Plan special events that publicize the achievements of the students in your program.
- Celebrate May as Sport and Physical Education Month.

head-on, using their imaginations to create new programs, new teaching methods, and new avenues that serve educational aims. Then educators need to find ways of promoting physical education (including these new programs) to parents, students, administrators, and fellow educators. The box above includes a few suggestions for promoting physical education.

Many states dictate maximum class sizes, but too often exceptions are granted for physical education. When school administrators believe that physical education is only play, with no instruction where cognitive learning occurs, physical educators may be expected to teach 50 to 60 students in each class. The first objective in this type of situation is to educate your principal about your curriculum and to invite decision makers to observe the quality of your program. Working with other professionals, you need to lobby against exceptions to maximum class size. The best rationale one can offer is the increased chance of injury when there is inadequate supervision and crowded instructional and activity conditions. Even with a normal size class, physical educators still face students with heterogeneous abilities. Skill grouping, use of lead-up or progressive games, and curricula that include both cooperative and competitive activities contribute to meeting students' diverse needs.

Discipline and behavioral problems may be the most recurring issue facing teachers. Rather than dissipating in an activity setting, these problems are often exacerbated. Some students with histories of misbehavior may seek to use physical education classes as opportunities to dominate others or show off. Physical educators must establish fair and impartial class policies in regard to these matters, and then enforce them consistently. Using timeouts as punishment, rather than exercises or laps, teaches respect for the rules. Rewarding appropriate behaviors with the opportunity to participate in favorite activities is even more effective for most students than punishments.

In overcoming these challenges, physical educators must be prepared to do a lot more than just teach their favorite sports and games. Each challenge is an opportunity to positively affect the lives of students.

SUMMARY

Physical activity programs are for everyone. They help people learn fitness and sports skills and incorporate them into their daily lives. It is hoped that students and exercise participants of all ages will increasingly enjoy their physical fitness activities, reach their goals, and adhere to their appropriately designed programs. Increasingly, public and private health and sports clubs, worksite programs, rehabilitation clinics, and retirement homes will meet the fitness and activity needs of adults. There will be a growing need for specialists in these areas. Advances in technology as well as the proliferation of research will continue to have widespread implications for physical education and exercise science in the future. School physical education programs will continue to evolve, with an emphasis on fitness activities and the development of the whole person. Educational reforms of standards, accountability, and assessments will significantly affect funding for school programs and lead to important changes. Although instructional constraints threaten the teaching/learning process, competent teachers must creatively find ways to surmount these barriers while being held accountable for helping each student achieve higher standards. Teachers and exercise and fitness specialists must take their responsibilities seriously to provide safe environments for learning and to act responsibly when injuries occur. Professional involvement and interchange among colleagues are two of the ways to combat job stress and career burnout.

CAREER PERSPECTIVE

RENÉ REVIS SHINGLES
Assistant Professor
Central Michigan University
Mount Pleasant, Michigan

EDUCATION
B.A., Health and Physical Education, University of North
Carolina at Chapel Hill
M.S., Physical Education: Athletic Training/Sports Medicine,
Illinois State University
Ph.D., candidate in psychosocial aspects of sport, Department
of Kinesiology, Michigan State University

JOB RESPONSIBILITIES AND HOURS
As a university assistant professor and certified athletic trainer, René teaches in a sports
medicine/athletic training curriculum accredited by the Commission on Accreditation of
Allied Health Education Programs. Courses taught include Introduction to Athletic Training, Therapeutic Exercise and Modalities, and Health Care Administration. In her supervision of the Injury Care Center, René coordinates the schedule, evaluates the student staff,
prepares the budget, takes inventory, keeps records, and writes reports. Her typical work
hours are 8:00 A.M. to 6:00 P.M. Some evening and weekend hours are also required for
class preparation, student evaluations, and center supervision.

SPECIALIZED COURSE WORK, DEGREES, AND WORK EXPERIENCES
NEEDED FOR THIS CAREER
Certification by the NATA Board of Certification and experience as a volunteer,
intern, or employed athletic trainer are essential prerequisites to teaching in this
area. Licensure or registration as an athletic trainer is required in some states.
René states that all athletic training courses, sport sciences classes such as exercise
physiology, and courses that taught instructional methodology have been beneficial
in her current position. A master's degree is the minimal academic credential for a
college position, although a doctor's degree in athletic training/sports medicine or a
related area is preferred.

SATISFYING ASPECTS
René enjoys sharing her experiences and developing relationships with students
who want to become athletic trainers. She finds it rewarding to work with and mentor
future professionals.

JOB POTENTIAL
She holds a tenure-track position that carries with it the opportunity to advance from
assistant to associate to full professor. Depending upon experience and academic
degrees held, assistant professors at her university get starting salaries of about $35,000.
Research, scholarly publications, and teaching proficiency are required for promotion
in rank and achievement of tenure. Salary increases and additional responsibilities are
usually associated with advancement.

SUGGESTIONS FOR STUDENTS

Obtaining a terminal (doctorate) degree is essential for teachers to advance in higher education. She advises students to get involved in professional organizations (such as the NATA and AAHPERD) and to appreciate and cultivate relationships with mentors.

REVIEW QUESTIONS

1. What are some of the values of physical activity programs?
2. What are several challenges facing professionals in recreation and leisure services?
3. Why do more students choose to specialize in fitness and exercise and sport science than prepare to teach physical education in the schools?
4. How have research and technology changed the quality of scholarship in physical education, exercise science, and sport?
5. How should middle school and secondary school physical education curricula differ?
6. What is accountability, and how does it relate to standards and assessment?
7. What four factors must exist for negligence to be proven?
8. What are several risk management strategies that you should use to ensure that the rights of participants in your program are being protected?
9. What are five contributing factors to career burnout?
10. What are several challenges facing school physical educators?

STUDENT ACTIVITIES

1. Talk with five of your friends about any individual exercise program that they are (or were) involved in. Summarize the factors that led to their quitting or adhering to their programs.
2. Write a one-page paper about your personal accountability in a job you have held in a field related to your major, such as lifeguard, sport official, camp counselor, or sporting goods salesperson. (If you have not had any of these experiences, talk with those who have and report their experiences.)
3. Ask a faculty member at your institution who led in the development of an undergraduate specialization why this program was established.
4. Secure a copy of the local elementary, middle school, and secondary school standards and curricula for physical education; analyze these to determine if the standards are being achieved through a progressive and sequential program.
5. Read two articles in any professional journals that describe how an expanded knowledge base and technology in physical education and exercise science have positively affected noneducational programs. Summarize in two or three sentences the impact each has made.

6. Describe two actual examples of people who have suffered from career burnout. What changes would you have recommended that might have prevented these situations from occurring?

7. Read two articles about negligent behavior by people in careers associated with physical activity. What action did they take or fail to take? What was the outcome of litigation, if there was litigation?

8. Complete a risk management assessment of a physical activity program, a sporting event, or a sports facility. List all potentially unsafe actions or situations.

SUGGESTED READINGS

Barrett KR: What does it mean to have a developmentally appropriate physical education program? *Phy Educ* 49(3):114, 1992. This article explains developmentally appropriate physical education. Teachers need to know that change occurs in an orderly, sequential fashion, that appropriate activities are age- and experience-related, and that teachers must be skilled observers of movements and its purposes.

Graham G (ed.): Developmentally appropriate physical education for children, *JOPERD* 63(6):29, 1992. In this nine-article feature, the authors describe the components of a developmentally appropriate program for elementary school children, which includes sequencing of games, dance, gymnastics, and fitness. Activities that should be excluded are also described.

Graham KC, Stueck P (eds.): Decisions for middle and high school physical education, *JOPERD* 63(7):65, 1992. This six-article feature argues that practitioners, supervisors, and professional preparation faculty need to work together more effectively for excellence in secondary physical education. They suggest ways to promote such cooperation.

Gray GR: Safety tips from the expert witness, *JOPERD* 66(1):18, 1995. This paper informs physical educators and coaches about how to avoid negligent actions and decisions through an understanding of how expert witnesses will testify in liability cases.

Melograno V: Quality physical education: setting the standards step by step, *Strategies* 5(6):15, 1992. The author identifies standards for quality physical education programs in the areas of curriculum, instruction, teachers, and administration. Strategies for implementing the proposed standards are included.

Mohnsen B (ed.): *The new leadership paradigm for physical education,* Reston, 1999, National Association for Sport and Physical Education. This book includes a wealth of information to help teachers develop and expand their capabilities as leaders in schools.

Siedentop D, et al.: Don't sweat gym! an analysis of curriculum and instruction, *J of Teach in PE* 13(4):375, 1994. School physical educators need to move away from the traditional methods of instruction if they are to change how physical education is accepted within the curriculum.

Spink KS, Carron AV: Group cohesion and adherence in exercise classes, *J Sp & Ex Psy* 14:78, 1992. This investigation found that selected aspects of group cohesion influenced female exercise participants' adherence behavior.

Strand B, Reeder S: Using heart rate monitors in research on fitness levels of children in physical education, *J of Teach in PE* 12(2):215, 1993. This study of heart rate intensity levels of middle school students as they participated in a variety of activities revealed that heart rate monitors have considerable potential in assessing fitness achievements of children.

Stroot SA: Contemporary crisis or emerging reform? A review of secondary school physical education, *J of Teach in PE* 13(4):333, 1994. A review of the literature reveals three themes that describe current perceptions about secondary school physical education. These include restructuring and reform, curriculum and instruction, and contextual factors in the secondary school setting.

CHAPTER

ISSUES IN SPORTS

11

KEY CONCEPTS

- Girls and women are increasingly involved in sports and have been aided by Title IX in these advances.
- Minorities, senior citizens, and individuals with disabilities, while enjoying greater activity, still struggle for equality in sports.
- Rather than emphasizing winning, the benefits and developmental goals of community youth sports and interscholastic athletics must be reinforced.
- As many intercollegiate athletic programs are besieged with problems associated with commercialized sports, colleges and universities must strive to ensure the attainment of educational outcomes.
- The Olympic Games provide opportunities for friendship among athletes of the world who are seeking to prove their physical superiority; yet, they are characterized by politics, nationalism, and excessive commercialization.

Sports participants seek to win. "We're number one" has seemingly become the United States' sports motto from youth leagues to professional teams. To produce the best teams, athletes are often expected to specialize in one sport, to accept coaches' dictates without question, to practice and train with deferred gratification, to excel or face elimination, and to circumvent the rules when necessary. Ethical behavior is often disdained or negatively regarded by coaches, teammates, and spectators since winning surpasses everything else in importance.

In contrast, cooperation, discipline, emotional control, fair play, self-esteem, and teamwork are the desired outcomes of sports. Athletes can learn these values as well as respect their opponents both on and off the field. And they can accept the officials' decisions without dispute. Even spectators can learn these values. Models of ethical behavior are especially important for young people, who typically imitate the attitudes and behaviors of school, college, professional, and Olympic athletes.

Sports are fun. Sports provide a setting for people to develop their own identities by learning about their capabilities and their limitations. Genuine satisfaction comes with making one's best effort regardless of the outcome. A revitalization of body, mind, and spirit through sports can renew one's perspective on life. Overly competitive and commercialized sports undermine this wholistic renewal and the character development that is an essential aspect of genuine sport. Administrators, coaches, athletes, and fans must ensure that experiencing the positive side of sports is the right of everyone by working to maintain these values.

Girls and women, minorities, senior citizens, and persons with disabilities, while being treated more equitably in sports today, still face discriminatory practices and biases. Public and private youth sports organizations, interscholastic programs, and elite competitions at the collegiate and international levels share some of these common problems and conflicts. Several of these controversial issues (see box on page 345) and some proposed solutions are discussed in this chapter.

GIRLS AND WOMEN IN SPORTS

Even though the Greeks excluded women from the ancient Olympic Games, and the founder of the modern Olympic Games viewed their role as cheering spectators, there has been a gradual acceptance of girls and women as sports participants. Traditionally, both physiological and societal factors contributed to the discriminatory treatment many girls and women experienced when they initially sought to compete in sports. Even though males beyond puberty have advantages in sports emphasizing speed, strength, and power, this does not justify the virtual exclusion from sports that females experienced in the past. Research demonstrates that most females are not as strong as men, are shorter and lighter, and have lower maximum oxygen uptakes. Women also tend to have smaller lung capacities, less vital capacities, and lower cardiac outputs. Yet many female athletes have surpassed the prejudicial limitations placed on them by running and swimming faster and longer than many men. They compete professionally against and with males, achieving high levels of muscular strength and endurance, and are proficient in sports skills once the domain of males only. The physical potential of girls and women is not yet known since girls and women must first have equal opportunities in sports to achieve their maximum potential. Contrary to the writings of the early 1900s, women do not risk sterility when they train strenuously and compete aggressively. Like males, females benefit in multiple ways when they achieve their physical potential.

Societal attitudes change slowly. Sports have traditionally been viewed in the United States as masculine—for males only. Familial and environmental influences have tended to establish fixed gender roles with regard to sports. For example, boys are usually given balls and outdoor toys, while girls usually receive dolls or quiet and passive toys. Early in life, girls learn that if they participate in sports they risk being called a tomboy or being viewed as less feminine or less attractive. Peer group pressure results in a role conflict, where choosing sports often make it more difficult to be accepted by one's peers. Therefore, many girls

THREATS TO THE INTEGRITY OF SPORT

Specialization in one sport, circumvention of rules to gain competitive advantages, pressures to win, and excessive commercialization are the major changes pervading competitive sport from the youth to the collegiate level. Due to these negative factors, many of the lofty values associated with sport, like fair play, have eroded.

The rationale for early and continued specialization in one sport is that only focused training can lead to victories and attainment of long-term goals such as Olympic medals, professional contracts, or college grants-in-aid. While children aspire for what over 99 percent will never achieve, they miss the enjoyment of playing various sports and risk overuse problems, such as injuries to the epiphysis. Interscholastic athletes are increasingly advised by coaches and parents to focus on only one sport, which again reduces fun and leads to overuse injuries. While some high school students still earn multiple varsity letters, the college dual sport athlete is almost an anachronism. The time and training required of intercollegiate athletes usually precludes participation in multiple sports.

Coaches often instruct their athletes in how to circumvent game rules without being penalized. At early ages, youth and school sport participants learn that faking an injury to get the clock stopped, calling an opponent's ball out when it helps you win, and lying about one's legal guardian in order to play on a desired team are acceptable, and even praised, behaviors. Later athletes may take anabolic steroids, accept money from a booster to ensure attendance at a certain university, or cheat on exams to maintain academic eligibility because these actions may contribute to victories.

Pressures to win are exerted on athletes of all ages by coaches, parents, and fans. In some coaches' overzealousness for victories, they excessively stress youngsters' arms and bodies, verbally and physically abuse children, and teach and model unethical behaviors. They also emphasize winning so much that by age 12, over 50 percent of all youth sport participants drop out because they are no longer having fun and developing skills. Too many parents try to live through their children by taking fulfillment from their children's sports achievements. Others may even withhold love from children who do not perform to parental expectations. Families have moved, parents have separated or been divorced, and other children in the family have been neglected—all in the pursuit of potential lucrative professional sports careers. Fans adore and reward athletes who win; yet, they speak disparagingly about and disassociate themselves from the less successful.

Commercialization in sport is both a reality and a necessity in our capitalistic society. Corporate and community funding, fans' financial support, and the media are not inherently bad. Problems occur, however, when these factors outweigh developmental and educational values. Communities may seek recognition and status through winning age-group Pop Warner National Championships or state basketball titles. Corporate sponsorships help youth, school, and college sports teams pay their expenses, yet how much control should these sponsors have in the hiring or firing of coaches or in the awarding of advertising space in sports arenas? Similarly, fans who donate huge sums of money to athletic programs often want more than preferential seating and parking. Television already dictates, or at least strongly influences, who gets broadcasted and when and where the teams compete. Many wonder how long television can charge sponsors increasingly higher prices for advertisements.

While certainly not the only changes, sport specialization, rule violations, pressures to win, and excessive commercialization have made a negative impact on competitive sports, at all levels. Combined, they pose threats to the integrity of these programs unless they are moderated, or potential abuses are controlled.

opt out. The more determined ones may compensate by always emphasizing a feminine appearance, by deemphasizing their athletic involvement (and their successes), and by selecting a sport that is viewed as more acceptable, such as golf, gymnastics, swimming, or tennis. The other alternative is to participate actively in sport, regardless of the consequences. Although few chose this route in the past, the situation is changing.

Television commercials that portray women as sports enthusiasts still include sexist overtones and innuendos. Newspapers and periodicals that publish sports stories on women seldom use them as lead stories and never cover them as extensively as they do male sports stories. Since women have lower salaries (today, women in the same jobs earn slightly over 70 percent of what men earn), they have less discretionary income to spend for sporting equipment and fitness club memberships. Over 50 percent of American women work outside the home. They usually enjoy less leisure time for recreational activities because of a combination of work, family, and household obligations. Tradition and sexism still prevent women from having equal access to public and private recreational facilities.

Today, more and more city recreation programs and private clubs are attracting women. The cultural emphasis on fitness has stimulated greater acceptance of women who not only look fit but are fit. Myths die slowly, and prejudicial attitudes are even more resistant to change. As girls' and women's sports performances improve, and as each generation of parents lobbies for greater equity, this issue in sports will come closer to resolution.

One leading reason girls and women have enjoyed expanded opportunities to play and compete has been Title IX of the 1972 Education Amendments. (The box on pages 347–348 includes data about changes in competitive and coaching opportunities for girls and women.) Because of this federal legislation, thousands of school and college females have achieved greater equity in sport. In 1992, the

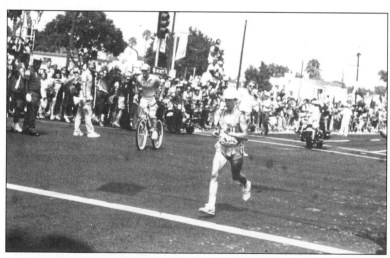

Joan Benoit won the initial Olympic marathon for women in 1984.
(Photo courtesy Kathy Davis.)

IMPACT OF TITLE IX ON SPORTS FOR FEMALES

High Schools*
Number of Participants

	1971	1977–1978	1984–1985	1991–1992	1999–2000
Girls	294,015	2,083,040	1,757,884	1,940,801	2,675,874
Boys	3,666,917	4,367,442	3,354,284	3,429,853	3,861,749

Most popular girls' sports (based on number of schools participating):

Basketball

Track and field

Volleyball

Softball (fast-pitch)

Cross country

Tennis

Soccer

Golf

Swimming and diving

Competitive spirit squads

Intercollegiate Sports (NCAA)†
Average number of sports for women:

1978: 5.61

1982: 6.59

1986: 7.15

1990: 7.24

1992: 7.09

1996: 7.50

2000: 8.14

Most popular sports:

Basketball

Volleyball

Tennis

Cross country　} tied

Softball

Female coaches of women's teams: (Since 1998, the number of head coaching jobs of women's NCAA teams has increased by 534; only 10 percent of these positions were filled by women.

1972: over 90%

1978: 58.2%

1982: 52.4%

(continued)

IMPACT OF TITLE IX ON SPORTS FOR FEMALES (CONTINUED)

1986: 50.6%

1990: 47.3%

1992: 48.3%

1996: 47.7%

2000: 45.6%

Female administrators of women's programs: (Females hold 34% of all administrative jobs in women's programs; yet, no females are involved in the administration of 23% of women's programs.)

1990: 15.9%

1992: 16.8%

1996: 18.5%

2000: 17.8%

*Data from the National Federation of State High School Associations.
†Data from a study by Vivian Acosta and Linda Carpenter, "Women in Intercollegiate Sport—A Longitudinal Study—Twenty-Three Year Update 1977–2000" © 2000 Carpenter/Acosta.

Wilma Rudolph, in 1960, became the first American woman to win Olympic gold medals in the 100 and 200 meter sprints.

Supreme Court ruled in *Franklin v. Gwinnett County Public Schools* that monetary damages were available under Title IX. The fact that victims can now be compensated for inequitable treatment for the first time may be just the incentive needed to force schools and colleges to eradicate discrimination. (See Chapter 9, page 276, for a timeline of the most important events related to the impact of Title IX on girls' and women's sports and the box on page 349 for a discussion of a recent landmark Title IX case.)

COHEN et al. v. BROWN UNIVERSITY

In November of 1996, the U.S. Court of Appeals for the First Circuit upheld a district court decision finding in *Cohen et al. v. Brown University* that Brown University and its athletic program had violated Title IX. Following the refusal of the U.S. Supreme Court to hear Brown University's appeal, the lower court ruling was upheld, with significant implications for support of equitable intercollegiate athletic programs for females. According to the 1998 settlement agreement, Brown University would be considered in compliance with Title IX as long as it retained its current women's sports programs and maintained a participation rate for female athletes within 3.5 percentage points of the percentage of female undergraduate students at the University. The settlement also stipulated that the university had to upgrade its women's water polo to varsity status and guarantee funding for four sports—gymnastics, fencing, skiing, and water polo—that had not received adequate support in the past.

Title IX's provisions relative to athletics have not been uniformly implemented because of gender biases, limited budgets and facilities, lack of coaches, and resistance to change. Women have benefited, however, by receiving approximately one-third of colleges' athletic budgets for extensive team travel, recruiting, coaches' salaries, medical treatment, publicity, and athletic grants-in-aid. School girls, too, have gained more teams, better-paid coaches, access to facilities, and other program supports such as new equipment and uniforms.

As these programs have expanded, however, control has shifted to men. Today, a much smaller percentage of women coach girls and women than before Title IX, and few women administer athletic programs for females (see the box on page 348). Among the factors contributing to the increasing number of men coaching girls and women are the following: too few women with expertise or interest in coaching; more equitable salaries for coaches of female teams than was the case prior to Title IX; unwillingness of many women to coach highly competitive teams; and hiring practices in which male athletic directors and school principals prefer to hire male coaches. When female and male athletic programs were combined, usually on the premise of equal opportunity, men were inevitably named to the top positions either because of seniority or because of the belief that they knew athletics better. Occasionally, though, a female is hired to administer an athletics program that competes at the highest collegiate level. Thus, a major issue confronting athletic programs is the need for more qualified female coaches and sport administrators who are given more opportunities to coach and manage teams as well as athletic programs.

EQUALITY FOR MINORITIES

Members of minority groups have found themselves sports outcasts throughout most of this nation's history. Prior to 1950, sports were rarely integrated, with a few exceptions such as Jack Johnson (boxing), Joe Louis (boxing), Paul Robeson (football), Satchel Paige (baseball), Jackie Robinson (baseball), and Jesse Owens (track). Following the Supreme Court's *Brown v. Board of Education* decision in 1954, school desegregation slowly began to open more school and college sports programs to minorities.

Throughout the years, minorities have experienced blatant discrimination in the form of quota systems (only a small number allowed on a team), position stacking (minorities competed for only a limited number of positions because certain others were unavailable to them), social exclusion from clubs and parties, disparity in treatment by coaches, weak academic counseling, and little tutorial help. Sometimes, minority athletes, because of their cultural and educational backgrounds, were ill-prepared for the academic demands of college; their athletic prowess had gotten them through a vocational or technical, rather than college-preparatory, high school curriculum. Many failed to earn college degrees, thus eliminating themselves from possible coaching positions when their dreams of professional stardom failed to materialize or ended abruptly.

Many minorities oppose the National Collegiate Athletic Association's rule that requires first-year athletes at its Division I institutions to have attained a minimum score of 820 on the Scholastic Assessment Test (SAT) or a 68 on the American College Test (ACT) and to have achieved a minimum standard of 2.50 grade point average in 13 core high school courses (English, mathematics, natural or physical science, social science, and additional academic courses). A sliding scale allows prospective student athletes to quality for grants-in-aid and competition with a GPA down to 2.00 along with test scores up to 1010 on the SAT and 86 on the ACT. Some argue that the SAT and the ACT are culturally biased against minorities and, therefore, the test requirements prove that the predominantly

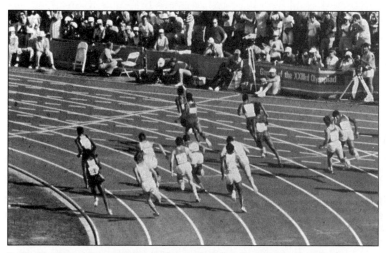

Carl Lewis, shown here receiving the baton (lane 5) in the gold-medal-winning 4 × 100 meter relay in the 1984 Los Angeles Olympic Games, has been called by some the greatest athlete ever. (Photo courtesy Paula Welch.)

white institutions want to limit the domination of minorities on some of their sports teams.

Whether the discrimination against minorities in sports is subtle or overt depends on the school or college, the team, and the leadership of both. Many interesting questions persist. Why are the starters on football and basketball teams predominately minorities when the student bodies are predominantly white? Why are minorities seldom members of tennis, swimming, golf, and gymnastics teams? Why do fewer minority team members who are marginal athletes receive athletic scholarships than comparably skilled whites? What is the status of the minority female athlete? Why are almost all head coaches and athletic directors white, especially when a high percentage of the football and basketball players are African American?

Some claim that minority athletes are bigger, stronger, and generally more highly skilled than white athletes? Research does not substantiate this. However, it is a fact that minority athletes' opportunities in elite and expensive sports have traditionally been limited, resulting in their devoting greater amounts of time and energy to the school-sponsored sports of football, basketball, and baseball. These· three sports also offer the remote potential for professional careers. Coaches often

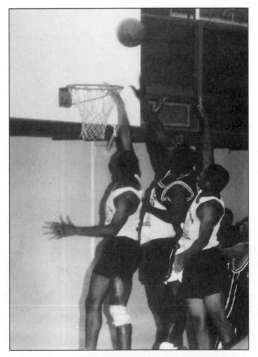

Formally underrepresented groups, when given the opportunity, often become dominant forces in sports. (Photo courtesy Maggie McGlynn.)

experience pressure to win. For them, recruiting the best athletes becomes imperative; yet in traditionally white institutions, they may also receive encouragement to have as many white players on their teams as possible, which may result in athletic scholarships being given disproportionately to marginal white athletes who play as substitutes, if they play at all.

High cost and the lack of opportunities have traditionally prevented many minorities from pursuing tennis, swimming, golf, and gymnastics. Private lessons, expensive equipment, club memberships, and travel requirements for quality competition discourage most minorities from entering these sports; the virtual absence of role models only reinforces the status quo. It should be noted that the minority female athlete must overcome both racial and sexual barriers to equity of sports opportunity. Her greatest opportunities, and hence achievements, have come in basketball and track.

Minority athletes, regardless of gender, sport, or level of competition, deserve to be treated fairly and equitably. All athletes should be expected to complete their academic work in schools and colleges and to earn their degrees in preparation for later life. Because of past discrimination, minorities may deserve to receive counseling to help them derive the most from their education and to learn marketable skills. Since prejudicial attitudes only change gradually, everyone must work together to eliminate discrimination in athletics. Coaches must not allow mistreatment of minorities on their teams, and administrators must ensure equity for all.

EQUALITY FOR SENIOR CITIZENS

Senior citizens have also had to overcome discriminatory biases in order to gain sporting opportunities. As the average age of the United States population increases, a greater awareness of the needs of seniors to exercise and to compete emerges. Persons past 60 years of age are walking, cycling, hiking, swimming, lifting weights, and engaging in a large number of sporting activities with the blessings of their physicians, who view such activities as good preventive medicine. This enthusiasm for exercise and activity has rekindled in many a desire to compete. The National Senior Games and masters events in national, regional, state, and local competitions are providing opportunities for former athletes and newly aspiring older athletes to achieve in sports in unprecedented ways. For example, in the first National Senior Games, which began in 1987, approximately 2,500 men and women competed in sports ranging from archery to volleyball. Held biennially, the National Summer Senior Games now attract over 12,000 competitors. Interest in other sports led to the establishment of the Winter National Senior Games in 2000. A listing of past competitions, the sports in which competitions are held, and affiliated state organizations can be found at www.nationalseniorgames.org. Whether competing for recognition or personal satisfaction, these older Americans are beneficiaries of enhanced strength, flexibility, endurance, and balance, factors that directly improve the quality of their lives. This activity also reduces the stress of lost spouses and friends and replaces loneliness with new friends and social opportunities.

Public and private recreational programs for older Americans are proliferating. For example, commercial health and fitness clubs offer water aerobics, exercise programs for individuals with arthritis, walking clubs, and other types of programs designed specifically for senior citizens. Many programs for seniors include cardiovascular, muscular strength and endurance, and flexibility components appropriate for individuals with histories of cardiac problems or chronic conditions requiring adaptations. Senior centers, either publicly funded or associated with residential areas, offer stretching sessions, a variety of recreational activities, and aerobic machines. Senior citizens are encouraged to continue their pursuit of life-long physical activity through age group competitions in tennis, golf, swimming, and many other sports. Through their votes and discretionary incomes, they are demanding and receiving more equitable access to recreational and sporting facilities.

EQUALITY FOR INDIVIDUALS WITH DISABILITIES

In recent years, persons with disabilities have increasingly desired equal opportunity to participate and compete in sports. The Amateur Sports Act of 1978 specified that the competitive needs of athletes with disabilities must be accommodated. The Education for All Handicapped Children Act of 1975 mandated that athletics be provided to school students with disabilities, and the 1990 Americans with Disabilities Act called for access to public recreational facilities for those previously denied it. These factors and an eagerness and

In 1984, the Olympic Games showcased the athletic achievements of athletes with disabilities. (Photo courtesy Paula Welch.)

determination to treat everyone equitably have led to a proliferation of organizations and competitions.

The Paralympic Games, which began in 1952, offer international competitions for individuals with spinal cord injuries. These games, which are now held every four years at the site of the Olympic Games, expanded from 130 athletes from 2 nations to 3,824 athletes from 122 countries at the summer 2000 Paralympic Games in Sydney. (See www.paralympic.org for more information about the history and activities of the International Paralympic Committee.) In 1976, the Paralympic winter games began, and visually impaired athletes were welcomed to its competitions. Since 1980, individuals with amputations and those with cerebral palsy have become competitors. The following list of sports attest to the abilities of these remarkable athletes: alpine skiing, archery, bocce, cross-country skiing, cycling, equestrian events, fencing, goalball, ice sledge hockey, ice sledge racing, judo, power lifting, sailing, shooting, soccer, swimming, table tennis, track and field, volleyball, wheelchair basketball, wheelchair rugby, wheelchair tennis, and wheelchair dance sport.

Since 1968, the Special Olympics has provided competitive opportunities for mentally retarded individuals. Although experts initially questioned this program, the overwhelming success of personal training and state, national, and international competitions have verified the importance of giving individuals with intellectual challenges the chance to achieve and to be recognized as winners. Official Special Olympics sports include alpine skiing, aquatics, athletics (track and field), badminton, basketball, bocce, bowling, cross-country skiing, cycling, equestrian events, figure skating, floor hockey, football (soccer), golf, gymnastics, power lifting, rollerskating, sailing, softball, speed skating, table tennis, team handball, tennis, and volleyball. The 10th Special Olympics World Summer Games for athletes with mental retardation was the largest multisport event in the world held during 1999. Nearly 7,000 athletes from more than 150 countries from around the world showcased their athletic talent.

YOUTH SPORTS

Around 50 million children and adolescents (ages 4 to 18) participate annually in youth sport competitions sponsored by cities, companies, and local and national organizations. These youthful athletes ride derby cars, horses, and dirt bikes; throw baseballs, softballs, footballs, basketballs, and roll bowling balls; hit golf balls, tennis balls, racquetballs, and table tennis balls; kick soccer balls; break boards; turn flips; swim; dive; wrestle; run; and compete in triathlons and many more sporting events. This proliferation of youth sports has been fueled by television, money, civic pride, the desire to produce national champions, parental overzealousness, and professional sports models.

The major issues facing youth sport programs are an overemphasis on winning, poorly trained coaches, parental interference, and eroded ethical values. When winning becomes the primary objective, other potential outcomes are lost. Coaches are usually the ones initially caught up in this win-at-all-costs attitude. To fulfill their own ego needs, coaches too often pressure their young players to play while injured, to violate the rules to their advantage, and to quit if they are not good enough. Also, coaches' lack of preparation may result in poorly taught skills, improper treatment of injuries, and inability to understand and to deal with children's developmental needs. Some coaches are even guilty of physically, mentally, and sexually abusing their young athletes.

While usually well intentioned, parents often impose their wishes on their children to play a particular sport or several sports. Too often parental aspirations to succeed in sports stem from their own needs rather than the children's needs. Children may experience considerable guilt because their parents invest huge amounts of time and money in lessons and competitions, which only pushes these young athletes to more desperately seek success. Parents too often reward results rather than effort and improvement. And when coaches and parents reinforce cheating to win, abusing officials and opponents, circumventing the rules, and stressing the outcome (winning) over the process (having fun and developing skills), important sporting values as well as essential personal virtues are lost. In addition, adult dominated sports rob children of the opportunity to make decisions, to learn give and take in sports, and to make good judgments.

With such a long list of problems, why do youth sports continue to grow in popularity? First, children in America have a genuine interest in and enthusiasm for sports. Second, the positive outcomes in most programs exceed the negative aspects. There are leagues, organizations, coaches, and parents who emphasize fun and participation and who ensure positive outcomes for the children physiologically and psychologically.

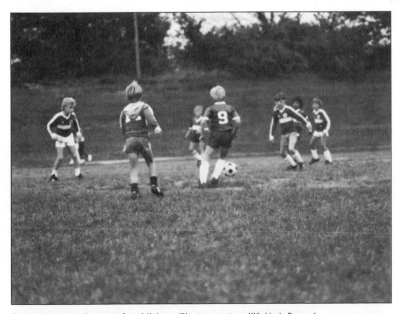

Soccer is a popular sport for children. (Photo courtesy Winkie LaForce.)

Through orientation programs, parents learn about program goals and how to help their children benefit most from their experiences. Program administrators need to emphasize the following:

- Everyone plays in every event and in rotating positions
- Certificates of participation and team outings are given as rewards instead of huge trophies and championship playoffs
- Children are asked what they want from their sports experiences to ensure attainment of these aspirations
- Coaches and parents stress and reinforce cooperation, teamwork, and sportsmanship
- Outcomes such as individual skill development, participation of everyone, development of intrinsic motivation, learning and playing several sports in varied positions, safe participation, and fun are emphasized.

Each year millions of girls and boys ages 8 to 18 years compete in the largest amateur sports program in the United States, the Junior Olympics. The Junior Olympics are organized by the Amateur Athletic Union and recognized by the United States Olympic Committee. These amateur athletes compete in more than 3,000 local meets, state championships, regional events, and national finals. The benefits from being a part of the Junior Olympics include making friends, having opportunities to travel, gaining a sense of achievement, and enjoying the excitement of the competitions. Youth also compete in state games, such as the Empire State Games (New York) and the Keystone State Games (Pennsylvania), which provide a variety of sports opportunities for children of all ages. Most of the athletes in these state games have developed their skills through youth and school athletic programs.

INTERSCHOLASTIC ATHLETICS

The National Federation of State High School Associations promotes interscholastic athletics as an integral part of the educational experiences of high school students. (See the "Case for High School Activities" at www.nfshsa.org/case.htm) Most physical educators have traditionally favored and supported interscholastic athletics because they believe that adolescents are able developmentally and emotionally to compete. School administrators stress the beneficial outcomes of fitness, sportsmanship, cooperation, self-discipline, and other values for the participants. From a broader perspective, interscholastic athletics enhances school spirit and, in many locales, enlists strong community support for the school.

Today, though, many interscholastic athletics coaches have not been properly prepared to coach. Several factors have contributed to this problem:

- Elimination of some physical education requirements and teaching positions;

- The addition of more specialized requirements for prospective physical education teachers, and a reduction of coaching-related courses in colleges;
- Physical educators not choosing to combine teaching and coaching careers;
- Physical educators ceasing to coach;
- More school sports teams, especially for girls, requiring coaches;
- Teachers of other school subjects seeking coaching positions.

One way to address this need is through the Program for Athletic Coaches' Education (PACE), which provides generic, practical information appropriate for entry-level interscholastic coaches. Basic principles and procedures are presented in the areas of philosophy, growth and development, sports medicine, psychology, litigation and liability, and sport management. (For more information, see www.mhsaa.com/administration/pace.html.)

The major problem in high school sports in the United States is an overemphasis on winning. Indicative of this compulsion are year-round conditioning programs and practices, students specializing in one sport, students playing while hurt, and coaches' jobs depending on winning records. Advocates of year-round conditioning programs stress that they are needed to develop proper skills, to stay competitive with other teams' athletes, and to increase chances for college grants-in-aid. Arguments against single-sport specialization include athletic burnout and overuse injuries; denied opportunities to acquire other skills, to play with other athletes, and to learn from other coaches; and exploitation by coaches concerned only with their teams.

The teacher/coach who must try to meet the demands of two full-time jobs is sometimes overwhelmed when school administrators, parents, and team supporters mandate winning. Coaching supplements are low when compared with these pressures, and the time expectations are high, although personal satisfaction and community and school recognition may compensate somewhat.

Another controversial issue facing interscholastic athletic programs is the "no pass, no play" policy adopted by some states. Generally, this policy requires that student players obtain passing marks in all (or most) courses taken during the previous grading period. Supporters state that the purpose of schools is education. Thus, participation on a team, or in any other extracurricular activity, is a privilege earned by those who achieve in the classroom. Advocates also claim that this policy will motivate students to achieve academically on a consistent basis. Lawmakers, school administrators, and most parents applaud the effectiveness of this policy because students' performances in their class work overall have improved. Opponents disagree. They claim that extracurricular activities, and especially sports, encourage some young people to remain in school. Experience, though, has shown that although a few students may only continue their education because of the appeal of sports participation, many students seem to be taking their schoolwork more seriously because of the "no pass, no play" policy.

The abuse of drugs is all too pervasive in schools. Most adolescents and children, including athletes, have ready access to tobacco, alcohol, marijuana,

Basketball had become a popular school sport nationally by the early 1900s
(Raylon School, Texas). (Photo courtesy Thomas L. Ward.)

amphetamines, cocaine, and other legal and illegal drugs. Unless coaches educate their athletes about the harmful effects of these drugs on their bodies, and
hence their performances, many interscholastic athletes will succumb to peer
pressure and use these drugs. Underage drinking, cigarette smoking, and the use
of smokeless tobacco are all too common among interscholastic athletes. Some of
these athletes also use anabolic steroids, resulting in immediate and irreparable
physiological damage. Taken to increase muscle bulk and size for appearance
and performance purposes, large dosages of anabolic steroids may interfere with
normal growth and development, lead to overly aggressive and irrational behaviors, cause sterility, and even kill the user.

     School athletic programs also face other problems such as spectator vio-
lence, unsportsmanlike conduct by coaches and athletes, cheating to maintain
academic eligibility, and program budget cuts. Because of skyrocketing costs,
due somewhat to injury and liability insurance and the provision of athletic programs for girls and persons with disabilities, many schools can no longer afford
to provide athletics as a right. Many high schools are adopting a pay-for-play
policy, which means that no longer will educational allocations finance athletic
teams; instead, any student who desires to participate on a team will have to
pay for the experience. Although this policy excludes students who are unable
to pay, this is an increasingly popular trend, especially in private schools.

INTERCOLLEGIATE ATHLETICS

Ever since the proliferation of college athletic programs for men in the late 1800s,
college faculties and administrators have been concerned about the potentially
detrimental effects of athletics on academic work. Associated problems then and

O RESEARCH VIEW

Citizenship Through Sports Alliance

The high school (National Federation of State High School Associations), college (National Junior College Athletic Association; National Association of Intercollegiate Athletics; National Collegiate Athletic Association), Olympic (United States Olympic Committee), and professional (Women's National Basketball Association; National Basketball Association; National Hockey League; Major League Baseball; National Football League) organizations joined forces in 1997 to establish the Citizenship Through Sports Alliance (CTSA). This alliance was formed because of concerns about the decline in sportsmanship and increase in unethical behaviors within sports in America, a deterioration that permeates competitions from the youth leagues to the professional leagues. This alliance seeks to promote the values realized through sportsmanship and ethical play in sports at all levels. The objective of the CTSA is to help sports participants become better citizens and learn those values necessary to teach and learn respect for self and respect for others. Among the character-building qualities that CTSA members espouse and seek to engender in their athletes are self-esteem, discipline, courage, responsibility, integrity, honesty, ethics, poise, pride, enthusiasm, teamwork, loyalty, compassion, tolerance, courtesy, fairness, and humility.

The CTSA advocates six principles that should characterize all sports programs:

- Value of diversity
- Drug-free athletes
- Value of sport
- Academic and social achievement
- Ethical conduct
- Nonviolence

Sports competitions should help instill and hone values essential for the development of respect for self and others as well as promote citizenship in this country.

now include students missing classes because of competing and traveling, receiving unearned grades, and being admitted even though underqualified. The National Collegiate Athletic Association (NCAA), the National Association of Intercollegiate Athletics (NAIA), and the National Junior College Athletic Association (NJCAA) have attempted to administer intercollegiate athletics on the basis of educational principles, although regulations concerning these issues largely rest with each institution. (See Research View box above.) The problem that each college faces is how to deal effectively with regulations when winning is almost synonymous with survival, especially at large institutions.

Winning teams appeal to spectators and lead to increased interest. More fans bring in larger gate receipts. More money contributes to hiring coaches with winning reputations and to recruiting and awarding grants-in-aid to better athletes, who combine to win more games. This cycle (winning = fans = money = winning = fans = money) repeats itself with alarming regularity and tends to spiral into an ever-widening circle. The resultant commercialization changes college athletics from an extension of the institution's educational mission to a business venture. When winning becomes the most important objective, rules are frequently violated, both during play and in the recruiting of athletes; sportsmanship, character development, and other values are often lost or at least deemphasized in the process. Increasingly, college and university presidents are addressing these problems by emphasizing academic outcomes over athletic goals, despite opposition by some coaches.

Why do intercollegiate athletics continue to thrive? There are three major reasons. First, intercollegiate athletics reflect Americans' attitudes, beliefs, and values. Many people believe that colleges have the responsibility to offer competitive sport opportunities for students, and they defend the concept that sports participation helps prepare the athletes for life by developing physical, intellectual, social, and moral skills. Second, the benefits already mentioned exceed the liabilities. Many people think that the problems listed above are sporadic rather than pervasive. They add that participants and spectators experience a cathartic

Intercollegiate football teams have become multimillion-dollar businesses in many institutions, thus challenging the accuracy of the concept of the student athlete. (Photo courtesy UNC Sports Information Office.)

release of tension and have fun, while college spirit and allegiance are greatly enhanced. Third, athletic teams are valuable public relations tools for institutions. College enrollments often increase as a result of successful athletic programs, especially in football and men's basketball. The provision of entertainment attracts large numbers of spectators to college athletic contests, with an accompanying surge in college loyalty that many claim positively affects legislative appropriations and private donations to academic departments, in addition to generous support for athletics.

Realistically, intercollegiate athletics, regardless of the extent of the challenges, will continue to thrive because of its entertainment value and benefits. To

Intercollegiate sports have the potential to help athletes develop their physical, mental, and social skills as long as these positive outcomes are taught and reinforced. (Photo courtesy State University of West Georgia Sports Information Office.)

accentuate the positive and to reduce the negative, the following actions are possible remedies:

- Sanction intercollegiate coaches and athletes who violate athletic regulations, especially in the areas of recruiting and scholarships, for the first offense; place violators on a two-year probation from coaching and competing for the second offense; ban violators from college coaching and from intercollegiate competition for life for the third offense.
- Withhold for a period of five years one grant-in-aid for every athlete who does not graduate within six years.
- Require that coaches of nonrevenue-producing sports be employed full-time (either within athletics or some other area of the institution).
- Base coaches' job security and salaries not on their won-lost records but on the fulfillment of their job responsibilities and the provision of positive experiences for their athletes.
- Restrict schedules of all sports to no more than two days of competition per week while classes are in session.
- Excuse athletes from classes no more than five days per academic year for travel and competition.
- Admit only those athletes who meet the academic standards of admission to the colleges they attend.
- Limit grants-in-aid to tuition, fees, and books, and award them only on the basis of need.

If some or all of these suggestions are implemented, intercollegiate athletics might become a more positive, educational experience for athletes.

The abuse of drugs by college athletes and the desire by the NCAA to curtail their use has led to drug testing at football bowl games and NCAA Championships (see the box on page 364). Although only a few athletes have been barred from competition because of their use of banned drugs, many claim that this testing and institutional drug-testing programs have deterred many athletes from the use of performance-enhancing drugs. Still, too many college athletes are guilty of perjury when they sign the pledge required by the NCAA stating that they do not use these substances. Even the drug education programs offered by colleges and universities have failed to eradicate this blemish on the reputation of intercollegiate athletics.

The use of anabolic steroids is especially dangerous. Besides providing unfair physical advantages, anabolic steroids can severely harm those who abuse them. These drugs may cause the users to behave violently on and off the field. Their abuse is often linked with an obsession to earn a starting position, to become a star player, or to get drafted into a professional league. Amphetamine abuse may also occur under the guise of increasing one's aggressiveness and effort. Cocaine, marijuana, tobacco, and alcohol are more likely to be used socially or for relaxation. As with other college students, most athletes' drug of choice is alcohol, even though most are underage drinkers. Coaches, therefore, face the challenge of educating their athletes about the negative effects of drug abuse as well as about the rules and values violated through their use.

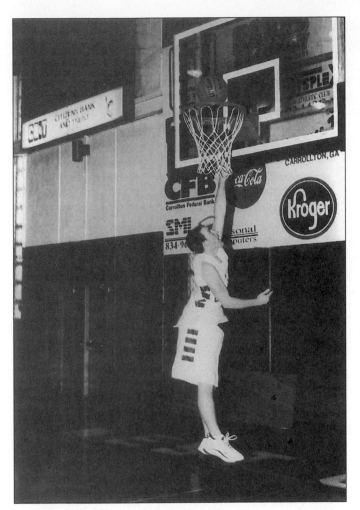

Competitive sports will continue to thrive in the twenty-first century. (Photo courtesy State University of West Georgia Sports Information Office.)

To preserve the integrity of intercollegiate sports, coaches and athletic administrators must also resolve issues of institutional control. Several institutions have failed to keep overeager supporters from giving money, cars, clothes, and other benefits to athletes. Although not illegal, these actions violate NCAA rules governing payments to athletes. In the intense recruiting battles for blue-chip athletes, coaches may convince admissions committees to lower entrance standards. Many institutions have been criticized for the low graduation rates of athletes, especially African Americans.

Some athletes' conduct also undermines the values thought to be associated with athletics. For example, actions such as taunting opponents and excessive celebrations illustrate that such behavior runs counter to the goals of fair play and respecting one's opponents. Coaches' physical and emotional abuse of players is another example of such destructive behavior. In addition, misdemeanors and felonies, such as driving under the influence of alcohol, using illegal drugs, and

DRUG TESTING

Sport governing organizations at the school, college, and professional levels, in an affirmation of their commitment to fair and equitable sports competitions, have specified that certain performance-enhancing drugs are banned. To prevent athletes from gaining artificial advantages through drugs or to deter athletes from the use of drugs that have been proven harmful to health, participants are required to submit to drug testing on a regular and/or random basis. Banned drugs include substances such as amphetamines, cocaine, and anabolic steroids. (See www.ncaa.org/sports_sciences/drugtesting/banned_list.html#stimulants for a complete list of the drugs banned by the NCAA.)

In order for student athletes to be eligible for intercollegiate competitions at NCAA institutions, they have to sign a consent form indicating that they understand the drug-testing program and are willing to participate in it. Member institutions must conduct a drug and alcohol education program once per semester to raise the awareness of student athletes about the harmful affects of drug use and to inform them about institutional and NCAA drug policies.

The Olympic Movement Anti-Doping Code governs the use of banned substances in the Olympic Games. This Code was developed because of increasing abuse of drugs to enhance the potential for winning medals in the Olympics despite the fact that doping contravenes the values and fundamental principles of Olympism and medical ethics. Since doping threatens the health of the athlete and the integrity of Olympic sport and its ideals, extensive drug testing pervades the Olympic Games and, unfortunately, results in disqualification of gold medalists and public exposure and sanctioning of guilty athletes, as seen repeatedly during the Sydney Games in 2000. Among the prohibited drugs in the Olympics are stimulants, narcotics, anabolic agents, and diuretics. Blood doping and other forms of pharmacological and chemical manipulation are also forbidden. (The USOC Guide to Prohibited Classes of Substances and Prohibited Methods of Doping can be found at www.usoc.org/usoc/drug2000.pdf.)

sexual assaults and rape, have negatively affected the image of athletes as well as institutions. Booster clubs or athletic foundations have also repeatedly paid off the contracts of coaches with whom they have become disillusioned for not winning enough games. Such actions always raise the question of who is in control of athletics. These examples describe situations at only a few of the nationally prominent universities that may have failed to maintain institutional control over their big-time athletic programs.

INTERNATIONAL SPORTS

Elite athletes around the world have numerous opportunities to compete in championship events annually as well as in special events, such as the Pan-American Games, the Asian Games, the British Empire and Commonwealth Games, and the World University Games. These events, open to athletes from the countries implicit in the games' titles, are conducted every four years except for the World University Games, which are held every two years. All of these are important competitions, but the most prestigious internationally are the Olympic Games (patterned after the ancient Greek spectacle). Since 1896 (and 1924 for the Winter

WEB CONNECTIONS

1. www.usoc.org
   The official web site of the United States Olympic Committee provides up-to-date information about the athletes and the activities of the national governing board for the Olympics in the United States.

2. www.paralympic.org
   Learn more about the International Paralympic Games, which are competitions for elite athletes with disabilities.

3. www.specialolympics.org
   The Special Olympics is an international program of year-round sports training and athletic competition for more than one million children and adults with mental retardation. Check out this site for a wealth of information about the history, philosophy, and programs of Special Olympics.

4. www.nfshsa.org
   The National Federation of State High School Associations provides leadership and national coordination for the administration of interscholastic activities. This site includes a wealth of information about the scope of operations of this oversight organization for high school sports.

5. www.aausports.net/mytp/templates/main.jsp?i=/org/AAU/aauprograms/jrolympicgames.text&cindex=-1
   Find out more about the events and activities of the Amateur Athletic Union's Junior Olympic Games at this site.

6. www.nationalseniorgames.org
   The National Senior Games Association promotes healthier lifestyles for seniors through education, fitness, and sports competitions and governs the Summer (in 18 sports) and Winter (in 5 sports) Senior Games.

7. www.ncaa.org
   Go to this site of the National Collegiate Athletic Association, which governs intercollegiate competition for its member institutions in 28 sports.

8. www.naia.org/
   Check out this site to find out more about the National Association of Intercollegiate Athletics, which governs intercollegiate competition for over 300 small colleges in 13 sports.

(continued)

9. www.njcaa.org
   Learn more about the National Junior College Athletic Association, which governs intercollegiate competition in 17 sports for its over 500 member two-year colleges.

10. www.womenssportsfoundation.org/templates/index.html
    This site provides comprehensive information about sports and fitness for girls and women.

Competitive opportunities in international sport include cycling.
(Photo courtesy Craig Premo.)

Games) athletes from around the world have competed every four years (except during World Wars I and II) under the direction of the International Olympic Committee (IOC) (see the box on pages 368–369). Since 1994, the Winter Games have been held in even-numbered years alternating with the Summer Games.

The Olympic Games have been subjected to numerous threats to their ideals, with politics being the chief detractor. From the inception of the Games through the attempt by the Nazis to prove Aryan supremacy in 1936 to the boycotts of 1976, 1980, and 1984, countries have attempted to use the Olympics to advance their political agendas and influence public opinion. The worst political situation occurred during the 1972 Munich Olympic Games when Arab terrorists massacred eleven Israeli athletes. The banning of some countries and the nonrecognition of others prove that the Olympic Games remain political. Athletes competing as representatives of their nations, the playing of national anthems during the awards ceremonies, national medal counts, team sports, and national uniforms constantly reinforce nationalism. Governments, financially and ideologically, continue to increase their involvement because international prestige and promotion of their political ideologies are at stake. Judging irregularities often result from political alliances, while increased use of drugs verifies the importance placed on winning.

Commercialism has grown exponentially. For example, the 1968 Mexico City Games cost $250 million to stage, while the 1980 Moscow Games reportedly cost over $2 billion. CBS paid $660,000 to broadcast the 1960 events; NBC televised the 1996 Olympic Games at a cost of about $800 million worldwide. One blatant example of the commercialism tainting the Olympics has been the bribes associated with site selection and privileged treatment of IOC members. The athletes are not immune to commercialism either. Although the Olympic Games were begun for amateur athletes competing for the love of sport, today most athletes are professionals, with each sport's governing federation specifying what competitors are allowed to accept monetarily. Many athletes receive money from their countries based specifically on how many medals and what types (gold, silver, or bronze) they win. The list could continue, but the point is that few, if any, Olympic athletes are amateurs in the sense of never having profited from their athletic skill.

In spite of these problems, the Olympic Games thrive and continue to increase in popularity. The development of friendships and the attainment of personal athletic goals are two of the many positive outcomes. Most disdain the boycotts, political maneuvering, unfair judging, and drug abuse, since these incidents only detract from the integrity of the Olympic Games. Commercialization of the overall staging and of the athletes themselves is a nuisance to be tolerated, rather than a reason to end the competitions. Many people advocate either reducing the number of events and entries or lengthening the Games and increasing the number of sites and sports. Several support reductions in the symbols of nationalism.

As other nations emphasized Olympic sport success, the United States found its traditional dominance lessening, often because of other nations' subsidization of elite athletes. A restructuring of amateur sports in the United States seemed

Jesse Owens, a Big Ten champion from The Ohio State University, won four gold medals in the 1936 Berlin Olympic Games. (Photo courtesy the University of Michigan.)

SUMMER OLYMPIC GAMES*

	Year	City	Nations	Events	Sports	Males	Females	Athletes
I	1896	Athens, Greece	13	42	9	311	0	311
II	1900	Paris, France	22	60	17	1319	11	1330
III	1904	St. Louis, MO	12	94	14	681	6	687
IV	1908	London, England	22	104	21	1699	36	2035
V	1912	Stockholm, Sweden	27	106	13	2490	57	2547
VI	1916	Berlin, Germany (canceled WWI)						
VII	1920	Antwerp, Belgium	27	154	21	2543	64	2607
VIII	1924	Paris, France	45	137	17	2956	136	3092
IX	1928	Amsterdam, Holland	46	120	14	2724	290	3014
X	1932	Los Angeles, CA	37	124	14	1281	127	1408
XI	1936	Berlin, Germany	49	142	19	3738	328	4068
XII	1940	Tokyo, Japan (canceled WWII)						
XIII	1944	London, England (canceled WWII)						
XIV	1948	London, England	59	138	17	3714	385	4099
XV	1952	Helsinki, Finland	69	149	17	4407	518	4925
XVI	1956	Melbourne, Australia	67	145	16	2958	384	3342
		Stockholm, Sweden (equestrian only)	29	6	1	145	13	158
XVII	1960	Rome, Italy	84	150	17	4738	610	5348
XVIII	1964	Tokyo, Japan	94	162	19	4457	683	5140
XIX	1968	Mexico City, Mexico	113	172	18	4750	781	5531
XX	1972	Munich, Germany	122	196	21	6659	1171	7830
XXI	1976	Montreal, Canada	92	199	21	4915	1274	6189
XXII	1980	Moscow, USSR	81	200	21	4320	1192	5512
XXIII	1984	Los Angeles, CA	140	223	21	5458	1620	7078
XXIV	1988	Seoul, Korea	160	237	23	6963	2438	9421
XXV	1992	Barcelona, Spain	169	257	25	7555	3008	10,563
XXVI	1996	Atlanta, GA	197	271	26	7060	3684	10,744
XXVII	2000	Sydney, Australia	199	301	37	Unavailable	Unavailable	11,000
XXVIII	2004	Athens, Greece						

WINTER OLYMPIC GAMES*

	Year	City	Nations	Events	Sports	Males	Females	Athletes
I	1924	Chamonix, France	16	13	5	281	13	294
II	1928	St. Moritz, Switzerland	25	13	6	366	27	393
III	1932	Lake Placid, NY	17	14	5	277	30	307
IV	1936	Garmisch-Parkenkirchen, Germany	28	17	5	680	76	756
V	1948	St. Moritz, Switzerland	28	24	6	636	77	713
VI	1952	Oslo, Norway	30	22	5	624	108	732
VII	1956	Cortina d'Ampezzo, Italy	32	24	5	687	132	819
VIII	1960	Squaw Valley, CA	30	27	5	502	146	648
IX	1964	Innsbruck, Austria	36	34	7	758	175	933
X	1968	Grenoble, France	37	35	7	1063	230	1293
XI	1972	Sapporo, Japan	35	35	7	927	218	1128
XII	1976	Innsbruck, Austria	37	37	7	1013	248	1261
XIII	1980	Lake Placid, NY	37	39	7	1012	271	1283
XIV	1984	Sarajevo, Yugoslavia	49	40	7	1127	283	1490
XV	1988	Calgary, Canada	57	46	7	1270	364	1634
XVI	1992	Albertville, France	65	57	7	1313	488	1801
XVII	1994	Lillehammer, Norway	67	61	7	1302	542	1844
XVIII	1998	Nagano, Japan	80	68	7	unavailable	unavailable	2,302
XIX	2002	Salt Lake City, UT						

*Courtesy of the United States Olympic Committee.

369

appropriate. Following the passage of the Amateur Sports Act of 1978, the United States Olympic Committee (USOC) established the United States Olympic Training Center in Colorado Springs, Colorado. It offered to National Governing Bodies for each Olympic sport its resources and facilities as training sites for athletes. The USOC has received some federal funding but relies largely on corporate sponsorships and private donations to support its work. Increasingly athletes in the lesser-known sports receive funding from the USOC to continue training year-round.

SUMMARY

Sports opportunities for girls and women and for minorities of race, age, or ability, while often limited in the past, are today more equitable, although some barriers exist that only time and an increased commitment to equity will remove. Youth sports too often overemphasize winning, as do high school sports. Yet most parents support their children's participation in sports because the positive outcomes outweigh the negative risks. Balancing educational values with business concerns remains the dilemma facing major college sports today. Abuses abound, yet the public continues to expect colleges to offer athletic programs as entertainment. Similarly, the Olympic ideals, whether real or imagined, seem to ensure people's support of the Olympic Games, as politics, nationalism, and commercialization provide insufficient reasons to cancel the spectacle. The pervasiveness of sports (see the box below) in the United States means that people believe that sports contribute far more to society than they detract from it. It is the responsibility of those who work in any of these sports arenas to ensure that the potential values to be learned and reinforced through participation in sports are realized by all.

SPORTS TIMELINE

Girls and Women in Sports
1972—Congress passed the Education Amendments that included Title IX

Equality for Minorities
1946—Kenny Washington and Woody Strode (Los Angeles Rams) became the first African Americans in the modern era to play in the National Football League
1947—Jackie Robinson (Brooklyn Dodgers) became the first African American in the modern era to play Major League Baseball
1950—Charles Cooper (Boston Celtics) became the first African American in the modern era to play in the National Basketball Association
1954—U.S. Supreme Court passes *Brown v. Board of Education*, which led to school desegregation with subsequently more equality of opportunity for African American students and loss of positions for African American coaches

(continued)

SPORTS TIMELINE (CONTINUED)

Equality for Senior Citizens
1987—National Senior Games began

Equality for Individuals with Disabilities
1952—Paralympic Games began to offer competitions for individuals with spinal cord injuries
1968—Special Olympics began to offer competitions for mentally retarded individuals
1978—Amateur Sports Act passed by U.S. Congress mandated meeting the competitive needs of athletes with disabilities
1990—Individuals with Disabilities Education Act passed by U.S. Congress (extended the provisions of Section 504 of the Rehabilitation Act of 1973 and the Education for All Handicapped Children Act of 1975 and subsequent amendments)

Youth Sports
1930—Pop Warner Football began
1939—Little League Baseball established
1950—Biddy Basketball formed
1964—American Youth Soccer Organization established
1967—Amateur Athletic Union's Junior Olympics began

Interscholastic Athletics
1922—National Federation of State High School Associations formed

Intercollegiate Athletics
1852—First intercollegiate sports competition for men held (rowing contest between Harvard and Yale)
1896—First intercollegiate sports competition for women held (basketball game between Stanford and California)
1906—National Collegiate Athletic Association established (began women's competitions in 1981)
1938—National Junior College Athletic Association formed (began women's competitions in 1976)
1952—National Association of Intercollegiate Athletics formed (began women's competitions in 1980)
1971—Association for Intercollegiate Athletics for Women established

International Sports
1896—Modern Olympic Games began
1924—Winter Olympic Games began
1978—Amateur Sports Act passed by U.S. Congress that totally restructured international sport in this country

CAREER PERSPECTIVE

MICHAEL DELONG
Head Football Coach
Springfield University
Springfield, Massachusetts

EDUCATION
B.S., Physical Education, Springfield College
M.A., Physical Education, University of North
Carolina at Chapel Hill

JOB RESPONSIBILITIES AND HOURS

The responsibilities of college and university coaches vary tremendously, depending
on the emphasis placed on the institution's program and the sport. Mike organizes and
administers an NCAA Division III football program, including directing a staff of two full-
time assistant coaches and 12 graduate assistants, recruiting student athletes, planning
games and practices, working directly with admissions and financial aid officers, raising
funds, developing community support, and carrying out on- and off-field coaching
duties. He also teaches four semester hours in-season and six to eight semester hours
out-of-season and advises physical education majors—a typical work load at a smaller
institution. Like most coaches, Mike's weekly hours, which vary from 85 in-season to 70
off-season to 30 during the summer, are demanding. Salaries are based on each coach's
experience and won/lost record, the institution and its reputation, and the sport. At the
NCAA Division III level, the salary range is $40,000 to $80,000 for head coaches and
$20,000 to $40,000 for assistant coaches.

SPECIALIZED COURSE WORK, DEGREES, AND WORK EXPERIENCES
NEEDED FOR THIS CAREER

Although college or university coaching does not require a master's degree, teaching at
smaller institutions may require attaining this degree. Physical education is the most
common major for coaches at both the undergraduate and graduate levels, although
many coaches have degrees in other disciplines. Opportunities to become head coaches
usually follow years of coaching high school teams, serving as effective graduate assistants or full-time assistant coaches, or completing successful college or professional playing careers. Volunteering to coach a youth, school, or club team may provide an entry
into this career. Mike recommends that prospective coaches emphasize exercise physiology, oral and written communication skills, problem-solving techniques, organizational
skills, motivational strategies, and theory and technique courses. He encourages prospective coaches as well as those already in positions to visit successful programs and to
learn from others.

SATISFYING ASPECTS

People may choose this career because they love a particular sport, want to continue
associating with it, enjoy teaching its skills and strategies, like to help athletes develop
their talents to their optimal levels, or any combination of these and other reasons. Mike
especially enjoys player/coach relationships, coach to coach interactions, and the

feeling of accomplishment as the team improves. Coaching can be tremendously satisfying, not only in terms of wins and losses, but in watching teams and players grow and mature. For Mike, helping individuals reach their goals is the most rewarding part of coaching.

JOB POTENTIAL

Mike states that to be secure in a college or university coaching position, winning is essential. If you perform within the rules, he says, you will be secure; if you do not perform within the rules, you can expect to be relieved of your duties. Promotion is also based on performance. Coaches who are proven workers have a good chance for advancement in the profession. Politics also plays a role, so it helps to know people. Since getting your foot in the door is difficult and highly competitive, a major part of the initial hiring process is knowing someone who can help you secure a full-time position. Once you have proven your abilities and made connections with people, things generally go a little easier. The job market is extremely competitive, especially for the best jobs. Patience and perseverance are two essential characteristics necessary for success.

SUGGESTIONS FOR STUDENTS

Mike states that coaching is a great career because of the fun and excitement. Coaches are surrounded by great people who like to work and play hard. The rewards of developing players and a team to perform to their fullest potentials are tremendous. Mike advises that prior to becoming a coach, make sure you are ready to make a full commitment, because the players you will coach deserve your best effort. Your family also must be aware of the sacrifices that they will have to make because of the time demands of this career. He adds that you need to be flexible and ready to overcome obstacles and setbacks; there are both extreme highs and extreme lows with which you must cope. The rewards of coaching are directly proportional to the effort you put into the team. If you give your best, in the long run, coaching is well worth the effort.

REVIEW QUESTIONS

1. What are three ways in which social factors inhibit girls' and women's involvement in sports?
2. What have been the positive and negative effects of Title IX on sports opportunities for females?
3. How have minorities faced discrimination in sports?
4. What are three common problems facing youth sports programs, and how would you recommend solving them?
5. What are three issues associated with interscholastic sports, and how would you recommend dealing with each?
6. What do "no pass, no play" and "pay-for-play" policies mean in relation to interscholastic sports?
7. What are three major problems facing intercollegiate athletics today, and how would you recommend solving them?
8. What is the meaning of the winning = fans = money = winning = fans = money cycle in sports today?

9. How does nationalism pervade the Olympic Games, and what are the positives and negatives of this?
10. How can sports contribute to value development?

STUDENT ACTIVITIES

1. Interview students about their attitudes toward girls and women in sport. Ask them what financial support women should receive, which team sports they should have, who should coach them, as well as other related questions. What changes have they observed in society's acceptance of girls and women in sport?
2. Interview two minority athletes on your campus. Ask them whether they have experienced any discrimination during their sports careers and, if so, have them describe it. Have they seen or experienced any changes in how they are treated today as opposed to how they were treated when they first began playing sports on the college level?
3. Based on your attendance at a youth sport event, what were the philosophy and values of that program? What should they have been? Was winning emphasized too much? What did you observe to indicate that winning was stressed too much?
4. Discuss whether the intercollegiate athletic program at your institution is a business or a component of education. Can it be both? If so, how?
5. List several possible changes that could improve the Olympic Games. Which of these are realistic alternatives?
6. Interview senior citizens who have participated in Senior Games or masters events or who are active sports participants. What are their reasons for competing and for being active? Has their involvement been lifelong, or is it a recent lifestyle change?
7. Stage a class debate addressing the topic "Athletics do/do not have a place in our educational system."
8. Attend a youth sports practice session and tabulate the number of times the coach(es) provide positive and corrective feedback, the amount of time spent on task such as in drills and observing skill demonstrations, and the methods used for learning motor skills.
9. Locate in a newspaper or magazine an illustration of biased journalism in the coverage of girls and women in sport. Discuss how this article depicts these athletes.
10. Interview a female who participated in sports prior to Title IX. Ask her what has changed in women's sports since that time.

SUGGESTED READINGS

Aicinena S: Youth sport readiness: a predictive model for success, *Phy Educ* 49:58, 1992. Readiness for organized sport participation in the proposed model is based on an interaction of sport-related fundamental skill development, motivation, socialization, and sport-specific knowledge.

Davis RW: The 1996 Atlanta Paralympics, *JOPERD* 67(6):59, 1996. The Paralympics, begun in 1952, has grown into quadrennial competitions in 17 events for over 3,500 international athletes with physical and sensory impairments.

Duderstadt JJ: *Intercollegiate athletes and the American University,* Ann Arbor, MI, 2000, University of Michigan Press. The author, who served as Michigan's president, shares his perspective about how intercollegiate athletics really operate in today's commercialized world. He offers suggestions for reform.

Fejgin N: Participation in high school competitive sports: a subversion of school mission or contribution to academic goals?, *Soc of Sp J* 11(3):211, 1994. Data from a national sample of 10th graders about the impact of athletic sports participation revealed positive effects on grades, self-concept, and educational aspirations and a negative effect on discipline problems.

Lidor R: Development of character through sports activities, *Int J Phys Educ* 35(3):91, 1998. After examining some of the theoretical aspects of moral education and selected research findings, the author contends that although it is espoused that sports build character, it is hard to educate people through sports because of the emphasis on winning.

Lumpkin A: Title IX update, in H. Appenzeller (Ed.), *Risk management in sport: Issues and strategies,* 1998, Durham, NC: Carolina Academic Press, pp. 313–320. The author provides a brief but comprehensive overview of the progress associated with Title IX of the Education Amendments of 1972.

Privett C: The Special Olympics: a tradition of excellence, *Except Parent* 29(5):28, 1999. In this part of a special section on sports and recreation for athletes with mental challenges, the author discusses the Special Olympics World Games. He includes the history of the games, the philosophy guiding the games, the opportunities offered by the games, the involvement of families, the 30th anniversary celebrations of the first Special Olympics of 1968, and a preview of the 1999 games.

Sports reform: college athletics in flux, *J of Coll and Univ Law* 22(1), 1995. This issue includes the text of the speeches of the symposium on intercollegiate athletics reforms, which was held at the University of Notre Dame on February 24–25, 1995. These presentations focused on subjects such as government attempts at regulating intercollegiate athletics, trends in NCAA regulation, and Title IX.

Sullivan KA, Lantz PJ, Zirkel PA: Leveling the playing field or leveling the players? Section 504, the Americans with Disabilities Act, and interscholastic sports, *J Spec Educ* 33(4):258, 2000. This article offers a systematic synthesis of the agency and court rulings that apply Section 504, the Americans with Disabilities Act, and the Individuals with Disabilities Education Act to interscholastic athletics. A framework provides insight into how these federal statutes pertain to the participation of students with disabilities in extracurricular activities.

Wilde TJ: Seeking equitable distribution of opportunities for intercollegiate athletic participation between the sexes, *J of Sp Mgmt* 9:300, 1995. This article describes Title IX case law and relevant legal principles before examining selected gender-equity initiatives. A three-for-one proposal is suggested as a way to satisfy the athletic interests and abilities of both genders.

Zimbalist A: *Unpaid professionals: commercialism and conflict in big-time college sports,* Princeton, NJ, 1999, Princeton University Press. The author discusses eight areas of concern in the intercollegiate sports industry such as the athlete as student and associated academic standards, treatment of athletes, corruption and erosion of values, and financing college sports. He concludes with 10 propositions for reform.

CHAPTER

12

LIVING ACTIVELY IN THE TWENTY-FIRST CENTURY

KEY CONCEPTS

- Life in the twenty-first century will differ dramatically from today's world and significantly impact the role of physical activity programs.
- Leadership is important for physical educators, exercise scientists, and sport professionals.
- A new name for the field of physical education reflects its changing image.
- The promotion of physical activity is essential for increasing participation levels.
- Physical activity is a highly valued part of life.

INTRODUCTORY SCENARIO I—LIVING IN 2050

At 7' 7", 275 pounds, Jimmy broke every national high school scoring and rebounding record during the 2049–2050 season. A basketball phenomenon, he touched off a recruiting frenzy that quickly exceeded sports fans' wildest imaginations. But to get Jimmy, everyone had to go through James, Sr., who had genetically engineered his son and then incessantly conditioned, fed, and trained him physically and mentally using the latest technologies and drugs. James, Sr. announced to the world that Jimmy's talents could be obtained but only for a huge price.

State University offered Jimmy a new car, a condo of his choice, a $100,000 per year salary, and a bonus to rename the basketball arena in his father's honor if Jimmy helped the semi-pro Golden Knights win the NCAA Championship.

The New York Kings, the leading professional basketball franchise, tried to entice Jimmy to leap to its league directly out of high school. They implored James, Sr. to allow Jimmy to sign a 30 million dollar per year, 20-year, no-cut contract. As an incentive, the Kings added a 50 million dollar bonus for each season Jimmy won the league's Most Valuable Player Award.

The NRA conglomerate (formerly Nike, Reebok, and Adidas) promised to introduce the Jamming Jimmy autograph shoe one month later if Jimmy signed its 1 million dollar per week endorsement agreement. Jamming Jimmy clothing and sports equipment would be marketed within six months, if he signed.

International Sports Marketing (ISM), however, succeeded in getting James, Sr. to grant it monopolistic control over Jimmy's career. Jimmy would play for State University for one year before joining the Kings. He would sign with NRA immediately and wear his autograph shoe at the University, but defer the 1 million dollars per week and other endorsements until he joined the Kings. All of the promised payouts were guaranteed; plus, ISM would negotiate for Jimmy an additional 10 million dollars per year in endorsements managed by ISM.

INTRODUCTORY SCENARIO II—LIVING IN 2050

By the mid-point of the twenty-first century most Americans' lives will be completely different from those lived by earlier generations, even as recently as a half-century earlier. Every school child's education is totally computer-based and individualized according to his or her learning style. Within this somewhat sterile learning environment, physical education, including dance and sport, has become essential for developing children's social, emotional, and physical skills. These daily school programs for youth from ages 3 to 20 focus on individualized fitness programs, environmentally-safe outdoor activities, and cooperative sports in addition to games developed and initiated by the students.

Parents are infused into the school environment—in the classroom and gymnasium—because the year-round school day starts at 7:00 A.M. and continues until 7:00 P.M. With more single-parent, non-Caucasian families, schools provide continuing education for parents, enrichment activities in extended day programs for children, and leisure-time activities for all ages. Social service and governmental agencies work with and through the schools to provide health care and counseling, recreational programs, and career education.

Within this technological society, a huge economic gap has developed. Those without advanced skills and knowledge provide services; those with these skills work in technology-based careers expanding the boundaries of knowledge as they lead the Information Age. Menial tasks, such as manufacturing, are completed by robots or through other nonhuman technologies. Restaurants have been replaced by food packets and pills to save time and money. Americans' fascination with the automobile has been eradicated and replaced by fast, efficient mass transit. Work requirements have increased with most employees choosing to spend an average of 50 hours per week on the job. Despite these work hours, with less time needed for transportation and eating, there is greater leisure time, which is being spent mostly in inactive pastimes such as searching the Internet and watching over 1,000 television channels.

The threat of heart disease, increasingly the number one killer, has finally begun to catch Americans' attention. Within the past decade, the percentage of adults engaged in physical activity has risen 50 percent, while 75 percent more school children are physically active. Extended school programs, private fitness

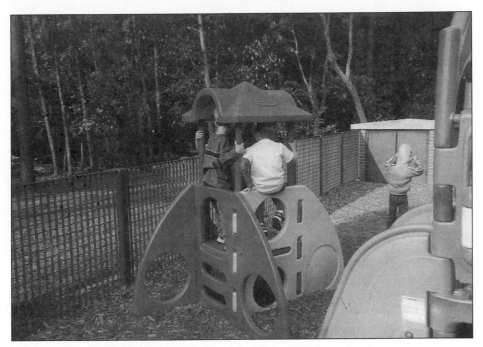

Children enjoy playing because they have fun.

and health centers, and the use of home exercise equipment have been credited with these dramatic improvements. The challenge for physical educators, exercise scientists, recreation directors, health educators, dance specialists, and sport leaders is how to promote the value of physical activity for all.

Are you ready for life in the twenty-first century? Do these scenarios accurately predict reality a half-century from now? This chapter's purpose is to describe what living in the twenty-first century may be like. This chapter will focus on building upon the fields of physical education, exercise science, and sport as described previously to help prepare you for the future.

Physical educators have often followed, rather than led, in Americans' participation in sports and activities. As a result, the importance and prestige of physical education in the schools and sports for all have suffered. Survival of school programs and educationally-based sports programs may be in jeopardy. To take a leading role in the sports and fitness movement, physical educators, exercise scientists, and sport professionals in various settings need to improve the quality of their programs and better publicize the potentially valuable outcomes of these programs. Fitness leaders must publicize and document the benefits of active lifestyles for all segments of the population. To add credibility to this advocacy, physical educators, exercise scientists, and sport professionals must become good role models of fitness.

Physical educators, exercise scientists, and sport professionals can guarantee accountability in instructional quality by making curricula and programs more humanizing to meet students' and clients' needs, keeping abreast of the knowledge explosion and applying this research-based information, providing equal opportunities for diverse populations, and refocusing athletics to ensure that educational outcomes are imperatives for the future.

LEADERSHIP IN PHYSICAL EDUCATION, EXERCISE SCIENCE, AND SPORT

Leadership is essential for individuals working in physical education, exercise science, and sport careers. Leadership can be defined as a behavioral process in which one person attempts to influence other people's behaviors toward the accomplishment of shared goals. Stated in another way, leadership is the creation of a vision of potential opportunities along with the empowerment of others who can translate that vision into reality.

Among the descriptors characterizing leaders are:

- Visionary
- Creative
- Risk-taker
- Global thinker
- Effective communicator
- Committed to excellence and high standards
- Energetic
- Self-confident
- Courageous
- Has integrity.

Each of these characteristics will be elaborated upon in the context of physical education, exercise science, and sport careers to help you understand the critical role each serves in developing and maintaining quality in our work.

A **visionary** establishes goals that answer the questions, "Where are we going?" "What do we want and why?" and "How will we get there?" In response to the first question, an exercise scientist wants to investigate several alternative cardiac rehabilitation programs to determine the most effective approach to prescribing exercise programs for patients. Relative to the second question, the goal of the sport manager may be to increase season ticket sales by 50 percent in order to use the increased revenues to make renovations to the football stadium. In response to the third question, the physical educator may choose to use heart rate monitors, aerobic exercise machines, and the *Physical Best* educational materials to help each student develop and maintain a personal cardiovascular endurance program. A visionary believes passionately in goals or aspirations and diligently works to achieve these. Fitness specialists are willing to spend long hours enhancing their knowledge, learning and using innovative instructional approaches, and expanding their physical activity program offerings in order to get participants to achieve their fitness goals. The visionary possesses charisma that sparks others' interest in and commitment to shared goals, so this characteristic is at the heart of leadership.

A leader is **creative** in determining how to achieve goals through the associated processes or steps. Creativity is evident in the planning of curricula, developing and implementing of a marketing plan for a fitness club or athletic team, and in organizing recreational activities for senior citizens.

The leader as a **risk-taker** believes that the action or direction to be taken is right even though it may appear to be difficult or seemingly impossible. The youth sport coach who asks unruly, boisterous, or vulgar parents to leave rather than allow the participants to be yelled at takes a huge risk. The exercise science researcher explores hypotheses that others have avoided because they take years to explore since the potential benefits outweigh the risks. A leader who is willing to take risks challenges the status quo and continually asks "Why not" and then proceeds to answer this question.

The leader who is a **global thinker** refuses to be confined by what has not yet been attempted. The fitness specialist working with senior citizens motivates them to challenge themselves to a higher level of fitness and sports proficiency. The professional sports team manager markets team merchandise internationally through new sales venues and innovative media approaches.

A leader who is an **effective communicator** shows a respect for others that includes being a good listener and a thoughtful respondent. The physical educator as leader models how each student is equally valued and has the potential to learn. The high school coach ensures that each athlete understands what contributions can and should be made in achieving the team's goals for the season.

Each leader is **committed to excellence and high standards** and demonstrates this through daily actions and words. Compromise in expectations and acceptance of inferior performances are not tolerated. The recreational professional insists that safe, organized, equitable, and enjoyable programs are provided for each participant. The exercise physiologist will not permit sloppy research or inaccurate reporting of research findings.

A leader who is **energetic** appears to work tirelessly. Each class of students, each group of clients, or each team receives the undivided attention and full commitment of the teacher, exercise specialist, or coach. It seems that the leader exudes energy to others because of a passionate desire to achieve the shared vision. Individuals in physical activity careers are normally role models for fitness, which energizes them to help others achieve a similar high quality of life.

The leader is usually so convinced of the rightness of the vision, that **self-confidence** is readily apparent. No one can deter the self-confident leader from proving that the chosen direction is in the best interests of the group. The personal trainer believes that every client can attain and maintain a physically active lifestyle. The teacher and the coach are knowledgeable in their sports and activities in ways that permeate and positively affect students and athletes.

The leader must be **courageous** in pursuit of the vision even when others raise questions or challenges. New teaching approaches or experimental research designs are seldom welcomed and frequently are derided. Yet regardless of the disclaimers or adversities faced, the courageous leader advances.

Unless the leader **has integrity,** the ruse will eventually be discovered. Values such as honesty, fairness, and beneficence are integral to gaining respect from others as well as eliciting their participation in attaining the vision of the physical education, exercise science, and sport professional.

WHAT WILL THE TWENTY-FIRST CENTURY BRING?

The world in the twenty-first century will continue to be different from preceeding eras, with numerous changes in the field of physical education, exercise science, and sport. What follows are several projections based on the continuation of current trends. They are divided into the categories of school programs, higher education, athletics, and exercise science and fitness careers. Consider whether these proposed changes and trends will become reality. How will they affect society and you and your career? Are these possibilities desirable? If not, what can be done to avert any undesired outcomes?

School Programs

- Physical education will achieve the established standards for student achievement and through performance assessment respond to the call for educational accountability.
- Physical education curricula will emphasize fitness development and maintenance as well as learning psychomotor skills and enhancing social and emotional skills.
- Physical educators will incorporate technology and computer skills into their programs to enhance learning.

The integration of technology into instruction helps students learn.

- Significantly more minority teachers will be recruited and retained to serve as role models for an increasing number of minority students.
- Coaching certifications will be required of all interscholastic coaches.
- Competency entrance and exit tests will be required of prospective teachers.
- Physical educators will continuously upgrade their instructional abilities and content knowledge.
- An appropriate reward system will be implemented to recognize excellence in teaching and coaching.
- Performance, more than longevity, will determine merit pay and career advancement.

Higher Education

- Five-year teacher education programs that include a master's degree will become the standard, while increasingly advanced education and certifications (beyond the bachelor's degree) will be required of sport and exercise practitioners.
- The number of graduates with specializations in fitness, exercise physiology, health education, athletic training, and sport management will increase.
- Elective physical education activity programs focusing on aerobic activities, weight training, outdoor activities, and lifetime sports will continue to thrive.

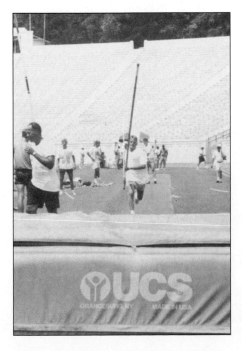

Just as the pole vaulter focuses on the goal ahead, physical educators, exercise scientists, and sport professionals must focus on what contributions they can make in the twenty-first century. (Photo courtesy Maggie McGlynn.)

- More and more college degrees will be completed "on line," using a variety of technologies.
- College students will be older, more career oriented, and more diverse in background.
- College professors will specialize even more in one of the exercise or sport sciences.
- More minority faculty members will be recruited and retained to serve as teachers of and mentors for minority students.
- Increased research productivity will be required for promotion and tenure, although scholarship will be defined more broadly.

Athletics

- Coaching certifications will be required of all youth sport coaches.
- The emphasis on winning in sports at all levels will intensify because of lucrative rewards.
- Value development will still be espoused, although only marginally attained.
- College athletics programs will become more commercialized and more dependent on financial subsidies from educational institutions, sponsors, and donors.
- Drug abuse will increase in athletics at all levels.
- The use of technological advances will enhance athletes' skills and performances.
- Competitive opportunities for girls, women, minorities, individuals with disabilities, and senior citizens in sports will continue to increase.

Sports will increasingly attract females who welcome the chance to display their skills. (Photo courtesy Maggie McGlynn.)

WEB CONNECTIONS

1. www.pesoftware.com/news.html
   This site provides monthly updates on trends to help infuse
   technology into K-12 physical education programs.

2. www.ed.gov/free/subject.html
   Check out the free instructional materials available from this site of
   the Federal Resources for Educational Excellence.

3. http://sportsvl.com/home.html
   This site for the Virtual Library of Sport links you with a wealth of
   Internet resources.

4. www.welcoa.org
   The Wellness Councils of America work with local councils and
   organizations to design and deliver corporate worksite wellness
   programs.

5. www.nal.usda.gov/fnic
   The Food and Nutrition Information Center of the United States
   Department of Agriculture's Research Service provides extensive
   information about nutrition and related resources.

6. www.americanheart.org
   This site of the American Heart Association offers extensive health-
   related information, resources, and links including those relative to
   exercise for all ages.

Exercise Science and Fitness Careers

- Fitness instructors and managers will help change participation levels
  of adults leading to significant lifestyle changes.
- Physical fitness and sport programs for senior citizens will expand
  dramatically.
- Businesses will increasingly provide fitness programs for their
  employees to help control escalating health care costs.
- Technology will significantly improve fitness equipment, recreational
  facilities, and physical activity programs.
- Extended day sport and physical activity programs for children, adolescents, and their parents will proliferate.
- Outdoor activities will continue to attract new enthusiasts.

- Consumers will become more discriminating in their purchases of fitness equipment, selection of sports to participate in, and nutritional choices to reduce calories, fat, and cholesterol.

- Baccalaureate and master's degrees, continual upgrading of skills and knowledge, and advanced certifications will be required of instructors and managers in exercise science and fitness careers.

THE TWENTY-FIRST CENTURY PHYSICAL ACTIVITY SPECIALIST

In education, those who follow you at your college or university will probably have to complete five years of course work if they choose a teaching career in schools. Such a requirement is a likely outgrowth of the emphasis on obtaining a liberal arts education before becoming certified as a teacher. Everyone, in all careers, will be expected—yes required—to continually retrain, upgrade, and recertify to keep abreast of the knowledge explosion. If you do not have the sophistication mandated by the Information Age, such as computer literacy for evaluating health risk profiles and prescribing and monitoring exercise programs, then you may not be competitive in the job market.

You must not only be an astute consumer yourself in this era of marketing mania, but you will be called upon to help those you teach or direct to discriminate between fact and fallacy. You must teach athletes what food or drugs to take or training regimens to follow in their quest for success. You must be prepared to differentiate between effective and ineffective exercise equipment and diets. Questions will be asked of you concerning whether certain behaviors in sports are ethical, whether the exercises provided by a certain fitness program or instructor are appropriate, and whether the schools, communities, or both should provide fitness programs for school-age children. You may need to become an advocate for "truth in advertising" because quackery in fitness, exercise, health, and nutrition abounds. Because of the increasing popularity of this broad field, many charlatans will eagerly take consumers' money and even cause them to risk their health and well-being unless you help the buyer beware.

Social issues continuing to influence our lives, such as aging and technology, will call for our involvement. Meeting the leisure needs of an older American populace will demand that fitness, recreational, and educational leaders develop and implement programs that are appropriate for their needs. We will not categorize people of retirement age or older as nonproductive or as nonenergetic. This segment of the population will demand to have its fitness needs met through seniors or masters competitions, daily walks in the malls, aerobics, bowling leagues, or golf. It will also be important to provide inexpensive physical activity opportunities for those on fixed incomes.

The technology of the twenty-first century will probably astound each of us. Incorporating technology into fitness programs through the use of blood pressure and heart rate monitors on exercise equipment, the use of computers to assess health risks and dietary problems, and the use of videotaping and computer analysis to improve sports performance allows technology to contribute to exercise safety and skill enhancement. Televised and videotaped exercise classes for home use, for school-age children, at the work-site, and in retirement homes may increase due to economic constraints and increased demand for fitness programs.

The environment will also continue to concern many people as they consider what possible irreparable damages our lifestyles may be heaping upon future generations. Backpackers, rock climbers, campers, and hikers will be challenged to enjoy nature while leaving it untarnished for those who follow. Ensuring urban green space and protecting state and national parks will be other ways in which recreation specialists will be able to leave a legacy.

CHANGING IDENTITY—FROM PHYSICAL EDUCATION TO EXERCISE SCIENCE AND SPORT STUDIES

When school and college programs involving the development of motor skills were initially developed in the late 1800s and early 1900s, they were called gymnastics or physical training. Gradually, though, the descriptive term for these programs was changed to physical education as an affirmation that this educational field could uniquely contribute to the psychomotor development of students. The term physical education continues to appropriately describe school and college programs that focus on participation in fitness, sports, and other physical activities. State requirements determine the number and length of physical education classes attended by school children where they learn fundamental movement skills, develop a variety of sports skills, and learn lifetime fitness practices. College elective and required programs in physical education continue to offer young adults the opportunities to learn new skills, increase abilities in preferred sports skills, and maintain personal fitness.

The term most often used by nonschool agencies, such as public recreational programs or private sports clubs, has never been physical education. Within the past few years, many of these and similar programs have identified themselves using terms such as fitness, physical activity, and wellness. Since they were not associated with educational institutions, the term physical education never appropriately explained their emphases on fun and healthy lifestyles.

Following the emergence of the specialty areas of exercise physiology, sport psychology, motor learning, and others in the 1970s, many in higher education began to question whether the name of physical education accurately encompassed the tremendous expansion in knowledge in these new fields. These professors did not want to be saddled with what was perceived as an outdated and constricting name, and especially one that came with the allegation of being nonacademic. Years of discussions and national surveys yielded dozens of proposed name changes, but no consensus for a new name for the field emerged. Several advocated for kinesiology; others preferred human movement or human performance as more inclusive of the various specialties. On college and university campuses, departmental names continue to vary widely as each seeks to find an identity that describes the scope of what they do and study.

Children are our future. They need to enjoy movement during their early years.

Most professionals in the fields associated with physical activity will agree that their professional history is built upon physical education. But they prefer to identify themselves as exercise physiologists, motor development specialists, biomechanists, fitness specialists, or athletic trainers. Like many university departments, this book has used the term exercise science to encompass these and related fields. Individuals in sport history, sport sociology, sport management, and sport philosophy also believe that sport studies more accurately describes what they do. So sport has been included throughout this book as a one vital component in the broad definition of this field. Less important than the preferred name is the commitment to contribute to the knowledge base associated with physical activity and to encourage all people to make physical activity a part of their lives.

PROMOTING PHYSICAL ACTIVITY

Accountability for program content is essential and will continue to grow in importance. Without quality and benefits accruing to those served, no program merits continuation. If children, club members, athletes, senior citizens, or corporate employees are not being taught the skills and knowledge that they seek through activity or sports programs, then elimination of the activity is warranted or at least replacement of the teacher or leader is mandated. Individuals hired to teach programs owe it to their participants to ensure learning. Abdication of this responsibility will lead to others being hired to do these jobs. For example, accountability in school physical education necessitates that every student achieve content

Karate is an example of a nontraditional activity enjoyed by people of all ages.
(Photo courtesy Don Ridgeway.)

standards established by the National Association for Sport and Physical Education. (See Chapter 1)

Linked closely with accountability is the importance of public relations. Traditionally, the perspective taken by individuals in school programs has been a willingness to serve but not a desire to publicize or market programs. Today, this attitude is archaic. Teachers and program leaders, regardless of setting, must publicize the benefits to those who participate in sport and physical activity. To enlist involvement and financial support, programs must be attractive and successful in meeting perceived needs. An additional outcome of this concerted effort to tell others what physical education and sport can do for them is that it brings together, rather than drives apart, all physical activity programs. Some examples of ways to promote physical activity and sport could be:

- Get your Governor or Mayor to proclaim May as Physical Fitness and Sport Month in your state or city.
- Conduct special events like a family fitness night, community fun run, or mall exhibitions of physical education during Physical Fitness and Sport Month.

- Celebrate National Employee Health and Fitness Day in May.
- Initiate daily fitness programs in schools and businesses to encourage everyone to participate in 10 minutes of stretching and 30 minutes of aerobic activities.
- Develop public service announcements for local radio and television stations that promote physical activity and include fitness tips.
- Write and publish a newsletter or local newspaper articles about popular physical activities, sports, and fitness.
- Involve the community in developing a fitness trail through the PTA/PTO or a local service organization.
- Ask the school and city libraries to display books about physical activity, sports, and fitness.
- Involve senior citizens with school-age children in inter-generational walks, dances, or other recreational activities.
- Plan special events in schools, businesses, and public agencies to celebrate National Nutrition Month (March), Family Health Month (October), and Heart Month (February).
- Celebrate National Girls and Women in Sports Day (first Thursday in February).
- Initiate a sports attire day each month to encourage everyone to dress for and participate in physical activity.

PHYSICAL ACTIVITY THROUGHOUT LIFE

The Madison Avenue promotion of physical activity has contributed to its over-whelming surge in popularity, especially for the middle and upper classes. Be-cause of social needs and feelings of self-worth, people of all ages are motivated by the media to join exercise and sports programs. Designer sports clothing and the latest technologically advanced equipment are essential. Club membership, attendance at sport camps, and making business and personal contacts on the golf course, as a sport spectator, or after-workout sessions are examples of this popular phenomenon.

The sports and fitness movement, recognized now as a part of the American way of life, rather than a fad, is initiating dramatic changes in physical activity programs. Consumer demand is readily evident for healthy lifestyles that seek to improve the quality of life through physical activity. Physical educators, exercise scientists, and sport professionals must share their knowledge about physiology, nutrition, psychology, and fitness and skill development. You will conduct your programs at the worksite as well as in public facilities and private clubs. While helping the corporate executive, you must not neglect lower-income individuals, whose levels of productivity and lifestyles can also be enhanced.

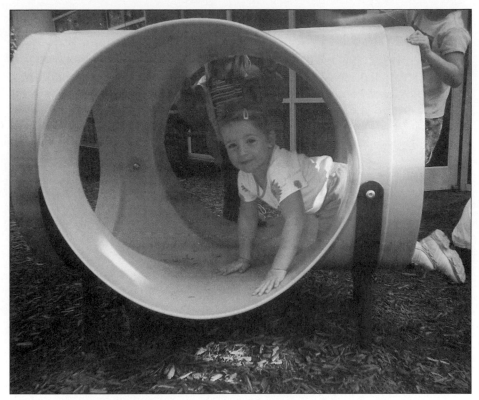

Physical activity begins early and spans our lifetimes.

The group whose needs probably will become paramount in the next century includes individuals 65 years of age and older. Between 1982 and 2050, the percentage of people in this age category will almost double (to over one-fifth of the population). As Americans live longer, they need lifetime recreational activities, not only to prevent disease and degeneration, but also as a way to enjoy happier, healthier lives.

Advances in medicine and technology not only help us live longer, but they greatly change our lives in other ways. Cures for cancer, AIDS, and other diseases, advances in heart surgery to prevent coronaries, and electronically stimulated movement of paralyzed limbs are but a few medical breakthroughs that lengthen and invigorate life. Fewer and fewer household and mundane tasks demand our time and energy, as machines free us from routine jobs. Although only some of our free time is currently spent developing fitness and enjoying sports and other leisure-time activities, free time will increase in the future. Technological advances directly influence our leisure time pursuits as well. Better designed running shoes, exercise cycles equipped to monitor fitness levels, biomechanical analyses of tennis strokes or other sport skills, and individualized

⟋ RESEARCH VIEW

In July of 1996, at the International Pre-Olympic Scientific Congress in Dallas, William L. Haskell presented a paper entitled "Physical Activity, Sport, and Health: Toward the Next Century." He stated that two of the major changes that will increasingly necessitate promoting physically active lifestyles during the next few decades are the impact of new technology on work and leisure time and the aging of the population. The key points stressed by Dr. Haskell were:

The Impact of Technology

- Much business and personal communications will occur electronically.
- The Internet will be used to transact business and for leisure pursuits.
- Most jobs will be sedentary, with limited physical exertion required.
- People will work more, have less leisure time, and thus, be less physically active.

The Aging Population

- The number of people aged 65 and older is projected to increase to 20 percent of the population by 2025.
- Many older individuals, although free of life-threatening diseases, are suffering from the consequences of years of physical inactivity and other negative health habits.
- Physical activity of moderate intensity on a regular basis can positively affect the quality of life, incidence of chronic, degenerative diseases, and mortality.

*Research Quarterly for Exercise and Sport 67 (Supplement to 3):S-37, 1996.

training paradigms already exist. Undoubtedly, advances in sporting equipment, clothing, and facilities will continue to enhance performance as well as pleasure. (See Research View box above)

The twenty-first century will expand the Information Age. Handheld personal computers, cellular phones, and satellite transmissions are only the beginning. With a service economy based on and mandating communications skills and technology as the norm, we will increasingly turn to sport, fitness, and leisure activities during nonwork hours for rest and stress reduction.

Computer technology already permits exercise scientists to assess fitness levels, to prescribe exercise paradigms designed to meet individualized needs, and to monitor the attainment of personal fitness goals. Using database management computer software, corporate fitness leaders can determine the impact of each

Intramural sports give college students opportunities to continue physical activity and competition.

exercise program offered by using attendance numbers and by recording fitness parameters. Sport managers can use computers to generate ticket sales solicitations and target marketing campaigns. Computer graphics, desktop publishing, financial forecasts for athletic programs and clubs, students' fitness report cards for parents, biomechanical analyses of athletes' skill performances, and computer-based play calling are a few examples of technological advances impacting our programs.

The realm of space travel and the establishment of space colonies broadens our perspective from this country to the importance of viewing how physical education, exercise science, and sport can influence the entire world. Our enthusiasm for sports and fitness is already altering attitudes in other countries. Many professionals share their sports expertise with people in other countries. Successful businesses worldwide model their corporate fitness programs on ours. All of these contribute to greater international understanding through the sharing of physical activity.

SUMMARY

Future physical activity leaders hold the keys to the acceptance and promotion of active and healthy lifestyles. Improved curricula based on standards that focus on meeting all students' fitness and lifetime sports and activity skill needs are imperative. The power and potential of physical education, exercise science, and sport are based on a commitment to physical activity, and our nation's health, and maybe even its existence, depends on this. Through technological advances, we must strive to improve the quality of life for ourselves and for others worldwide in the twenty-first century.

CAREER PERSPECTIVE

WINIFRED WARREN LAFORCE
Executive Vice President and General Manager, Events
Capitol Sports Management
Raleigh, North Carolina

EDUCATION
B.A., Education, University of Florida
M.A., Reading and Language Arts, University of North Carolina
at Chapel Hill
M.A., Physical Education with specialization in Sport
Administration, University of North Carolina at Chapel Hill

JOB RESPONSIBILITIES AND HOURS

The job responsibilities of the Executive Vice President and General Manager of
Events Capitol Sports Management include overseeing all the events of Capitol
Sports Management. This includes a new Olympic-style multisporting event being
created by the company to be hosted in 2003. This event will focus on masters compe-
tition for several thousand adult athletes from the United States expected to participate
in 15 sports. Winkie was the Executive Director of the State Games of North Carolina
from 1988 to 1990. From 1990 to 1993 she served as President of North Carolina
Amateur Sports. She then moved to Atlanta to serve as Director of the Sports
Department for the 1996 Centennial Olympic Games. She also consulted for the 2000
Olympic Games in Sydney, Australia, and the 1999 Pan American Games in Winnipeg,
Canada. In January 1998, Winkie led North Carolina's effort to bring the 2007 Pan
American Games to the Triangle area. During this period, she guided a team of over
600 volunteers, and with the assistance of many corporate citizens, raised over a half
million dollars for the bid effort.

SPECIALIZED COURSE WORK, DEGREES, AND WORK EXPERIENCES NEEDED FOR THIS CAREER

Although no specific degree is required for a sport management career, experiences that
include managing people and details are vitally important. Winkie believes that management and business courses that include learning about motivation and goal setting are
critical to successfully fulfilling job expectations.

SATISFYING ASPECTS

Winkie loves to work with people and to see the culmination of their combined efforts
in a successful event. Managing sporting events requires working with hundreds of
people including community leaders, staff members, and volunteers who coordinate
the competition sites and the sports with corporate sponsors who support the events.

JOB POTENTIAL

Given the increasing popularity of sporting events, opportunities abound for sport
managers who are willing to gain skills and knowledge starting in entry-level positions.
Salary increases, job security, and career advancement depend on experience, proven
performance, and networking.

SUGGESTIONS FOR STUDENTS

Winkie suggests that you willingly start at a low salary in order to "get your foot in the door." Make yourself invaluable to your employers by working hard (including weekends). With such diligence, you can move to the top. Since sport management careers remain male oriented, says Winkie, women have to work harder and longer to be recognized for their merit; however, when this recognition is achieved, a woman may have an advantage in this professional environment.

REVIEW QUESTIONS

1. What factors will influence society and you in your career as you enter the twenty-first century?
2. What changes are projected for school programs in the twenty-first century?
3. What changes are projected for college and university programs in the twenty-first century?
4. What changes are projected for athletic programs in the twenty-first century?
5. What changes are projected for exercise science and fitness programs in the twenty-first century?
6. How will technology affect physical activity programs in the future?
7. Should physical education change its name, and why?
8. What are several strategies for promoting physical activity for all?
9. Why are even more physical activity programs for senior citizens essential in the future?
10. What is the greatest challenge you will face in your career within the next few years?

STUDENT ACTIVITIES

1. Find five magazine advertisements that validly use physical activity or fitness in marketing their products. Find five magazine advertisements that make outlandish claims about their fitness-related products.
2. Interview three people who teach physical activities in any type of program. Ask them what they think the problems and challenges are for people in their careers or similar careers. What suggestions for improvement do they have?
3. Describe the program offerings of an elementary school, secondary school, college activity program, health club, or recreation department that you think meets the needs of the individuals currently being served. Will these needs differ by 2010? If so, how will these needs be met?
4. Write a two- or three-page paper describing "Living in the Year 2020" when you will be around the midpoint of your career.

SUGGESTED READINGS

Baker JAW, Pan DW, Wade MG: Multidimensional scaling: the name revisited, *Int J Phys Educ* 33(2):76, 1996. In this study, 85 chairpersons of physical education departments were asked to rate attributes associated with 13 potential departmental titles. All except the physical education/teacher education group preferred the name of sport and exercise science.

Edginton CR, Davis TM, Hensley LD: Trends in higher education: implications for health, physical education, and leisure studies, *JOPERD* 65(7):51, 1994. Access, delivery systems, privatization, curricular innovation, accountability, strategic thinking, and entrepreneurship are among the trends that will impact the future of health, physical education, and leisure studies programs.

Harrington WM: Our collective future: a triumph of imagination, *Quest* 51(3):272, 1999. This Thirty-Third Amy Morris Homans Commemorative Lecture deals with the collective future of physical education. Harrington presents a scenario for 2015 that optimistically predicts that the physical education profession will thrive in the future if professionals collectively plan for the future.

Haskell WL: Physical activity, sport, and health: toward the next century, *Res Q Exer & Sp* 67:37, September, 1996 supplement. In this section of a special issue on physical activity, sport, and health, the writer discusses the key issues for taking advantage of the growing scientific evidence that regular physical activity is beneficial. He states that the two major changes that will increase the need to promote physically active lifestyles are the impact of new technology on work and leisure time and the general aging of the population.

Hill J, McLean DD: Technology and leisure, introduction: defining our perspective of the future, *JOPERD* 70(8):21, 1999, and Introduction: possible, probable, or preferable future? *JOPERD* 70(9):15, 1999. In these two articles, the authors discuss the relationship between, and integration of, technology and leisure as well as possible implications of how technology will impact leisure in the future.

Jordan D (ed.): Promoting active lifestyles—a multidisciplinary approach, *JOPERD* 64(1):34, 1993. This seven-article feature describes an Exercise and Nutrition for Lifetime Wellness course; facilities and equipment designed for children, seniors, and people with disabilities; changing perceptions of aging; fear as a constraint to females' activity; teaching students with disabilities; aquatic programs; and assessment. These all affect the promotion of active lifestyles.

Kretchmar RS: The challenge of telling our story effectively, *Quest* 51(2):87, 1999. The future of physical education, exercise science, and sport in higher education requires professionals to communicate powerfully and effectively in describing what they do.

Saunders RP, Fee RM, Gottlieb NH: Higher education and the health of America's children: collaborating for coordinated school health, *Phi Delta*

Kappan 80(5):377, 1999. Good health behaviors, say researchers, are linked with academic results and the reduction of specific dangerous behaviors of students. Coordinated school health programs can increase these positive outcomes.

Zeigler EF: From one image to a sharper one! *Phys Educ* 54:72, Spring 1997. The traditional field of physical education must select and support an appropriate name (with attendant knowledge, skills, and scholarship) and coalesce around the professional competencies associated with working with physical activity programs.

Zeigler EF: The profession must work "harder and smarter" to inform those officials who make decisions that affect the field, *Phys Educ* 56(3):114, 1999. Professionals must promote activity throughout a person's life. The author suggests 13 principles that should guide programs in the twenty-first century.

Appendix A

SELECTED PHYSICAL EDUCATION, EXERCISE SCIENCE, AND SPORT JOURNALS

Journal	Publisher/Contact Information	Article Type
ACE Fitness Matters	American Council on Exercise 5820 Oberlin Drive, Suite 102 San Diego, CA 92121-3787 1-800 825-3636 www.acefitness.org	Information about a variety of fitness issues
Adapted Physical Activity Quarterly	Human Kinetics Publishers Box 5076 Champaign, IL 61825-5076 1-800-747-4457 www.humankinetics.com/products/ journals.journal.cfm?id=APAQ	Scholarly papers related to physical activity for special populations
American Fitness Magazine	Aerobics and Fitness Associations of America 15250 Ventura Boulevard, Suite 200 Sherman Oaks, CA 91403-3297 1-800-446-2322 www.afaa.com/10010ASP?1=&1=4	Popular articles about fitness, nutrition, and health
American Journal of Clinical Nutrition	American Society for Clinical Nutrition, Inc. 9650 Rockville Pike, Rm. 2310 Bethesda, MD 20814-3998 301-530-7024 www.ajcn.org	Practical articles dealing with nutritional issues
American Journal of Health Education	American Association for Health Education 1900 Association Drive Reston, VA 20191-1599 1-800-213-7193 www.aahperd.org/aahperd/publications- AJHE.html	Scholarly and applied research in topics in health education
American Journal of Physiology	American Physiological Society 9650 Rockville Pike Bethesda, MD 20814 301-530-7180 www.ajpcon.org	Scholarly articles about research in physiology
American Journal of Sports Medicine	American Orthopaedic Society for Sports Medicine 230 Calvary Street Waltham, MA 02453 781-736-0707 www.sportsmed.org	Scholarly articles in sports medicine
Clinical Exercise Physiology	Human Kinetics Publishers Box 5076 Champaign, IL 61825-5076 1-800-747-4457 www.humankinetics.com/products/ journals/journal.cfm?id=CEP	Applied research in exercise physiology in clinical settings

Journal	Publisher/Contact Information	Article Type
Clinics in Sports Medicine	W.B. Saunders Curtis Center, 3rd Floor Independence Square West Philadelphia, PA 19106-3399 215-238-7800 www.harcourthealth.com/fcgi-bin/ displaypage.pl?isbn=02785919	Academic and scholarly articles in sports medicine
Exercise and Sport Sciences Reviews	American College of Sports Medicine 401 W. Michigan Street Indianapolis, IN 46202-3233 317-637-9200 www.acsm-essr.org	Reviews of scientific, medical, and research-based topics in sports medicine and exercise science
Fitness Management Magazine	Fitness Management 4160 Wilshire Blvd. Los Angeles, CA 90010 323-964-4800 www.fitnessworld.com/publish/fr/ subscriptions.html	Popular articles about fitness and fitness products
Health and Fitness Journal	American College of Sports Medicine 401 W. Michigan Street Indianapolis, IN 46202-3233 317-637-9200 www.acsm-healthfitness.org	Scientific research, education, and practical applications of sports medicine and exercise science
Journal of Aging and Physical Activity	Human Kinetics Publishers Box 5076 Champaign, IL 61825-5076 1-800-747-4457 www.humankinetics.com/products/ journals/journal.cfm?id=JAPA	Research associated with physical activity and aging
Journal of Biomechanics	Elsevier Science Ltd. P.O. Box 800 Kidlington, Oxford OX5 1DX England www.elsevier.nl/inca/publications/ store/3/2/1/	Scholarly articles dealing with sport biomechanics
Journal of Applied Biomechanics	Human Kinetics Publishers Box 5076 Champaign, IL 61825-5076 1-800-747-4457 www.humankinetics.com/products/ journals/journal.cfm?id=JAB	Research associated with biomechanics in sport, exercise, and rehabilitation
Journal of Applied Physiology	American Physiological Society 9650 Rockville Pike Bethesda, MD 20814 301-530-7164 www.the-aps.org/publications/journals/ pub_jap_home.htm	Scholarly and applied articles in physiology
Journal of Applied Sport Psychology	Association for the Advancement of Applied Sport Psychology c/o Faculty of Kinesiology University of Western Ontario London, ON N6A 3K7, Canada 519-661-4118	Scholarly articles related to sport psychology

Journal	Publisher/Contact Information	Article Type
Journal of Athletic Training	National Athletic Trainers' Association 2952 Stemmons Fwy. Dallas, TX 75247-6196 214-637-6282 www.journalofathletictraining.org	Education and research about the prevention, evaluation, management, and rehabilitation of injuries
Journal of Cardiopulmonary Rehabilitation	Lippincott-Raven Publishers 227 E. Washington Square Philadelphia, PA 19106 215-238-4200 www.lww.com/productdetailresults/ 1,2265,33811462,00.html	Scholarly works dealing with cardiac rehabilitation
Journal of Leisure Research	National Recreation and Park Association 22377 Belmont Ridge Road Ashburn, VA 20148 703-858-0784 http://stores.active.com/cgi-bin/ NRPA.storefront/3ad79642116d9f34271 840463d15067c/Product/View/ 2003&2DP	Dedicated to the creation of new knowledge and understanding in the leisure services field
Journal of Motor Behavior	Heldref Publications 1319 Eighteenth St., N.W. Washington, DC 20036-1802 202-296-6267 www.heldref.org/html/jmb.html	Scholarly articles dealing with motor behavior
Journal of the Philosophy of Sport	Human Kinetics Publishers Box 5076 Champaign, IL 61825-5076 1-800-747-4457 www.humankinetics.com/products/ journals/journal.cfm?id=JPS	Research and theory about the philosophic thought in sport
Journal of Physical Education, Recreation and Dance	American Alliance for Health, Physical Education, Recreation and Dance 1900 Association Drive Reston, VA 20191-1599 1-800-213-7193 www.aahperd.org/aahperd/publications-joperd.html	Research and applied articles associated with physical education, recreation, and dance programs
Journal of Sport Behavior	University of South Alabama Mobile, AL 36688-0008 334-460-7131	Research articles about sport
Journal of Sport and Exercise Psychology	Human Kinetics Publishers Box 5076 Champaign, IL 61825-5076 1-800-747-4457 www.humankinetics.com/products/ journals/journal.cfm?id=JSEP	Research in the interactions of psychology with exercise and sport performance
Journal of Sport History	North American Society for Sport History c/o Ronald Smith P.O. Box 1026 Lemont, PA 16851-1026 www.nassh.org/index1.html	Scholarly research about sport history
Journal of Sport Management	Human Kinetics Publishers Box 5076 Champaign, IL 61825-5076 1-800-747-4457 www.humankinetics.com/products/ journals/journal.cfm?id=JSM	Research about the theory and application of sport management

Journal	Publisher/Contact Information	Article Type
Journal of Sport Rehabilitation	Human Kinetics Publishers Box 5076 Champaign, IL 61825-5076 1-800-747-4457 www.humankinetics.com/products/ journals/journal.cfm?id=JSR	Scholarly information about rehabilitation from sport injuries
Journal of Sport and Social Issues	Sage Publications, Inc. 2455 Teller Road Thousand Oaks, CA 91320 805-499-0721 www.sagepub.com	Research-based articles about sport within the social context
Journal of Strength and Conditioning Research	National Strength and Conditioning Association 1955 N. Union Blvd. Colorado Springs, CO 80909 719-632-6722 www.nsca-lift.org/publications.htm	Optimizing physical performance through applied exercise science research
Journal of Teaching in Physical Education	Human Kinetics Publishers Box 5076 Champaign, IL 61825-5076 1-800-747-4457 www.humankinetics.com/products/ journals/journal.cfm?id=JTPE	Descriptive, theoretical, and research articles about the teaching of physical education at all levels
Measurement in Physical Education and Exercise Science	American Association for Active Lifestyles and Fitness 1900 Association Drive Reston, VA 20191-1599 1-800-213-7193 www.erlbaum.com/Journals/journals/ MPEE/mpee.htm	Research articles associated with measurement and assessment in physical activity programs and settings
Medicine and Science in Sports and Exercise	American College of Sports Medicine 401 W. Michigan Street Indianapolis, IN 46202-3233 317-637-9200 www.acsm-msse.org	Articles from basic and applied science, medicine, education, and allied health fields
Palaestra	Challenge Publications, Ltd. Box 508 1948 Riverview Drive Macomb, IL 61455-0508 309-833-1902 www.palaestra.com	Articles about sport, physical education, and recreation for those with disabilities
Parks and Recreation	National Recreation and Park Association 22377 Belmont Ridge Road Ashburn, VA 20148 703-858-0784 http://stores.active.com/cgi-bin/ NRPA.storefront/ 3ad79642116d9f34271840463d15067c/ Product/View/2.004&2DI	Articles of general and applied interest
Pediatric Exercise Science	Human Kinetics Publishers Box 5076 Champaign, IL 61825-5076 1-800-747-4457 www.humankinetics.com/products/ journals/journal.cfm?id=PES	Reporting about scientific knowledge of exercise during childhood

Journal	Publisher/Contact Information	Article Type
Quest	Human Kinetics Publishers Box 5076 Champaign, IL 61825-5076 1-800-747-4457 www.humankinetics.com/products/ journals/journal.cfm?id=QUEST	Research about contemporary issues in physical education in higher education
Research Quarterly for Exercise and Sport	American Alliance for Health, Physical Education, Recreation and Dance 1900 Association Drive Reston, VA 20191-1599 1-800-213-7193 www.aahperd.org/aahperd/publications-rqes.html	Scholarly research in the exercise sciences
SCHOLE: A Journal of Leisure Studies and Recreation Education	National Recreation and Park Association 22377 Belmont Ridge Road Ashburn, VA 20148 703-858-0784 http://stores.active.com/cgi-bin/ NPRA.storefront/ 3ad79642116d9f34271840463d15067c/ Product/View/2005&2D1	Scholarly inquiry into all aspects of parks, recreation, and leisure education
Sociology of Sport Journal	Human Kinetics Publishers Box 5076 Champaign, IL 61825-5076 1-800-747-4457 www.humankinetics.com/products/ journals/journal.cfm?id=SSJ	Research, critical thought, and theory in the sociology of sport
The Sport Psychologist	Human Kinetics Publishers Box 5076 Champaign, IL 61825-5076 1-800-747-4457 www.humankinetics.com/products/ journals/journal.cfm?id=TSP	Applied research in sport psychology
Strategies: A Journal for Sport and Physical Education	National Association for Sport and Physical Education 1900 Association Drive Reston, VA 20191-1599 1-800-213-7193 www.aahperd.org/aahperd/publications-strategies.html	Applied sport and physical education articles
Strength and Conditioning Journal	National Strength and Conditioning Association 1955 N. Union Blvd. Colorado Springs, CO 80909 719-632-6722 www.nsca-lift.org/publications.htm	Articles about resistance training, sports medicine and science, and other issues of interest to strength and conditioning professionals
The Physical Educator	Phi Epsilon Kappa Fraternity 901 W. New York Street Indianapolis, IN 46202 317-637-8431	Scholarly articles about physical education
The Physician and Sportsmedicine	McGraw-Hill Companies 4530 W. 77th Street Minneapolis, MN 55435 612-835-3222 www.physsportsmed.com	Scholarly articles about medical aspects of sports

Journal	Publisher/Contact Information	Article Type

Therapeutic Recreation	National Recreation and Park Association
	22377 Belmont Ridge Road
	Ashburn, VA 20148
	703-858-0784
	http://stores.active.com/cgi-bin/
	  NRPA.storefront/
	  3ad79642116d9f34271840463d15067c/
	  Product/View/2006&2D1
		Scholarly works in therapeutic recreation

Appendix B

CERTIFYING ORGANIZATIONS

Aerobics and Fitness Associations of America
15250 Ventura Boulevard, Suite 200
Sherman Oaks, CA 91403-3297
1-800-446-2322
www.afaa.com/10000.asp

American Sport Education Program
Box 5076
Champaign, IL 61825-5076
1-800-747-4457
www.asep.com

American College of Sports Medicine
401 W. Michigan Street
Indianapolis, IN 46202-3233
317-637-9200
www.acsm.org

American Council on Exercise
5820 Oberlin Drive, Suite 102
San Diego, CA 92121-3787
1-800-825-3636
www.acefitness.org

American Red Cross (national headquarters)
431 18th Street, NW
Washington, DC 20006
202-639-3520
www.redcross.org

The Cooper Institute
12330 Preston Road
Dallas, TX 75230
1-800-635-7050
www.cooperinst.org

National Athletic Trainers' Association
2952 Stemmons Fwy.
Dallas, TX 75247-6196
214 637-6282
www.nata.org

National Strength and Conditioning Association
1955 N. Union Blvd.
Colorado Springs, CO 80909
719-632-6722
www.nsca-lift.org

Young Men's Christian Association of the USA
101 North Wacker Drive
Chicago, IL 60606
312-977-0031
www.ymca.net

Glossary

Academic discipline   a formal body of knowledge discovered, developed, and disseminated through research and inquiry

Accountability   asserts a political right that demands that an individual or institution be held responsible to achieve a specified action

Accreditation   process of measuring institutions' attainment of established program standards to ensure quality

Actual notice   refers to the removal of known hazards by a responsible person

Adapted physical education   program for exceptional students who are so different in mental, physical, emotional, or behavioral characteristics that, in the interest of quality of educational opportunity for all students, special provisions must be made for their proper education

Aesthetics   is the philosophical area that focuses on the artistic or beautiful aspects of anything, including movement

Affective objective   educational outcome that focuses on the development of attitudes, appreciations, and values, including both social and emotional dimensions

Agoge   educational system for Spartan boys

Agreement to participate   signed acknowledgment of a participant's knowing, understanding, and appreciating risks associated with an activity

Allied fields   the areas of dance, health, and recreation that share some purposes, programs, and professionals with physical education, exercise science, and sport

Arete   all-around mental, moral, and physical excellence valued by the Greeks

Assessment   refers to a measure of knowledge, skills, and abilities that leads to the assignment of a value or score

Assumption of risk   refers to participants knowing, understanding, and appreciating the risk associated with their activity

Athletics   organized, highly structured, competitive activities in which skilled individuals participate

Axiology   deals with the value of things and discovering whether actions are good or virtuous

Battle of the systems   controversy raging in the 1800s over which system of gymnastics was most appropriate for Americans

British Amateur Sport Ideal   belief in playing the game for the game's sake

Burnout   decreased performance quality and quantity resulting from stress, job repetitiveness, lack of support and reward, and overwork

Calisthenics   term used in the 1800s to describe Catharine Beecher's program of exercises designed to promote health, beauty, and strength; also used synonymously with general exercises today

Categorical imperatives   refers to the belief that moral duties are prescriptive and independent of consequences

Cognitive objective   educational outcome that emphasizes the acquisition, comprehension, analysis, synthesis, application, and evaluation of knowledge

Comparative negligence   apportions damages when a negligent plaintiff and a negligent defendant played some part in the injury

Constructive notice   refers to hazards that a responsible person should have noticed and eliminated

Contributory negligence   refers to behavior by the plaintiff that contributed to the injury

Dance   bodily movements of a rhythmic and patterned succession usually executed to the accompaniment of music

Deontology   an ethical theory that advocates that actions must conform to absolute rules of moral behavior

Eclecticism   refers to a combination of several philosophies into a consistent and compatible set of beliefs

Education of the physical   a belief that physical education's unique contribution within education should be to develop individuals' physical fitness and sport skills

Education through the physical   a belief that physical education should uniquely contribute to the education of the whole person through physical activities

Epistemology   the branch of philosophy that examines what people know and how and why they hold certain beliefs

Ethics   the branch of philosophy that deals with good and bad, moral duty and obligation, and principles of conduct; also, the study of moral values

Exercise   to practice, to strengthen, or to condition through physical activity

Exercise physiology   the study of bodily functions under the stress of muscular activity

Exercise science   describes the scientific analysis of the human body in motion and can broadly encompass exercise physiology, biomechanics, kinesiology, anatomy, physiology, motor behavior, and some aspects of sports medicine

Existentialism   twentieth-century philosophy that centers on individual existence and advocates that truth and values are arrived at by each person's experiences

Games   activities ranging from simple diversions to cooperative activities to competitions with significant outcomes governed by rules

General supervision   refers to action required whenever activity is occurring by those for whom the person is responsible

Grand tourney or melee   combats fought under conditions of war between two teams of knights

Greek ideal   unity of the "man of action" with the "man of wisdom"

Gymnasium   site for intellectual and physical activities for Greek citizens

Gymnastics   term used to describe Greek athletics, European systems of exercises with or without apparatus, and a modern international sport

Health   soundness of body, mind, and soul, or one's general well-being

Health-related fitness   refers to attaining the level of well-being associated with the heart function (cardiovascular endurance), muscular function (strength and endurance), and flexibility as a deterrent to debilitating conditions

Hygiene   the science of preserving one's health

Idealism   philosophical theory that advocates that reality depends on the mind for existence and that truth is universal and absolute

Inclusion   the integration of children with disabilities into classes with nondisabled students

Intramurals   recreational and competitive activities participated in by students within an institution or employees within a company

Jousting   event at medieval tournaments in which two mounted knights armed with lances attempted in a head-on charge to unseat each other

Leadership   describes a behavioral process in which one person attempts to influence other people's behaviors toward the accomplishment of shared goals

Leisure   time free from work or responsibility that may be used for physical activity

Light gymnastics   Dioclesian Lewis' program based on executing Beecher's calisthenics along with handheld apparatus

Metaphysics   refers to the nature of things, or how actions or events are related to each other

Motor control   an area of study that deals with the neurophysiological factors that impact human movement

Motor development   the maturation of the neuromuscular mechanism that permits progressive performance in motor skills

Motor learning   the study of cognitive processes underlying motor acts and associated with skill acquisition through practice and experience

Movement education   child-centered curriculum emphasing movement challenge and encouraging problem solving and guided discovery

Muscular Christianity   philosophy that moral values can be taught through sport

Nationalism   pervasive theme stressing promotion and defense of one's country that was the desired outcome of several European systems of gymnastics in the 1800s

Naturalism   a belief that the scientific laws of nature govern life and that individual goals are more important than societal goals

Negligence   describes the legal claim that a person fails to act as a reasonable and prudent person should, thereby resulting in injury to another person

New physical education   curriculum focused on developing the whole individual through participation in play, sports, games, and natural outdoor activities

Normal school   an institute for the training of teachers

Paidotribe   the first physical education teacher who taught Greek boys wrestling, boxing, jumping, dancing, and gymnastics at a palaestra

Palaestra   Greek wrestling school where boys learned wrestling, boxing, jumping, dancing, and gymnastics

Pancratium   an event in Panhellenic festivals that combined wrestling and boxing skills into an almost-anything-goes combat

Panhellenic games   festivals open to all Greeks in which athletic contests were a focal point

Pentathlon   a five-event competition that included the discus throw, javelin throw, long jump, stade race, and wrestling

Philosophy   the pursuit of wisdom

Physical activity   all movements that can contribute to improved health

Physical education   a process through which an individual obtains optimal physical, mental, and social skills and fitness through physical activity

Physical fitness   combination of cardiovascular endurance, muscular strength and endurance, flexibility, body composition, agility, balance, neuromuscular coordination, speed, and power

Play   amusements engaged in freely, for fun, and devoid of constraints

Pragmatism   American movement in philosophy emphasizing reality as the sum total of each individual's experiences through practical experimentation

Profession   a learned occupation that requires training in a specialized field of study

Psychomotor objective   educational outcome that emphasizes the learning of fundamental movements, motor skills, and sports skills

Realism   philosophical system that stresses that the laws and order of the world as revealed by science are independent from human experience

Recreation   refreshing or renewing one's strength and spirit after work; a diversion that occurs during leisure hours

Renaissance   a period from the fifteenth to seventeenth centuries marked by a renewed appreciation for classical culture

Skill-related fitness   refers to achieving levels of ability to perform physical movements specific to a sport, such as serving a tennis ball effectively, or a physical activity, such as executing safe and proper technique in a step aerobics class

Specific supervision   refers to mandated action required whenever a higher level of risk is associated with the activity of the persons for whom the adult is responsible

Sport   physical activities governed by formal and informal rules that involve competition against an opponent or oneself and are engaged in for fun, recreation, or reward

Sport and exercise psychology   the study of human behavior in sports, including an understanding of the mental processes that impact motor skill performance

Sport biomechanics   the study of the effects of natural laws and forces on the body through the science and mechanics of movement

Sport history   descriptive and analytical examination of significant people, events, organizations, and trends that shaped the past

Sport management   the study of the management of personnel, programs, budgets, and facilities in various sports settings

Sport pedagogy   the study of how to enhance instructional content, the learning process, and the achievement of learning outcomes

Sport philosophy   the search for, and the analysis of, truths, values, and actions of sport

Sport sociology   the study of the social units and processes within the sporting context

Sports medicine   the study and application of the prevention, treatment, and rehabilitation of sports injuries; also called athletic training

Stade race   a footrace in Panhellenic games run the length of the stadium

Standard   a uniform criterion or foundational element used to measure quality

Teleological   refers to theories that focus on the end results or consequences of occurrences

Thermae   facilities in Rome for contrast baths of varying water temperatures and other leisure activities

Utilitarianism   refers to the goal of creating the greatest good for the largest number of people

Wellness   mental, emotional, spiritual, nutritional, and physical factors that lead to healthy behaviors

Credits

Chapter 1

Unit one photo courtesy Corbis.

P. 6, Reprinted from *Moving into the Future—National Standards for Physical Education* with permission from the National Association for Sport and Physical Education, 1900 Association Drive, Reston, VA 20191-1599.

P. 8, Photo, Reprinted with permission of the University of Tennessee Press. From Kozar AJ: *R. Tait McKenzie, the sculptor of athletes,* 1975, The University of Tennessee Press.

P. 19, Reprinted with permission of the American Alliance for Health, Physical Education, Recreation and Dance, 1900 Association Drive, Reston, VA 20191-1599.

Chapter 3

P. 68, Reprinted with permission of the American Alliance for Health, Physical Education, Recreation and Dance, 1900 Association Drive, Reston, VA 20191-1599.

P. 73, Box, Reprinted with permission of the Southern District of the American Alliance for Health, Physical Education, Recreation and Dance, 1900 Association Drive, Reston, VA 20191-1599.

Chapter 4

P. 114–115, Box, Reprinted with permission of the National Athletic Trainers' Association, 2952 Stemmons Frwy, Dallas, TX 75247-6196.

Chapter 5

PP. 141–144, Reprinted from *Quality Coaches, Quality Sports: National Standards for Athletic Coaches* with permission from the National Association for Sport and Physical Education, 1900 Association Drive, Reston, VA 20191-1599.

Chapter 7

P. 223, Puzzle, Reprinted with permission of Jane Jenkins.

Chapter 8

P. 226, Reprinted with permission of Human Kinetics Publishers, Inc., Champaign, IL 61825-5076.

P. 242, This article is reprinted with permission from the *Journal of Physical Education, Recreation and Dance,* April 1960, p. 27. The journal is a publication of the American

Alliance for Health, Physical Education, Recreation and Dance, 1900 Association Drive, Reston, VA 20191-1599.

Chapter 9

P. 255, *NEA Proceedings,* 32:621, copyright 1893, National Education Association. Reprinted with permission.

Chapter 10

Unit Three photo courtesy PhotoDisc.

P. 316–317, Box, Reprinted from "Developmentally Appropriate Physical Education Practices for Children" with permission of the National Association for Sport and Physical Education, 1900 Association Drive, Reston, VA 20191-1599.

Chapter 12

P. 347 (high schools), National Federation of State High School Associations. (2000). (available from P.O. Box 690, Indianapolis, IN 46206). pp. 347–348 (intercollegiate sports), Acosta R.V. and Carpenter L.J. (2000). Women in intercollegiate sport—a longitudinal study twenty-three-year update 1977–2000 (available from the authors, P.O. Box 42, West Brookfield, MA 01585–0042).

P. 368–369, Box, Data provided by the United States Olympic Committee, One Olympic Plaza, Colorado Springs, C0 80909 and International Olympic Committee, Château de Vidy, Case Postale 356,1007 Lausanne, Switzerland.

Index